A VERY INDEPENDENT COUNTY

Parliamentary elections and politics in
County Armagh, 1750–1800

Last night at nine o'clock Mr Brownlow was voted duly elected in the House by a majority of one. The numbers were 119 to 120. ... I am assured by a member of the House, that they came down charged with resolutions for sending the sheriff of Armagh to Newgate and on voting the Primate [George Stone] guilty of undue influence etc., etc., if they had happened to have the majority.

Thomas Waite (Under-secretary in Dublin) to Sir Robert Wilmot (Secretary resident in London) reporting the mood of the opposition to government during Francis Caulfeild's petition to the Irish parliament against William Brownlow's victory in the Armagh county by-election contest of 1753.

[I] stood forth determined to the utmost of my power, to promote that independent interest which I could wish to see flourish in your's and every other county. As I find that that interest can more effectually be supported in the person of another gentleman, I shall ... resign my pretensions ... and shall most heartily co-operate with the independent gentlemen of the county in supporting that candidate who is so deservedly the object of their wishes.

William Richardson's notice of withdrawal as candidate for an Armagh county seat in the 1776 General Election in the *Belfast News-Letter*, 26–30 January 1776.

Mr Cope ... takes this opportunity of assuring his friends, that on his canvass he has been successful to a degree the most flattering; and that he is determined to support those respectable and independent gentlemen, who, on this occasion have done him the honour of supporting him against a combination of interests, that threatened the independence of this respectable county.

Robert Camden Cope's election notice of candidature for the 1795 Armagh county by-election in the *Northern Star*, 26–29 December 1794.

A VERY INDEPENDENT COUNTY
Parliamentary elections and politics in County Armagh, 1750–1800

C.F. McGleenon

ULSTER HISTORICAL FOUNDATION

For Kathleen

This publication has been supported by the Ulster Local History Trust. Ulster Historical Foundation is also pleased to acknowledge support given by the individual donors and subscribers. All contributions have made this publication possible.

First published 2011
by Ulster Historical Foundation
49 Malone Road, Belfast BT9 6RY
www.ancestryireland.com
www.booksireland.org.uk

Except as otherwise permitted under the Copyright, Designs and Patents Act 1988, this publication may only be reproduced, stored or transmitted in any form or by any means with the prior permission in writing of the publisher or, in the case of reprographic reproduction, in accordance with the terms of a licence issued by The Copyright Licensing Agency. Enquiries concerning reproduction outside those terms should be sent to the publisher.

© C.F. McGleenon
ISBN: 978-1-903688-93-9

Print manufacture by Jellyfish Print Solutions
Design by FPM Publishing

Contents

ABBREVIATIONS	vii
ACKNOWLEDGEMENTS	ix
LIST OF PATRONS	x
LIST OF SUBSCRIBERS	xi

	Introduction	1
1	Establishment of a political élite in County Armagh 1605 to 1749	6
2	A resurgence in high politics in County Armagh in the 1750s	38
3	High politics in Armagh 1760–75: the dynamics of two general elections; socio-economic protest; the viceroyalties of Townshend and Harcourt	84
4	The general election of 1776; dispositions of Armagh MPs 1777–8; Volunteer politics 1778–83	143
5	The 1783 general election contest; Armagh MPs in parliamentary issues; the Armagh 'disturbances' 1783–90	180
6	The 1790 general election poll; the struggle for political control of County Armagh 1790–6	222
7	The election contests of 1797 and 1799; contention over Union in County Armagh 1798–1800	249
	Conclusion	274

APPENDICES

I	List of elections to Armagh county 1715–1800	280
II	List of elections to Armagh borough 1715–1800	282
III	List of elections to Charlemont borough 1715–1800	284
IV	Brief biographical details of MPs returned to Armagh constituencies 1715–1800	286

BIBLIOGRAPHY	297
INDEX	308

FIGURE 1: Map of County Armagh *c*. 1710 showing baronies and main holdings — 30

TABLE 1: Numbers of non-resident voters at the 1753 Armagh county by-election — 53

TABLE 2: Political interests and distribution of votes in the Armagh county by-election of 1753 — 54

Abbreviations

Bartlett & Hayton, *Penal Era and Golden Age*	Thomas Bartlett and D.W. Hayton (eds.) *Penal Era and Golden Age (Belfast,* 1979)
BNL	*Belfast News-Letter* (Belfast 1737–)
Cal HO papers	*Calendar of home office papers*
Cal SP Ire	*Calendar of state papers of Ireland*
COFLA	Cardinal Tomás Ó Fiaich Library & Archive, Armagh
Commons' jn. Ire.	*Journals of the house of commons of the kingdom of Ireland*, (Bradley ed., 1613–1791, 28 vols, Dublin, 1753–91; reprinted and continued, 1613–1800, Grierson ed., 19 vols, Dublin, 1796–1800)
DCLA	Dublin City Library & Archive
DDA	Dublin Diocesan Archive, Dublin
DEP	*Dublin Evening Post* (Dublin, 1732–1875)
EHR	*English Historical Review*
FJ	*Freeman's Journal* (Dublin, 1763–1924)
HJ	*Hibernian Journal* (Dublin, 1771–1821)
HMC	*Historical Manuscripts Commission*
IHS	*Irish Historical Studies* (Dublin, 1938–)
Ir Econ & Soc Hist	*Irish Economic and Social History* (Dublin and Belfast, 1974–)
Johnston, GB & Ire	E.M. Johnston, *Great Britain and Ireland, 1760–1800: a study in political administration* (Edinburgh, 1963)
Johnston-Liik, *Irish parliament*	E.M. Johnston-Liik, *History of the Irish parliament 1692–1800: commons, constituencies and statutes* (6 vols, Belfast, 2002)
KAO	Kent Archives Office, now Centre for Kentish Studies
MP	Member of parliament
NAI	National Archives of Ireland, Dublin

NLI	National Library of Ireland, Dublin
NS	*Northern Star* (Belfast, 1792–7)
PRO	Public Record Office, London
PRONI	Public Record Office of Northern Ireland
QUB	Queen's University, Belfast
RIA	Royal Irish Academy, Dublin
RIA Proc	*Proceedings of the Royal Irish Academy* (Dublin, 1836–)
Seanchas Ardmhacha	*Seanchas Ardmhacha: Journal of the Armagh Diocesan Historical Society* (Armagh, 1954–)
TCD	Trinity College, Dublin
UJA	*Ulster Journal of Archaeology* (3 series: 1853–62, 9 vols; 1895–1911, 17 vols; 1938–)
ULS	*Ulster Local Studies* (Belfast, 1976)

Acknowledgements

I am indebted to the patience of many academics who gave freely of their time to discuss Armagh politics in the eighteenth century, particularly Professor Brian Walker and Professor David Hayton of Queen's University, Dr Allan Blackstock and Dr Eoin Magennis, and Dr Anthony Malcomson, Dr Roger Strong, Dr Bill Crawford and Dr Brian Trainor who pointed me to relevant archives and encouraged me to publish research findings.

I am grateful to the staff of libraries and archives who courteously facilitated my research: Armagh Public Library (particularly Carol Conlin and Lorraine Frazer), Armagh County Museum (Roger Weatherup, Dr Greer Ramsey, Sean Barden), Armagh Local Studies Library (particularly Mary McVeigh and Catherine Gartland), Armagh Regimental Museum, Belfast Central Library, Cardinal Tomás Ó Fiaich Library and Armagh Diocesan Archive (particularly Joseph Canning, Kieran McConville and Roddy Hegarty), Dublin City Library and Archive (formerly Gilbert Library), Dublin Diocesan Library (particularly Dr David Sheehy), Linen Hall Library, Belfast, Manuscripts Department of Trinity College, Dublin, National Archives of Ireland, National Library of Ireland, Nottingham Archives Office, Public Record Office of Northern Ireland, Queen's University Library, Belfast, the Royal Irish Academy, Dublin (particularly Dr Bernadette Cunningham).

I appreciate the moral support of Rt Rev. Monsignor Raymond Murray and other members of the management committees of the Cardinal Ó Fiaich Library and Archive and Cumann Seanchais Ard Mhacha, who welcome all research and publication of Armagh's history. I am also grateful for the practical help of friends such as Angela McCrystal and Dr Bronagh McGleenon who advised on word-processing, Vincent Braniff who often rescued the technology to produce the manuscript and for the patience of my wife Kathleen who endured the untidiness of the researcher's study.

Finally I would like to thank Fintan Mullan, Executive Director of Ulster Historical Foundation, for his courtesy and guidance on publication, and patrons and subscribers who contributed to the costs of production.

NEIL McGLEENON

List of Patrons

Ulster Historical Foundation is pleased to acknowledge the support of the following patrons who made a generous contribution towards the production costs of this publication.

Ulster Local History Trust

Finn Dental Care, Ballybofey, Co. Donegal

Caoimhe McGleenon, Drumcondra, Dublin
Curran Commercials, 130 Markethill Road, Armagh
Donegal Animal Hospital, Letterkenny
Terry Eakin, Lane Cove, NSW, Australia
J.D. Hunter and Co. Supermarket, Markethill, Co. Armagh
Johnstons of Mountmorris, Armagh
Killeen Hardware, Killycopple Road, Armagh
Gerry Hennessey, Ballybofey, Co. Donegal
Anthony Magill, Belfast, Co. Antrim
Michael McNeely, Roanoke, Virginia, USA
O'Neill Family, 'Donard', Windsor Hill, Newry
Dr Brian Trainor, Belfast, Co. Antrim
Pamela Ottaviano, Perth, WA, Australia
Rafferty and Co., Solicitors, 83 Hill Street, Newry

List of Subscribers

The Foundation would like to acknowledge the following list of individuals and organisations who subscribed to this publication.

Ron Anderson, Madison, WI, USA
The Bailey Family, Bournemouth, Dorset
Sean Barden, Armagh
Wesley and Pat Beasant, Newtownabbey
Dr Allan Blackstock, Belfast
Patricia Bogue, Dungannon
Fr John Bradley, Dungannon
Vincent and Mary Braniff, Shanecracken, Markethill
Ann Buchanan, Parksville, BC, Canada
John Butler, Armagh
Joseph Canning, Mountnorris, Armagh
Helen Cockle, Chorleywood, Herts
James and Noreen Colhoun, Keady
Sean Conlon, Markethill
Constant Family, Swansea, Wales
Joanne Cox-Brown, Ruddington, Nottingham
Mrs May Cox-Brown, Sherwood, Nottingham
Cumann Seanchais Ard Mhacha, Armagh

Henry Daly, Portadown
Deirdre de Fráma, Bessbrook, Newry
Patrick Devlin, Downpatrick
Michael and Val Farrell, Newry
Anne Fay, Abingdon, Oxfordshire
Benedict and Ellen Fearon, Portadown
Dr Eoghan Fearon, Ballymacnab, Armagh
Fr John Flanagan, Rock, Dungannon
John Foy, Rockfield House, Ballybofey
Dr Mary Goss, Newry
Rosalind Hadden, Portadown
House of Commons Library, Westminster, London
Denis and Sheila Hughes, Armagh
Wilson Johnston, Markethill
Evelyn Kennedy, Newry
Colin and Rosaleen Kerr, Mullaghbrack House, Markethill
Thomas Lee, Collone, Armagh
Pádraig Mac Floinn, Gilford, Craigavon

An tAth. Brian Mac Raois, Chapel Hill, Carlingford

Dónal MacArtáin, Newry

Mons. Ambrose Macaulay, Belfast

Dr Eoin Magennis, Warrenpoint

Markethill and District Historical Society

Frank McCann, Downpatrick

Mary Jo McCann, Muskegon, MI, USA

Nan McCone, Markethill, Armagh

Kieran E. McConville, Cullyhanna, Armagh

Mrs Mary Rose McCourt, Warrenpoint

Angela McCrystal, Belfast

Emily and John McEldowney, Kilrea

Thomas McGeown, Portstewart

Phil McGinn, Armagh

Patrick McGleenon, Lurgan

Patrick and Sadie McGleenon, Keady, Armagh

McGleenon Family, Malone Road, Belfast

Brian McGrane, Portadown

Keith and Mary McKay, Newry

Michael and Carmel McKeown, Newry

Felix and Anne McNally, Newry

Michael McShane, Silverbridge, Newry

Brendan and Elizabeth McStravick, Lurgan

Seamus Mallon, MP, MLA, Markethill, Armagh

R.J. Morris, Duns, Berwickshire

Gerard, Margaret and Monica Murphy, Newry

Brendan and Philomena Murphy, Castleconnell, Limerick

Pat and Dympna Murtagh, Keady

Fergus D. Nixon, Loughgall, Armagh

Cardinal Ó Fiaich Library and Archive, Armagh

Réamon Ó Muirí, Armagh

Joseph and Margaret O'Hara, Bishopstown, Co. Cork

Dr Rory O'Hanlon, Carrickmacross, Monaghan

Poyntzpass and District Local History Society

Robert J. Robinson, Toronto, Ontario, Canada

Rev. D.C. Scott, Markethill, Armagh

Brian Toal, Mullynure, Armagh

Harry Toner, Limavady

Dr Sean Treanor, Newry

Dr Fionnuala M. Watters, Armagh

Ronnie and Matti West, Hamiltonsbawn, Armagh

Damian Woods, Dungannon

Fr Michael Woods, Tandragee, Armagh

Three such grantees, associates of Fiennes's party and with Staffordshire connections – Powell, Rolleston and Dillon – disposed of their holdings quickly. William Powell, equerry and overseer of the king's stable at Tutbury, soon sold his 8,700 acres grant at Ballyoran (Portadown) to Cambridge graduate Rev. Richard Rolleston who had already received a grant of over 3,000 acres at Teemore in 1610. The financially over-stretched Rolleston was soon obliged to re-sell the Ballyoran estate to Richard Cope of Drumilly. Rolleston's mortgaged Teemore holding had passed to Francis Annesley by 1622. Richard Cope re-sold part of Ballyoran estate to Michael Obins, retaining half for his two sons. Having survived the Civil War, Henry Cope built Loughgall Manor house across the lake from Richard's Drumilly house. From these two family seats developed the separate political interests of Cope of Loughgall Manor – the larger – and Cope of Drumilly. The Copes of Loughgall Manor would increase the family estate in 1738 with the purchase of the 2,000 acre Mountnorris estate,[24] and would play a leading part in Armagh politics in the eighteenth century.

Rev. James Matchett, a Norfolk clergyman, was unable to find English tenants or erect buildings on his *c.* 3,500 acres holding at Kernan, between Ballyoran and Brownlow's-Derry. Matchett was collated rector of the parishes of Drumcree and Kilmore in 1616. His holding had passed to servitor Sir Oliver St John of Ballymore by 1619.[25] John Dillon developed two villages of settlers at Mullabane and Hockley on his 5,000 acres at Castle-Dillon. But the Dillon family seemed to be constantly pressed for capital. Dillon mortgaged part of the estate to Lord Charlemont who foreclosed; and his grandson Henry Dillon sold the rest in 1664 to Samuel Molyneux. The Molyneux family had been Protestant refugees from Flanders *c.* 1570 who settled at Swords. Samuel Molyneux bought Castle-Dillon as family seat for his descendants. Samuel was father of the famous William Molyneux who succeeded his father in 1696 but survived him by only five years. The sphere of Molyneux political interest remained around Dublin, and it was not until the mid-eighteenth century when William's nephew Sir Capel Molyneux, third baronet, settled at Castle-Dillon that the Molyneux family became a force in Armagh politics. This was boosted by the purchase of most of Teemore estate from Annesley *c.* 1738 bringing Molyneux holdings to *c.* 5,000 acres.[26]

SCOTTISH UNDERTAKERS IN FEWS FROM 1610

The Scottish undertakers in Fews barony in 1610 were fewer and, with one exception, granted smaller holdings, than their English counterparts in Oneilland. These five Lowland Scots from around Edinburgh were friends of James I. Largest grant was to courtier Sir James Douglas from Linlithgow parliament of James II would be used by opponents in elections during the eighteenth century to smear Brownlow's descendants as crypto-Catholic. In 1706, Arthur Brownlow purchased the adjoining Waldron manor of Richmount in West Oneilland. Richmount included over 5,000 acres granted in 1610 to undertaker John Heron of Lincolnshire which had passed into Waldron ownership by 1630, plus Waldron's acquisition of much of the Shanagoolan proportion on his northern border.[20] Brownlow's holdings in Oneilland from 1706 probably exceeded 20,000 acres, and enabled the family to continue as a leading player in Armagh politics in the eighteenth century.

The holding of over 11,500 acres granted to Norwich undertaker William Stanhawe at Shanagoolan, on the south western shore of Lough Neagh contained much bog and wood. It was not developed according to plantation stipulations and its tenants were mainly Irish. Following John Waldron's acquisition of much of it in the 1620s, the remainder was re-named Clontylew. The male Stanhawe line at Clontylew seems to have died out in the Civil War period and by 1676 an Eleanor Stanhawe had married Edward Obré bringing Obrés to Clontylew where the name continued until 1907.[21] Obré votes – though few – would be sought in parliamentary elections in the eighteenth century.

The manors of Mullalelish and Legacorry granted to Francis Sacheverel of Reresby, Leicestershire comprised *c.* 7,500 acres. Sacheverel's fortified houses at Legacorry and Mulladry were badly damaged in the Civil War and the family taken prisoner. About 1654, Ann Sacheverel, only surviving member of the Sacheverel family, married Edward Richardson of Pershore, Worcester, a major in the army who had come to Ireland in 1642. The Richardsons were re-granted the property at the Restoration and erected a new mansion at Legacorry (Richhill). Major Edward Richardson served Armagh as high sheriff on three occasions between 1655 and 1665 and represented the county with Hans Hamilton of Monella (Hamiltonsbawn) from 1661 in Charles II's parliament. He was succeeded in 1690 by his oldest son, professional soldier William (1656–1727) who served as Armagh county member in William and Mary's short first parliament 1692–3 and in George I's parliament.[22] Richardsons would be a leading force in Armagh politics throughout the eighteenth century.

Other undertaker families had disposed of their original holdings of 1610 in Oneilland before 1753. A grant of over 8,000 acres was allotted to Sir Richard Fiennes, Lord Saye and Sele, earmarked in London as leader of the Oneilland planters. But Fiennes died in 1613 and his manors of Derrycreevy and Drumilly were acquired by fellow Oxfordshire landowner Sir Anthony Cope of Hanwell for his younger sons, Henry and Richard who developed separate estates, increasing them with acquisitions from impecunious neighbours.[23]

William, second Baron Charlemont, secured and extended the influence of the family dynasty by a network of marriages.[14] Second Viscount Charlemont's tenure of the estates covered a long and stormy period in Irish history from 1671 to 1726. He zealously espoused the Williamite cause. No MP was returned from Charlemont borough to the Jacobite parliament of James II in 1689 which attainted Lord Charlemont.[15] The 1689 attainder on Lord Charlemont was reversed by King William's parliament in 1692 and he was appointed governor of Armagh and Tyrone.[16]

ENGLISH UNDERTAKERS IN ONEILLAND FROM 1610

In 1610, the general plantation scheme allocated holdings in Oneilland to ten English undertakers of varied background. Only Brownlows – and the female line of Stanhawes and Sacheverels – of those original grantee families, survived on their Armagh plantation estates until 1753. John Brownlow and his son William of Nottinghamshire – with friends in government circles – were granted the East Oneilland manors of Dewcorran and Ballynemoney.[17] Towns were developed on the two manors which were united into a single holding of almost 13,000 acres and renamed 'Brownlow's-Derry' by Sir William Brownlow in the 1620s. Sir William served as high sheriff of Armagh in 1623 and as MP from 1639–1660. He married Eleanor, daughter of Sir Cahir O'Dogherty and an Old English mother, and their eldest daughter and heir, Lettice, married Patrick Chamberlain from an Old English family of Nizelrath, County Louth. The latter couple's eldest son, Arthur Chamberlain (1645–1710), succeeded to Brownlow's-Derry estate in 1660, assuming the name Brownlow as stipulated in Sir William's will. Arthur was appointed high sheriff of County Armagh in 1679. His re-appointment in 1686, during Tyrconnell's regime, was surprising as was his return for and attendance at the Jacobite parliament of 1689 as county member for Armagh county when Brownlow was one of only six Protestant members attending. His Pale Old English ancestry may have been a factor. The other county member in 1689 was the Catholic Walter Hovenden from a branch of an Old English family from County Offaly residing in Tyranny barony in 1689.[18]

Arthur Brownlow's opposition to Jacobite proposals in James II's parliament induced violent response and he was forced to withdraw – disguised in Quaker attire for his safety.[19] When the political tables were overturned at the Boyne, he was returned in 1692 as Armagh county member for the new Protestant parliament of William and Mary. He also served in their second parliament of 1695 and in Queen Anne's new parliament of 1703. But his brief attendance in the predominantly Catholic

FORMATION OF ARMAGH AND CHARLEMONT PARLIAMENTARY BOROUGHS IN 1613

As part of Stuart anglicisation policy, additional parliamentary boroughs were created as double-member constituencies, like the counties. Armagh and Charlemont were incorporated by James I on 26 March and 28 April 1613. Armagh's charter designated a 'body corporate or free borough', the body corporate to consist of a sovereign, twelve burgesses and the assembly of the borough, the sovereign and burgesses electing two parliamentary representatives. The Protestant primate was patron and controlled the return of the two Armagh borough MPs. The sovereign was usually the primate's seneschal or land agent and the twelve burgesses his relations or trusted friends chosen by him. The primacy was an English political appointment which normally guaranteed political harmony between church and state and a supply of MPs supportive of government. Fifteen of the nineteen Protestant primates between 1552 and 1800 were English born and led the 'English interest' in Ireland.[11] Like Armagh, the franchise of Charlemont corporation borough rested in an electorate of thirteen who returned its two MPs. Its patrons were the Caulfeild family. First patron was Captain Tobias Caulfeild (1565–1627) a distinguished army officer from Oxfordshire who had served Queen Elizabeth in Europe before accompanying Essex to Ireland where he held Charlemont Fort in 1602. Caulfeild's high reputation as servitor was rewarded from the spoils of victory in the Nine Years War with holdings in five Ulster counties *before* the official scheme of Ulster plantation 1608–20 which reserved Orior barony for nine other leading servitors. In 1607 Caulfeild was granted 'the fort and town of Charlemont ... (also) the extensive and scattered grange lands of the medieval Abbey of SS. Peter and Paul of Armagh city'.[12] Charlemont's holdings of over 20,000 acres in Armagh were distributed throughout the county from north to south alongside holdings re-granted to, but later forfeited by the O'Neills of Tyranny, Upper Fews and Upper Orior and O'Hanlons of Orior.

Their extensive holdings and patronage of Charlemont parliamentary borough enabled the Caulfeild family to become a leading force in Armagh and national politics in the seventeenth and eighteenth centuries. The 'close' borough seats of Charlemont were bestowed to family members, kinsmen, in-laws and politically like-minded protégés. Their vast estates also provided a significant political interest in the election of county members. Toby Caulfeild was a figure of political importance within and without the county. He was returned as Armagh county member to James I's Irish parliament in 1613. Created Baron Charlemont in 1620, he died unmarried in 1627 when the title and estate passed to his nephew Sir William Caulfeild.[13]

and Scottish undertakers, servitors – mainly English and a few Palesmen, native Irish, the Protestant primate, other Protestant church authorities, and Trinity College Dublin. The new county was subdivided into five baronies to facilitate administration: Oneilland in the north – later subdivided further into East and West Oneilland, Orior in the east – later subdivided into Lower (north) and Upper (south) Orior, Tyranny in the west, Armagh in the centre, and Fews in the south west – later subdivided into Lower and Upper Fews.[7]

While the plantation scheme for all six escheated counties followed a common pattern, each county had its own peculiarities. In County Armagh separate baronies were allocated to different categories of settlers – to avoid friction between grantees – which would later influence the electoral process. Ten principal English undertakers were placed in Oneilland where their holdings amounted to $c.$ 21 per cent of the total county acreage. Five Lowland Scottish undertakers located in Fews barony comprised some 5 per cent of the county total. Also in Upper Fews was the huge holding of Sir Turlough MacHenry O'Neill of over 33,000 acres re-granted to him before the plantation settlement. The holdings of other Irish grantees – chief of whom were Art MacBaron and Henry MacShane O'Neill with $c.$ 7,000 and 5,000 acres respectively in Upper Orior and various families of O'Hanlons – were located in Orior, between the holdings of serving military officers. Servitors were granted over 9 per cent of the county total in Orior which, when added to over 9 per cent granted to high-profile servitors prior to the plantation scheme from secular and former monastic holdings scattered over the county, made the servitor proportion some 18.6 per cent of the total acreage $c.$ 1610. Irish grantees held $c.$ 25 per cent of the total acreage though much of their holdings would pass to new planters during the course of the seventeenth century.[8]

Although the creation of new freeholders boosted the electorate of the Irish parliament in the early-seventeenth century, less than half the total acreage of Armagh county was freehold land held by English and Scottish settlers. Major reasons were the 25 per cent still in Irish hands and 28 per cent in church and college non-freehold land throughout County Armagh. Over 15 per cent of the total acreage in Armagh county was owned by the Protestant archbishop and just under 5 per cent between the dean of Armagh, vicars choral, and other ecclesiastical proprietors. The plantation scheme also allocated another 7 per cent, in Armagh barony, to endow Trinity College Dublin, and $c.$ 0.5 per cent in Orior for the proposed Armagh Royal School.[9] While church and college property constituted most of the land in Armagh barony, some was scattered over all baronies.[10]

parliamentary electioneering and politics. This emphasises the influence of the distribution of settlement in the county of the various religious denominations, and of a buoyant market economy on Armagh politics and the electioneering process

DISTINCTIVE POLITICAL AND SOCIO-ECONOMIC FEATURES OF THE ARMAGH POLITICAL ÉLITE FOUNDED IN THE SEVENTEENTH CENTURY

The origin of the Irish parliament was medieval.[3] The basis of the franchise in the Irish counties, established by the act of 1534 (33. Henry VIII c.1) was the forty-shilling freehold i.e. property worth forty shillings a year after payment of rent and other charges, and either owned outright or leased for lives – as opposed to years. Registered forty-shilling freehold was the lowest level of qualification pre-1829, giving each freeholder a single vote in by-elections and two votes in general elections where two members were returned.[4]

A significant period in the development of parliamentary representation in Armagh dated from the reign of James I. Following the Nine Years War, the Dublin government sought to bring Gaelic Ulster under the control of the crown with a series of administrative measures intended to anglicise society in the six escheated counties. In 1605, the former medieval territory of *Airthir* was shired by Lord Lieutenant Arthur Chichester in the English manner into County Armagh, a small inland county of *c.* 512 English square miles and *c.* 328,000 acres – including 'profitable' and 'unprofitable' land – bordered by Lough Neagh on the north and by counties Louth on the south, Down on the east – separated from Armagh in the south east near Newry by the River Clanrye, Monaghan on the south west, and Tyrone on the north west – separated from Armagh by the River Blackwater.[5] The drumlin geography of much of Armagh county contained rich soil except for the mountainous area in the south (Upper Orior, Upper Fews and south Tyranny) and a flat boggy area in the north.[6] These features influenced the patterns of settlement and political development in the seventeenth and eighteenth centuries.

With its militant Gaelic lords in exile – the O'Neills who had controlled the west of *Airthir* and the O'Hanlons the east – the aim was to reduce the status of Gaelic chiefs remaining from lords to landlords and raise lesser landholders to rent-paying freeholders. To replace Gaelic law and custom, a new uniform system of law and local government was introduced including circuit judges, assizes, local justices of the peace and a high sheriff appointed annually, mostly from the new English settlers. A major part of the anglicisation process was the change in landownership, with the escheated lands of departed Gaelic chiefs re-distributed between English

1
Establishment of a political élite in County Armagh 1605 to 1749

INTRODUCTION

In the Armagh by-election poll of 1753, it has been calculated that twenty landed families controlled the return of the great majority of freeholder votes. By 1789, it was estimated that twenty two landed families in the county similarly influenced election returns.[1] Sir Charles Coote's survey of 1802 listed ninety nine 'landed proprietors' in the county.[2] However, under the distinctive arrangement of land distribution in the Ulster Plantation scheme, many proprietors in Coote's list were holders of non-freehold church and college lands which did not qualify for the franchise. This chapter explores the distinctive features of land ownership and settlement in Armagh in the seventeenth and eighteenth centuries which influenced the emergence of electoral interests; and attempts to identify defining periods and planter families who established a political élite in County Armagh prior to 1753. It is argued that the infrastructure for its political power-base was laid in the Ulster Plantation scheme of James I and strengthened in further waves of settlement in the seventeenth century. This political élite emerged and developed in parliamentary elections in the eighteenth century.

The distinctive socio-economic-political changes brought about in Armagh society by the Ulster plantation scheme are explored. Key political settler families who survived in County Armagh will be profiled – from the Ulster Plantation through the periods of Cromwellian and Restoration settlement, Williamite wars, the Whig-Tory power-struggle 1701–15, and the period of Whig political supremacy and relative tranquility from 1715 to mid-century. Political stirrings at mid-eighteenth century are examined and the emergence of several ambitious political players identified.

A socio-economic profile of County Armagh in the second half of the eighteenth century is included to illustrate the distinctive features of the society in which elections occurred and how they impinged upon the late eighteenth and early nineteenth centuries was through a working relationship characterised by mutual respect rather than any oppressive power, through consensus rather than coercion.[10] Exploration is made in the following chapters to discover evidence of coercion, deference, consensus and independence of the electorate in Armagh elections, and the incidence of political issues as significant factors. The narrative is also examined for the political dispositions of Armagh MPs to court, country and patrons.

Notes

1. D.W. Hayton, 'Introduction: the long apprenticeship', in *Parliamentary History*, xx (2001), p. 20.
2. *Commons jn. Ire.* (Bradley ed., 28 vols, Dublin, 1782–95; Grierson ed., 19 vols, Dublin, 1796–1800).
3. Gosford papers: personal, political and general correspondence, 1745–1867 (PRONI, D/1606/1/1/1–260).
4. *HMC Charlemont* MSS (2 vols, London, 1891–4); Royal Irish Academy, Original correspondence of James, late earl of Charlemont, arranged J.P. Prendergast (2nd series, 10 vols, 1867; hereafter RIA, Charlemont correspondence).
5. E.M. Johnston-Liik, *History of the Irish parliament 1692–1800: commons, constituencies and statutes* (6 vols, Belfast, 2002, hereafter Johnston-Liik, Irish parliament).
6. A.P.W. Malcomson, *John Foster, the politics of the Anglo-Irish Ascendancy* (Oxford, 1978; hereafter Malcomson, *Foster*), p. 1.
7. Sir Lewis Namier, *England in the age of the American Revolution* (London, 2nd ed., 1961), pp 19–20.
8. 'County Armagh Poll Book, 1753', (copy in Johnston Collection, Armagh Public Library, PRONI, T/3324/2B/Acc.12465 – hereafter 'Armagh Poll Book, 1753'); *A second letter from a free citizen of Dublin to a free-holder of the county of Armagh, Dublin*, 1753 (Foster pamphlet, xiii, 4, Special Collections, QUB Library).
9. J.H. Whyte, 'Landlord influence at elections in Ireland, 1760–1885' in *EHR*, lxxx (Oct. 1965), pp 740–7.
10. Peter Jupp, 'County Down elections 1783–1831' in *IHS*, xviii (Sept. 1972; here after Jupp, 'County Down elections'), pp 177–206; B.M. Walker, 'Landowners and parliamentary elections in County Down, 1801–1921', in Lindsay Proudfoot (ed.) *Down: history and society* (Dublin, 1997) pp 297–325.

Chapter six researches the 1790 contest for the county seats: pre-election negotiations in winter-spring by four potential candidates and the poll in May. Changes in borough seats and returns of Armagh gentry for seats outside the county are outlined. Dispositions of Armagh MPs to major parliamentary issues over the period 1790–6 are identified. With the traditional opposition in Armagh continuing in the 1790 parliament, attempts to establish a pro-government caucus in Armagh are traced, with the Armagh county by-election contest of 1794–5 examined as a test of political strength between families supporting and those opposing the Dublin administration. Analysis is undertaken of the resumption of sectarian disturbances in 1794 and the links between popular movements and the politics of law and order. Further analysis is made of the application of the politics of national security in Armagh under the twin threats of insurrection and invasion in 1796.

Advanced republicanism and the politics of protest dominating Armagh politics in the first half of 1797 threatened the scheduled general election but army intervention held the ring for an election to be held. Chapter seven researches the background to, and course of, the third general election contest in succession, exploring how it was used to launch the parliamentary careers of eldest sons of Armagh's two peers, how their entry was challenged by other leading political interests in the county and how far the increased electorate following the Catholic Relief Act tipped the balance of power to influence a change of personnel in county seats. Returns for boroughs are also outlined. Dispositions of Armagh MPs in key national issues over 1798–9 are explored: proposals for parliamentary union, appeals to public opinion in Armagh; and how the campaign for union impinged on yet another contest in the county by-election of 1799. Nowhere was the struggle for union fought more fiercely than in County Armagh. The final rounds of the Armagh campaign in 1800 are researched in detail.

Evidence is sought for the nature and scope of landlord-tenant relations in Armagh elections in the second half of the eighteenth century. Earlier research has argued that, pre-1793, the scarcity value of freeholder votes and their use as a dividend of Protestant ruling class power, led to docility and apathy in Irish elections which, generally, were not about political issues but inter-family rivalries between coalitions of local gentry jousting for power and prestige. And though the Catholic Relief Act of 1793 raised the Irish county electorate from over 40,000 to over 100,000 – increasing to *c.* 200,000 by 1820 – there was still no real challenge to landlord control of the electorate until *c.* 1826.[9] More recent research has found that a key method by which County Down landlords controlled election returns in

The general elections of 1761 and 1768, and related political issues, are researched in chapter three. While neither election went to a contest, the other trappings of general elections elsewhere in Ireland and Britain were present in County Armagh: the scramble for election pacts, preliminary canvass and pre-poll tactics, illustrating the processes by which Armagh members were returned to parliament in the second half of the eighteenth century. The dynamics of electioneering are explored and the multiple relationships involved: between landlords, between candidates and landlords, between candidates and freeholders, between landlords and freeholders, and between candidates and the Dublin administration. The reaction in County Armagh to the national campaign for limited parliaments between the two general elections in the 1760s and the dispositions of the Armagh MPs in parliamentary divisions in the Townshend and Harcourt viceroyalties are examined. The impact of local economic discontent and outbreaks of violence by Oakboys in 1763 and 1772 are investigated.

The presence of five candidates – some new to electioneering – for two county seats in the 1776 general election and returns for Armagh city and Charlemont parliamentary boroughs, are analysed in chapter four. With the dissolution of the successful partnership of two traditional leading families in the previous two general elections, independent politics in the county took a giant step forward with 'a man of no property' as high profile candidate for a county seat. The involvement of Armagh MPs in key parliamentary issues is traced and their dispositions in parliamentary divisions over 1777–8 identified. The growth of Volunteering in Armagh and its part in the campaigns for free trade and a new parliamentary constitution are emphasised. Divisions within Armagh Volunteer politics in the national issues of renunciation and fencible regiments over 1782–3 are examined as factors influencing the scheduled election.

The first poll in Armagh for thirty years in the general election of 1783 for the two county seats is outlined in chapter five, and why the independent candidate lost much of his support of 1776, is explored. Returns for borough seats are examined including change of personnel in both Armagh primate-borough seats. The government found little respite from the independence and opposition of most Armagh MPs in the 1783 parliament. Their involvement in key national issues is researched, including continuing pressures from Volunteer politics and the campaign for parliamentary reform in 1783–5, the proposed legislation to improve Irish trade and commerce and the election of a new speaker in 1785, the regency crisis of 1789, and concurrent civil disturbances in Armagh county 1784–90.

As the 1790 election approached, the Armagh ruling élite, fearing continuing sectarian disturbances, sought – in vain – to avoid a contest.

editions,[2] and contemporary newspapers and pamphlets in charting the narrative of elections, issues, events and division lists in key parliamentary votes. Correspondence and memoirs of the leading political families, particularly those of the Gosford peers[3] and first earl of Charlemont,[4] and archival material from the memoirs and correspondence of the Irish lord lieutenants, chief secretaries and contemporary political observers are scanned for information. The publication in 2002 of Johnston-Liik's collective biography of the Irish parliament has been an invaluable source of cross-reference for biographical details of Armagh MPs and other members connected with elections and key issues in the county, and guide to parliamentary and division lists.[5]

Identification of MPs returned for Armagh county to the Irish parliament reveals the dominance of families, a dynastic trend which characterised the parliamentary representation of the Anglo-Irish Ascendancy[6] and English parliamentary history.[7] Leading Armagh political families of the eighteenth century had their roots in the establishment of a Protestant ruling élite in the seventeenth century following the Ulster plantation. Chapter one profiles this élite and identifies the families of Brownlow, Richardson and Cope as dominating county election returns in the first half of the eighteenth century. It traces a new generation from these and other landed families who sought electoral opportunities to challenge for county seats in mid-eighteenth century. Specific families also dominated returns for Charlemont parliamentary borough. Charlemont, under the patronage of the Caulfeild family – later the Charlemont peers – from the early seventeenth century, was represented by family members, relations and in-laws: Caulfeilds, Moores of Drumbanagher and Stewarts of Ramelton, County Donegal. In contrast, seats for Armagh city borough, under the patronage of the Protestant archbishops of Armagh, were allocated to various government office-holders in need of a parliamentary place. The profile also identifies distinctive socio-economic features of County Armagh influencing political relationships and behaviour 1750–1800.

In chapter two, induction of the new generation of aspiring politicians to the electioneering process is traced in a dry run for a general election in 1752 and in the celebrated 1753 by-election. The rare availability of a poll-book facilitates analysis of the latter contest in terms of organisation and voting patterns, the identification and quantification of political interests in the county and distribution of votes from each, polling tactics and major electoral issues. The archive of documentation on the background to the 1753 by-election also reveals the interaction of Armagh politics with ideological and national issues. This contest provided comprehensive, if alarming, learning experiences at local and national levels for the ruling élite, candidates and many of the electorate,[8] resulting in re-defined electoral working relationships between landlords and freeholders for thirty years.

Introduction

This book is a study of parliamentary elections and related high politics in an Irish county in the second half of the eighteenth century. Following a preliminary examination of the evolution of County Armagh as a political community – defined by its own Protestant political élite, its freeholder county electorate and its parliamentary boroughs – it focuses upon parliamentary elections in County Armagh to the Irish parliament in the period 1753 to 1800. The main thrust is research of the elections; but politics, and social and economic issues between elections influencing election issues and outcomes, are also examined. The momentous political initiatives at national level during this buoyant period in the history of the Irish parliament were reflected in electoral hyper-activity in County Armagh. For the first half of the eighteenth century, none of four general elections and two county by-elections had required a poll to decide the return of its MPs. In the second half, three general elections out of six, and three county by-elections out of four, went to a poll.

Recent advice on how to proceed in reconstructing a history of electoral and high politics in eighteenth century Ireland is followed as a working model for researching County Armagh

> Discovering who the members were, and understanding the processes by which they came to be elected, are two of the most important stages towards a proper reconstruction of the political history of the parliament. We need also to know what members said, and what they did, when they eventually arrived in College Green.[1]

The latter areas of research include how members voted in key parliamentary divisions and how far they were involved in major national issues. This study investigates the inter-action between electoral politics, contemporary national issues and high politics in County Armagh. It also explores the incidence of private and public interests as motivating the political decisions of Armagh families.

Key sources of reference in identification of Armagh MPs returned are the journals of the Irish house of commons – both Bradley and Grierson who received some 7,000 acres in the medieval precinct of Clancarny. Henry Acheson, from Gosford, Haddingtonshire, courtier and unrequited creditor to the crown, was granted *c.* 2,000 acres in the adjoining precinct of Coolmilis. Three other courtiers were granted holdings situated between Coolmilis manor and Armagh borough. Sir James Craig from Leith was granted over 2,500 acres at Magheryentrim, William Lauder from East Lothian, *c.* 2,500 acres at Kilrudden, and Claude Hamilton from Haddingtonshire, *c.* 2,000 acres at Edenaveys.[27]

In 1611 Henry Acheson purchased the large holding of his southern neighbour, Douglas, following the latter's complaints to James I that he suffered daily robberies by Irishmen. Such depredations may have been due to Clancarny manor's location in the former territory of the MacDonnell galloglass who had been evicted from their holdings to neighbouring precincts such as the primate's lands in Ballymoyer or smaller holdings in Orior barony.[28] Shortly afterwards, Sir Archibald Acheson acquired his brother Henry's estate in Armagh in addition to the Corodownan manor he had acquired from John Brown near Arvagh, County Cavan in 1613. By 1619 John Hamilton from Ayrshire, brother of Sir James Hamilton of Clandeboye, had exchanged his Clony estates in County Cavan for the proportions of Craig, Lauder and Claude Hamilton in County Armagh. Thus leaders of the Scottish settlement in Lower Fews from 1619 were Sir Archibald Acheson with some 9,000 acres and John Hamilton with over 6,500 acres.[29]

Sir Archibald Acheson had developed and protected his Irish estate with a fortified house and armed Scottish tenants in 1622.[30] But his successors, Patrick and George struggled with insolvency and attacks from the native Irish. Third Baronet George survived bankruptcy and insurrection when the Ulster Plantation scheme temporarily collapsed in 1641. His Scottish origins may have saved his life when Sir Phelim O'Neill's forces laid waste the manors of Clancarny and Coolmilis on his march from Newry to Armagh.[31] But Sir George survived to revive his estates in the 1650s, serve as high sheriff of Armagh and Tyrone in 1657 and preside over returns of the hearth money roll of January 1666 in Armagh.[32] First of the Acheson family to be returned for parliament was fourth Baronet Sir Nicholas who succeeded to the estate in 1685. He had widened the family political network in 1686 when he married Anne, only daughter of Sir Thomas Taylor of Kells, ancestor of the marquess of Headfort.[33] He espoused the Williamite cause and was accused, with others in the Markethill area, of treason by James II's 'patriot parliament'.[34] His name appears in signatories of an 'association' of support for William and Mary against the Jacobites on 28 March 1696.[35] Sir Nicholas Acheson served as MP for County Armagh 1695–9. He was succeeded in 1701 by his young son Arthur.

Following John Hamilton's death in 1639, his eldest son Hans inherited his estates in Armagh and Cavan. Hans Hamilton attained the rank of lieutenant-colonel in the Civil War. He served as county MP from 1661, afterwards being knighted by Charles II.[36] Acquisition of forfeited O'Neill land in Tyranny barony at the restoration land settlement of 1666–8, made Sir Hans Hamilton one of the largest landowners in County Armagh, but an improvident one who left huge debts on his death in 1681. His descendants were equally improvident and his grandson Hans had to sell much of the Hamiltonsbawn estate to the Grahams of Ballyheridan and the remainder to the Achesons in the early eighteenth century. The outcome was that the Hamiltons disappeared as a political force in Armagh and were replaced by the Achesons, last of the original Scottish undertaker families in Fews barony.[37]

SERVITORS AND NATIVE IRISH IN ORIOR FROM 1610

Holdings granted to servitors in Orior barony were, on average, similar in size to those of Scottish undertakers in Fews but some were increased by acquisitions. Principal among ten prominent servitors in Orior was the St John family in Ballymore, descended from English military officer Sir Oliver St John of Wiltshire. Knighted in 1599 for services in the Nine Years War, Sir Oliver was appointed master-general of ordnance 1606–14 and lord-deputy 1616–22. He was granted Ballymore manor in 1610, estimated at almost 5,000 acres, where he developed a town, castle, bawn and water-mills at Tandragee on the River Cusher on the former stronghold of the O'Hanlons, medieval lords of Orior. By 1619 St John had added Matchett's manor of Kernan at Seagoe, Oneilland. In 1620 Sir Oliver St John was created Viscount Grandison of Limerick. When he died without issue c. 1630, the title continued – via his niece Barbara St John married to Edward Villiers – with the earls of Jersey, but the estate was bequeathed to other St John kinsmen. By then the St John estate in Armagh comprised over 8,000 acres and would serve as an important interest in eighteenth-century elections.[38]

The Orior manors of Tawnavaltiny and Ballyclare granted to military servitors Sir John Bourchier and Francis Cooke in 1610 were examples of holdings which changed hands quickly, would be combined and divided again. Sir John Bourchier was returned as MP for County Armagh in 1613 but died two years later without issue. His parliamentary seat passed to Sir Francis Annesley, constable of Mountnorris, and his Irish estate to his younger brother Henry. By 1619 Henry Bourchier had acquired both holdings estimated at c. 6,500 acres.[39] Knighted in 1621, Sir Henry succeeded his cousin as fifth earl of Bath in 1637–8. He married Lady

Rachel Fane, daughter of Francis, first earl of Westmorland, and died without issue in 1654, leaving the combined manors of Clare and Tawnavaltiny to his widow. Lady Fane bequeathed the property in 1680 to her brother Henry Fane and it passed to his son Charles in 1705.[40] The Fane estate would remain a key interest in eighteenth-century elections.

The manor of Drumbanagher, estimated at over 2,500 acres, was granted to Sir Garret Moore (1566–1627), former captain in the Nine Years War. Sir Garret, created first Viscount Drogheda in 1621, was a different type of servitor, in being a Palesman and second generation to Ireland, the son of Sir Edward Moore who had come from Kent in the late-sixteenth century to make a fortune in Ireland with estates at Mellifont. Sir Garret's fifth son, Arthur, was the first Moore to reside at Drumbanagher.[41] The Moores exemplified many families who developed and used the Protestant ascendancy network to achieve public office. The friendship and inter-marriages of Moores and Caulfeilds would lead to seats for the Moores in Charlemont borough in the seventeenth and eighteenth centuries. Viscount Garret's eldest son, Sir Edward Moore of Mellifont was the first member chosen for the Irish parliament by Charlemont borough under its new charter of 1613. The other Charlemont seat was given to Faithfull Fortescue, Moore's neighbour at Dromisken. Arthur Moore, married to Dorothy, daughter of Sir John King of Boyle, succeeded his brother as MP for Charlemont 1634–5. His grandson John Moore (1675–1752) was proprietor of the Drumbanagher estate at the turn of the seventeenth century.[42] The Moore family of Drumbanagher would be deeply involved in Armagh politics in the second half of the eighteenth century.

Lieutenant Charles Poyntz of Iron Acton, Gloucestershire, was granted *c.* 700 acres at 'Brenoge', re-named Acton, as reward for a successful action at nearby Curriator Pass in the O'Neill Wars. Poyntz proved a very active and influential settler, building a large fortified house and Poyntzpass town, and turning a small holding into a large one by leasing six adjacent townlands from the archbishop of Armagh and purchasing others in Lower Orior.[43] The Book of Survey and Distribution calculated the Poyntz estate to have grown to *c.* 2,000 Irish acres by 1676, probably an under-estimate.[44] Charles Poyntz served as high sheriff of Armagh in 1613 and a burgess of Newry in the town's first charter 1613–4. Knighted in 1630, he was elected MP for Newry borough in 1638. He was imprisoned there from the outbreak of the Civil War until freed in 1642 when the town was re-taken by Lord Conway and General Monroe. The Poyntz family was well-connected by marriage. Sir Charles's sister Elizabeth married Thomas Butler whose son became duke of Ormonde. Sir Charles married Christina Puleston, sister of Dame Mary Whitechurch of Loughbrickland and Killevy. When their great grandson Lucas Poyntz died without issue in 1707, the Poyntz estate devolved to his two aunts, Sarah married to Major

Charles Stewart of Ballintoy, County Antrim, and Christina to Roger Hall of Narrowwater Castle, County Down. In 1709 the whole manor of Acton passed to the Stewart family when Rev. Archibald Stewart bought out his aunt Christina Hall's share for £2,000 cash. The Stewarts continued to reside in Ballintoy until the 1760s.[45] The Stewart interest at Acton would play a supporting role in elections in the second half of the eighteenth century.

Mullaghglass of over 2,500 acres on the border between Lower and Upper Orior was granted in 1610 to former muster-master Sir Thomas Williams in lieu of pay.[46] This holding soon passed to Captain Anthony Smith, and later, through marriage of a descendent of Smith, to the West family of Ballydugan, County Down. The Mullaghglass estate was purchased in 1676 from Roger West by Francis Hall of Narrow-water and remained in the Hall interest throughout the eighteenth century when it would be canvassed by Armagh parliamentary candidates.[47]

West of Mullaghglass lay the holdings of Lord Audley and Sir Francis Annesley which had passed into the possession of others by 1753. Annesley succeeded Captain Henry Adderton in 1612 as constable of the fort of Mountnorris, adding its attached land to his own small holding to provide him with almost 2,000 acres. The Annesley family was created Viscounts Valentia in 1621, Lords Mountnorris in 1628 and earls of Anglesey in 1661. Having purchased most of the manor of Teemore from the impecunious Richard Rolleston, the Annesley estate probably exceeded 5,000 acres by the beginning of the eighteenth century. In 1738 the Mountnorris holding was sold to the Cope family of Loughgall and the Teemore proportion to the Molyneux family of Castle-Dillon.[48]

Acquisitive undertaker George Tuckett, created Lord Audley of Orior and earl of Castlehaven, increased his holding of c. 1,500 acres at Tullyhappy with the huge holding of Art MacBaron O'Neill at Forkhill c. 1625, and Marmaduke Whitechurch's former monastic lands at Killevy, amounting in all to over 9,000 acres, some of which he sub-let to Rory O'Moore of Kildare and Dundalk until the latter fled following his part in the 1641 insurrection. Under the Act of Settlement in 1662–3, this Orior holding was confirmed the property of Lady Elizabeth Audley the Dowager Castlehaven who bequeathed it to her nephew Baptist Noel.[49] It remained in the Noel name until it passed c. 1730 in the female line to the Wigley family who sold it to Richard Jackson in 1749.[50] Because of its location and preponderance of Catholic tenants, the electoral potential of the Jackson holding was limited before 1793.

Over 7,000 acres in County Armagh attached to the dissolved Cistercian abbey of St Patrick and St Mary in the Lordship of Newry, were re-granted to Arthur Bagnal in 1613 and Edward Trevor, by patent, in 1615. In the early-eighteenth century, the Lordship of Newry passed to a cadet branch in Kent of the Nedham (Needham) family. Though absentee landlords, the Nedham political interest in Armagh was canvassed in eighteenth-century elections.[51]

FURTHER SETTLEMENT IN COUNTY ARMAGH 1650–1700

The second wave of settlement following the Civil War and Restoration land settlement in the period 1650–80 transferred most of the lands still in native Irish hands in 1641 in Orior, Fews and Tyranny to new settlers. Largest holdings confiscated were those of Sir Henry O'Neill in Upper Fews, Hugh Boy O'Hanlon in Orior, and Sir Phelim O'Neill, his brother Tirlough Og and their cousin Tirlough MacBrian in Tyranny. Major grantee, ex-soldier Thomas Ball, lieutenant in Cromwell's army, received land in several counties including Armagh where he acquired former native Irish holdings in the baronies of Fews and Orior. Other recipients were Sir Hans Hamilton and his cousin William who acquired much land forfeited by the O'Neills of Tyranny at the restoration land settlement.[52]

The Restoration land settlement which brought new settlers and boosted the estates of others, had limited long-term effect on parliamentary returns. Financial difficulties of Sir Hans Hamilton and his descendants, would seem to have left the fortunes of the estate and its electoral potential in terminal decline at the end of the seventeenth century.[53] The preponderance of Catholic tenants on the Ball estates undoubtedly contributed to the paucity of electors.[54] Location of estates in south Armagh limited their electoral potential until 1793. The proportion of Lord Charlemont's holdings in the southern half of the county reduced his electorate, and the availability of two MPs returned for Charlemont borough may have reduced the family's political drive for county seats. Acheson's political interest in Clancarny was similarly restricted. In the seventeenth century, English settlers in north Armagh preponderated the return of county MPs to the Irish house of commons. (See Appendix 1)

The large-scale settlement of English and Scottish settlers in the seventeenth century changed the relative sizes of the religious denominations in Ulster counties thereby creating social and political tensions. Not only did the Protestant proportion increase to a majority over Catholics but, itself, became increasingly divided between Church of Ireland and Dissenters. While the category Dissenters in the seventeenth century comprised Presbyterians, Independents, Anabaptists and Quakers, Ulster Presbyterians – based on irregular waves of Scottish immigrants from the beginning of the seventeenth century – were by far the most numerous. While the main settlement of Scottish Presbyterians was in Antrim and Down, a significant number settled in Armagh, particularly in mid and south county.55 In 1679 Catholic Archbishop Oliver Plunkett, reported from south Armagh:

> Presbyterians are very numerous in these parts ... one could travel twenty-five to thirty miles in my area without finding have-a-dozen Catholic or Protestant [Church of Ireland] families but all Presbyterians i.e. strict Calvinists.56

A final great wave of Scottish immigration swept over Ulster in the 1690s. To the earlier Presbyterian settlement in Armagh city, facilitated by the tolerant attitudes of Primates Hampton, James Ussher, Bramhall and Marsh, was added the development of Presbyterian congregations in Lurgan and areas in mid and south-county such as Markethill, Clare, Keady, Mountnorris and Creggan which would influence political events in the eighteenth century.57

*****

DEVELOPMENT OF POLITICAL INTERESTS AND PARLIAMENTARY RETURNS IN THE FIRST HALF OF THE EIGHTEENTH CENTURY

RETURNS FOR ARMAGH BOROUGH, 1703–49 (SEE APPENDIX 2)

The party political complexion of the Irish administration continued to be determined in London by the English government's appointment of the Irish viceroy and Irish primate – both Englishmen throughout the eighteenth century. But, with the stormy English Tory-Whig politics and changes of government in Queen Anne's reign replicated in Ireland, harmony between executive and legislative in Ireland was occasionally disrupted.58 From 1708, Whig lord lieutenant, Thomas Wharton, intensified political conflict by replacing Tories with Whigs in the Irish administration and attempting to repeal the Sacramental Test of 1704. The appointment of Tories, Lord Ormonde as lord lieutenant in 1710 and, particularly, Sir Constantine Phipps as a lord chancellor, reversed the process and provoked the Whigs. A series of bitter disputes ensued: the Tory-dominated privy council's refusal to ratify the election of a Whig lord mayor of Dublin in 1711, the Whigs' campaign to have the hated Phipps removed from office, and the election of Irish Whig leader Alan Brodrick in opposition to Tory Lord Lieutenant Shrewsbury's candidate, Sir Richard Levinge in 1713.59

The pattern of returns of members for the two parliamentary boroughs in County Armagh continued in the eighteenth century. The primate determined the MPs elected for Armagh borough at elections. The choices of MPs by all eight English born Protestant primates in the eighteenth century – from Marsh to Stuart – were, normally, supporters of the 'English interest' in Ireland and provided a steady supply of supporters of the Dublin administration. Occasionally, a change of monarch and/or party in power could disrupt continuity in local and national affairs of church and state. Church-Whig Narcissus Marsh who was translated by Queen Anne from Dublin to Armagh in 1702, was described 'though zealously attached to Church of England, [he] displayed a spirit of liberality towards Dissenters'.[60]

Marsh's successor in 1713 was high churchman Thomas Lindsay, appointed by the High Tory interest at the end of Queen Anne's reign – to Jonathan Swift's approval. Lindsay was shunned by the Whigs who came to power with George I and received none of the customary patronage associated with the primacy. He attempted to force Armagh city Dissenters from their meeting-house on see-land to a site outside the city. But the Dissenters were sufficiently numerous in the city to resist eviction. Their strength in Armagh city and the bitterness they held towards the ruling High Church-Tory corporation, were revealed in evidence at a hearing by Armagh magistrates against rioters in Scotch Street on 17 March 1717 when local butcher James Henderson with other named Presbyterian comrades had assaulted prominent local magistrates Chapell and Thomas Dawson, sovereign Thomas Ogle and several other Tory gentlemen. Sectarian-political motivation behind the attacks was evident in the catch-cries of the assailants reported in depositions: 'Scour the Tories and Papists, for they are much alike; and damn the Church of England people, for the most of them are Jacobites. [61]

In the decades after 1714, bitter rivalry divided the Whig-promoted 'English interest' and the 'Irish interest' in the Irish episcopate. The successors of the marginalised Lindsay after 1724 were all ardent Whigs. Hugh Boulter kept Walpole briefed and the Irish episcopal bench stocked with Englishmen in opposition to the 'Irish interest' led in turn by William King, archbishop of Dublin 1703–29, and Theophilus Bolton, archbishop of Cashel 1730–44. Boulter's successors, John Hoadly 1742–6, and George Stone 1747–65, younger brother of Newcastle's secretary Andrew Stone and protégé of Lord Lieutenant Dorset, continued Boulter's Whig watchdog role for the 'English interest' in Ireland. In 1760, the twenty two strong Irish episcopate was evenly divided between Irish born and English born. Three of the four Irish archbishops had been introduced from England.[62]

Thus MPs chosen for Armagh borough from the beginning of the eighteenth century shared the political ideology of, and took direction from their primatial patrons in supporting, or not, the government of the day.

Government supporters Marmaduke Coghill and Samuel Dopping were brought in by Marsh from 1703–13.[63] Both voted with the government on the mayoralty vote in 1711. When Coghill switched to a TCD seat in 1713, Primate Marsh brought in his inveterate Whig brother Epaphroditus for Armagh, possibly as a defiant gesture by the dying primate against the encroachments of ultra-Tories. While Dopping and Coghill supported government candidate Levinge for speaker on 25 November 1713, Marsh did not. Both Coghill and Dopping were blacklisted as Tories by the Whigs in 1714. In the general election of 1715 Primate Lindsay brought in blacklisted Tory Silvester Crosse and professional soldier Charles Bourchier; and when Bourchier died in 1716, Lindsay brought in another blacklisted Tory, John Eyre of Galway. Thus during the Irish Whig ascendancy of George I's reign, two blacklisted Tories represented Armagh borough.[64]

At the 1727 general election Boulter took the opportunity to redress the situation by returning English Whigs and lawyers Sir Edward Knatchbull and Ambrose Philips for Armagh borough as active supporters of the Dublin administration.[65] Knatchbull was nephew of recently appointed Lord Chancellor Thomas Wyndham. Phillips, former secretary to the Hanover Club, had accompanied Boulter to Ireland as his secretary and whose secretarial and legal services Boulter shared with Wyndham. Phillips, who advanced to judge of the prerogative court in 1733 and its registrar from 1734–47, did not neglect his parliamentary constituency, bringing in heads of a bill in 1736 to repair the road between Armagh and Newry.[66]

When Phillips was dying in 1749, Undersecretary Thomas Waite asked Chief Secretary Edward Weston to canvass Primate Stone on his behalf for an Armagh borough seat:

> The borough is absolutely in my lord primate's disposal, and I think I am well {?} with His Grace, that I could ask the favour of him to appoint me without meaning the imputation of being forward. But I do not care to stir till I know your sentiments and I wish you would favour me with them by return of post, that I may apply to His Grace in time, if you have no objection to it.[67]

But Waite's enquiries were too late as this Armagh seat was already bespoken to Stone's friend and drinking companion Lieutenant-general Philip Bragg.

RETURNS FOR CHARLEMONT BOROUGH 1703–49 (SEE APPENDIX 3)

The two Charlemont parliamentary seats were retained among family members as far as possible for most of the eighteenth century. This policy was facilitated by the Caulfeild network of marriages. In Queen Anne's first parliament in 1703, second Viscount Charlemont who had resumed his military career abroad, returned his brother, retired soldier Colonel John Caulfeild of Tullydowey, County Tyrone and his eldest son James who managed the family estate from Castle-Caulfeild, County Tyrone. When James travelled abroad in 1705, he was granted permission by parliament – exceptionally – to resign his seat in favour of his brother-in-law John Davys, married to Anne Caulfeild. Colonel Caulfeild died in 1707 and his Charlemont seat given to George Dodington, chief secretary to Lord Lieutenant Pembroke from July to October 1707–8, though absent from further sessions of parliament. James Caulfeild returned to parliament in Queen Anne's second parliament of 1713 with Andrew Lloyd, secretary to Lord Chancellor Phipps. The Charlemont MPs supported government on most issues during Queen Anne's parliaments. James Caulfeild, Andrew Lloyd, and John Davys – by then MP for Carrickfergus borough – who supported Levinge, were later blacklisted as Tories.[68]

In the parliament of George I, James Caulfeild was returned again, this time with the experienced Humphrey May as his partner. When May died in 1722, he was replaced by James Caulfeild's younger brother John, a chancery clerk in the lord privy seal's office with residences in Dublin and London, who held the Charlemont seat from 1723 to 1760. When James Caulfeild succeeded as third Viscount Charlemont in 1726, his Charlemont seat went to his brother-in-law John Moore of Drumbanagher married secondly to Mary Caulfeild in 1724 who held it until his death in 1752.[69] The third viscount's wife was Elizabeth Bernard of Castle Bernard, Bandon. He died in 1734 and their second son James was only six years old when he succeeded as fourth viscount. The third viscount's young widow married her young cousin Thomas Adderley, County Cork, but died in childbirth in 1743. Adderley assumed the responsibility of managing the Charlemont estate and its political interest until the young fourth viscount came of age, occupying a Charlemont seat after Moore's death.[70]

LEADING POLITICAL INTERESTS AND RETURNS FOR COUNTY SEATS 1703–49

At the beginning of the eighteenth century, the principal contenders for the two Armagh county seats, by virtue of the size and location of their estates, were Brownlow, Hamilton, Cope and Richardson. The Caulfeilds and Achesons were ruled temporarily out of contention, the former by the undeveloped electoral potential of their estates resulting from second Viscount Charlemont's absence abroad on military duties and a seeming satisfaction of his sons with Charlemont borough seats, the latter by an heir too young to stand for parliament. MPs returned for Armagh county seats in Queen Anne's parliament of 1703 were Arthur (Chamberlain) Brownlow and Sir Hans Hamilton.[71]

Arthur Brownlow was an astute politician and experienced parliamentarian, steering an adroit course between parliamentary parties and religious denominations. Having conformed to the Church of Ireland to inherit the Brownlow estates, he displayed a religious tolerance to Catholics and Dissenters, granting tenancies to Presbyterians and Quakers to found meeting-houses in Lurgan. Arthur's entrepreneurship was evidenced in his development of Lurgan as a linen centre and purchase of Richmount manor making the Brownlow estate amongst the largest in County Armagh. In Queen Anne's first parliament he was regarded as a supporter of government until his death in 1711. Arthur Brownlow was succeeded in the family estate and parliament by his son William who consistently supported government: in the Dublin mayoralty vote of 1711, and favouring Levinge and Phipps in 1713. Though blacklisted as Tory, William retained his county seat in the parliaments of George I and George II until his death in 1739.[72] There followed a break in Brownlow parliamentary service as William Brownlow's eldest son, William junior, was a minor in 1739 and no further vacancy occurred in Armagh county seats until 1753.

Sir Hans Hamilton's fortunes were very different. The estate he had inherited in 1703 was already in financial difficulties due to bad management and the situation was exacerbated by Hamilton's absence as professional soldier on the continent resulting in the sale of much of the estate to pay debts. Arthur Graham of Ballyheridan bought most of it in 1708 and the Achesons purchased the remaining portions at Hamiltonsbawn in 1724 and Mount Hamilton (Ardgonnell at Middletown) in 1750. It was the end of the Hamilton family as a force in Armagh politics and a fillip to the rise of the Achesons. Hamilton was not returned for an Armagh county seat in 1713, resorting to a Carlingford borough seat for his final period as MP.[73]

Robert Cope of Loughgall Manor came in for Hamilton in Queen Anne's second parliament. Cope had made his parliamentary debut at a by-election in 1711 for Lisburn borough on Lord Conway's interest and proved himself a reliable supporter of government in the mayoralty and Levinge divisions.[74] Cope, well-connected in Armagh political society – his first wife was Arthur Brownlow's daughter Letitia – was assisted by Tory interests to take an Armagh county seat in tandem with his brother-in-law William Brownlow in 1713 over rival candidate William Richardson of Richhill. Cope was not returned to the Whig parliament of George I in October 1715. When Tories who had signed county addresses in support of Phipps were asked to apologise to the house of commons, Cope's explanation to parliament for signing an Armagh petition opposing a parliamentary address for the removal of Phipps, failed to satisfy the house of commons, and he was placed in the custody of the sergeant–at–arms.[75]

William Richardson, though he had served as Armagh county member in William and Mary's first short parliament, was not returned in their second. Brought in by the Hill family for Hillsborough in Queen Anne's first Irish parliament, Richardson was one of the few members of the Armagh gentry to oppose government. A Tory campaign prevented his return for Armagh county in 1713, but, in 1715, Whig Richardson replaced Cope as County Armagh member, serving until his death in 1727. His nephew, William Richardson, was returned for an Armagh county seat following William Brownlow's death in 1739, holding it until his death in 1758.[76]

Following the October 1715 general election, the Irish Tory party was purged from high office and reduced to a group of about thirty in the house of commons. While in custody in Dublin, Robert Cope was befriended by fellow Tory, Dean Swift who continued visits to Loughgall Manor in 1717 and early 1720s until Cope turned his political coat and made peace with the Whigs. The occasion of Cope's political conversion was the change in attitude by Dublin Castle following the appointment of Lord Lieutenants Grafton in 1720 and Carteret, 1724–7 who encouraged rehabilitation of previously proscribed Tories.[77] Cope recovered his Armagh county seat at the general election of 1727, was accepted into government ranks, appointed to a number of government posts in the 1730s and was a leading government spokesman in the gold currency debate of 1737. His purchase in 1738 of the Annesley estate at Mountnorris in Orior, and the manor of Grange in Oneilland, aggregated one of the largest political interests in County Armagh.[78]

When Robert Cope trimmed to the Whigs, Swift transferred his friendship and visitations between 1728 and 1730 to Sir Arthur and Lady Acheson and their Tory friends, Henry Jenny and Henry Leslie, at Markethill. Acheson had acquired his Tory leanings from his in-laws having, in 1715, married Anne, heiress of Rt Hon. Philip Savage, Tory chancellor of the Irish exchequer in Queen Anne's parliament. Towards the end of Anne's second Irish parliament, Savage attempted to transfer his exchequer post to Acheson. However, the lords justices in George I's new Irish parliament successfully contested the appointment of Acheson 'who has ever been esteemed a professed Jacobite' and the post went to Sir Ralph Gore.[79] Arthur Acheson, thirteen years old when his father Nicholas died 1701, did not enter parliamentary politics until he was brought in for Mullingar borough in 1727. He served as governor of Armagh from 1709 until his death in 1748.[80]

Sir Arthur Acheson's son Archibald (1717–90) would enhance the economic and political profile of the Acheson estate in rising prosperity brought on by growing population and financial insulation of the expanding linen industry in the second half of the eighteenth century. He was affluent and well-connected by marriage in 1740 to Mary, daughter of his northern neighbour John Richardson, and their children married into the gentry. As kinsman of the marquess of Headfort, and in-law of the Copes of Loughgall, the Frenchs of Monivea and Kings of Roscommon – all political families – it is hardly surprising that Sir Archibald Acheson took an active interest in politics.[81] He represented the University of Dublin from 1741 but by the early 1750s had an eye on the more prestigious County Armagh seat of the ageing and ailing Robert Cope.

MEDIUM-SIZE AND SMALL SUPPORTING INTERESTS c. 1750

No single family on its own from the above leading interests had sufficient freehold votes to win a county seat and pre-election alignments were necessary between candidates, supplemented by promises from supporting electoral interests of lesser and absent gentry. This middle-range category included the interests of St John, Molyneux, Graham, Hall, Nedham, Stewart, Moore, Fane, Rev. Walter Cope and Lord Orrery.[82] The size and location of the St John estates in County Armagh had the potential to produce significant numbers of voters in mid-eighteenth century but co-ownership and absenteeism must have diminished that electoral potential thereafter. When proprietor Sir Francis St John of Longthorpe, Northants died in 1756, two daughters succeeded as co-heiresses to his County Armagh estates of Ballymore in Orior and Kernan in Oneilland. One daughter was unmarried, the other was wife of Sir John Bernard of Brampton Park, Huntingdon.[83]

Flamboyant young third Baronet Sir Capel Molyneux (1717–97) was active in Armagh politics serving as high sheriff of County Armagh in 1744 but was denied the Armagh county seat he coveted. Sir Capel used the ascendancy network to social and political advantage. His sister's marriage to John Garnett, bishop of Clogher would bring Molyneux a borough seat at Clogher from 1761, and, when that was unavailable, the reputation of his ancestors facilitated a TCD seat. Sir Capel was committed to the family tradition of colonial nationalism espoused by his uncle William Molyneux and to patriot politics.[84] The Molyneux interest and Sir Capel's own involvement played important supporting roles in Armagh elections in the second half of the eighteenth century.

The size and location of the Graham holding purchased from Hamilton retained the potential to produce a significant number of voters in mid-eighteenth century. The interest of Alexander Stewart's Acton estate would be canvassed from 1752 despite the non-residence of its proprietor. When Stewart's attempts to develop a colliery and quay at Ballintoy led to bankruptcy and sale of his Ballintoy estate, he changed residence to Acton in the 1760s which enhanced its supporting political interest. Roger Hall's Mullaghglass estate, and the Armagh portion of the Nedham estate centred on Lisdrumgullion manor west of the River Clanrye at Newry, were other supporting interests sought by Armagh candidates 1752–1800.[85] The Drumbanagher estate, inherited in 1697 by John Moore (1675–1752) was not large enough to give the family a leading electoral interest in County Armagh in the eighteenth century. But that did not deter Moore who continued the family tradition of networking the Protestant ascendancy through intermarriage to further a parliamentary career. His second marriage to third Viscount Charlemont's sister Mary facilitated his return for a Charlemont borough seat from 1727 until his death in 1752.[86] The Moore family would be deeply involved in Armagh elections 1752–1800.

The political interest of Rev. Walter Cope, Sir Archibald Acheson's brother-in-law, at Drumilly from 1724 to 1787 played an active supporting role in Armagh elections. That of the Fane estate was also in demand though under-developed. When first Viscount Charles Fane's son Charles died in 1766 without issue, the title expired and the estate was divided between the first viscount's two sisters – Tawnavaltiny portion to Mary married to Jerome Count de Salis in 1739 and Ballyclare portion to Dorothy who married John, earl of Sandwich in 1740 – with some specified lands included in jointure to Fane's widow.[87] Thenceforward its electoral potential, already restricted by non-residence, became further hampered by circumstances of divided ownership and jointure arrangements.[88] Lord Orrery's Caledon estate which straddled the River Blackwater with a much greater acreage in County Tyrone, was acquired in 1738 through the second marriage of John Boyle, fifth earl of Cork and Orrery, to Margaret, heiress daughter of John Hamilton of Caledon. The small portion of the holding in County Armagh had enough freehold votes to have Sir Archibald Acheson canvass Lady Orrery for them in 1752.[89]

A third category of electoral interests in County Armagh in the eighteenth century contained those with less than ten freehold voters, but sufficiently numerous to be canvassed by election candidates. These were located in various baronies. The Ball family sold some of the family's vast estates in Upper Fews to the Tipping family of Beaulieu and Bellurgan, County Louth, in 1745. Both interests, however, were restricted in electoral development by location.[90] Property around Armagh city and Blackwatertown in Armagh barony inherited by the Dawsons of Dawson's Grove, County Monaghan – earls of Dartrey and Cremorne – could produce a few freehold votes though most of it was non-freehold leased from the archbishop of Armagh.[91] Other small political interests worth canvassing in the second half of the eighteenth century included: the holdings in Upper Orior barony of Jackson and Seaver, the Oneilland holdings around Portadown of Obins at Ballyoran, Workman at Mahon and Blacker at Carrickblacker; the Oneilland holdings of Verner at Churchhill and Obré at Clontylew and the holdings of Strong at Tynan and Bond at Bondsville in Tyranny. The Bonds were linen merchants in Armagh from the late seventeenth century, different generations of whom served as high sheriff of Armagh.[92]

SOCIO-ECONOMIC FEATURES OF COUNTY ARMAGH IN THE EIGHTEENTH CENTURY

By the last quarter of the eighteenth century County Armagh was regarded in contemporary surveys as the most populous county in Ireland in proportion to its size.[93] Estimates of the population – reported to be 'in progressive increase' – varied c. 1790 from 120,000 to 125,000 based on 21,983 houses in the 1790 hearth-money roll at 5.5 'souls to a house'.[94] The incomplete religious census for County Armagh in 1766 had returned 13,698 households.[95] An estimated five occupants per household, gives a county population of c. 68,500, probably an under-estimate.

The 1766 returns also revealed a relatively close numerical division between 7,327 Catholic and 6,371 Protestant households. Catholics clearly outnumbered Protestants in southern Armagh parishes such as Creggan in Upper Fews and Jonesborough and Killevy in Upper Orior; the ratio was reversed in north Armagh parishes such as Drumcree, Kilmore, Loughgall in Oneilland, and Ballymore in Lower Orior; and numbers of each denomination were fairly evenly divided in mid-Armagh parishes such as Armagh, Mullaghbrack and Loughgilly. Not all parishes returned a numerical break-down between Established Church and Dissenter households, but those that did revealed that Established Church households in Loughgall were four times as numerous as Dissenters, while Dissenter families outnumbered, even more overwhelmingly, those of the Established Church in Loughgilly, Derrynoose and Killevy parishes.[96] A census of Armagh city in 1770 found 209 'Popish' families, 162 Established Church and 131 Presbyterian families.[97]

Other accounts reported expansion of Protestant denominations in north and south Armagh. In 1733, landed proprietors Alexander Hamilton, Edward Tipping, James McCullough, Adam Noble and Randal Donaldson invited Presbyterians to settle on their thinly inhabited estates around Newtownhamilton in Upper Fews and asked Rev. Alexander McCombe, licentiate of the presbytery of Killileagh, County Down, to become their minister. McCombe was ordained minister at Fews Barracks of Creggan congregation which he served actively until his death in 1797. Numerous

Presbyterian families from the Lecale area of County Down and from Dundalk were attracted to the Newtownhamilton area where they developed a Presbyterian colony over the next forty years. Evidence of expansion of the Established Church in Upper Fews in the same period was Primate Robinson's division of the former parish of Creggan into Creggan and the separate Newtownhamilton parish in 1773.[98] About a century after a community of Quakers had settled around Lurgan in the late seventeenth century, Methodists became established in north Armagh following John Wesley's preaching circuit in summer 1771 and his appointment of correspondent Thomas Wride of Salisbury as assistant.[99]

Armagh's population was distributed more widely than in the bordering County Down whose larger mountainous tracts were almost uninhabited. Even the highest and roughest country in south Armagh sustained population. Generally, the soil was fertile – particularly in the flatter northern baronies of Armagh and Oneilland – with even most of mountainous Upper Orior and Upper Fews fit for some husbandry and tillage. The bogland on the southern shore of Lough Neagh provided domestic fuel though insufficiently to fuel the domestic linen industry. The Newry Canal had been constructed in the 1730s to carry coal from the Tyrone collieries southwards but by the 1770s was conveying English coal via Newry, northward into County Armagh.[100] Contemporary surveys reported that land was in demand and rented holdings small. In 1776 Arthur Young estimated that Armagh farms in general were between five and twenty acres, and smaller than Monaghan farms.[101] Twenty four years later the average size of farms in the county was estimated as c. 5 acres. Factors cited were the increasing population, early marriages, subdivision, and the concentration of families in the linen domestic industry leading to farming activity on smallholdings becoming supplementary to linen manufacturing in the rural economy. Farms in the Fews mountain area which afforded pasturage for young cattle, tended to be larger.[102] While there were no extensive or exclusive dairy-farms in County Armagh, some larger farms produced firkins of butter for sale in Armagh market and in Newry market for export.[103] The economy of Upper Orior and Fews looked south to Newry and Dundalk for markets, that of mid and northern Armagh used Armagh city, Lurgan and towns further east.

Some of the mountainous land in south Armagh was colonised for rough grazing. Armaghbreague, whose turf fuelled the local linen bleaching process, was limed from limestone quarries around Armagh city and Dundalk.[104] Generally, Armagh holdings seldom amounted to twenty acres and often did not exceed one or two. The smallest were used merely for non-market provisions of potatoes, oats, milk, beef, bacon, poultry and eggs for occupants employed in linen manufacture. Farms under five acres tended to have only one milch-cow. Tillage of holdings *c.* five acres was divided on average as follows: one fifth to potatoes, one twentieth to flax, seven twentieths to oats and four tenths to grass.[105]

Contrary to traditional views, subsistence farming did not necessarily force the occupants of smallholdings into a subsistence economy. While food produced on smallholdings was usually for home consumption and not for market, even cottier labourers were involved in marketing activities. Wages were calculated in money terms for a number of days at a daily wage rate, and when the rent for land and cabin was deducted, the residual was bartered in cash. Thus the smallest holdings combined subsistence and commercial economies. Generally, a market-oriented rather than a subsistence economy prevailed in County Armagh in the second half of the eighteenth century, enhancing the independence and prosperity of its inhabitants. This trend was supported by the rapid development of the linen industry which kept a commercial economy buoyant and relations between landlords and tenants sufficiently trusting for the former to grant leases to smallholders and permit increasing subdivision, confident that rents could be paid.[106]

Agriculture was seen as secondary to linen manufacture in the county's economy. The latter was regarded as the main factor for the general prosperity in County Armagh 'where the lower class of people are wealthy, industrious, civilized and tolerably well educated', much more so, it was claimed, than in some neighbouring counties west of it, because of Armagh's development of fine linen webs.[107] Linen manufacture was fairly widespread throughout the county, extending, by the 1770s, south into the Callan valley and the mountainous area of Armaghbreague, with a linen market in Newtownhamilton.[108] The finest materials tended to be woven and marketed in north Armagh. Master-weavers, styled 'manufacturers', who employed many weavers, spent much of their time at markets procuring yarn for their journeymen or selling their webs. Where they settled on a farm, they frequently established a cluster of families employed by them. Most houses had two or three looms.[109] The estimated total value of bleached and unbleached linens marketed in 1771 was £280,000; and sales in the brown linen markets of County Armagh in 1783 were £288,600 – highest in Ulster.[110] In 1809, a return from the linen board showed that 15,000 acres had been sown in flax in Armagh, the highest amount in Ireland.[111] Recent research estimates that sales in the brown linen markets of County Armagh had risen to £431,600 in 1803. It also attributes the development of market towns such as Armagh, Lurgan, Tandragee, and new towns like Keady and Newtownhamilton, to the influence of the domestic linen industry. Armagh towns, the buildings in them and the network of roads preserve evidence of the prosperity of County Armagh in the last quarter of the eighteenth century.[112]

The growing prosperity of Armagh in the second half of the eighteenth century would alter the structure of land tenure. Landlords were prepared to grant freehold leases to growing numbers of farmer-weavers on smallholdings who, increasingly, could afford to pay rent. They preferred to lease their estate directly to occupiers – who had a stake in improving the holding – rather than to a middleman or single tenant who would sub-let to tenants for short-term years with less commitment to improvement. Coote reported that 'the occupying tenant had no lazy middleman between him and his landlord'.[113] The closest Armagh came to middlemen were those lessees of large tracts of church and college property, mainly in Armagh barony, leased for no more than twenty one years and sub-let for fewer. Arthur Young reported that under-tenants on church-lands had leases for fourteen years but for three lives on other lands which made 'a visible difference in culture'.[114] Coote reported that leases of freehold land varied in tenure: 'The more general term is for one life and twenty-one years, some few for a life or lives only, and very few indeed are leased in perpetuity'.[115] As the second half of the eighteenth century progressed, the prosperity and increase in freehold leases promoted increasingly widespread interest and involvement in Armagh political life.

CONCLUSION: WAVES OF SETTLEMENT, SURVIVAL AND POLITICAL FOUNDATIONS, 1609–1749

The establishment of a political élite in County Armagh in the seventeenth and early-eighteenth centuries was a slow and arduous process. Wars fought in Ireland in the seventeenth century were followed by opportunities for English and Scottish planters to obtain grants of cheap land: the Nine Years' War was followed by the Ulster Plantation of six escheated counties; mid-century, the Cromwellian and Restoration settlements brought further changes in possession, as did the Williamite Wars at the end of the century. But many plantations encountered difficulty in establishing roots. Huge tasks faced seventeenth century planters: to build manor-houses with defensive structures, develop town communities loyal to the crown, maintain law and order and keep a watching brief on the Irish grantees, now in reduced numbers, estates and power – with the aim of fulfilling government strategy of constructing a network of plantation manors across the county. While the government supplied inexpensive land, grantees were expected to use their own capital to develop estates, attract British settlers and build towns. Many lacked the necessary capital for such development in a hostile countryside. Some of the early grantees returned to Britain because of insolvency or intimidation by dispossessed Irish. Only those with sufficient capital and determination braved it out. Some of these

Figure 1: Map of County Armagh *c.* 1710 showing baronies and main holdings

increased their Irish estates by buying adjacent holdings while others exchanged estates. For many, the seventeenth century in Ireland was a struggle for survival. Those who survived to the eighteenth century developed political interests, combinations of which produced the Armagh county MPs.

By the eighteenth century a community of Protestant families had been established and dominated the return of the two county MPs. While the Protestant primate and Lord Charlemont determined the return of the members for Armagh and Charlemont parliamentary boroughs respectively, both county seats were open to a freeholder electorate. A new infrastructure for a political power-base had been laid in the plantation settlements at the beginning of the seventeenth century when the discrete placement of the different categories of settlers in the various baronies made Armagh county a microcosm of the Ulster Plantation.

The reasons particular Armagh families produced MPs are complex. While size of holding was important, there was no necessary correlation between acreage and electorate of estates. The electoral strength of a property was multi-factorial, a function of acreage, location, denominational composition of tenants, usual residence of the proprietor and the intensity of his political drive and activism. At the highest end on a continuum of electoral strength were the estates of English undertakers in north Armagh with a preponderance of Protestant tenants and residential and politically active proprietors like Brownlow, Cope and Richardson, reflected in their diligent registration of freeholders.[116] At the lowest end were the estates of south Armagh where tenants were mainly Catholic, and non-freehold church and college lands mainly in the baronies of Armagh and Tyranny. Here landlords had less political incentive to create or register numerous small freeholdings until the late eighteenth century when Catholics could vote.

Despite the existence of a political power-base in the eighteenth century, County Armagh was politically dormant prior to mid-century. This, in part, reflected the political position in Britain and Ireland. The dynastic upheavals of the late seventeenth and early eighteenth centuries had subsided and the attendant stormy party politics abated. The tactics of Walpole and his political colleagues in smearing all Tories as Jacobites had been sufficiently successful in securing the Hanoverian succession and a Whig political supremacy in state and church – in both kingdoms.[117] And the tranquility in Ireland pervaded both the Protestant ruling élite and a disenfranchised Catholic rising middle class anxious not to have their discreet prosperity disturbed. Thus, in 1745, Undersecretary John Potter in Dublin Castle could assure Resident Secretary Sir Robert Wilmot in London of the negligible effect on Ireland of the Young Pretender's landing in Scotland:

... There has not been the least disturbance here nor any likely to so be. The Papists of property are afraid of a commotion as what may cause only present confusion, in which, they'll suffer and be made the catspaw of France.[118]

The political tranquility in County Armagh in the 1730s and 1740s was also partly the result of a generation gap in some leading political families relative to electoral opportunities. The paucity of elections after 1715 and lack of obvious eligible candidates among the leading political families in County Armagh in the second quarter of the century resulted in a quiet political life in the county. In England, the Septennial Act of 1716 – with the stated aim of reducing the incidence of 'animosities and divisions' and resultant violence of elections in the community – substituted a seven-year maximum duration of parliament for the three-year maximum laid down by the Triennial Act of 1694, thwarting the hopes of Walpole and Newcastle to return to the seventeenth-century practice of parliaments without any time limit.[119] In Ireland, however, political tranquility was enhanced by parliaments running the lifetime of ruling monarchs.

In Armagh, elections were uncontested and political life tranquil during the first half of the eighteenth century. Three families, Brownlow, Cope and Richardson, shared the Armagh county seats and, unsurprisingly, were the most numerous lessors of the 834 County Armagh freeholders registered c. 1738.[120] But there was political apathy among other Armagh landlords who had little political or economic incentive to create or register small freeholders. The Achesons, ostracised from government circles by associations with Tory in-laws and Dean Swift, had little hope of a county seat, reflected in the token thirty freeholders or so registered by Sir Arthur. In 1739, Sir Arthur Acheson saw a county seat go to his son Archibald's brother-in-law William Richardson following Brownlow's death. Archibald had to settle for a Dublin University seat which he held 1741–60. In 1739, William Brownlow junior and the Caulfeild boys were under-age. Thus family circumstances and lack of electoral opportunity would dictate that high politics remained dormant in County Armagh until the late 1740s.

Notes

1 C.F. McGleenon, 'The 1753 County Armagh by-election revisited', in *Eighteenth Century Ireland*, vol. 21 (2006), p. 98; enclosure from Arthur Acheson to R. Johnston, 19 June 1789 (PRONI, Gosford papers, D/1606/1/1/139A).

2 Sir Charles Coote, *Statistical survey of the county of Armagh* (1804, Dublin; hereafter cited as Coote, *Survey*), pp 122–9.

3 S.J. Connolly (ed.), *The Oxford companion of Irish history* (Oxford, 1998; here after Connolly, *Oxford companion*), pp 428–30, 204.

4   Johnston-Liik, *Irish parliament*, i, 91, 95.
5   Kay Muhr, 'Territories, people and placenames in County Armagh' in A.J. Hughes & William Nolan (ed.) *Armagh, history and society: interdisciplinary essays on the history of an Irish county* (Dublin, 2,001) pp 295–8; R.J. Hunter, 'County Armagh: a map of plantation, *c.* 1610', (ibid., hereafter Hunter, 'County Armagh'), pp 276, 284–6; *Armagh county guide*, (Belfast, 1969), pp 21, 49.
6   D.A. Beaufort, *Memoir of a map of Ireland* (Dublin, 1792; hereafter Beaufort, *Memoir*), pp 16–19; Coote, *Survey*, pp 5–6; Edward Wakefield, *An account of Ireland, statistical and political* (2 vols, London, 1812; hereafter Wakefield, *Account*), p. 13.
7   Hunter, 'County Armagh', pp 265–8.
8   Ibid., pp 284–6. Estimated sizes of plantation holdings here are based on Hunter's calculated inclusive OS acreage converted from the exclusive, 'profitable' acreage specified in government grants *c.* 1610.
9   Ibid., pp 284–6.
10 Coote, *Survey*, pp 122–3.
11 James Stuart, *Historical memoirs of the city of Armagh* (Newry, 1819; hereafter Stuart, *Armagh*), pp 345–6, 640–6; R.J. Hunter, 'Towns in the Ulster plantation' in *Studia Hibernica*, xi (1971), p. 79.
12 J.C. Erck (ed.), A *repertory of enrolments on the patent rolls of chancery in Ireland commencing with the reign of James I* (Dublin, 1852), p. 327.
13 John Lodge, *The peerage of Ireland* (7 vols, London, 1789; hereafter Lodge, *Peerage of Ireland*), iii, 84–90; Francis Hardy, *Memoirs of the political and private life of James Caulfeild, earl of Charlemont* (2nd ed., 2 vols, London, 1812; here after Hardy, *Charlemont*), i, 2; M.J. Craig, *The Volunteer earl, being the life and times of James Caulfeild, first earl of Charlemont* (London, 1948; hereafter Craig, *Volunteer earl*), p. 7.
14 Lodge, *Peerage of Ireland*, iii, 90–7; Peter Townsend (ed.), *Burke's peerage, baronetage and knightage* (105th ed., London, 1970; hereafter *Burke's peerage*), p. 571. Second Baron Charlemont (1587–1640) married Mary King – daughter of Sir John King of Boyle Abbey, ancestor of the earls of Kingston – by whom he had four sons and three daughters, all of whom became well-connected politically, notably his third son William, first Viscount Charlemont (1624–1671) married to Sarah second daughter of second Viscount Moore of Drogheda, youngest son Thomas to Anne another daughter of Lord Moore, and youngest daughter Margaret to Sir George Acheson of Markethill. In 1678 second Viscount William married Anne, only daughter of James Margetson, archbishop of Armagh.
15 Lodge, *Peerage of Ireland*, iii, 99–101.
16 Thomas Davis, *The patriot parliament of 1689* (3rd ed., London, 1893; hereafter Davis, *Patriot parliament 1789*), p. 158; Craig, *Volunteer earl*, pp 17–8.
17 Rev. George Hill, *An historical account of the Plantation of Ulster at the commencement of the seventeenth century, 1608–20* (Belfast, 1877; hereafter Hill, *Plantation*), pp 259–85; Philip Robinson, *The Plantation of Ulster* (Dublin, 1984; hereafter Robinson, *Plantation*), pp 195–213.
18 T.G.F. Paterson, 'County Armagh in 1622, a plantation survey' in *Seanchas Ardmhacha*, iv, no. 1 (1960–1; hereafter Paterson, 'County Armagh in 1622'), pp 118–9; T.G.F. Paterson, 'The Chamberlains of Nizelrath, the Brownlows' in *The County Louth archaeological journal*, xi (1947), pp 182–5; J.J. Marshall, 'The Hovendens, foster brothers of Aodh O'Neill, prince of Ulster (earl of Tireoghan)' in *UJA*, 2nd series, xii (1906), pp 4–12, 73–83; J.G. Simms, *The Williamite Confiscation in Ireland 1690–1703* (London, 1956), pp 179, 187.

19   J.G. Simms, *Jacobite Ireland* (London, 1969), p. 75.
20   Paterson, 'County Armagh in 1622', pp 118–9, 123–4; R.G. Gillespie (ed.), *Settlement and survival on an Ulster estate, the Brownlow leasebook 1667–1711* (Belfast, 1988; hereafter Gillespie, *Brownlow leasebook*), pp xxix, lx.
21   Paterson, 'County Armagh in 1622', pp 124–6.
22   Ibid., p. 127; *Commons' jn. Ire.* (Bradley), i, 556; ibid., ii, 440. The medieval placename Legacorry was changed later to Richardson's Hill, shortened to Richhill, and that of Monella to Hamiltonsbawn.
23   Paterson, 'County Armagh in 1622', pp 120–21.
24   Ibid., pp 120–2.
25   Ibid., p. 119.
26   Ibid., pp 128–9; J.G. Simms, *William Molyneux of Dublin 1656–98* (Dublin, 1982), pp 11–12; F.J. Bigger, 'Castledillon and the Molyneux family', in the *Belfast News-letter*, 12 Oct. 1923; hereafter *BNL*.
27   M. Perceval-Maxwell, *The Scottish migration to Ulster in the reign of James I* (London, 1973; hereafter Perceval-Maxwell, *Scottish migration*), pp 153, 170, 324–9.
28   Donald Schlegel, 'The MacDonnells of Tyrone and Armagh' in *Seanchas Ardmhacha*, x, no. 1 (1980–1), pp 193–219; *Cal. S.P. Ire.* (1629), pp 454–5; Paterson, 'County Armagh in 1622', pp 129–32.
29   Perceval-Maxwell, *Scottish migration*, pp 196–7; Hunter, 'County Armagh', p. 284.
30   Paterson, 'County Armagh in 1622', p. 115.
31   H.H. Moore, *Three hundred years of congregational life, the first Presbyterian Church, Markethill, County Armagh* (Armagh, 1909; hereafter Moore, *First Presbyterian, Markethill*), pp 37–8.
32   L.P. Murray, 'The County Armagh Hearth Money Rolls, A.D. 1664' in *Archivium Hibernicum*, viii, (1941), p. 120.
33   Lodge, *Peerage of Ireland*, vi, p. 82.
34   Moore, *First Presbyterian, Markethill*, pp 41–2.
35   *Commons' jn. Ire.* (Bradley), ii, 822.
36   Ibid., i, p. 556.
37   Paterson, 'County Armagh in 1622', pp 130–1; Harold O'Sullivan, 'Land confiscations and plantations in County Armagh during the English Commonwealth and Restoration periods, 1650 to 1680' in Hughes and Nolan, *Armagh, history and society* (hereafter O'Sullivan, 'Land confiscations'), pp 374–5.
38   Paterson, 'County Armagh in 1622', pp 136–8; Hunter, 'County Armagh', p. 284.
39   Ibid.
40   Ibid.
41   Paterson, 'County Armagh in 1622', pp 133–4.
42   *Commons' jn. Ire.* (Bradley), i, 8; Countess of Drogheda, *The family of Moore* (Dublin, 1906; hereafter cited as Drogheda, *Moore*), pedigree chart.
43   Paterson, 'County Armagh in 1622', pp 134–5.
44   Book of Survey and Distribution, County Armagh (PRONI, MIC/532/SM21/Reel 5, hereafter 'Book of Survey and Distribution, County Armagh').
45   Paterson, 'County Armagh in 1622' p. 135; conveyance of Acton, 2 Aug. 1709 (PRONI, Hall papers, D/1540/1/5).
46   Hill, *Plantation*, p. 311.
47   Paterson, 'County Armagh in 1622, pp 132–3; Edward Parkinson, The Wests of Ballydugan' in *UJA*, 2nd series, xii, (1906), pp 137–8.

48 Paterson, 'County Armagh in 1622', pp 122–3.
49 O'Sullivan, 'Land confiscations', pp 340, 352–3.
50 'County Armagh leading interests' (PRONI, ENV/5/1, pp 5, 14).
51 Hunter, 'County Armagh', pp 281, 284; Coote, *Survey*, pp 376–7; A.P.W. Malcomson, *Isaac Corry, 1755–1813* (Belfast, 1974; hereafter Malcomson, I*saac Corry*), p. 1.
52 O'Sullivan, 'Land confiscations', pp 333–80.
53 Paterson, 'County Armagh in 1622', p. 131; O'Sullivan, 'Land confiscations', pp 370–5.
54 Rev. W. Ball-Wright, *Records of Irish families of Ball compiled from public and private sources* (Dublin, 1887), pp 38–48; O'Sullivan, 'Land confiscations', pp 357–60.
55 S.J. Connolly, *Religion, law and power, the making of Protestant Ireland 1660–70* (Oxford, 1992, hereafter Connolly, *Religion, law and power*), p. 161.
56 Letter 203, to Cerri no pl., 15 May 1679, in John Hanley (ed.), *The letters of Saint Oliver Plunkett 1625–81, archbishop of Armagh and primate of all Ireland* (Dublin, 1979), pp 529–30.
57 Presbyterian Historical Society of Ireland (ed.), *A history of congregations in the Presbyterian Church in Ireland 1610–1982* (Belfast, 1982), pp 296–8, 635–8, 658; S.R. Jones, 'Presbyterianism in County Armagh' in Hughes and Nolan, *Armagh: history and society*, pp 393–701; T.G.F. Paterson, 'Presbyterianism in Armagh', *Seanchas Ardmhacha*, xix, no. 2 (2003; hereafter Paterson, 'Presbyterianism'), pp 140–6; Stuart, *Armagh*, pp 309, 323, 380, 393.
58 David Hayton, 'The beginnings of the "Undertaker system"'(hereafter Hayton, 'Undertaker system') in Bartlett and Hayton,, *Penal Era and Golden Age*, pp 32–54; David Hayton, 'Ireland after the Glorious Revolution' in PRONI, *Education Facsimiles* 221–240 (Belfast, 1976), pp 2–25.
59 Patrick McNally, *Parties, Patriots and Undertakers: parliamentary politics in early Hanoverian Ireland* (Dublin, 1997; hereafter McNally, *Parties*) pp 63–4.
60 Stuart, *Armagh*, p. 393.
61 Ibid., pp 394–6; Paterson, 'Presbyterianism', p. 146, claims that at that time Presbyterians were numerically stronger than either members of the Church of Ireland or Roman Catholics in the city; 'Examinations against some rioters in Scotch Street, Armagh in May 1717' (PRONI, Dio/4/5/3).
62 A.P.W. Malcomson, *Archbishop Charles Agar, churchmanship and politics in Ireland 1760–1810* (Dublin, 2002; hereafter Malcomson, *Agar*), pp 134–8, 138; A.P.W. Malcomson, *Primate Robinson* (Belfast, 2003; hereafter Malcomson, *Robinson*), pp 1–3; McNally, *Parties*, p. 148.
63 *Commons' jn. Ire.* (Bradley), iii, 3, 935; iv, 3.
64 Parliamentary lists (PRONI, Southwell papers, T/2827/2) and (PRONI, Blenheim papers, T/3411/1); Johnston-Liik, *Irish parliament*, iii, 225, 442–3, 554; iv, 76, 125–6; v, 193.
65 *Commons' jn. Ire.* (Bradley), v, 415.
66 Johnston-Liik, *Irish parliament*, v, 37; vi, 62–3.
67 Waite to Chief Secretary Weston, 1 June 1749 (PRONI, Wilmot papers, T/3019/1339).
68 *Commons' jn. Ire.* (Bradley) iii, 3, 353, 869, 935; parliamentary lists (PRONI, Southwell papers, T/2827/2); parliamentary lists (PRONI, Blenheim papers, T/3411/1); Johnston-Liik, *Irish parliament*, iii, 389–90; iv, 18–9, 69; v, 99.
69 *Commons' jn. Ire.* (Bradley), iv, 3; v, 1, 415; Johnston-Liik, *Irish parliament*, iii, 390; v, 230, 299.

70 Lodge, *Peerage of Ireland*, iii, 102; *Commons' jn. Ire.* (Bradley), viii, 303.
71 *Commons' jn. Ire.* (Bradley), iii, 3.
72 Gillespie (ed.), *Brownlow leasebook*, pp xi-lxiv; *Commons' jn. Ire.* (Bradley), iii, 3, 869; parliamentary lists (PRONI, Southwell papers, T/2827/2), parliamentary lists (PRONI), Blenheim papers, T/3411/1).
73 Paterson, 'County Armagh in 1622', p. 131; Johnston-Liik, *Irish parliament*, iv, 335–6.
74 Parl. lists, 1711–3 (PRONI, Southwell papers, T/2827/1, 2); Johnston-Liik, *Irish parliament*, iii, 505.
75 *Commons' jn. Ire.* (Bradley), iii, 869, 935.
76 Parliamentary lists, 1711–3 (PRONI, Southwell papers, T/2827/ 1, 2); Johnston-Liik, *Irish parliament*, vi, 158; *Commons' jn. Ire.* (Bradley), ii, 440; iii, 6; iv, 3.
77 J.G. Simms, 'Dean Swift and County Armagh', (hereafter Simms, 'Swift') *Seanchas Ardmhacha*, vi, no. 1 (1971) p. 132; McNally, *Parties*, pp 82–3.
78 *Commons' jn. Ire.* (Bradley), v, 415; Johnston-Liik, *Irish parliament*, iii, 505; Paterson, 'County Armagh in 1622', p. 122.
79 Simms, 'Swift', pp 134–40; Johnston-Liik, *Irish parliament*, iii, 52–3; Jonathan Swift, 'A vindication of His Excellency John, Lord Carteret, from the charge of favouring none but Tories, High-churchmen and Jacobites, 1730', in Walter Scott, (ed.), *The works of Jonathan Swift D.D., dean of St. Patrick's, Dublin, containing additional letters, tracts and poems not hitherto published, with notes and a life of the author* (2nd ed., Edinburgh, 1824), vii, 495–9.
80 *Commons' jn. Ire.* (Bradley), v, 864.
81 Lodge, *Peerage of Ireland*, vi, 83–4. Sir Archibald's brother Arthur was married to Jane King of the Roscommon family, his sisters Anne to Rev. Walter Cope of Drumilly and Nichola to Robert French MP of Monivea, County Galway.
82 Table 2 below lists leading County Armagh political interests in the 1753 by-election.
83 County Armagh leading interests (PRONI, ENV/5/1, pp 15, 16); Paterson, 'County Armagh in 1622', pp 136–7.
84 Paterson, 'Castledillon', in E.E. Evans (ed.), *Harvest Home* (Dundalk, 1956; hereafter Evans, *Harvest home*), pp 134–40; Paterson, 'County Armagh in 1622', pp 123, 129; County Armagh leading interests (PRONI, ENV/5/1, p. 13).
85 Paterson, 'County Armagh in 1622', pp 131, 135; Alexander Stewart to Sir Archibald Acheson, Oct. 1758 (PRONI, Gosford papers, D/1606/1/1/19); County Armagh leading interests (PRONI, ENV/5/1, pp 12, 14); Malcomson, *Isaac Corry*, p. vi.
86 Drogheda, *Moore*, pedigree.
87 Paterson, 'County Armagh in 1622', p. 138.
88 County Armagh leading interests (PRONI, ENV/5/HP/2/1, p. 10).
89 Lord Orrery to Mr Southerne, 29 June 1738, in Countess of Orrery (ed.), *The Orrery papers* (2 vols, London, 1903) i, 339; Lady Orrery to Acheson, 2 May 1752 (PRONI, Gosford papers, D/1606/1/1/ 6, 7).
90 County Armagh leading interests (PRONI, ENV/5/HP/2/1, pp 7, 16).
91 Peter Collins, *County Monaghan sources in the Public Record Office of Northern Ireland* (Belfast, 1998; hereafter Collins, *County Monaghan sources*), p. 40; Lodge, *Peerage of Ireland*, vi, 78–9; County Armagh leading interests (PRONI, ENV/5/HP/2/1, pp 6–7, 11, 14, 16–7); Malcomson, *Foster*, p. 283.
92 County Armagh leading interests (PRONI, ENV/5/HP/2/1, p. 14); George Seaver, *History of the Seaver family formerly of Heath Hall in the county of Armagh and their connections* (Dundalk, 1950), p. 65; Paterson, 'County

Armagh in 1622', pp 125–6; Evans, *Harvest home*, p. 123; *BNL*, 18 Jan. 1760; *Armagh Gazette*, 9 July 1998; Ponsonby to Acheson, 21 Dec. 1758 (PRONI, Gosford papers, D/1606/1/1/20B).
93   Beaufort, *Memoir*, p. 18 argues that County Dublin with more people to acreage, must be excluded from comparison because it included the capital.
94   Beaufort, *Memoir*, p. 18; Coote, *Survey*, p. 246.
95   'Returns to the Irish house of lords on the state of Popery', copied by Tennison Groves (PRONI, T/808/15266; hereafter '1766 religious census').
96   Ibid.
97   Census of Armagh City (PRONI, T/808/14938, 14977).
98   John Donaldson, *Account of the barony of Upper Fews in the county of Armagh*, 1838 (reproduced by Creggan Historical Society, 1993), pp 4–5, 11–16; W.D. Killen, *History of congregations of the Presbyterian Church in Ireland* (Belfast, 1886), pp 107–8.
99   'Copy of [Methodist] plan of the Armagh Circuit in 1771' (PRONI, Lutton papers, MIC/74/1).
100 Coote, *Survey*, pp 25–34, 72–3.
101 Arthur Young, *A tour of Ireland, 1776–9*, ed. A.W. Hutton (London, 1892, 2 vols; hereafter Young, *Tour*), i, 120.
102 Coote, *Survey*, pp 136–7; Beaufort, *Memoir*, p. 18.
103 Thomas Bradshaw (ed.), *Bradshaw's Directory of Newry, Armagh* (Newry, 1819), p. xxi.
104 'Robert Stevenson's view of County Armagh, 1795'; hereafter 'Stevenson's Armagh' (PRONI, Massereene-Foster MSS, D/562/1270).
105 Coote, *Survey*, p. 176; Wakefield, *Account*, i, p. 324.
106 W.J. Crawford, 'Economy and society in south Ulster in the eighteenth century', *Clogher Record*, viii, no. 3 (1975), pp 241–58.
107 Coote, *Survey*, pp 262–3.
108 'Stevenson's Armagh' (PRONI, Massereene-Foster MSS D/562/1270).
109 Coote, *Survey*, pp 138, 262, 260–72.
110 'Stevenson's Armagh' and table by John Greer, Inspector-General, *c.* 1784 (PRONI, Massereene-Foster MSS, D/562/1270, 5596).
111 Wakefield, *Account*, i, 683.
112 W.J. Crawford, 'Evolution of towns in County Armagh' in Hughes and Nolan, *Armagh: history and society*, pp 861–72; George Taylor & Andrew Skinner, *Maps of the roads of Ireland* (Dublin, 1778 – IUP reprint, Shannon 1969), pp 22–27; *The post chaise companion or traveller's directory through Ireland* (1st ed., Dublin, 1786), pp 34–9; 43–50; 455, 460–2, 481–6; *The traveller's guide through Ireland* (Dublin, 1794), pp 11–15.
113 Coote, *Survey*, p. 119.
114 Young, *Tour*, i, 120.
115 Coote, *Survey*, p. 144.
116 List of County Armagh freeholders *c.* 1738 (PRONI, T/2731/1; hereafter Armagh freeholders list, 1738).
117 Basil Williams, *The Whig supremacy, 1714–1760* (2nd ed., Oxford, 1962), pp 72–81, 182–5, 294–5.
118 Potter to Wilmot, 24 Oct. 1745 (PRONI, Wilmot papers, T/3019/698).
119 Frank O'Gorman, *Voters, patrons and parties, the unreformed electoral system of Hanoverian England 1734–1832* (Oxford, 1989; hereafter O'Gorman, *Voters*), pp 11–12.
120 Armagh freeholders list, 1738.

2
A resurgence in high politics in County Armagh in the 1750s

INTRODUCTION: A NEW GENERATION OF POLITICIANS

As mid-eighteenth century approached, a new generation of young politicians was emerging in Armagh as more of the leading political families had sons who had reached, or were approaching their majorities and thus eligible to mount a challenge for the county seats of the ageing Cope and Richardson at the first vacancy. Chief among these were: Francis Caulfeild (*c.*1732–75), younger brother of the young James, fourth Viscount Charlemont, William Brownlow (1726–94) and the more experienced, but still young Sir Archibald Acheson (1718–90). As the number of potential candidates for parliamentary seats increased, electoral activity quickened, and leading interests sought political alignments.

The first sign of burgeoning political ambitions appeared in local politics when rivalries precipitated in 1748 over the coveted governorship of Armagh. As titular head of the county and 'principal conservator of peace', the governor, appointed by the Dublin executive, was the most prestigious officer in each county. This martial office had been established in the 1660s to raise and command a county militia when the county policing service by the magistracy required assistance to face possible threats from internal rebellion and/or foreign invasion. With the removal of the Jacobite scares, military mobilisation of the county militia was infrequent by the mid-eighteenth century. But the office remained one of great honorific importance to contemporaries signifying political seniority in the county and, normally, was held for the lifetime of the appointee.[1]

When Sir Arthur Acheson, governor since 1709, died on 17 February 1748, Thomas Adderley, stepfather and advisor to the Caulfeild family, proposed that the post be 'kept open' until Lord Charlemont came of age on 18 August 1748. Sir Archibald Acheson and William Richardson who had also applied for the post, made a counter-proposal that the government should appoint one of them as pro-tem governor until Charlemont was of age. Adderley opposed their proposal arguing that if it was implemented, Charlemont, when eligible to fill the post, could appear to be 'under an obligation' to the temporary incumbent he would replace. The impasse was resolved when the lords justices accepted the argument of Robert Cope that he (Cope) was older, longer-serving MP and had more property than either Acheson or Richardson, and as deputy governor for many years had more right to the temporary post than either; but would forego a temporary appointment for a mere six months and support the decision to leave the post 'open' until 18 August.[2]

The dispute over the appointment of a new governor had aroused political consciousness in a range of Armagh families and given notice that opportunities would be sought in parliamentary elections in the 1750s. And Armagh politicians would be drawn by George Stone, archbishop of Armagh, into the national political struggles between 'court' (pro-government) and 'country' (opposition) parties of this period. Stone, the most politically oriented primate of the eighteenth century, had come to Ireland as chaplain of Lord Lieutenant Dorset in 1730 and risen rapidly to the primacy of the Church of Ireland in 1747. Following the return of his patron the duke of Dorset for a second ministry as lord lieutenant in 1750, Stone began a power-struggle with Speaker Henry Boyle, chief undertaker and head of the Irish interest in the Irish parliament.[3] Stone's coterie of political friends included Lieutenant-general Philip Bragg, Lord George Sackville, Dorset's son and chief secretary, Robert Maxwell, second secretary and envoy between Stone and the English ministers, and Captain Robert Cuninghame, aide-de-camp to Stone. The political intrigues, entertaining, and private lives of Stone and his 'minions' inspired a stream of political squibs bringing the primacy into temporary disrepute.[4]

DRESS-REHEARSAL FOR A GENERAL ELECTION IN 1752

The desire for Armagh county seats was revealed in an abortive canvass in 1752. This began when sitting member William Richardson and young William Brownlow unexpectedly declared a coalition of interests for the next general election at the Armagh Lent assizes of 1752.[5] While the assizes were a common venue in England where candidates for shire elections were agreed and announced, the timing of the Richardson-Brownlow announcement smacked of sharp practice. Declarations before the returning officer had announced an election date were disliked as cavalier, provocative and disruptive of the peace; and precipitate electioneering was usually counter-productive.[6] In the absence of official news of an election and given George II's rude health, though approaching seventy, the premature announcement by Richardson and Brownlow annoyed Acheson and Adderley.

However, once the Richardson-Brownlow election pact had been announced, other Armagh candidates felt obliged to follow and were drawn into alignments and widespread preliminary canvasses. These election pacts and subsequent preparations for a general election contest in Armagh for the first time in the eighteenth century, typified and exemplified procedures for county elections in contemporary Britain; and set a precedent for later Armagh county elections. They illustrated the alignments between political interests, considered a necessary part of electioneering. In general elections, with the possible exceptions of the duke of Leinster in Kildare and the earl of Shannon in Cork, no Irish county had a single proprietor with a sufficiently large interest to return both county members unaided.[7] In Armagh no interest was sufficiently developed to return even one member at county elections, though eight interests were deemed large enough by their proprietors to consider contention of county elections at various times in the second half of the eighteenth century: viz. Brownlow, Cope, Richardson, Acheson, Caulfeild, from the leading interests, and Molyneux, Stewart and Moore from the medium-size category. In general elections, these candidates depended upon partnerships and resulting 'splitters' from their partner; or, at least, 'plumpers' which prevented second votes going to opponents, to win a county seat.[8]

The electorate of 834 in Armagh c.1738 had risen to almost 1,200 by 1753.[9] It was a significant rise in a period when landlords were still cautious of indulging in the political agronomy of maximising the political potential of their estates – by leasing out small forty-shilling freehold parcels – to their economic cost.[10] Long leases at fixed rents were uneconomic and thus unpopular with landlords at any time but particularly so in a period of rising rents; and, as elsewhere, most Armagh landlords were reluctant to sacrifice economic to political considerations. The consequence was a quest for alignments at election time giving rise to canvassing as sounding device to help candidates decide whether to stand a poll, with its demands on finance, organisation, time and effort. A preliminary canvass – begun as early as possible – determined candidates, whether a contest was necessary, and was instrumental in reducing the number of contests.[11] The increasing number and fluidity of electoral alignments in Armagh county, encouraged more prospective candidates to canvass before declaring for elections.

Annoyed at the premature Richardson-Brownlow declaration in 1752, Acheson flounced into an arrangement with Adderley that he (Acheson) would run in tandem with young Francis Caulfeild at the next general election. It was a surprising alignment considering their earlier rivalry in 1748 and gap in political ideology between families of Tory and Whig reputations and was hardly guaranteed to last very long. Acheson was also smarting that Richardson had stolen a march on him by negotiating the promise of the interest of absentee landlord Sir Francis St John. He attempted electoral damage limitation by writing, belatedly, to St John announcing his own candidature and asking for St John's second vote. St John confirmed that he had 'ingaged' (sic) himself to Richardson in the event of a county election when he had last visited Tandragee but would now write to his agent Counsellor Samuel Blacker of Tandragee directing him to ask the freeholders to split their votes between Richardson and Acheson at the next election.[12] It was a magnanimous gesture to an old family friend as landlords, agents and voters all disliked breaking initial pledges.[13]

Canvassing continued over spring and summer 1752, raising many general electioneering issues. In May 1752 Sir Capel Molyneux wrote to his neighbour Rev. Walter Cope at Bath where the latter and wife Anne – Acheson's sister – were taking the waters. Molyneux asked the curate to forward the list of freeholders on the Drumilly estate to Acheson to be registered as voters. Cope informed Acheson that he would furnish a list of his freeholders but added that Acheson could risk waiting until Cope returned home to expedite registration.[14] The reference to registration illustrated the concern with meeting the legal deadline for registering freeholders with the county clerk of the peace,[15] and was a harbinger of future controversy. When Acheson canvassed Lord Orrery of Caledon for the small part of his interest in County Armagh, Orrery, from Marston House on his Somerset estate, promised to instruct his agent Robert Ellis junior, 'to give all my little interest [Caledon] in the County Armagh' to Acheson.[16]

Where Acheson was not closely acquainted with a landlord he asked a mutual friend – sometimes one from outside the county – to affect an introduction. Thus he persuaded Judge Michael Ward of Castleward, County Down to recommend him to the absentee Sir Francis Nedham whose south Down estate extended into Armagh county. Acheson's letter of thanks to Ward alluded to canvassing protocol, referring to the importance of obtaining the approval of the gentry as a pre-requisite for winning more widespread popular support.

> ... As you must well know, what vast consequence it is to candidates, to have upon their first setting out, the principle (sic) gentlemen of a county in their interest, and what a vast influence it has upon the inferior rank of people.[17]

So infectious was election fever in 1752 that Alexander Stewart – newcomer to the Armagh political scene and still resident in Ballintoy – indicated his own ambition for an Armagh county seat when promising to support the Acheson-Caulfeild general election partnership with the proviso that if Caulfeild should withdraw, Acheson would support Stewart as candidate.[18]

The 1752 episode was extraordinary in Armagh psephology. Perhaps the campaign for an imaginary general election which continued for most of the year – a general election would not occur for another nine years – may be attributed to an emerging generation of young politicians flexing their electoral muscles in impatient anticipation of some future general election not yet fixed. The real contest came the following year, not in a general election, but in a celebrated county by-election.

THE STORMY 1753 ARMAGH BY-ELECTION CONTEST

THE CANVASS

News in early 1753 of the terminal illness of Robert Cope brought preparations for a county by-election. Cope's seat was of particular interest to political aspirants since both his sons, his heir Rev. Anthony Cope – 'Nanty' to acquaintances – and younger son Arthur were not contenders. Adderley immediately proposed Francis Caulfeild as candidate and canvassed Acheson who continued his 1752 alignment with Caulfeild. Acheson's presence in the Caulfeild camp attracted the support of Molyneux and others. Adderley and Caulfeild in Dublin depended heavily on Acheson and Molyneux in Armagh for information and access to local political interests such as those of Nanty Cope and absentee landlords Lord Fane – difficult to contact because he was in Europe on diplomatic duties – and Sir Francis St John.[19]

By-election preparations in Armagh took on a new dimension when the leaders of the court and country parties at national level took sides and Armagh became another arena in the on-going national power-struggle – even before Robert Cope's death. In February, Adderley and Caulfeild had canvassed both Primate Stone and Speaker Boyle but were promised support only by Boyle. Stone informed Chief Secretary Lord George Sackville he would be supporting Brownlow.[20] Already the Armagh by-election was anticipated by outside observers on 10 March as a trial of strength between Stone and Boyle, considered all the more significant by the probability of it coinciding with a by-election in Galway: 'If Mr. Cope drops, there will probably be a tight contest in the county of Armagh. Young Caulfeild has declared his purpose to set up … There is another vacancy in the county of Galway.'[21] On 17 March Robert Cope died, and within the week Brownlow and Caulfeild publicly declared themselves candidates for his county seat.[22]

Speaker Boyle's support for Caulfeild was undoubtedly repayment for Adderley's inclusion in fellow Corkman Boyle's country camp. Boyle promised Acheson that he would canvass absentees on Caulfeild's behalf but warned him that his support would alienate Stone:

> ... however prudently his G[race] may act on this occasion, I think you may venture to assure yourself that his attachments will not be to your side of the question; the part he well knows me to have taken would be a sufficient bar to that, had he no other motive to an opposition to it.[23]

Boyle had correctly predicted Stone's reaction and the primate joined Brownlow in a temporary marriage of convenience.

The acquisition of the Cope interest was a major coup for the Brownlow camp, as the support of the previous incumbent's heirs held a special significance, like the concept of goodwill. But more importantly, the Cope estates had one of the largest electorates in the county. Its loss was a shock to the Caulfeild camp who had been confident of receiving it since Rev. Nanty Cope, three days before his father's death, had written a highly confidential letter to Acheson asking for a meeting in Dublin after his father's funeral.[24] But the court party moved fast to win the Cope interest for Brownlow through negotiation by Henry Singleton, lord chief justice on the north east circuit.[25] Probably the inducement which secured Cope's interest for the court party was the promise of the deanery of Armagh. Dean James Aughmuty died on 18 April 1753. On 8 June 1753, Dublin Castle announced Rev. Anthony Cope's appointment to the vacancy. By then Cope was abroad 'owing to ill-health and upon extraordinary affairs'.[26]

The importance of Cope's interest may be gauged by the efforts and methods of each camp to obtain it and by subsequent recriminations in a paper war over its destination. The Caulfeild camp continued to seek it up to the eve of the poll and accused Cope of breaking his pledge of support, and Cope's agents of putting late pressure on tenants to vote for Brownlow.[27] Brownlow's acquisition of the Cope interest had seemed to offset the loss of that of Acheson whose choice of side had puzzled and disappointed the court party. Stone was jubilant: 'I believe the Armagh election will hardly admit of a poll. If I had meditated any revenge upon Sir Archibald Acheson for his strange behaviour, he has been so good as to execute it upon himself'.[28]

The widespread court network had also secured Sir Francis St John's Armagh interests for Brownlow when Bishop Richard Trevor of Durham visited St John with a plea from Lord Abercorn – Brownlow's kinsman – and secured his interest. This time Acheson's communication to St John was too late, for, unlike the previous year, St John had not the option of splitting his vote and was not prepared to break his pledge to Brownlow.[29]

Counsellor Samuel Blacker, St John's Armagh estate agent, confirmed that St John had previously instructed him to recommend Brownlow to his freeholders, instructions which he (Blacker) regretted but was obliged to follow.[30]

But not all St John's tenants were prepared to take electoral direction from an absentee landlord. The conflict between St John's April pledge to Brownlow and his estate agent Samuel Blacker's expressed attraction to Caulfeild political principles was reflected in a divided voterate. A pro-Caulfeild pamphleteer lauded a declaration by St John tenants rejecting pressure to vote for Brownlow.[31] In the poll, 68 votes from St John estates went to Caulfeild against 44 votes to Brownlow. The influence of Blacker was greater in Ballymore manor where he resided than in Kernan. Overall, it was public rejection by tenants of landlord electoral direction similar to that on Cope's Mountnorris estate, but on an even greater scale.

St John's painful experience of having to choose between friends was adroitly evaded by veteran churchman Rev. Henry Jenny of Armagh, former Tory friend of Dean Swift and Acheson's father, Sir Arthur, and distantly related to Brownlow and Caulfeild. Approached by both candidates for his small interest, he retained a position of neutrality by deciding '... never to give my vote against either of them.'[32]

Canvassing continued over the spring and summer of 1753. The Caulfeild camp trawled the social network for votes. Acheson, turning a national interest to local advantage, persuaded Speaker Boyle to use his friendship with the family of Thomas Tipping's wife to plead Caulfeild's cause for the Mounthill interest which brought a few Tipping votes at the poll.[33] But the social connections of the Caulfeild camp had fewer Armagh freeholders than had the Brownlow connections.

PRE-POLL TREATING, HOSPITALITY, EXPENSES, FAVOURS OBTAINED

Drawing from the English pattern of electioneering,[34] canvassing in the 1753 Armagh by-election was supported by a range of social activities: dinners, treating of voters, their accommodation at inns and public houses, music, band parades and election favours. Different social levels were targeted. In the 1752 campaign for a pseudo-general election Acheson's tactics for winning influential friends included an invitation to Judge Michael Ward to stop over in Acheson's recently renovated mansion house at Markethill when visiting Armagh on his North East Circuit of Ulster. Through Ward, Acheson further extended an invitation to Lord Chief Justice Henry Singleton, who also covered this circuit.[35]

In British elections, treating of voters was traditional, and neglect or refusal by candidates to treat was taken as an insult. Thus freeholders expected to be wined and dined at the candidate's expense, and accommodated at inns or other public houses if travelling a distance. Election dinners were common and usually accompanied by music and parades.[36] Such occurred in Lurgan on 16 April 1753, when Brownlow used the occasion of the eighth anniversary of the duke of Cumberland's victory at Culloden Moor to combine a display of loyalty to the Hanoverian dynasty with an election dinner at his house near Lurgan for over two hundred local linen weavers. Toasts were drunk to George II and his son, the Protestant cause, the linen industry, and County Armagh. After dinner the guests assembled in the courtyard, each wearing the Brownlow favour of a blue cockade. A band then struck up and led a parade into Lurgan where the toasts were repeated in an election rally.[37] Appealing to Brownlow's linen connections, the election rally had also appropriated Protestant, loyalist and royalist sentiments to its own political cause. Brownlow, based within the county, was better placed to mount such election dinner rallies than his Dublin-based opponent.

Treating caused election expenses to soar over the summer of 1753. An account of Brownlow's election expenses reveals an outlay exceeding £1,500 – well before the poll opened. Bills were sent from numerous proprietors for treating and entertaining freeholders in their own areas such as: Portadown, Armagh, Mountnorris, Richhill, Tandragee, Loughgall and Clare in addition to Lurgan. The Brownlow camp had moved quickly to treat Cope's freeholders from the recently promised Mountnorris interest and three proprietors from Mountnorris were paid a total of £84/18s./9d on 8 April 1753. A bill of £285/7s./6d. from six Loughgall proprietors was settled in May. Between April and August, Brownlow paid ten named individuals from Richhill a total of £377/14s./9d. for treating Richardson's freeholders, another ten Tandragee proprietors £365/11s./6d. for entertaining St John freeholders, and £53/12s./8d. to one in Clare for treating Fane freeholders. Five bills from Armagh proprietors for bills totalling £150/15s./10d., and three more from Portadown totalling £94/3s./2d. were also received between June and September. And these were only some of Brownlow's pre-poll expenses.[38] Although no similarly detailed account is available, it may be assumed that Caulfeild's outlay for this period was no less. Lord Charlemont would later record that, while he was still abroad on his Grand Tour, Adderley, had spent some £1,000 out of estate funds on election expenses, which sum was undoubtedly only part of Caulfeild's total expenses.[39] Expenses would rise even more steeply from late October during the poll, with increased treating and the provision of transport and accommodation for voters resident at some distance from the polling centre in Armagh city.

Election year was an opportune time for communities as well as individuals to press for favours, and for political magnates and their candidates to impress voters with their influence with government. Two Armagh towns petitioned the lords justices at this time. On 20 July, Dublin Castle announced the award of two additional fair-days to Armagh borough to be held on 20 May and 20 November each year.[40] A petition from James McCullough of Camoley to the lords justices for two fairs per year plus a weekly market was also granted by Dublin Castle's announcement on 13 August which fixed fairs in Cullaville for 26 April and 26 October and a weekly market 'on every Friday for ever'.[41] The political stock of Stone and the Brownlow camp would also have been enhanced when the primate's application for government grant-aid to make a waggonway to bring coal from Drumglass colliery near Coalisland to Dublin via the newly developed Newry canal, was awarded £4,000 on 8 November 1753.[42]

THE PAPER WAR

Ammunition used by competing interests in eighteenth century English elections included 'a veritable torrent of rival publicity – squibs, poems, songs, cartoons, handbills, letters, and advertisements'.[43] The Armagh by-election of 1753 brought an exchange of propaganda pamphlets between the rival electoral camps. The first was from the Caulfeild camp. It was in the guise of a letter from a 'Dublin free citizen' to a County Armagh freeholder advising him on how to choose a worthy representative to parliament and purporting to be neutral in allegiance. It appealed for change from the traditional stereotype of 'the knight of the county [who] ruled the roost ...led his company in fox-hunting through the cornfields ... [was] grand man of the grand jury', to a responsible 'representative' of the electorate. [44]

Only towards the end of the pamphlet did the writer allow his mask of neutrality to slip when he outlined 'negative qualities' in candidates to be avoided. Though Brownlow was not named, the negative qualities alluded to rumours about Brownlow's ancestors and his political allies. The writer attacked any candidate with ancestors of dubious loyalty to civil institutions – a reference to former rumours of Brownlow's having Jacobite and Papist affiliations. He also warned against candidates of haughty, distant and inaccessible disposition, an allusion to Brownlow's shy and reserved personality.[45] Free Citizen's exhortation to 'avoid a man debauched in morals' would seem to have referred to Primate Stone who was subject to a hate campaign,[46] and a criticism of Brownlow's electoral association with Stone.

A follow-up letter from 'Free Citizen of Dublin' dropped all pretence at neutrality. It praised the tenants of Sir Francis St John for their remonstrance against landlord direction to vote for Brownlow. It then proceeded to smear Brownlow and his ancestors as crypto-Catholics. Brownlow's grandfather was condemned for serving in the 'Popish parliament' of James II which 'your competitor's ancestors {the Caulfeilds} wisely and bravely disclaimed and refused to send representatives there from Charlemont borough'. Brownlow, himself, was attacked for his education abroad under a 'Popish mother', his misconduct there, neglect of his tenants and friendship with 'Papists and their Masshouses', which was contrasted with Lord Charlemont's support for the arts abroad, his relief of the poor at home, and his championing the cause of Protestantism in Rome. The second letter concluded by urging Caulfeild's supporters to be proactive in spreading the Whig doctrine of independent voting and not to be merely satisfied with sporting their favours of orange cockades.[47]

The Brownlow camp responded with a twenty seven page pamphlet presented as a letter of electoral advice from an Armagh freeholder, using the pen-name Brother Freeholder, to his fellow freeholders. Voters were warned of the slander against Brownlow – 'scurrilous stories and vile arts of defamation ... published in print, in memorials and letters ... poison ... from the press'.[48] Caulfeild was attacked for his lack of land and freehold, his lack of education, and for being politically under age. Brother Freeholder refuted the previous accusations against Brownlow and his forbears. He argued that Brownlow's grandfather, Arthur Brownlow, had attended James II's Patriot Parliament at great danger to himself to oppose anti-Protestant legislation until forced to flee parliament, in disguise and guarded by his tenants, in peril of his life. Though advised to escape and join King William's forces in England, Arthur had remained in Lurgan with his tenants, was later returned to serve in William's first Irish parliament, and had survived charges brought against him by Williamites with eyes on his estates.[49]

The pamphlet then answered criticisms against Brownlow's father, William senior viz. that he had 'favoured a malignant party {High Tory Chancellor Phipps}' and had been sympathetic to the Old Pretender and the 1715 Rebellion. It was conceded that William senior had made an error of judgement in supporting Phipps which he later retracted and apologised to the house of commons when he realised Phipps's 'dangerous tendency'. But Brother Freeholder rejected accusations of treason against William senior who, it was asserted, had remained loyal to the Hanoverian cause in 1715. William Brownlow senior's record of public service was lauded: as county MP, member of the Linen Board, improving landlord, sincere member of the Established Church yet tolerant of Protestant dissenters and loyal supporter of the Hanoverian cause; and was contrasted with the Caulfeild family's recent poor record of public service, referring to the cloud of disaffection over a Caulfeild who had been dropped from Carteret's government.[50]

Brother Freeholder then refuted the accusations against the current William Brownlow of being 'a Papist and Jacobite' because he had spent his youth in France and Italy with his mother who had 'perverted to Popery'. These assertions, it was argued, were distortions of the truth. Young Brownlow, on medical advice, had been taken by his mother to the south of France. There his mother had converted to Catholicism. But to avoid their mother's influence, young William and his sisters had gone to Naples to where the son of a Protestant clergyman had been sent from Armagh to tutor them. William had remained six years in Italy until he was twenty two, uninfluenced by Catholicism and innocent of scandalous behaviour in Rome of which he had also been accused in the pro-Caulfeild pamphlet. Brother Freeholder reminded readers that Caulfeild's older brother, Lord Charlemont, had also been abroad for most of his adolescence and was sceptical of claims of Charlemont's promotion of Protestantism in Rome – except, perhaps, 'through toasts in drinking'! Voters were assured that Brownlow had returned home when his health was restored, untainted by Catholic influence. He argued that if candidate William Brownlow was popular with Catholics, it was because the Brownlow family had traditionally been 'tolerant of all professions and persuasions' and not because it was of the Catholic faith – of which, in any case, William, his father, and grandfather were not members.[51]

The allegations by the pro-Caulfeild 'Free Citizen' of Brownlow's neglect of Lurgan and of the poor at home during his sojourn abroad, were also repudiated by 'Brother Freeholder' who asserted that the Brownlow and St John families had provided extraordinary relief to the poor of their estates, especially in two seasons of scarcity and sickness. The charge of haughtiness and inaccessibility was similarly rejected with Brownlow described as a temperate and thinking man with strict regard for the truth and not given to ingratiation.[52]

The pro-Brownlow pamphlet, forced on the defensive by the pro-Caulfeild pamphlets to refute the accusations against Brownlow and his ancestors, concluded by providing reasons why Armagh freeholders should choose Brownlow rather than Caulfeild. The former, by virtue of his extensive property in County Armagh, was committed to promoting trade and wealth there, unlike Caulfeild who had 'not a foot of land' and had only an eye to government sinecure. The Brownlow family's record of public service surpassed that of the Caulfeilds of whom, Lord Charlemont, by title, was excluded from the house of commons and the younger branches of the family were untried. Brownlow was older and more experienced than Caulfeild. Brownlow's residence in Armagh guaranteed his presence to prevent oppression and administer justice among his tenants at the assizes and sessions, while Caulfeild had neither house, land, authority nor influence in the county but 'with a scanty portion provided for him, must seek a subsistence in the army'. The property factor was further emphasised when readers were reminded that none of the four borough members had any property and thus it was important that county members should have the independence of a property stake which gave freedom from a political patron. Lord Charlemont's parliamentary influence should not be extended by the election of his brother to a county seat since the earl already controlled the two Charlemont borough members – Thomas Adderley, his stepfather, and his uncle the Hon. John Caulfeild who lived in London on a post of £200 per annum and did not even attend the Irish house of commons.[53]

The above pamphlets led to others, in which many of the previous accusations and arguments were re-visited. A recurring theme in the pro-Caulfeild accusations was that the Brownlow family had denounced Dissenters and favoured Catholics and seemed aimed at appropriating the Dissenter vote for Caulfeild and alienating Brownlow from it.[54] In turn, the pro-Brownlow pamphlets attempted to undermine Caulfeild's appeal to the Dissenter vote. Brother Freeholder alleged intolerance by Caulfeild's ancestors in refusing the Dissenters permission to build a chapel on Charlemont land when they (the Dissenters) were obliged to turn to the tolerant Primate Boulter who allowed them to build on see land. He also updated alleged Caulfeild intolerance by accusing Caulfeild of opposing removal of the Sacramental Test; and contrasted the moderation of Brownlow and his religious toleration of all.[55]

Another anonymous pamphleteer, claiming to be an Armagh freeholder and clergyman, made public his reasons for asking to be released from a prior pledge of neutrality, to vote for Brownlow: abhorrence of excessive insults to the Established Church, to William Richardson and others by Caulfeild supporters and Free Citizen's pamphlets.[56] And yet another, under the pen-name 'Thomas Tell-tale', claiming to be a gentleman in Armagh – yet, tellingly, published in Dublin – accused the Caulfeild camp of attempting to delay the start of the poll by robbing the northern mail of the Armagh election writ.[57]

ROBBERY OF THE ELECTION WRITS

A series of sensational incidents marked the preparations for the Armagh poll. A warrant for the writ was issued by parliament on Tuesday 9 October.[58] It was one of a number issued for by-elections round the country including Monaghan borough to replace deceased Baptist Johnson, and in Galway, to replace both deceased county members, Frederick Trench and George Warburton. In the early hours of Wednesday morning, as the Armagh writ was being transported northwards, it was stolen from the mail-coach in an armed holdup near Swords. Both the Dublin *Universal Advertiser* and the *Belfast News-Letter* carried the story:

> Last Wednesday morning about 3 o'clock, the post-boy carrying the north mail was stopped by two persons near Clogheran Church and carried into a bye-lane where one of them cocked a pistol at the post boy's breast, and made him turn his head to the carriage, while the other cut open the mail, and thereout took the Armagh and Monaghan bags from which they took out such packets as they thought proper, and then went off undiscovered.[59]

The Brownlow camp suspected the robbery of the Armagh writ was part of a conspiracy by the opposition to delay the Armagh poll. A motive for the delay would have been to enable many pro-Caulfeild freeholders who had registered at the quarter sessions of 3 May, to have completed the legal six-months qualifying period of possession for eligibility to vote stipulated in the statute of 1745.[60] William Richardson, in a letter to his father-in-law, referred to the affluent appearance of the highwaymen 'two men in gentlemen's apparel, well-mounted' – implying they were not the archetypal highwayman. He also emphasised the subsequent delaying tactics of Caulfeild's friends in parliament to hinder the issue of a warrant for a replacement writ by an attempted filibuster led by Speaker Boyle – whose remit it was to issue warrants to the Clerk of the Crown to make out writs:

> I got intelligence of it [the robbery] very early and moved the House for a new writ, which I obtained after some debate. The S{peaker} did appear as if he had no mind to put the question, and raised several difficulties in order to delay till the next day, and had a great mind to fight upon that question. But our friends ... did not think fit to divide upon it, which threw a great damp upon those gentlemen that are inclined to favour our antagonist.[61]

Richardson's persistence succeeded and Boyle was ordered on Wednesday 10 October to issue his warrant to the clerk of the crown to make out a new writ – 'of the same tenor and date of the former'.[62] This time Richardson personally despatched the writ to Armagh from Dublin Post Office by express under a double armed guard. The second writ arrived safely with Armagh Sheriff Meredyth Workman on Thursday 11 October, but was there stolen from the mail-bag – giving further credence to Richardson's conspiracy hypothesis. Upon this news, Richardson called with Lord Lieutenant Dorset who promised to call a privy council meeting and issue a proclamation with large reward for the writ's recovery.[63]

Thomas Tell-tale's letter on 13 October expressed shock and disgust at the armed robbery of 'the king's mail [which was] held sacred [robbed by] well-dressed gentlemen', and, not too obliquely, accused the Caulfeild camp of the crime in order to delay the election. The plan had misfired, argued the writer, because the robbery had been perpetrated too near Dublin, thus facilitating prompt replacement of the writ. He further argued that public revulsion against this scandalous deed should guarantee Brownlow's election.[64] The writer had not then heard of the theft of the second writ in Armagh. It is not clear whether the latter crime was solved, but the measures taken by the lord lieutenant and privy council enabled Sheriff Workman to open the poll on 26 October 1753.

THE POLL, 26 OCTOBER TO 09 NOVEMBER 1753

The rare availability of a poll book enables an analysis to be made of voting tactics and patterns in the 1753 Armagh by-election. Poll books were introduced in 1696 when sheriffs in England and Ireland were first required to openly record voting details in parliamentary elections on a county basis, and continued until 1872 when they were effectively abolished by the Ballot Act. Before the secret ballot, voters were required to declare publicly to the county high sheriff who was returning officer, their electoral preference and other information which was recorded in the poll book. From 1727 to 1793, only male Protestants with a freehold valued at least forty shillings a year and registered at least six months prior to the poll, were eligible to vote.

A hand-written copy of the 1753 Armagh poll book was made in a bound quarto volume in 1898 by Lieutenant Colonel George Hamilton Johnston from the original, then in the possession of Lord Gosford, and later presented to Armagh Public Library by Johnston's younger brother Henry.[65] Information was arrayed in seven columns. The first column listed the names of voters with each entry numbered from 1 to 1181.[66] Under the heading 'trade', the second column listed the occupation of each voter; his 'abode' was given in the third; and the address and valuation of his freehold recorded in the fourth. His vote was recorded by a B (for Brownlow) in the fifth column or a C (for Caulfeild) in the sixth.

The seventh column, headed 'Observations', listed the objections by each candidate, or his legal representative, to his rival's votes. Rarely can an election contest have experienced as many objections. Most reflected the issues raised in the pamphlet war. All votes for Caulfeild were challenged by Brownlow as voting for a minor; but the charge of Caulfeild, though still a student, being under age was not substantiated, and those votes polled. Objections to two voters for Brownlow and one for Caulfeild as being minors were also overruled. One voter for Brownlow was accused of being a rioter but his vote was polled. Twelve voters for Brownlow and two for Caulfeild were challenged on a range of religious grounds – of being

Papists, or married to Papists, or having children who were Papists residing with them, or of attending Mass, or of 'not having conformed properly' – but all these objections were overruled. The freehold qualification of several voters was challenged on various grounds: of being registered after the six month deadline, a few as being fictitious e.g. as having been sold or passed to a son. The majority of these objections were upheld. The heavy incidence of objections was undoubtedly notice by both sides – probably on the advice of court and country factions in Dublin – that the result of the poll would be referred to parliamentary appeal by the defeated party.

Johnston's copy of the poll book also contained an introductory note revealing continuation of the Caulfeild camp's tactics of delaying the start of the poll. This referred to objections by a Mr. Blacker[67] and Sir Archibald Acheson to the poll beginning after the scheduled starting time of 11.00 am, and by Thomas Verner, Caulfeild's agent, against Sheriff Workman tossing up for 'point of place between candidates' – the latter objection resolved by agreement that candidates change positions each day. Caulfeild won the toss for first poll; but before a vote was polled, Brownlow objected to Caulfeild being under age, whereupon a vote was cast for Caulfeild – probably in defiance of Brownlow's objection.[68] Ironically, this vote undermined Caulfeild delaying tactics; for, when Acheson objected to the poll being opened as late as 1.15 pm, his objection was overruled on the grounds that a vote had already been polled for Caulfeild, and the court proceeded.

ANALYSIS OF THE POLL

The poll lasted thirteen days from Friday 26 October to Friday 9 November inclusive. Polling continued daily, except on Sundays. Following the delayed start on opening day, the poll was scheduled to open daily at 8.00 am. Each candidate introduced groups of five voters alternately on the opening day, and groups of ten subsequently. Thus each day concluded with the poll level until the thirteenth day when Caulfeild's poll was exhausted after 20 votes on that day, against the 114 polled by Brownlow, and Workman declared Brownlow the winner. Caulfeild requested a scrutiny but when he did not appear for this the following morning, Brownlow was confirmed elected with 637 to 543 votes.

Comparison between columns three and four of the poll book reveals the remarkable number of 121 voters, representing over 10 per cent of the poll, with freeholds in County Armagh who resided outside the county and returned to vote in 1753. It is further evidence of national interest and intervention in this by-election. Voters travelled, not only from the contiguous counties of Down, Louth, Antrim, Tyrone and Monaghan, but also from the more distant counties of Londonderry, Fermanagh, Kildare,

Kilkenny and Wexford, and from the cities of Dublin and London. Table 1 shows the numbers of residents outside County Armagh who returned to vote at the by-election and the distribution of their votes.

PLACE OF RESIDENCE	BROWNLOW	CAULFEILD	TOTAL VOTES
Newry Town	6	30	36
Dublin	16	7	23
County Down (outside Newry)	14	6	20
County Louth	7	4	11
County Antrim	8	2	10
County Tyrone	3	5	8
County Monaghan	5	2	7
County Londonderry	0	1	1
County Fermanagh	0	1	1
County Kildare	1	0	1
County Kilkenny	1	0	1
County Wexford	1	0	1
London	0	1	1
TOTALS	62	59	121

Table 1: Numbers of non-resident voters at the 1753 Armagh county by-election

Hon. John Caulfeild MP for Charlemont borough and chancery clerk in the Lord Privy Seal's office returned from London to vote alongside his brother Rev. Charles Caulfeild, rector of Donaghhenry, County Tyrone, for their nephew. An advertisement by candidate Francis Caulfeild in a Dublin newspaper appealed for electoral support from Armagh freeholders resident in Dublin.[69] The poll book reveals that 23 prominent Armagh gentry travelled from Dublin city, though only seven voted for Caulfeild.

County Down provided the highest return of non-resident voters with 56 votes, 36 of which went to Caulfeild and 20 to Brownlow. Many were Newry merchants such as Edward and Isaac Corry. High profile gentry from north west Down, including Archdeacon George House, Arthur Workman and John Birch of Waringstown voted for their neighbour Brownlow, while those in south Down voted mainly for Caulfeild and included Roger Hall of Narrowwater, Arthur Acheson of Mourne and John Stevenson of Hallsmill. From 11 gentry travelling from County Louth, Brownlow received 7 votes: William Henry Fortescue of Randalstown [Reynaldstown], Abraham Ball and Robert Levinge of Drogheda, William Warren and James Farlow of Dundalk, John Trewman of Kilcurly and Francis Eastwood of Oaktate. Thomas Tipping JP of Beaulieu, Malcolm

McNeale of Ballymascanlon, John Turnley of Castlebellingham and Thomas Coulter of Dundalk voted for Caulfeild. From voters who journeyed to Armagh from other bordering counties, Brownlow polled 8 of 10 votes from County Antrim residents, 5 of 7 from County Monaghan residents, and 3 of 8 from residents of County Tyrone. Overall, the 121 votes from non-residents divided: 62 to Brownlow, 59 to Caulfeild.

POLITICAL INTEREST	BROWNLOW	CAULFEILD	TOTAL
William Brownlow:			
1. Manor of Brownlow's-Derry	202	0	
2. Manor of Richmount	42	0	244
Rev. Anthony Cope			
1. Loughgall Manor	97	1	
2. Manor of Mountnorris	33	30	161
William Richardson	123	4	127
Sir Francis St John			
1. Manor of Ballymore	10	39	
2. Manor of Kernan	34	29	112
Sir Archibald Acheson	0	96	96
Lord Charlemont	0	74	74
Sir Capel Molyneux	4	68	72
Captain Arthur Graham	23	22	45
Roger Hall	0	37	37
Sir Francis Nedham	0	30	30
Alexander Stewart	0	23	23
Rev. Walter Cope	1	19	20
Lord Fane	16	2	18
Lord Orrery	0	15	15
John Moore	0	13	13
John and Thomas Ball	8	1	9
Thomas Tipping	0	8	8
Richard Jackson	0	6	6
Edward Obré	5	0	5
Thomas Morres Jones	3	1	4
Minor gentry, merchants, professionals	32	23	55
Unidentified other interests	4	2	6
TOTAL POLL	637	543	1,180

Table 2: Political interests and distribution of votes in the Armagh county by-election of 1753[70]

Information recorded in the poll book does not in itself identify the controlling landlord interests in 1753. However, most of such identification was possible through comparison of the townland address of the freehold recorded in column four against lists of townlands in landlord estates in surveys of tenants as in plantation settlements of the seventeenth century, Griffith's Valuation of the mid-nineteenth century and modern research on estate and family history in County Armagh.[71] Twenty landlord electoral interests controlling multiple votes have thus been identified in Table 2, accounting for 1,119 votes or almost 95 per cent of the 1753 poll. In addition to those twenty magnates, were independent minor gentry and landed proprietors with freehold registered for less than four votes. These latter were often agents, professional lawyers, merchants and affluent clerics who had acquired landed holdings in single townlands, and are categorised as 'Minor gentry, merchants and professionals'. Their holdings, numbering 55, tended to be clustered around the towns of Armagh and Newry, or interspersed between the church-lands in the baronies of Armagh and Tyranny. Townlands recorded by 6 voters remained unidentified, and are categorised as 'unidentified other interests'.

The leading interest in the Armagh 1753 by-election was that of William Brownlow, with 244 votes polled from his two estates in Oneilland barony. The concentration of English Protestant settlers in north Armagh together with a tradition of Brownlow family involvement in parliamentary politics for over one hundred years, contributed to making its electoral interest best developed in the county. Most of his votes, 202, emanated from the original family manor of Brownlow's-Derry in East Oneilland at Lurgan. Another 42 votes were returned from his Richmount estate in West Oneilland. No freeholder on Brownlow holdings voted for Caulfeild.

The second highest interest was the 161 votes returned from Rev. Anthony Cope's estates of Loughgall Manor and Grange Oneilland in north Armagh and the manor of Mountnorris comprising 15 townlands in Loughgilly and Kilcluney parishes in mid-Armagh. The late Robert Cope's involvement in parliamentary politics over forty years had resulted in the Cope interest being well developed and eagerly sought by both sides in 1753. The freeholders on his Oneilland estates followed direction and 97 out of 98 votes were cast for Brownlow. However, his Mountnorris freeholders – heavily Dissenter[72] – were less willing to follow direction. When they sent a signed memorial to Dean Cope in England requesting permission to be allowed to vote for Caulfeild, Cope's agents allegedly came to Mountnorris on the eve of the poll and threatened to distrain rent which was over-due – probably through hanging gale – from tenants objecting to voting for Brownlow.[73] It was a clear case of a landlord's attempted coercion of tenants to vote against their will. And clearly many resisted. At the poll, just under half of the voters on Cope's Mountnorris estate defied landlord pressure and voted for Caulfeild.[74] The Caulfeild camp's appeal for the Dissenter vote in the propaganda war may have influenced the Mountnorris vote. And freeholders there may have been further influenced by political pressures from the surrounding mid-Armagh holdings of Charlemont, Acheson, Stewart, Hall and Moore, all supporting Caulfeild, and resentful of Cope's seeming eleventh hour volte-face on the destination of his interest.

William Richardson's manors of Mullalelish and Legacorry at Richhill produced the third highest return with 127 votes, 123 of which went to Brownlow. This was a reasonable poll from an estate of some 7,500 acres. It was another example of the effects of a north Armagh family's tradition of participation in local and parliamentary politics since 1661, and William Richardson's position as sitting county member in 1753.

Absentee landlord Sir Francis St John's combined manors of Ballymore at Tandragee, and Kernan at Portadown, produced a fourth highest return of 112 votes. This was a reasonable poll, given St John's non-residence, and may have been the product of political activity arising out of the conflict between the landlord's personal direction and his agent's dissident influence on the estate electorate. This conflict between St John's pledge to Brownlow and his agent Samuel Blacker's attraction to Caulfeild political principles was reflected in a pro-Caulfeild pamphlet praising a declaration by St John's tenants rejecting landlord pressure to vote for Brownlow, 'though the style of it shakes some people vastly ... expressions of freedom ... are the proper garb of truth'.[75] Such 'expressions of freedom' influenced the poll where 68 of the total 112 votes went to Caulfeild. It was a public rejection by tenants of landlord electoral direction similar to that on Cope's Mountnorris estate, but on an even greater scale. Blacker's influence was greater on the Ballymore estate where he resided, and the division there was 39 votes to Caulfeild against 10 votes to Brownlow. The division among Kernan freeholders favoured Brownlow marginally by 34 votes to 29.

The 96 votes from Sir Archibald Acheson's estates of Coolmalish and Baleek in mid-Armagh plus detached holdings at Ardgonnell near Middletown, and Hamiltonsbawn, provided the fifth highest return in the poll. The Acheson estates may be estimated at c. 8,000 acres in 1753. If 96 votes seem a modest return for so large an estate and for a landlord of Acheson's political ambitions, an explanation, perhaps, was the location of his larger Baleek manor of 4,495 acres stretching into south Armagh and a greater proportion of Catholic tenants than on more northerly estates.[76]

To Caulfeild, whose main source of votes should have been his brother Lord Charlemont's vast estates in Armagh, a return of 74 votes from these must have been a disappointment. A combination of factors contributed to so low an electoral return from so huge an estate, stretching from Upper Orior barony, through the former monastic granges in Lower Fews and around Armagh City, to the holding at Charlemont in the north west and across the River Blackwater into County Tyrone. This location resulted in the estate comprising large tracts of poor land and a high percentage of Catholic tenants, particularly in the south, which reduced the number of enfranchised tenants in 1753. Further, lack of involvement in Armagh county elections by generations of the Caulfeild family, and absence of eligible contestants in recent generations of the nuclear family, had left the Caulfeild political interest underdeveloped. Added to this was the continued residence of the Caulfeild family outside County Armagh, distancing it from personal contact with the Armagh electorate and thus hindering efficient preparation for the contest. Nor could the youth and election inexperience of Francis Caulfeild have inspired confidence, a point stressed by opposition pamphlets, as evidenced in his belated registration of freeholders. The sixth largest political interest in the county was a very weak position from which to challenge for a county seat.

The only other political interest returning over 50 votes was that of Sir Capel Molyneux of Castle-Dillon, a landlord with political ambitions of his own. His combined Mullabane and Teemore estates amounting to *c*. 5,000 acres, produced a respectable 72 votes, seventh highest, in 1753. His Mullabane estate was surrounded by Armagh City on the south, Loughgall on the north west and Richhill on the north east, thus exposing his freeholders to the political pressures of Brownlow supporters on all sides. But, a committed supporter of Acheson and Caulfeild, Molyneux controlled the overwhelming majority of his freeholders, 68 of whose votes went to Caulfeild.

Thirteen other political interests in County Armagh in 1753 produced returns varying from 45 to 4 votes. The largest of these was the 45 votes of the Graham holding in mid-Armagh. The Grahams were descended from a Scottish family who had come to Ireland in the seventeenth century as military servitors, and a branch had settled in Ballyheridan townland near Armagh City.[77] In 1707–8 Arthur Graham purchased most of the bankrupt Hamilton estate stretching eastward from Ballyheridan to Hamiltonsbawn.[78] The Graham estate had gained its significant political interest from the Hamilton family's involvement in parliamentary service at the turn of the seventeenth century. At the time of the 1753 by-election, the landlord was another Arthur Graham, an army captain residing in Dublin who had sufficient interest in Armagh politics to travel north to vote for Brownlow. His brother Rev. Isaac Graham of Hockley, voted for Caulfeild. Their difference of choice was replicated in the Graham electorate which divided at the poll: 23 votes to Brownlow and 22 to Caulfeild, a division probably resulting from the captain's non-residence and the opposing pressures on Graham freeholders from surrounding magnates, Acheson and Richardson.

The next four highest interests in 1753 went to Caulfeild. Two County Down magnates had holdings in County Armagh around Newry. Roger Hall of Mount Hall, Narrowwater, possessed the manor of Mullaghglass with eight townlands north east of Newry in Lower Orior which produced 37 votes. Marching Mullaghglass was the holding of the Nedham family with 30 votes.[79] The interest of Alexander Stewart of Acton, personal friend of Acheson, produced 23 votes. In 1753, Rev. Walter Cope was curate of Loughgilly parish with a glittering career in the church still ahead of him. Though a cousin of Rev. Anthony Cope, he sided with his brother-in-law Sir Archibald Acheson to whom, in 1752, he had promised the electoral interest (amounting to 20 votes) of his holding of nine townlands at Drumilly, Loughgall.[80]

Next highest were the interests of two absentees – Lord Charles Fane's in Lower Orior and Lord Orrery's in Tyranny on the Armagh-Tyrone border. A return of 18 votes from Fane's large estate of *c.* 6,500 acres in the manors of Tawnavaltiny and Ballyclare was very low due to Lord Fane's continued absence abroad on diplomatic service. As Fane's manors were close to Brownlow's Lurgan estates, 16 votes went to Brownlow against 2 to Caulfeild. In contrast, Lord Orrery's relatively small Armagh holding produced a reasonable return of 15 votes. Most of the fifth earl of Orrery's northern estate was in County Tyrone with his seat in Caledon, but he possessed five townlands south of the River Blackwater in County Armagh. Orrery responded to Acheson's request for support in 1752 and his votes all went to Caulfeild in 1753.

The only other return to reach double figures was from John Moore's manor of Drumbanagher in Lower Orior. Moore's holding of *c.* 2,500 acres produced a mere 13 votes putting it in fifteenth place. It was a very low return from a long-established family with political ambitions and wide political connections, including Caulfeild, to whom all his votes went in this by-election.

Four of the lowest five returns were from the baronies of Upper Fews and Upper Orior. In sixteenth and seventeenth places were the 9 votes and 8 votes respectively from the Ball and Tipping families. The members of the Ball family lived in various counties outside Armagh and returned to vote,[81] though 8 votes to Brownlow and 1 to Caulfeild were a meagre return from the extensive Ball estates. All 8 votes from the neighbouring Mounthill estate of Thomas Tipping who resided at Beaulieu, Bellurgan, County Louth[82] went to Caulfeild following Speaker Boyle's canvass. Three other holdings produced small multiple votes. Two were situated in Upper Orior. The huge estate recently purchased by Richard Jackson produced a mere 6 votes for Caulfeild in 1753. The holding of Thomas Morres Jones at Jonesborough returned 3 votes for Brownlow and 1 for Caulfeild.[83] The location and preponderance of Catholic tenants on those four holdings reduced their electoral potential in 1753. At the other end of the county, Edward Obré's small holding at Clontylew in West Oneilland produced 5 votes for the neighbouring Brownlow.[84]

A further 55 voters can be identified as independent minor landed gentry, merchants or professional personnel such as agents, lawyers or senior clerics. Many resided in towns or cities, separated from their property which tended to be located in townlands around Newry and Armagh. A significant number was also to be found in townlands between non-freehold churchlands in the baronies of Armagh and Tyranny. Ten voters in this category with freehold south of Newry divided at the poll: 7 votes for Brownlow,[85] 3 votes for Caulfeild.[86] The pattern was similar around Armagh City where 9 of the 11 votes went to Brownlow.[87]

There was no major electoral interest in Tyranny barony because of the vast amount of churchlands there. However, a number of minor gentry, merchants and professionals had acquired townlands and property there by the mid-eighteenth century. Twenty votes from Tynan parish were divided evenly between the two candidates. Votes for Brownlow included those of the Rev. James Strong[88] and Rev. Benjamin Barrington[89] of Tynan, Rev. Robert Levinge of Doogary, William Irwin of Mountirwin, and two County Monaghan residents viz. Francis Lucas with registered freehold at Sheitrim and Richard Graham with property at Rawes. Among supporters of Caulfeild were the Bond family at Tullybrick,[90] Robert Pringle of Doogary and Thomas Verner – Caulfeild's agent who resided in Dublin but had property at Kiltubbrid.

Fourteen holdings of other minor gentry were scattered elsewhere throughout Armagh county. Their proprietors divided at the poll as follows. In West Oneilland, three members of the Clarke family of Ardress – social friends of the Caulfeild family – and Charles Nicholas of Tallbridge in nearby Cranagill voted for Caulfeild. But Dublin-based Thomas Townly Dawson also with freehold at Cranagill, voted for Brownlow. Further east around Portadown, Richard Workman of Corcrain, William Blacker of Carrick, Dr Hugh Hill and David Hunter of Ballynaghy, and Hugh Robinson of Ballyhannon voted for Brownlow, while Arthur McCann of Ballydonaghy supported Caulfeild. In Lower Orior, Henry Harden of Harrybrook, Clare, voted for Caulfeild. Two minor gentry with freehold near Newtownhamilton in Lower Fews barony were James McCullough of Camly, or Camoley, who voted for Brownlow, and Dublin resident Alexander Hamilton JP who used his freehold at Tullyvallen to vote for Caulfeild.

POLLING TACTICS

A feature of the poll evident in the poll book was the chronology of voting. The spread of voters would seem to have been planned by both camps. Both candidates withheld most of their own freeholders until the final three days of the poll, and polled the freeholders of their electoral partners on specific days before then. Thus Brownlow held 196 freeholders – *c.* 80 per cent – from his own estates in reserve until the final three days. Some 86 per cent of Caulfeild's freeholders also voted on those days. Approximately 66 per cent of Richardson's freeholders polled on the fifth, sixth and seventh days. Most of Acheson's freeholders voted over two days: some 34 per cent on the eighth day and another 40 per cent on day eleven. Approximately 31 per cent of Molyneux's freeholders voted on the third day, though the attendance of the remainder was spread evenly over the other twelve days. Attendance at the poll by Rev. Anthony Cope's freeholders varied according to estate. Some 83 per cent of his Mountnorris freeholders attended over the first and second days. None of his freeholders from Loughgall Manor voted on those days. Their attendance was spread over the remaining eleven days, with *c.* 48 per cent voting on days seven and eight. The incidence of voting also varied on the St John estates. Approximately 53 per cent of freeholders on his Ballymore estate attended on the fourth and fifth days; *c.* 60 per cent of his Kernan freeholders voted over the second, third, fifth and sixth days.

This pattern of attendance on specific days also held for the smaller interests, showing widespread discipline and control by patrons over voters. Sixty per cent of Rev. Walter Cope's freeholders attended on the seventh day, *c.* 67 per cent of Lord Fane's freeholders on the fourth day, 40 per cent of Graham's freeholders on the third day, *c.* 49 per cent of Hall's freeholders on the fourth and fifth days, 50 per cent of Nedham's freeholders on the second and sixth days, *c.* 62 per cent of Moore's freeholders on the sixth day, and *c.* 67 per cent of Lord Orrery's freeholders on the fifth and twelfth days.

Another tactic deployed by both camps was to include high profile members of the gentry as prestige voters each day in order to impress the electorate. Many were public representatives, justices of the peace, and some were members of parliament. Caulfeild opened with Sir Archibald Acheson MP, JP, deputy governor of Armagh and former high sheriff in 1751, followed by Sir Capel Molyneux, high sheriff in 1744 and descendant of the famous patriot family. These were followed by prominent freeholders from Cope's Mountnorris estate, undoubtedly to flaunt their dissidence against Cope, Brownlow and Stone. Likewise Brownlow opened with his electoral partner William Richardson MP, JP, and high sheriff of Armagh in 1737. He followed with a parade of prominent gentry. Some resided outside the county, including Richard Chapel Whaley, high sheriff of Armagh in 1742, now resident in Dublin, William Henry Fortescue of Randalstown, County Louth, MP for County Louth, high sheriff in 1746,[91] Thomas Ball of Wexford, high sheriff of Armagh in 1749, Hunt Chambré of Athy, Richard Workman, Captain Arthur Graham, Richard Magenis and Thomas Townly Dawson all of Dublin. Prominent local gentry appearing for Brownlow on the first day of the poll were William Irwin of Mountirwin, William Blacker of Carrickblacker, Edward Obré of Clontylew, George Bell of Armagh, Isaac Corry of Newry, and prominent clergymen Rev. Benjamin Barrington and Rev. James Strong of Tynan.

Similar tactics were deployed on the second day. Caulfeild continued with more dissident Mountnorris freeholders and some status gentry voters including Thomas Tipping JP of County Louth, Rev. William Godley JP of Mullabrack, Richard Jackson JP and Thomas Seaver of Killevy, Joshua McGeough of Drumsill, Alexander McComb of Altnamackin, Henry Harden of Harrybrook, and Henry Clarke of Annasamry. Brownlow, in turn, introduced further status names – some local, some non-resident – and a number of freeholders from Cope's Mountnorris estate to counterbalance those who had voted for Caulfeild.

And so the pattern continued with each candidate introducing some prestigious names on each day alongside rank and file freeholders from the various interests. On the thirteenth and final day of the poll, Friday 9 November, Caulfeild, despite his inclusion of the high-profile names of Joseph Johnston JP of Knappagh, Samuel McGeough of Newry and Leonard Dobbin of Ballynewry, could muster only 20 votes which were soon out-distanced by Brownlow's 114 votes finishing flourish with freeholders from his own estate supported by members of the gentry including John Johnston JP of Derryhale, Thomas Morres Jones of Moneyglass and Jonesborough, and William Workman of Portadown.

The poll book does not show the total numbers who were refused or were unable to vote. It has been noted earlier that tactics of the Caulfeild camp were to delay the opening of the poll in order to have his forty-shilling freeholders, registered on 3 May 1753, eligible to vote in the autumn by-election. However, these delaying tactics were thwarted by High Sheriff Workman's interpretation of the six-month qualification period stipulated in the statute of 1745. The *Belfast News-Letter* reported that 369 votes for Caulfeild were refused by Workman on 5th and 6 November, and a total of 447 votes over the five days, Monday to Friday, 5–9 November. These figures were also reported by the Dublin patriot newspaper *Universal Advertiser*.[92] Caulfeild would later claim that he was deprived of the votes of 448 freeholders registered on 3 May who attempted to vote on the 5 to 9 November, by Workman's interpretation that ineligibility on the opening day of the poll applied for the duration of the poll. Workman's ruling that 'the whole time for taking the poll was to be considered as one day' in effect ended Caulfeild's chances of winning.[93]

FESTIVITIES AND VIOLENCE DURING THE POLL

Contemporary accounts of the Armagh by-election painted a picture of a colourful, dispute-riven, rowdy and at times riotous affair with no quarter given either at the polling-booth or in the streets of Armagh. One aspect was the festive nature of the occasion. A large crowd gathered in Armagh city for the poll with hostelries packed with rival gangs of voters wearing the orange favours of Caulfeild and blue of Brownlow. Many were accommodated in bed-and-board establishments charged to the two candidates. Both sides had street musicians to rally supporters. Caulfeild had three drummers, Brownlow, a musical quintet from the Belfast stage and two trumpeters who toured Armagh city in a specially painted musical carriage. After the daily poll, the rival candidates retired to dinner at their respective headquarters each evening with their election agents and supporting gentry while freeholders ate and drank in a variety of public houses patronised by their own side.

Expenses soared during the thirteen days of the poll. By its completion Brownlow had already spent £5,434/13s/9d,[94] with the further expense of defending a parliamentary petition to come. Caulfeild's election expenses, though no detailed account is available, must have been similar. To treating of freeholders were added the expenses of travelling and accommodation arrangements. Attendance at the poll of non-residents was costly. Caulfeild's advertisement in the *Universal Advertiser* outlined arrangements for Dublin-based voters:

> Coaches will be ready for his [Caulfeild's] friends at the White Hart in Bolton Street and accommodation prepared for them at the Man of War, Crown and Thistle in Drogheda, Gainer's at Dunleer, The Feathers at Dundalk, McCord's at Newry and Mrs Henderson's at Markethill …[95]

Between October 1753 and April 1754, Brownlow paid numerous bills from Armagh hostelries for entertaining voters including Thomas McCann, Sam and Jane Bellew, a Mr. Ogle, Robert McKinstry, William Hall, George Burleigh, Tim Coyns, James Gellespie, Daniel Canavan, Charles McTrew, James Conlon and Robert Jones. Also paid by Brownlow were Patt Wilson and Chris Byrne for journeys to Newry, Catherine Heasty and John Timmons for supplying ale, Ob. Wisdom, a Dublin barber attending the Armagh poll and Mr. McCann for hire of a horse to transport him, a host of proprietors for providing lodgings including accommodation for the five musicians from the Belfast stage and two other trumpeters. Sundry expenses included Gardiner's bill for blue ribbon, William Dickie's bill for printing, James Edall's bill for poll books, bills for horse hire, carpentry, painting, and compensation for a lost saddle.[96]

The occasion also had a violent dimension with physical intimidation of opponents by rival gangs of supporters who roamed Armagh's streets, chanting provocative catch-cries and attacking each other with cudgels and cobblestones. All this brought a renewal of the paper war with a pro-Caulfeild letter accusing a mob of Brownlow supporters comprising 'weavers, quill-boys and blackguards' from Lurgan running amok in Armagh, breaking windows, trampling on orange cockades and using taunts such as 'B[rownlow] forever! Scour the Whigs, and down with the Orange-cockades'.[97] A pro-Brownlow pamphlet accused the Caulfeild side of introducing physical intimidation from the first day of the poll when a servant of Richard Chapel Whaley was assailed by Caulfeild supporters on the public street, and continued next day when one of Brownlow's servants was beaten with a cudgel. It further alleged that a Caulfeild mob had been summoned by drumbeat that evening and attacked opponents before being routed by a pro-Brownlow gang.[98] An earlier pamphlet from the same source accused Alexander Stewart and John Bond of leading a march of Caulfeild supporters with cocked pistols, and taunting opponents with offensive slogans such as: 'C[aulfeil]d forever, and B[rownlo]w in the river'.[99]

A newspaper report attributed the early violence to Brownlow supporters, or, specifically, fifty to sixty weavers who entered Armagh City on Saturday 27 October from 'a neighbouring place' and terrified the inhabitants.[100] When an enquiry into Saturday's disturbances was being held in Armagh courthouse on Monday 29 October, recriminations, refusals by both sides to disband the drummers and musicians, and chants of rival gangs outside, disrupted proceedings to such an extent that High Sheriff Workman had to adjourn at 3 pm. The evening violence returned in the worst night of rioting in Armagh. Drunken mobs armed with cudgels and quarter-staffs attacked each other and bystanders, and used cobblestones to break the windows of houses of entertainment and private houses accommodating opponents.[101] More recriminations and 'a great altercation' followed in court on Tuesday 30 October. However, on this occasion, the drums were officially banned, and both candidates agreed to appeal to the public for peace. This initiative was successful in maintaining order for the present. But disturbances were anticipated for the week beginning 5 November when Caulfeild introduced his freeholders registered on 3 May who were refused by Workman; and when Caulfeild continued to tender their rejected votes each day subsequently. But the expected disturbances did not materialise and the fragile peace held.[102]

The contest slowly built to a climax. On Friday 9 November, after one round of ten freeholders being introduced by each side, the poll was tied. Then when Caulfeild could only find another eight freeholders, Brownlow produced '97 ten pounders out of his own estate alone' – a traditional clinching bid to which Caulfeild could not respond. The final tally was taken and the poll concluded on a tally of 637 votes for Brownlow against 543 for Caulfeild, giving victory to the former on a majority of 94.[103] Both candidates were chaired from the courthouse. The drums sounded again and the truce was broken in a final purging street battle. It began between a minority on each side with sticks, but, fortified by alcohol, developed into a general battle in which firearms were produced and shots fired. A pro-Brownlow account reported that a Brownlow tenant was dangerously ill and another had lost an eye having been shot in the face. The 9 November fracas was a final confrontation. The last observation in the Saturday 10 November account was: 'The two competitors are gone off this morning, and we have peace at last'.[104]

CAULFEILD'S PETITION TO PARLIAMENT AND THE NATIONAL POWER-STRUGGLE, NOVEMBER TO DECEMBER 1753

That the 1753 by-election in Armagh was used as another campaign in the continuing power-struggle between Primate Stone and Speaker Boyle was evident in several factors. The intervention from Dublin was significant in the numerous election pamphlets published there, and in the number of Armagh freeholders resident in Dublin who attended the poll in Armagh. The orchestration of objections by both camps against electors were clear signals that the loser would continue the struggle via a parliamentary petition to overthrow the result and stage-manage a show-down between the parties of Stone and Boyle by which time national political issues would long have superseded local ones. At the beginning of the Armagh poll in late October, Chief Secretary Sackville had emphasised the importance of victory for Brownlow, the government's adopted candidate, as a means of keeping the opposition at bay. He believed the country party would join with Lord Kildare in attempting to attack the government on two issues: the expulsion of former Surveyor-general Arthur Jones-Nevill from the house of commons for incompetence and the defeat of Brownlow in the Armagh by-election. Sackville warned Pelham 'This {expulsion of Jones-Nevill} and the Armagh election are the two points upon which they threaten to show a great majority'.[105]

On 17 November Caulfeild petitioned the house of commons against the by-election result. Sackville's report to residential Under-secretary Sir

Robert Wilmot in London, conveys the importance attached to the issue by both country and court parties:

> Mr. Brownlow takes his seat this day, and I am told the speaker's son moves the petition against him. Brownlow will be well supported, and I verily believe for the first time that the speaker will lose an election point in the house of commons. If that should happen it would more effectively hurt his interest than ten other questions.[106]

On the day Caulfeild's petition was placed before parliament, Sackville was encouraged by the government's success in a first division over Jones-Nevill by 118 to 115 from which result 'people will be convinced that the speaker is not invincible'.[107] But Sackville was all too aware how the opposition would use the Armagh petition to undermine the government generally and Stone in particular: 'And the Armagh election is their [the country party] next great object, and at the rate they are going on I will not be surprised if they carry it [and] attack the primate personally'.[108]

The following is a summary of four main charges in Caulfeild's petition against the result of the poll. Firstly it was argued that Rev. Anthony Cope had promised his interest to Caulfeild but later had been induced to break his pledge by a promise of the deanery of Armagh; whereupon Cope had directed his agents to coax and threaten all his freeholders to vote for Brownlow. Caulfeild alleged 132 of Cope's tenants had thus been bullied into voting for Brownlow.[109] Secondly, when tenants on Cope's Mountnorris estate signed a memorial to Cope in England requesting leave to vote for Caulfeild, they had been visited on the eve of the poll and bullied by Cope's emissaries to vote for Brownlow, under penalty of being pressed for immediate payment of rent not due until 10 November – all of which, the petition argued, was an unwarranted interference in a parliamentary election, and had forced many pro-Caulfeild tenants to vote for Brownlow or to stay at home. Thirdly, Brownlow's supporters were blamed for the riots in Armagh city on 27 and 29 October.

Fourthly, Cauldfeild's petition accused High Sheriff Workman of partiality in conducting the election: of opening the poll unreasonably soon on 26 October before eight hundred freeholders registered on 3 May were eligible to vote on 3 or 4 November; and adjourning the poll one hour early on opening day at the request of Brownlow's side, allegedly to facilitate Brownlow's agents to intimidate further Cope freeholders waiting to vote for Caulfeild. It was alleged that details of Cope's tenants supporting Caulfeild were entered incorrectly in the clerk of peace's book resulting in objections from the Brownlow side at the poll being upheld by Workman who refused these votes and any review of the original entries. Yet, it was argued, Workman had accepted some 129 votes for Brownlow despite objections by the Caulfeild side that these voters had no, or insufficient, freehold qualification. Further, it was alleged that Workman had accepted 19 votes for Brownlow from persons who were 'Papists' or had connections with the 'Popish religion'. Finally, between 5 to 9 November, Workman had refused 448 votes for Caulfeild which had been registered on 3 May which he adjudged did not satisfy the six-month qualification period prior to the start of the poll on 26 October, and Workman had so dated the final indenture, although he had signed it on 10 November; nor had Workman agreed to accept the 3 May registered votes provisionally, dependent upon a later decision regarding their validity by the house of commons.[110]

How far was Caulfeild's case to parliament valid? The first three charges had little merit. While Caulfeild's argument that freeholders on Cope's Mountnorris estate resented Cope's volte-face is supported by the fairly even division of votes at the poll despite late pressure from Cope's agents, and while it was regarded as a breach of protocol for a landlord to reverse his pledge of support, it was not illegal for him to change his mind. Evidence of intimidation of Caulfeild supporters was neither specific nor conclusive. The *Universal Advertiser* reported that when some Cope freeholders refused to pledge votes for Brownlow 'their cattle were instantly drove [sic] to the pound some days before their rent became due'.[111] But reportage by this patriot newspaper tended to be pro-Caulfeild during the election. An absence of named witnesses suggests that either criminal intimidation did not occur at Mountnorris, or was effective. It could also be assumed that the violence in Armagh city during the poll was not one-sided.

Accusations of partiality in crucial decisions taken by High Sheriff Workman merit more scrutiny. The role and functions of the high sheriff were complex. The shrievalty was a key county office in eighteenth century Ireland with the occupant appointed annually by the Dublin executive. Responsibilities of the post were onerous and included choosing juries, convening the quarter sessions and assizes, custody of prisoners, and acting as chief returning officer for the county during parliamentary elections when he had power to make a range of executive decisions.[112] A sine qua non of appointment was ownership of land in the county, and normally, residence on it[113] since the high sheriff required considerable local knowledge and familiarity with members of the magistracy and grand jury.

Because of its demanding duties, the shrievalty was not always desired by the county gentry and regarded by some as something of a poisoned chalice, especially in parliamentary election year when the high sheriff was precluded from candidature for county member. Service could also involve high expenses incurred in entertainment and in fees for clerks and deputy sheriffs who carried out the day-to-day administration. Such expenses were not all refunded by the exchequer as, for instance, deputy sheriffs were appointed by the high sheriff and were not patent officers.[114] Dublin Castle attempted to spread the burden of service as high sheriff as widely as possible among the gentry of the county. Thus in the eighteenth century forty eight different Armagh families filled the office, twenty three of whom served only once. Highest frequencies of service were by the families of Cope of Loughgall – seven terms, Clarke of Summerisland and Dawson of Armagh city – five terms each, Ball of the Fews, Bond of Middletown, Johnston of Gilford and Richardson of Richhill – four terms each, Workman of Portadown and Brownlow of Lurgan – three terms each, and Acheson of Markethill – two terms. The relative infrequency of service in the shrievalty by the Brownlow and Acheson families was undoubtedly due to their contemporaneous service as members of parliament; while no member of the Caulfeild family held the post, probably as a result of continued residence in Dublin in the eighteenth century.

At first sight, it seemed as if High Sheriff Workman was partial towards Brownlow at the 1753 poll. All branches of the Workman family voted for Brownlow. His critical decision to disallow the votes of freeholders registered on 3 May at any stage during the election – based on his ruling that votes ineligible at the start of the election on 26 October would remain ineligible for the duration of the election – penalised Brownlow less than Caulfeild,[115] and thus seemed blatantly partisan. The issue was less simplistic. Workman had come under increasing pressures as the six months qualification period neared completion to accept the 3 May registered votes from 3 November. Sackville reported to Wilmot in London: 'Mr. Caulfeild's friends have used every method to create delay, and have by riots and trifling objections continued the poll to this time, when the new registered voters may be offered as having a right.'[116] Court and country parties in Dublin anxiously awaited Workman's ruling on whether to admit the new voters to the poll. Sackville assured Wilmot that Dublin lawyers were of the opinion that 'the election means the day upon which the poll begins' and, on that interpretation, Lord Chancellor Jocelyn, Attorney General Flood, Solicitor General Tisdall, and Recorder of Dublin Stannard were all of the opinion that the 'new registered voters' had 'no right' to vote in this election poll.[117] Workman undoubtedly consulted this legal opinion at the highest level before he decided to reject the 'new registered voters' at the poll from 3 November.

The legal implications of Workman's decision were far-reaching and adjudged by Sackville to be the issue which would decide the outcome of the anticipated petition to the house of commons: 'If the sheriff persists in rejecting them, the dispute in the house of commons will probably turn on that point of law.'[118] However, once a petition had been accepted by the house of commons, the outcome of the Armagh election would depend less on legal precedent than on a head-count between the supporters of the court and country parties. Flushed with their victory in having Jones-Nevill expelled from parliament on 22 November, Speaker Boyle's country party now used Caulfeild's petition as more ammunition to attack the primate and increase the pressure on government. Under-secretary Thomas Waite reported from Dublin Castle to Wilmot in London: 'The party continue their denunciations and threatenings against my lord primate, Brownlow, and the Galway members.'[119] And, to rub salt into the court party's wounds, Caulfeild was introduced to Lord Lieutentant Dorset at a levee on 25 November.[120]

On 3 December, Brownlow was ordered by the house of commons to give evidence[121] and presented his case to the committee of privileges and elections on 6 December. His submission argued that the by-election poll would have concluded before the 3 November but for the delaying tactics of the Caulfeild side to enable some 400 freehold votes, mostly from the Charlemont estate and registered at the quarter sessions of 3 May, to be included in the poll; and it had been correct to disqualify those votes from the poll. Brownlow further alleged that Caulfeild was an under age 'minor' and thus ineligible to stand as a parliamentary candidate. He also alleged that several persons in the Caulfeild camp had used 'undue means' to procure votes.[122]

Caulfeild's petition assumed huge national importance as evidenced in two separate communiqués written on the same day. When reporting the introduction of Caulfeild's petition for hearing on 6 December, Waite warned Wilmot:

> I hear it said everywhere that if the Patriots, as they are called, have anything of a majority against Brownlow they are to vote the primate an enemy to the country and to address the king to remove him from the government and from his majesty's councils. If they carry this election, no doubt is made of their carrying the one for Galway, and the next consideration will be what is to become of the money bill that is altered.[123]

Waite's second letter of 6 December re-emphasised why the government must defeat Caulfeild's petition and have Brownlow's election upheld:

> ... had we suffered the Armagh election without dispute to have been given up to the speaker, who declared aloud that Brownlow should not sit because he was reputed a friend of the primate's and that anybody who professed himself his friend should be the object of the resentment of that party which was resolved to govern this country without control ... if that had been our conduct, we should have been left at the mercy of the speaker, my Lord Kildare, and the prime sergeant, and all English influence would have been at an end.

Waite reported that little progress had been made on the opening day of the hearing and that the outcome would be very close.[124]

On Saturday 8 December, Henry Meredyth, first clerk to the chief secretary and secretary to the primate, and Benjamin Barrington, Stone's first chaplain, were called to give evidence to the hearing. Waite considered that being confidants of the primate, neither should have been pressed 'to divulge his master's secrets' and regarded their summons an unseemly ploy by the speaker's party to humiliate the primate. He also reported that Sackville thought the coming vote would be 'a hard run thing by both sides.'[125] That evening a division by the hearing committee upheld Brownlow's election by 122 votes to 118 – though Waite warned that the opposition would try again on Monday when the report was made to the house of commons.[126] The opposition strove on Sunday 9 December to win over votes. It persuaded two government supporters of Saturday to absent themselves from the vote on Monday, and Johnny Macarell, member for Carlingford who had been absent on Saturday, to attend and vote for Caulfeild's petition on Monday. On Monday 10 December 1753, the government survived on a vote of 120 votes to 119 to have Brownlow declared duly elected.[127]

Recriminations by the Caulfeild camp revealed just how fortuitous Brownlow's survival had been. Adderley later referred to the break-down of deals involving the Armagh and Galway petitions when proposals to trade withdrawal of support for the Galway petition in return for support for Caulfeild's petition, and a proposed 'pairing' of abstentions by Sir Archibald Acheson and his brother-in-law Robert French of Monivea, did not materialise.[128] He also castigated John Preston's eleventh hour breach of promise. Preston, member for Navan, had voted against Caulfeild's petition in committee but had promised to absent himself from the Monday vote. Then he had been persuaded and brought to the parliament at 8.00 pm by Sir George Forbes, member for Mullingar, to vote for Brownlow. Had Preston been absent the vote would have been tied and Speaker Boyle could have given his casting vote in favour of Caulfeild's petition.[129]

Adderley also lamented the vagaries in attendance at the parliamentary votes for Caulfeild's petition: the absence through illness or desertion, of Caulfeild supporters such as Stephen Bernard, member for Bandon-bridge, Acheson Moore, member for Bangor, and Galbraith Lowry, member for Tyrone county. He contrasted the effort made by Tom Butler, ailing member for Belturbet who was persuaded by his brother Lord Lanesborough to obey Stone's summons to attend and vote against the petition – just days before his death; and the loyalty and luck of Brownlow's uncle, Hon. George Hamilton, member for St Johnstown, County Donegal, who had caught all connections from London just in time to vote for his nephew on Hamilton's first visit to the Irish parliament since his election to it in 1727.[130]

A special importance to the government of victory over the Armagh petition was that it repelled an attack by the patriot opposition on the primate in his own diocese. That importance was confirmed on the following day when the petition against the Galway by-election result was withdrawn.[131] Waite apprised Wilmot that the Armagh vote had been a narrow escape from a determined and vindictive opposition:

> I am assured by a member of the House that they came down charged with resolutions for sending the sheriff of Armagh to Newgate and for voting the primate guilty of undue influence etc., etc., if they had happened to have the majority.[132]

The patriot opposition had its revenge on 17 December 1753 when the altered money bill concerning the disposal of the surplus in the treasury was defeated by 118 votes to 123 after a ten hour debate.[133]

MOBILISATION OF A PATRIOT OPPOSITION IN COUNTY ARMAGH 1754–9

Following the rejection of the money bill, Lord Lieutenant Dorset removed patriot dissidents from the Dublin administration in January 1754.[134] The response of the patriot opposition was to accelerate its campaign in the country. New patriot clubs and independent freeholders and 'free citizens' societies were founded, and addresses made to members of parliament to promote an 'Irish interest' against the 'English interest' personified in Primate Stone. Pamphlets and essays, resolutions and toasts at dinners and supportive addresses from grand juries and assizes, all lauding patriot ideals, were published in sympathetic newspapers such as the recently founded *Universal Advertiser*.

A long pamphlet issued in the name of the County Armagh Patriot Club called for continued patriot vigilance which, it alleged, had challenged the Dublin administration for justice for the 'Irish interest' which had been compromised on four recent occasions. The Linen Bill of 1751 when altered by the British government, had been rejected by the Irish house of commons despite the betrayal of an Armagh 'Tale-monger' and MP – an allusion to William Richardson – who, it was alleged, had attempted to fudge the issue by minimising the significance of the English changes. Secondly, Dublin Castle was accused of double standards in the administration of justice: though Jones-Nevill, friend of Stone and Sackville, had been expelled by the house of commons for corruption, a bill compelling him to make restitution had been rejected by the privy council on the recommendation of the lord lieutenant. In contrast, Bellingham Boyle and the other sacked dissidents were deprived of their pensions.

Thirdly, in the Armagh by-election, it was alleged that Stone's use of church preferment had obtained the vital electoral interest of Rev. Anthony Cope for Brownlow, and the partiality of Workman had cheated Caulfeild of legal votes. Fourthly, the pamphlet lauded the rejection of the Money Bill as 'the glorious event of the 17 December 1753'.[135]

Reference in this pamphlet to the abuse received by Protestant dissenters in the Armagh 1753 by-election, suggests that the author may have been William Bruce, patriot and Dublin Presbyterian printer and pamphleteer:

> No wonder, gentlemen, that the Protestant dissenters that outnumber their brethren of the Established Church in this county, and were on this occasion remarkably on the side of Whiggish independence, should be rancorously abused by the enemies of this glorious cause, and particularly by a certain lying ecclesiastical retainer to the over-grown ecclesiastick [sic].[136]

Armagh patriots were heavily involved in rallies. In January 1754, Thomas Adderley and other Armagh 'free citizens' were lauded at a county patriot meeting in Roscommon.[137] At a dinner in Dublin on 15 February, patriots toasted included Charlemont borough members Adderley and Hon. John Caulfeild, while 'Rotten Stone' was condemned.[138] On 25 February, a meeting of 'independent freeholders' in Cavan thanked Sir Archibald Acheson, who possessed a second estate in Arvagh, for his patriotic contribution in the recent political debate.[139] James Bell, secretary of the 'Free and Independent Club of the County of Armagh' advertised its quarterly dinner-meeting for 16 April in Thomas Stringer's Hotel in Armagh.[140] The choice of the ecclesiastical capital as venue was undoubtedly an act of defiance to the primate, its political patron.

Armagh county members Brownlow and Richardson were eclipsed by the patriot campaign of 1754. Their names fleetingly re-appeared when the linen drapers and traders around Lurgan, having drawn up an address of thanks to the lord lieutenant on 29 March for his intervention to support the credit of banks, requested Richardson – in Brownlow's absence – to present it to Dorset who publicly thanked them.[141] It was an expression of appreciation to their local linen patrons and to the government for stabilising fiscal agencies. However, the omission of linen weavers from the address suggested a class division in the Armagh linen industry between an emerging middle class of entrepreneurs supporting government and a lower class of weavers supporting the patriot opposition. Ironically, many of those weavers had provided the electoral muscle for Brownlow as late as the previous autumn by-election contest.

In the spring of 1754, Dorset's changes in personnel to prop up the Irish administration with more reliable servants had a mixed reception and limited effects. New Prime Sergeant Eaton Stannard was described as 'a man of more vanity than ambition'; a weary Lord Chief Justice Henry Singleton – 'old, infirm and worn-out ... ready to drop into his grave' – was promoted to master of the rolls; and the Rt Hon. Arthur Hill – another choice 'to gall his adversaries' – replaced Henry Boyle as chancellor of the exchequer.[142] The Rt Hon. William Yorke was moved to succeed Singleton, Robert Marshall succeeded Yorke and Lord Forbes was appointed to the joint post of quarter-master and barrack-master general[143] – probably reward for his eleventh-hour services to the late parliamentary vote on the Armagh petition on 10 December 1753.

The star of the three Armagh patriot MPs i.e. who either resided or represented seats in the county, continued to rise. At the dinner-meeting of the Armagh Independent Freeholders Club in Thomas Stringer's Hotel on 16 April, special thanks were unanimously returned to Sir Archibald Acheson, and acknowledgements to the Hon. John Caulfeild and Thomas Adderley for 'steady adherence to the same [independent] principles in the last session of parliament.'[144] The rotation of venue and chair of meetings identified key areas and leaders of patriot opposition in the county as Armagh City, Tandragee, Acton, Newry, Portadown and Lurgan. The next meeting, held in November at the house of Robert Martin in Tandragee with Sir Archibald Acheson in the chair, supported 'the principles of freedom', Speaker Boyle and the government employees dismissed from office for 'attachment to the true interest of their country', and condemned those who deserted that interest, including the 'ambitious' primate and members of parliament under his influence.[145]

A meeting fixed for John McCord's Newry hostelry on 17 December to be chaired by Francis Caulfeild, was too large and adjourned to the market-house. This rally of Armagh residents in and around Newry celebrated with cheering, bonfires, illuminations and gun-fire. After-dinner toasts wished 'success to Mr. Caulfeild and Sir Archibald Acheson, Bart. at next election for the county according to the principles of this club; success to Roger Hall, Esq. ... for the town of Newry.' Other toasts included those to Armagh patriot members and patrons of electoral interests such as Lord Charlemont, Sir Francis St John and Sir Francis Nedham who had opposed Stone and the government in the 1753 by-election. Stone, Rev. Anthony Cope et al. were roundly condemned:

> May all clergymen and others who would sell their interest and distress their tenants for acting as freemen be disappointed, and meet with the contempt they deserve; may Caiaphas [sic] and all his adherents who would sell the liberties of this country, meet with Laud's fate.

Next meeting was fixed for Charles Casey's house in Portadown on 13 January 1755 with Sir Capel Molyneux in the chair.[146]

The patriot campaign continued in 1755. The Patriot Club of Newry was instituted on 1 January with Down county MP in the chair and follow-up meetings arranged.[147] On 7 February, freeholders from Alexander Stewart's manor met at James Tegart's inn in Acton village to form themselves into a new patriot club to support opponents of government. Following the usual toasts, special thanks were reserved for Stewart's magnanimity in allowing them freedom to vote for the candidate of their choice in the 1753 by-election, and a follow-up meeting fixed for 16 April at the same venue.[148] This date commemorated the duke of Cumberland's victory at Culloden and was also chosen by Lurgan inhabitants for an initial patriot meeting. However, unlike 1753 when the Lurgan commemoration was celebrated at Brownlow's house, in 1755 it was held at the house of Thomas Hill where resolutions similar to those at the other patriot club meetings and the names of Brownlow and Richardson – still under a cloud in patriot eyes – were omitted from toasts. Included was a toast to the marquis of Hartington, now tipped to replace Dorset as lord lieutenant.[149]

As the patriots grew in strength, Dorset's position appeared increasingly untenable. In spring 1755, an estimate of interests in the Irish house of commons identified 125 members 'on the country side' against 116 'on the court' side'.[150] This situation became all the more worrying for the English government with the growing threat of war with France, who, it was thought, might use Ireland as side-door for an invasion of England.[151] Following the death of Henry Pelham, main supporter in the English administration of Stone and Sackville, the duke of Newcastle and Legge[152] considered that the duke of Devonshire who was related by marriage to Henry Boyle and to the Ponsonby family, might effect a reconciliation and working arrangement with the Irish patriots. In March 1755, Devonshire's eldest son Lord Hartington was appointed to replace Dorset as lord lieutenant of Ireland with Colonel Henry Seymour-Conway, brother of Lord Hertford, as his chief secretary.[153]

On 1 May 1755, it was reckoned that ten members were still 'personally attached' to Stone, and 'entirely directed by him'. These included Armagh county members Brownlow and Richardson.[154] Identified 'in the dissenting interest' of opposition were Sir Archibald Acheson, independent member for Dublin University, Thomas Adderley and Hon. John Caulfeild.[155] Following Hartington's arrival in Ireland in May 1755, the Armagh families of Acheson and Caulfeild enjoyed better relations with the Dublin administration. Hon. John Caulfeild agreed to support the new administration.[156] Lord Charlemont, who had socialised with Hartington on his European tour,[157] was persuaded by Adderley on his return to act as mediator between Boyle and Dublin Castle.[158] Boyle and Malone were restored to favour, and Viscount Jocelyn and the earls of Kildare and Bessborough appointed as lords justices. Patriot opposition eased in the counties. The meeting of the Free and Independent Club of the county of Armagh re-scheduled for 16 April 1755 in Portadown, was cancelled and a newspaper notice announced the Club to be dissolved.[159] A letter in the *Universal Advertiser* rejoiced at the appointment of Hartington who was described as 'of the old Whig stamp' whose grandfather had opposed all High Churchmen and Papists.[160] In March 1756 Acheson was asked and agreed to support Hartington's brother-in-law John Ponsonby in an election for the speakership.[161] In June, the lords justices appointed Acheson deputy governor of County Armagh.[162] Primate Stone and his party had quietly become the new opposition directing from his Leixlip residence the dissent of friends such as Brownlow, Pery, Maxwell et al. in the house of commons.

However, allegations over 1756–7 that the new political arrangement had been reached by double-dealing for office, pension and honours between many of the principals brought public disillusion with high politics. Pery's conspiracy theory of 1757 referred to a 'cabal' of former patriots, including the Boyle family, Malone and Carter, and the primate and Ponsonby family, all involved in secret deals, and claimed that Stone's withdrawal from the power-game was but a tactic before his return to the field of play in a pre-arranged game-plan.[163] Things turned sour in Charlemont's negotiations when he discovered secret deals including Boyle's negotiation of the title earl of Shannon and an annual pension for thirty one years for vacating the speakership. Effigies of Boyle and Malone were burned for their perceived sell-out in March 1756 followed by a serious riot in Dublin.[164] A disillusioned Charlemont recorded: 'these frequent apostacies had been used by the corrupt as an inexhaustible source of ridicule and even of argument against true patriotism ... there are many hypocrites.'[165] He resolved to be a committed 'freeman' of independent views untied to either court or country party but truly 'patriotic' i.e. doing what was right for Ireland.[166]

Brownlow became an adherent of independent country politics and joint-leader with Pery of the 'new patriots' in the house of commons – 'a member who is an honour to it', according to Pery's account to Bedford[167] – opposing all political jobbery until his death in 1794. By 1756, Brownlow seemed to have distanced himself from Stone. When Lord Lieutenant Hartington who had succeeded to fourth duke of Devonshire in December 1755 became first lord of the English treasury in the Pitt-North coalition, he appointed the fourth duke of Bedford as his successor. Bedford's Chief Secretary Richard Rigby tended to dominate the new lord lieutenant's decisions. Stone returned to power in March 1758 as a lord justice in Bedford's re-built administration.[168] But Brownlow remained in opposition, developing a reputation of patriot spokesman. Pery and he proposed a motion to abolish the practice of paying military fees to the chief secretary, under-secretary and first clerk and to replace it with fixed salaries. It was a bloodless victory as the three officials concerned welcomed the change, and the measure was carried on 16 January 1758 nemine contradicente.[169]

About this time, Acheson would also seem to have become disillusioned with politics in high places. In December 1757 he proposed a house of commons enquiry into the management of the revenue service, controlled by the Ponsonby family. Speaker John Ponsonby – whose appointment Acheson had supported in 1756 – regarded Acheson's motion as an attack on the integrity of the Ponsonby family, and a lack of confidence by Dublin Castle when Rigby supported the motion and acted as teller of the votes in favour.[170] Most of the balloted members of the committee of enquiry were supporters of the Revenue Board and found no fraud or mismanagement when they reported in April 1758.[171] But the very holding of an enquiry had placed a strain on the Ponsonby family role in and contribution to the administration.

In 1759, Bedford and Rigby availed of an opportunity to secure Acheson's support for the administration when Rigby informed him that Bedford was recommending Rev. Walter Cope, Acheson's brother-in-law, to the king for appointment to the vacant deanery of Dromore.[172] Acheson reciprocated by sponsoring recruits to Captain Walsh's company of Colonel Aldercorn's new regiment at Armagh.[173] It was an initiative appreciated by both Charlemont who as governor of the county had asked his deputy to encourage Protestant recruitment to new regiments to defend Ireland in an impending war,[174] and Bedford who had on-going problems raising Irish troops; and one soon shown to be opportune by Pitt's intelligence that the target of French attack was to be Ireland.[175] Acheson's services were further recognised when Bedford appointed him a trustee of the Linen Board in replacement for recently deceased Henry Singleton.[176]

From mid 1755, county member Richardson withdrew increasingly from active parliamentary politics, confining initiatives to promoting the local linen industry, including his support for a resolution from the body of linen drapers that all unbleached linen lengths must be fully exposed to buyers at market to avoid fraud.[177] Problems in his personal life may have contributed to his withdrawal from politics. His wife, Isabella Mussenden, had died young in November 1753. The attacks on his character by pamphleteers may have affected his own health and he died suddenly, aged forty nine, in his Dublin house in February 1758. In the resulting by-election Armagh politicians were unwilling to risk the experiences of 1753 being repeated, and Francis Caulfeild was returned quietly for Armagh county without a contest.[178] Indeed, the ferocity, violence and expense associated with the 1753 poll remained long in the memories of Armagh politicians who subsequently strove to avoid contested elections.

The final parliamentary election in Armagh in the decade of the 1750s was held following the death in early June 1759 of General Philip Bragg.[179] Primate Stone took the opportunity to enhance his stock with the lord lieutenant by choosing Bedford's son, the Hon. Francis Russell, marquis of Tavistock, as Bragg's replacement for Armagh borough.[180]

CONCLUSION: STORMY ELECTIONEERING IN THE 1750s

Following a half-century with few parliamentary elections and no contests, by mid-eighteenth century a new generation of young aspiring politicians in County Armagh was eager to participate in the electoral process. The number of families emerging to challenge for the prestigious county seats increased significantly. Brownlow, Cope, Richardson, Acheson and Caulfeild – in descending order of electoral strength – were willing to field a candidate if available, and the ambitious Molyneux, Moore and Stewart waited for a suitable opportunity to compete or pick up a borough seat outside the county. In Armagh, county seats seemed to be more open than in neighbouring counties where larger but fewer political magnates dominated returns. The eagerness of these families and others was manifested in a phoney general election campaign in 1752 and in the celebrated by-election of 1753. Both campaigns followed the English model of preliminary negotiations between political magnates, resident and absentee, to agree election partnerships; the canvass of the landed gentry for electoral voting interests; the canvass of freeholders by candidates; and the negotiations by the Dublin administration to recruit supporters of government from elected members. Other practices at election-time included the English customs of festivities and treating, which voters expected and were resentful where omitted.

An issue which has aroused debate in historical research has been how far the relationships between landlords and their tenants in eighteenth century elections were based on unquestioning subservience or on mutual trust and respect. The fact that the attendance of tenants at the Armagh poll over thirteen days was so well organised by landlords and/or agents could be interpreted as supporting a traditional view that tenants were always subservient to their landlords at elections. However, the revolt of significant numbers of tenants on the Cope and St John estates, at the poll or by abstention, is clear evidence that they would defy the direction of landlords they deemed to have broken conventions. This division at the Armagh poll illustrated, as research on early eighteenth century Cheshire elections has argued,[181] that landlord influence and tenant independence could coexist not only within the same county but even within the same community. It also suggests that relationships, generally, were based on mutual trust –

rather than on subservience and intimidation – which landlords breached at the risk of tenant defiance at the poll.

Another lesson learned by Armagh landlords in 1753 was the huge expense and potential for violence associated with a poll. Thus defeated candidate Caulfeild was allowed to take a county seat unopposed at a subsequent County Armagh by-election in 1758. And the leading political magnates and magistrates in the county would strive to avoid a contest in future county elections.

A feature of the 1753 Armagh by-election was that local and national politics became inextricably intertwined with leading national political interests using the Armagh election as another campaign in the on-going national power-struggle between Speaker Boyle and Primate Stone. Accordingly, the paper war, attempts to delay the start of the poll, transport of non-resident voters and the subsequent petition to parliament, were largely orchestrated from Dublin. The outcome was a narrow victory for Brownlow and the Stone party who had formed an improbable electoral partnership as did Caulfeild with Acheson, both alignments unlikely to survive in the long-term. The national dimension to the Armagh by-election was continued post-election in the mobilisation of a patriot interest in County Armagh, 1754–9.

Notes

1   D.M. Beaumont, 'The gentry of the King's and Queen's Counties, Protestant landed society 1690–1760' (2 vols, unpublished Ph.D. thesis, TCD; hereafter Beaumont, Thesis), ii, 58.
2   Adderley to Charlemont, 22 Feb. 1748 (*HMC Charlemont*), i, 181.
3   Malcomson, *Agar*, p. 135.
4   James Walton (ed.), *"The King's business": letters on the administration of Ireland, 1740–1761, from the papers of Sir Robert Wilmot* (New York, 1996, hereafter Walton, *The King's Business*), pp xxxvii–xliv.
5   Acheson to St John, 21 Apr. 1752 (PRONI, Gosford papers, D/1606/1/1/4).
6   O'Gorman, *Voters*, pp 128–9.
7   E.M. Johnston, *Great Britain and Ireland, 1760–1800, a study in political administration* (Edinburgh, 1963; hereafter Johnston, *G.B. & Ire.*).
8   J.A. Phillips, *Electoral behaviour in unreformed England, plumpers, splitters and straights* (Princeton, New Jersey, 1982; hereafter Phillips, *Electoral behaviour*), p. 20. 'Splitters' were a voter's pair of votes cast in a general election divided between election partners; a 'plumper' was a single vote cast from a voter's pair of votes in a general election where the other vote was discarded.
9   Armagh freeholders list, 1738; County Armagh Poll Book, 1753, Johnston Collection, Armagh Public Library (PRONI, T/3324/2B/Acc.12465; hereafter 'Armagh Poll Book, 1753').
10 Malcomson, *Foster*, p. 29.
11 O'Gorman, *Voters*, pp 90–105.

12 Acheson to St John, 21 Apr. 1752 (PRONI, Gosford papers, D/1606/1/1/4); St John to Acheson, 30 Apr. 1752 (ibid., D/1606/1/1/5).
13 O'Gorman, *Voters*, pp 93–4.
14 Rev Walter Cope to Acheson, 1 June 1752 (PRONI, Gosford papers, D/1606/1/1/8). Rev Walter Cope had married Anne Acheson in 1742.
15 Johnston, *G.B. & Ire.*, pp 122–3.
16 Lord Orrery to Acheson, 23 May 1752 (PRONI, Gosford papers, D/1606/1/1/7).
17 Acheson to Judge Ward, 22 June 1752 (PRONI, Ward papers, D/2092/1/8/1).
18 Ibid.
19 Adderley to Acheson, 3 Mar. 1753 (PRONI, Gosford papers, D/1606/1/1/11B); Molyneux to Acheson, 10 Mar. 1753 (ibid., D/1606/1/1/11C). Second Viscount Charles Fane of Basildon, Berkshire, was Whig MP for Tavistock, and ambassador at Turin and Constantinople. He had inherited the Armagh manors of Clare and Tawnavaltiny in 1744.
20 Stone to Sackville, 11 Mar. 1753, *Report on the manuscripts of Mrs Stopford-Sackville of Drayton House, Northamptonshire*, (*HMC*, 2 vols, London, 1904–10; hereafter *HMC, Stopford-Sackville*), i, 192–4.
21 William Bruce to Justice Ward, 10 Mar. 1753 (PRONI, Ward papers, D/2092/1/8/1).
22 *BNL*, 23 Mar. 1753
23 Boyle to Acheson, 22 Mar. 1753 (PRONI, Gosford papers D/1606/1/1/12).
24 Cope to Acheson, 14 Mar. 1753 (ibid., D/1606/1/1/11A).
25 Molyneux to Acheson, 29 Mar. 1753 (ibid., D/1606/1/1/14). Henry Singleton was chief justice of the common pleas 1740–53 and master of the rolls 1754–9.
26 J.B. Leslie, *Armagh clergy and parishes* (Dundalk, 1911; hereafter Leslie, *Armagh clergy*), p. 22; *BNL*, 12 June 1753.
27 *Case of the Hon. Francis Caulfeild, Esq.* (RIA, Haliday Collection, 3B53–56/219, hereafter *Case of the Hon. Francis Caulfeild*).
28 Stone to Sackville, 16 Apr. 1753 (*HMC, Stopford-Sackville*), i, 194–6.
29 St John to Acheson, 3 Apr. 1753 (PRONI, Gosford papers D/1606/1/1/15).
30 Blacker to Acheson, 26 Apr. 1753 (PRONI, Gosford papers D/1606/1/1/16).
31 *A second letter from a free citizen of Dublin to a freeholder of the county of Armagh, Dublin, 1753* (QUB Library, Special Collections, Foster pamphlets; hereafter *A second letter*), xiii, 4.
32 Jenny to Acheson, 27 Mar. 1753 (PRONI, Gosford papers, D/1606/1/1/13); Rev. Henry Jenny, served as prebendary of Mullabrack 1707–33, archdeacon of Armagh 1733–8 and rector of Armagh 1738–58.
33 St John to Acheson, 3 Apr.1753 (PRONI, Gosford papers, D/1606/1/1/15); Speaker Boyle to Acheson, 22 May 1753 (ibid., D/1606/1/1/17A).
34 O'Gorman, *Voters*, p. 100.
35 Acheson to Ward, 22 June 1753 (PRONI, Castleward Letterbook 8, p. 13, D/2092/1/8/1).
36 O'Gorman, *Voters*, pp 152, 155.
37 *BNL*, 20 Apr. 1753.
38 Account of 1753 election expenses (PRONI, Brownlow papers, D/1928/A/2/2/ pp 10–13; hereafter 'Brownow's election expenses 1753').
39 Memoirs (*HMC, Charlemont*), i, 5.
40 *BNL*, 24 July 1753.
41 Ibid., 17 Aug. 1753.
42 *Commons' jn. Ire.* (Bradley), ix, 389.

43 O'Gorman, *Voters*, p. 129.
44 *A letter from a free citizen of Dublin to a freeholder in the county of Armagh* (QUB Library, Foster Collection, Dublin, 1753; hereafter *A letter from a free citizen*), vol xiii.
45 Ibid.
46 Walton, *The King's Business*, pp xxxvi –xlv.
47 *A second letter from a free citizen of Dublin to a freeholder in the county of Armagh by the author of the first* (RIA, Haliday, Tracts, Dublin, 1753; hereafter *A second letter from a free citizen of Dublin*), No. 27. Box 212.
48 *Seasonable advice to the freeholders of Armagh by a brother freeholder* (QUB Library, Foster Collection, Dublin, 1753; hereafter *Seasonable advice*), vol xiii.
49 Ibid., pp 7–10
50 Ibid., pp 17–21.
51 Ibid., pp 24–7.
52 Ibid.
53 Ibid.
54 *A fifth letter from a free citizen of Dublin to a freeholder of the county of Armagh, containing an examination of a pamphlet entitled Seasonable Advice & c. and recommended to the perusal of those who would form a fair and clear judgement of the candour and veracity of the author of that paper* (RIA, Haliday, Tracts, Dublin, 1753, hereafter A fifth letter), vol. 250, No.4, pp 6–7.
55 *Observations on the free citizen's fifth letter; by the author of The Seasonable Advice* (RIA,Haliday, Tracts, Dublin, 1753, hereafter *Observations*), vol. x, Box 210, No. 1, pp 25–8.
56 *A letter from a freeholder of the county of Armagh to a friend in Dublin, bearing date October 31st, 1753* (ibid.), Box 212, No. 15.
57 *A letter from a gentleman in the county of Armagh to his friend in Dublin; occasioned by the late robbery of the northern mail* (ibid., 13 Oct. 1753; hereafter *Thomas Tell-tale's letter*), No. 2.
58 *Commons' jn. Ire.* (Bradley), ix, 319.
59 *BNL*, 16 Oct. 1953.
60 *The Statutes at Large Passed in the Parliaments Held in Ireland, 1310–1800* (20 vols, Dublin, 1789–1800; hereafter *Irish Statutes*).
61 William Richardson to Daniel Mussenden, 13 Oct. 1753 (PRONI, Mussenden papers, D/354/1029). Richardson was married to Isabella Mussenden, daughter of Belfast businessman and banker, Daniel Mussenden.
62 *Commons' jn. Ire.* (Bradley), ix, 322.
63 Richardson to Mussenden, 13 Oct. 1753 (PRONI, Mussenden papers, D/354/1029).
64 *Thomas Tell-tale's letter*.
65 'County Armagh Poll Book, 1753'. The Johnston family came from Kilmore House, County Armagh.
66 However, as the vote of '328 John Ralston' was not polled following an objection that the townland declared at the poll differed from that registered – though mistakenly left among those listed in the poll book – the actual poll was 1,180.
67 This was probably Counsellor Samuel Blacker JP of Tandragee and Portadown, who was Sir Francis St John's recalcitrant agent and admirer of the politics of the Caulfeild family.
68 This vote may have been cast by Acheson whose name is listed first in the poll book.

69   *Universal Advertiser* (hereafter UA), 23 Oct. 1753.
70   The information in Table 2 is abstracted by the author from the 'County Armagh Poll Book, 1753'.
71   For these various sources see Chapter 1, particularly Hill, *Plantation*; Hunter, 'County Armagh'; Paterson, 'County Armagh in 1622'; O'Sullivan, 'Land confiscations'; Gillespie, *Brownlow leasebook*; 'Book of survey and distribution, County Armagh'. Also Richard Griffith, *Valuation of the several tenements ... in the county of Armagh*, Dublin, 1864; hereafter Griffith, *Valuation*; Ian Maxwell, *Researching Armagh ancestors. A practical guide for the family and local historian* (Belfast, 2000; hereafter Maxwell, *Researching Armagh ancestors*).
72   'The 1766 Religious Census', shows that Dissenter families overwhelmingly outnumbered those of the Established Church in Loughgilly parish.
73   *Case of the Hon. Francis Caulfeild.*
74   See Table 2.
75   *A second letter from a free citizen of Dublin*, p. 4.
76   *General report on the Gosford estates in County Armagh 1821 by William Greig*, F.M.L. Thompson and D. Tierney ed. (Belfast, 1976; hereafter *Greig's Report*), pp 20, 57, 65.
77   Genealogy of the Graham family, Johnston collection, Armagh Public Library.
78   Paterson, 'County Armagh in 1622', p. 131
79   The Nedham family of Beckenham. Kent, possessed estates in south Down and most of Newry and its environs, and controlled one Newry borough seat from 1727–76. Their Armagh holdings lay west of the Newry River in nine townlands.
80   Nineteen of Rev. Walter Cope's twenty votes in 1753 went to Caulfeild. The dissenting vote of William Williamson of Greenagh townland went to Brownlow, possibly explained by only part of Greenagh townland being in Cope's manor.
81   In 1753, Thomas Ball lived in Dunganstown, County Wexford, John Ball at Three Castles, County Kilkenny, and Abraham Ball at Drogheda, County Louth; see Rev. W. Ball Wright, *Records of Anglo-Irish families of Ball* (Dublin, 1887), p. 44.
82   Tipping became MP for County Louth in 1755 after another bitterly contested 'court' and 'country' clash, see Malcomson, *Foster*, pp 116–7.
83   Jones resided on his main holding at Moneyglass, County Antrim.
84   This estate had passed down from the marriage in the seventeenth century of Edward Obré to Elinor Stanhawe, heiress to the dwindling plantation estate.
85   Brownlow supporters included Newry merchants Isaac and Edward Corry, Archibald Macartney and William Ogle of Fathom; and minor gentry Hunt Chambré of Athy and Killevy, Matthew Henderson of Dublin and Derrybeg, and Richard Chapel Whaley of Dublin and Lislea.
86   Votes for Caulfeild came from Thomas Seaver of Armagh and Killevy, Joseph Foxall of Dublin and Killevy, and Malcolm McNeale of Ballymascanlon, County Louth, and Killeen.
87   Among Brownlow supporters with freehold in, or near, Armagh City were Dublin residents Richard Dawson (MP, banker, alderman of Dublin and father of Lord Cremorne of Dawson Grove, Co. Monaghan), John Maxwell and John Gibson; Armagh City merchants George Bell, John Barnes, Thomas Dobbin, James Richardson and William Steele; and Rev. Charles Carthy, headmaster of Armagh Royal School.
88   Rev. Dr James Strong of 'Fairview', later Tynan Abbey, was curate of Tynan 1741–c .1761.

89 Rev. Benjamin Barrington, prebendary of Tynan 1747–59, rector and alderman of Armagh 1759–68, dean of Armagh 1763–8 and chaplain to Archbishop Stone, vicar of St. Anne's, Dublin 1768–73, rector of Bray 1773–4.
90 Edward Bond, an Armagh linen merchant bought the townland of Tullybricketra from John Hamilton in 1708 and renamed it Bondville. His descendants Edward and Henry were in residence in 1753.
91 W.H. Fortescue was the first and only earl of Clermont.
92 Undoubtedly it was the time consumed by this dispute which reduced the poll on these two days to 26 votes and 30 votes respectively; see *BNL*, 16 Nov.1753; *UA*, 10 Nov. 1753.
93 *Case of the Hon. Francis Caulfeild.*
94 'Brownlow's election expenses 1753', pp 10–13.
95 *UA*, 23 Oct. 1753.
96 'Brownlow's election expenses 1753', pp 10–13.
97 *An extract of a letter from Armagh, dated October the 31st, 1753* (RIA, Haliday collection, Dublin, 1753 3B53–56/220; hereafter *An extract of a letter from Armagh*, 31 Oct. 1753).
98 *An impartial account of the whole proceedings at Armagh during the election, with the causes of the late disturbances at that place, dated 10 November 1753* (PRONI, Chilham papers, T/2519/4/225; hereafter *An impartial account, 10 Nov. 1753*).
99 *A letter from a gentleman at Armagh to his friend in Dublin, giving a true and impartial account of the late disturbances at this place, dated 5 November 1753* (PRONI, Chilham papers, T/2519/4/224; hereafter *A letter 5 November*).
100 *UA*, 3 Nov. 1753.
101 *An extract of a letter from Armagh*, 31 Oct.
102 *An impartial account, 10 Nov. 1753.*
103 *The case of William Brownlow, Esq. – To be heard before the Honorable Committee of Privileges and Elections, the 6 December, 1753* (PRONI, Chilham papers, T/2519/4/227; hereafter *Case of William Brownlow*).
104 *An impartial account, 10 Nov. 1753.*
105 Sackville to Pelham, 28 Oct. 1753 (PRONI, Newcastle papers, T/2863/1/58).
106 Sackville to Wilmot, 16 Nov. 1753 (PRONI, Wilmot papers, T/3019/2205). The 'Speaker's son' was Richard Boyle, MP for Dungarvan.
107 Sackville to Wilmot, 17 Nov. 1753 (ibid., T/3019/2206).
108 Sackville to Pelham, 27 Nov. 1753 (PRONI, Newcastle (Pelham) papers, T/2863/1/61).
109 *Case of the Hon. Francis Caulfeild.*
110 Ibid.
111 *UA*, 3 Nov. 1753.
112 There are examples in the eighteenth century where Armagh high sheriffs lived outside the county e.g. Tipping of Bellurgan, Hall of Narrowwater, Johnston of Gilford, and Jones of Moneyglass.
113 Beaumont, Thesis, ii, pp 57–73.
114 Ibid., pp 61–3.
115 Caulfeild claimed that of *c.* 800 freeholders who had registered on 3 May, two-thirds were Caulfeild supporters, see *Case of the Hon. Francis Caulfeild.*
116 Sackville to Wilmot, 4 Nov. 1753 (PRONI, Wilmot papers, T/3019/2197).
117 Ibid.
118 Ibid.

119 Waite to Wilmot, 2 Dec. 1753 (ibid., T/3019/2214).
120 Same to same, 6 Dec. 1753 (ibid., T/3019/2216)
121 *Commons' jn. Ire.* (Bradley), ix, 413.
122 *Case of William Brownlow.*
123 Waite to Wilmot, 6 Dec. 1753 (PRONI, Wilmot papers, T/3019/2217).
124 Same to same, 6 Dec. 1753 (ibid., T/3019/2218).
125 Same to same, 8 Dec. 1753 (ibid., T/3019/2219).
126 Same to same, 8 Dec. 1753 (ibid., T/3019/2220).
127 Same to same, 11 Dec. 1753 (ibid., T/3019/2223); *Commons' jn. Ire.* (Bradley), ix, 418.
128 Adderley to Charlemont, 10 Feb. 1755 (*HMC Charlemont*), i, 203–4; *Commons' jn. Ire.* (Bradley), ix, 413.
129 Same to same, 29 Dec. 1753 (*HMC Charlemont*), i, 188–9.
130 Same to same, 29 Dec. 1753 (*HMC Charlemont*), i, 188–9.
131 Waite to Wilmot, 11 Dec. 1753 (PRONI, Wilmot papers, T/3019/2223).
132 Ibid.
133 Same to same, 18 Dec. 1753 (ibid., T/3019/2226).
134 Registrar of the Prerogative Court Bellingham Boyle, Master of the Rolls Thomas Carter, Prime Sergeant Anthony Malone, and joint Quarter-Master and Barrack-Master General Michael O'Brien Dilkes were sacked, see *BNL*, 22 Jan. 1754.
135 *A layman's sermon preached at the Patriot Club of the County of Armagh which met at Armagh, the 3rd September 1755* (RIA, Tracts, 1749–64, Dublin, 1755; hereafter *A layman's sermon*), vol x, Box 220, No. 9.
136 Ibid. p. 19.
137 *BNL*, 25 Jan. 1754.
138 Ibid., 26 Feb. 1754.
139 Ibid., 12 Mar. 1754.
140 Ibid., 26 Mar. 1754.
141 Ibid., 5 Apr. 1754.
142 *HMC Emly MSS, 8th Report, appendix 1* (London, 1891; hereafter *HMC Emly*) pp 178–80.
143 *BNL*, 26 Apr. 1754.
144 Ibid.
145 Ibid., 22 Nov. 1754.
146 Ibid., 27 Dec. 1754. The meeting scheduled for 13 January 1755 was later postponed to 16 April, but seems not to have taken place.
147 Ibid., 7 Jan. 1755.
148 Ibid., 4 Mar. 1755.
149 Ibid., 22 Apr. 1755
150 O'Hara to O'Hara, 1 May 1755 (PRONI, O'Hara papers, T/2812/10/3).
151 Molyneux to Acheson, 19 Apr. 1755 (PRONI, Gosford papers, D/1606/1/1/17E).
152 Henry Legge was chancellor of the exchequer in England from April 1754 to November 1755, and friend and political ally of the Devonshires
153 Waite to Wilmot, 15 Mar. 1755 (PRONI, Wilmot papers, T/3019/2529).
154 NLI, O'Hara's survey of the Irish house of commons, 1755 (O'Hara papers, MS. 14299, Mic. P. 1576). Other Stone adherents were John Maxwell, member for Co. Cavan, his son Robert Maxwell, member for Lisburn, Robert Cuninghame, member for Tulsk, E.S. Pery, member for Wicklow, William Richardson, member for Augher, Owen Wynne Jr, member for Co. Sligo, and the

Fortescues of Co. Louth. General Philip Bragg, member for Armagh borough was included among others 'divided in affection between the primate and Lord Bessborough's family'.
155 Ibid.
156 Ibid.
157 Hardy, *Charlemont*, ii, 19.
158 Craig, *Volunteer earl*, pp 106–7.
159 *BNL*, 27 May 1755.
160 *UA*, 24 May 1755.
161 Ponsonby to Acheson, 13 Mar. 1756 (PRONI, Gosford papers, D/1606/1/1/17G).
162 *BNL*, 29 June 1756.
163 *HMC Emly*, pp 174–81.
164 Eoin Magennis, 'In search of the "Moral Economy": food scarcity in 1756–7 and the crowd' in Jupp, Peter and Magennis, Eoin (ed.) *Crowds in Ireland c. 1720–1920* (Basingstoke, 2000; hereafter Jupp & Magennis, *Crowds in Ireland*), p. 193.
165 Memoirs (*HMC Charlemont*), i, note I, p. 6.
166 Hardy, *Charlemont*, i, 94–9.
167 *HMC Emly*, p. 178
168 Waite to Wilmot, 14 Mar. 1758 (PRONI, Wilmot papers, T/3019/3341).
169 Rigby to Wilmot, 15, 17, 19 Jan.1758 (ibid., T/3019/3306, 3307, 3308). The three officials were Chief Secretary Richard Rigby, Undersecretary Thomas Waite and First Clerk Henry Meredyth.
170 *Commons' jn. Ire.* (Bradley), x, 158.
171 Ibid. pp 262–71.
172 Rigby to Acheson, 17 May 1759 (PRONI, Gosford papers, D/1606/1/1/22B).
173 *BNL*, 4 Sept. 1759.
174 Charlemont to Acheson, 21 June 1759 (PRONI, Gosford papers, D/1606/1/1/22C).
175 Rigby to Wilmot, 19 Oct. 1759 (PRONI, Wilmot papers, T/3019/3630).
176 *BNL*, 30 Nov. 1759.
177 Ibid., 26 Sept. 1755.
178 Ibid., 7 Apr. 1758.
179 Waite to Wilmot, 8 June 1759 (PRONI, Wilmot papers, T/3019/3592).
180 *Commons' jn. Ire.* (Bradley), xi, 287.
181 S.W. Baskerville, Peter Adman and K.F. Beedham, 'The dynamics of landlord influence in English county elections, 1701–1734: the evidence from Cheshire', *Parliamentary History*, xii, (1993), p. 136.

3

High politics in Armagh 1760–75: the dynamics of two general elections; socio-economic protest; the viceroyalties of Townshend and Harcourt

INTRODUCTION: DEATH OF GEORGE II AND PREPARATIONS FOR A GENERAL ELECTION

By 1760 the leading political activists in County Armagh were Sir Archibald Acheson and William Brownlow. Francis Caulfeild, following his return as county member in 1758 would seem to have taken little active part in Armagh's political affairs. Primate Stone, embarrassed by the court-martial of his close friend and political ally Lord George Sackville for cowardice at the battle of Minden, was also keeping a low political profile.[1] Acheson had been won over to the support of government by Lord Lieutenant Bedford's favours and by a sense of duty as deputy governor of the county, to rally to the nation's defence under threat from France. County governor, Lord Charlemont, would seem to have adopted a similar stance.

Brownlow, however, continued his spirited patriot opposition. In January 1760 he joined with Pery and over thirty others to support Hely-Hutchinson's motion attacking the raising of regiments. The motion was defeated but generated so much ill-feeling in the house of commons that a duel between Brownlow and Lord Drogheda – who was then recruiting a regiment of light dragoons at Charlemont Fort[2] – was only averted by Pery's intervention.[3] Chief Secretary Rigby bemoaned the persistence of opposition to levies despite Bedford's blandishments to rally support, and identified its leaders:

> ... chiefly of Lord Tyrone's friends, who are in every question against the government, Mr. Pery, Mr. Brownlow, and that set of gentlemen who have been loaded with favours from the d. of Bedford but who

seem insensible to anything but popularity, and Mr. Hely-Hutchinson with a few lower eternal opposers.[4]

Opposition was suspended during the scare over Thurot's occupation of Carrickfergus on Thursday 21 February and members returned to their county militias.[5] Companies from the counties of Antrim, Down and Armagh marched to Belfast to oppose the French. From Armagh, companies from Lurgan, Lylo, Richhill, Armagh City, and Tandragee totalling 525 men arrived in Belfast between Friday and Sunday. A Lurgan troop of 140 dragoons was the first of these to arrive on Friday afternoon under the command of First Lieutenant James Forde until Brownlow, their captain, arrived from Dublin. Rev. George Cherry commanded Tandragee company in the absence of its captain Samuel Blacker in Dublin.[6] With Carrickfergus retaken, the house of commons passed a vote of thanks to the militias of those counties.[7]

The death of King George II on 25 October 1760 meant the first general election in Ireland for thirty-four years – though Armagh had the experience of the phoney general election of 1752 and the by-election contest of 1753 – and landed gentry and men of property with political ambition for a parliamentary seat prepared for a canvass. The experience of sitting members in the Irish house of commons like Brownlow, Acheson, Adderley, Francis Caulfeild and Hon. John Caulfeild, gave them some advantage over newcomers. Aspiring candidates saw a parliamentary seat as an advancement in prestige and access to sources of patronage and influence in appointments to government places, church offices and commissions in the armed forces.

In 1760–61, fearful memories of the disorder and violence at the 1753 by-election poll overshadowed the thinking of Armagh gentry and magistrates who hoped to avoid a recurrence. Candidates had also learned from the experience of 1753 that the votes of freeholders could not be taken for granted and that discontented freeholders might withhold their votes or give them to the opposition. The sources of such discontent could vary from dislike of an unpopular candidate to a feeling of being bullied or ignored or refused treats by their own landlord. Thus candidates were aware of the importance of canvassing all potential freehold voters and of wooing rather than attempting to bully freeholders into voting for them.

Some candidates might have anticipated the intervention of a patriot campaign to pressurise them – against their natural inclinations – into supporting a programme of parliamentary reform. The 1761 general election afforded reformers a rare opportunity to pressurise candidates to seek a reduction in the duration of Irish parliaments which currently ran the life of the monarch unlike that of the English parliament limited by the Septennial Act of 1716. Candidates could be faced with conflicting pressures of deciding whether to reject patriot demands for shorter parliaments and alienate the popular vote or promise to support a campaign which ran counter to their own interests.

The virtual retirement of Primate Stone to Bath removed him from the centre of Irish politics which he had dominated in the mid-1750s. But there were other political churchmen seeking promotion in or to the archdiocese of Armagh who were willing to use political patronage for their preferment. And the borough of Armagh remained a reserve option for friends of the primate and Dublin administration in need of a parliamentary seat. Obversely, the borough of Charlemont served friends of the earl of Charlemont who were of patriot persuasion.

The administration of Bedford and Rigby, having completed four years, neared its end in the winter of 1760–61. Both were still in office for most of the initial canvassing and negotiations for candidature in the general election but had been replaced when the writs were issued on 7 April 1761. A good working relationship between Permanent Secretary Robert Wilmot in London and Under-secretary Thomas Waite in Dublin had provided continuity for the administration of Ireland since their appointment in the 1740s. From August 1765, Richard Jackson, MP for Coleraine and under-secretary to Lord Lieutenant Hertford, would provide information on the strength of parliamentary support for government. Their experience of and service to Ireland was invaluable due to the frequent changes – and absences – of lord lieutenants and chief secretaries. During the parliament of 1761–8, Ireland would be governed by no fewer than six lord lieutenants – two of whom would not visit Ireland – and nine chief secretaries; and the business of delivering majorities in the Irish parliament was undertaken by Speaker John Ponsonby and friends in return for the lion's share of government patronage.

Four dynamics would drive preparations for the general election in the counties: negotiations between the landed gentry to agree election partnerships, the canvass by candidates of the landed gentry for election voting interests, the relationship between candidates and freeholders, and the negotiation by the Dublin administration to recruit supporters of government from elected members. Other forces influencing election outcomes and subsequent administrations were the politics of patronage, of popularity and of protest, and the quest for parliamentary reform.

NEGOTIATIONS AND CANVASS FOR ARMAGH COUNTY SEATS IN THE 1761 GENERAL ELECTION, OCTOBER 1760 TO APRIL 1761

Opinions were divided on how soon the general election should be called after the king's death. Lord Farnham advised the chief secretary that the Irish parliament had four months from the monarch's death until election writs were required to be issued.[8] The lords justices advised an early issue of the writs – to avoid disorder from drawn-out elections – with the general election to be completed within forty days of commencement in December 1760 i.e. before the appointment of new county sheriffs on 12 February 1761.[9] By late February 1761, when Daniel Kelly of Dawson's Grove was appointed high sheriff for County Armagh and Sir Archibald Acheson high sheriff for Cavan[10], the writs had still not been issued. In late February, too, rumours had Bedford's resignation imminent, and Waite hoped, for the chief secretary's sake, that 'this decision is far enough off (for Rigby) to enjoy the profits of office a little longer'.[11]

News of the king's death heralded the start of electioneering in Ireland well before an election date was fixed, sending John Ponsonby back to Ireland.[12] With the accession of a healthy young king, a parliamentary seat was a particularly valuable acquisition in Ireland where parliaments still ran for the lifetime of the monarch. The market for seats was brisk 'with talk of 70 to 100 new members in parliament and seats offered at £1,500 – £2,000'. Lord Chancellor John Bowes observed: 'Venality exceeds decency.'[13]

This time, Charlemont decided he would manage his brother's election campaign. On hearing of George II's death, he immediately offered Brownlow first refusal of a conjunction with Francis Caulfeild for Armagh county in the coming election. Brownlow could not have been impressed by a grating clause in Charlemont's letter which seemed to ask Brownlow to pay the election expenses of *both* candidates: 'But then, as in the last election, I was at the whole expense in supporting our joint interests, in this I shall expect that you in your turn will take that burden wholly upon yourself.'[14] When Brownlow did not immediately accept Charlemont's proposition, the earl applied to Acheson who also declined to rush into partnership with Caulfeild. Acheson's rejection resulted in a bitter row and recriminations between Charlemont and Acheson which would continue over the winter months.[15] Charlemont's immediate reaction to the rebuff by his brother's former political ally, was to return to Brownlow with his offer. But his second application to Brownlow received the same fate as the first, as the latter's intention was to partner Acheson.[16]

In the 1760s, Brownlow and Acheson shared sufficient common electoral ground to form an election partnership. There were no major political or ideological issues to keep them apart as in the money bill dispute of 1753 when Acheson was opposed to the establishment of Primate Stone and Dublin Castle and Brownlow was its electoral tool. Nor were there differences of affiliation between them in the 1760s as there would be in the 1770s when Acheson would feel more comfortable as supporter and beneficiary of government and Brownlow would see his parliamentary role at the forefront of the patriot opposition. The key objectives of both in 1761 were to avoid the alarming violence and exorbitant expense which had marred the 1753 contest.

In November 1760 three candidates in County Armagh declared for the anticipated general election. Sitting member Brownlow appealed to 'the gentlemen, clergy and freeholders' on his record of representation 'uninfluenced by any selfish views'. The other county member, Francis Caulfeild, made it clear where his hopes of electoral support now lay: 'I now find it necessary to address myself particularly to those who are inclined zealously and vigorously to contend for supporting the independency of this county'. He identified the barriers to his return as 'conjunctions powerful and unnatural' but trusted the electorate not to be 'disposed to receive both representatives from a superior hand, with patient submission.'[17]

Caulfeild rightly feared the entry of third candidate, Acheson – his industrious election supporter in 1753. Seven years on, Acheson was determined to enhance his political status with a county seat and knew the vulnerable seat was that of Caulfeild. He published an early election notice to 'the gentlemen, clergy and freeholders' of the county, on 'the advice of several friends' for his candidature 'for the good of the kingdom in general and of this county in particular.'[18] His reference to 'several friends' was no empty election rhetoric. Acheson had influential political friends both beyond and within Armagh county. At national level his friends in 1760 included Rigby and Bedford, Primate Stone, Lord Newtown and the Butler family, Lord Farnham and the Maxwell family – both with interests in Cavan – and the earl of Kildare.

In May 1760, when an anonymous MP attacked the chief secretary and lord lieutenant in *Faulkner's Dublin Journal*, Acheson had defended them and informed Rigby who had written from London thanking Acheson for his continued kindness and service to Bedford and himself.[19] Primate Stone, according to Dean Anthony Cope, held Acheson 'in great esteem and speaks of you as a worthy and honest man'.[20] Barry Maxwell, Lord Farnham's brother and candidate for a County Cavan seat, sought Acheson's interest of his second estate at Arvagh, as did Lord Newtown sitting county member for Cavan.[21] The earl of Kildare, replying to a written canvass from Acheson conveyed by Dean Walter Cope, assured Acheson that he had earlier requested his cousin Roger Hall of Narrowwater to keep his Mullaghglass interest in Orior barony free for Acheson in the event of the latter standing for election; but would write to Hall again. Kildare was optimistic of an easy victory for Acheson.[22]

The 'conjunction' of Brownlow and Acheson feared by Caulfeild was agreed in November 1760. This partnership was considered by both partners and by the other leading interests in the county as the best guarantee of keeping the peace and avoiding the violence of 1753. Brownlow argued for *resident* county members: 'that those gentlemen who reside in the county, and do the business of it are best entitled to its favours'. To copper-fasten the alignment, Brownlow asked Acheson to contact the absentee Sir John Bernard and his agent Samuel Blacker for all of the Tandragee vote most of which had so sensationally defected to Caulfeild in 1753; and, in turn, he (Brownlow) would approach Colonel Graham and other friends for similar support.[23] Dean Anthony Cope endorsed the new partnership whose strength, he argued, should convince Charlemont to abandon any plan for opposing it.[24] The growing support for the partnership provided a significant lead to other interests in the county such as James Johnston who promised his vote and 'any additional service' to Acheson.[25]

Charlemont's hopes for Caulfeild now lay in assistance from former committed supporters such as Sir Capel Molyneux. Molyneux was visiting his brother-in-law Dr John Garnett, bishop of Clogher, to negotiate a vacant seat for Clogher parliamentary borough for himself. His acceptance of the Clogher seat, however, was tied to the condition that he give his Castle-Dillon interest to Acheson and Brownlow. Thus Charlemont's application was again rejected, this time by an embarrassed Molyneux.[26] It was another bitter disappointment for Charlemont that his former patriot ally should have been bought over to the government side, a deal confirmed when Molyneux wrote to thank Bedford for recommending him for the Clogher borough seat.[27]

The Caulfeild camp was also missing the organisational assistance of Thomas Adderley, former mentor to the young Caulfeild family. Charlemont had dismissed his stepfather from charge of his affairs in the summer of 1760. Among reasons given was his disapproval of Adderley's conduct in parliament which clashed with Charlemont's policy.[28] Following Charlemont's rejection of his stewardship, Adderley had turned to building a new political interest for himself in his native Innishannon, County Cork. With eyes on a borough seat for Bandon-bridge, Adderley pocketed his pride and asked Charlemont to approach the duke of Devonshire, who could influence the destination of the Bandon-bridge seats, on Adderley's behalf. If successful, Adderley added, his current seat in Charlemont borough would be freed for Charlemont's disposal; if unsuccessful he (Adderley) would pay Charlemont 'six or eight hundred or such further sum as may be sufficient' to retain it. Adderley also advised

Charlemont to apply for the interests of Lord Orrery at Caledon, Lord Fane at Clare and Sir John Bernard at Tandragee. He added that he had attempted to bespeak the Tandragee interest for Charlemont after Sir Francis St John died, but the new proprietor had been non-committal.[29]

Charlemont's sharp reply showed no desire to be reconciled with his stepfather and revealed his growing frustration and desperation in his county election plans. He informed Adderley that he had considered allocating the Charlemont borough seats, not to Adderley, but to 'my uncle John and Harry Moore' and rebuked his stepfather for having insulted him with an offer of money for a Charlemont borough seat. The letter also revealed that the earl was losing confidence in his brother's chances of retaining the county seat as evidenced in his new intention of holding a Charlemont borough seat in reserve: 'Affairs have since turned out so ill in county matters that I now find myself obliged to reserve a seat for my brother'.[30]

However, Charlemont was still not prepared to give Acheson and Brownlow the satisfaction – or the Armagh establishment the peace of mind – of a free election run by Caulfeild's withdrawal from the county election contest. Indeed, further pressure emerged in late autumn with demands on candidates to support a measure of parliamentary reform. An unsigned advertisement called for a meeting on 16 December of all prospective voters at Thomas Stringer's hostelry in Armagh to discuss strategies for limiting the duration of parliaments and how to pressurise election candidates accordingly.[31] This advertisement was followed, ten days later, by an open appeal 'to all the free electors in Ireland' to put pressure on election candidates to oppose 'perpetual parliaments' and press for parliaments of shorter duration. The latter notice pointed out the current anomaly between England's septennial parliaments and Ireland's parliaments lasting the length of the monarch's reign. Irish voters were urged to use the present opportunity to pressurise candidates to seek parity of duration.[32]

The advertisements above were indications that the patriot movement was involving itself in the general election campaign. Also returned to the political fray was the radical Dr Charles Lucas, who had been forced to flee the country when the Irish house of commons had voted him 'an enemy to his country' for alleged seditious writings in 1749.[33] Lucas who was still in political exile in London but negotiating to return to Dublin as candidate for Dublin City, was in correspondence with Charlemont in November 1760 and had sent a pamphlet to the Irish press.[34]

The three candidates for the Armagh county seat remained in the field over the winter months locked in an acrimonious campaign. In December 1760 Acheson complained to Rigby in London of underhand tactics being perpetrated against him. Rigby sympathised for 'such shallow and such low politics as were used against you' but assured Acheson that these had rebounded against the perpetrators.[35] In February, 1761, Acheson's appointment as high sheriff of Cavan created for him the possible logistical problem of a clash of dates between general election contests in Armagh where he was standing and Cavan where he was presiding.[36]

The anticipated close of Bedford's administration also brought a scramble for last-minute favours. Primate Stone's memorandum to Bedford about jobs for his protégés, included encouragement to promote Dr Benjamin Barrington, rector of Armagh and Hon. Henry Maxwell, dean of Kilmore and Lord Farnham's brother.[37] Stone's agent Henry Meredyth asked that Rigby be reminded 'to do something' for his nephew Lieutenant John Meredyth in Bagshawe's regiment;[38] Robert Cuninghame, a close friend of Stone sought confirmation of promotion;[39] and, for his support for the privy council money bill, Rigby reported that 'Lord Kildare is made a marquess with a promise of a dukedom whenever a duke is made'.[40]

Some who were promoted attempted to squeeze the last drops of benefit from the lord lieutenancy. Bishop Richard Robinson who, though expressing gratitude to Bedford for his translation from Ferns to Kildare, asked permission to retain his former patronage of the borough of Old Leighlin by nominating his own candidates in the coming election despite his successor Dr Jackson's intention to do likewise.[41] An incensed Rigby, referring to Robinson's 'jesuitical shuffling letter', asked Bedford: 'Was there ever a greater rascal than this bishop?'[42] and Bedford censured Robinson's conduct in the matter.[43] By then, Bedford and Rigby had been replaced by Lord Halifax and William Gerard Hamilton, appointed 3 April.[44] But Robinson was forced to recant and to withdraw his candidates for Old Leighlin; and Bishop Jackson's candidates, John Bourke and Francis Andrews, were returned.[45]

The above episode is not the only example of Robinson's political designs from the arrival of John Garnett and he in Ireland in 1751 as Lord Lieutenant Dorset's two chaplains – a key initial post for promotion in the hierarchy of the Irish Established Church. From 1751 he was one of a coterie of political figures including Dorset, Lord George Sackville, and Archbishop Stone who was his career advisor and probably grooming Robinson for the primacy from an early stage. In 1751, Dorset recommended Robinson to George II for a bishopric which, the duke of Newcastle had advised Dorset: 'His Majesty was pleased to grant, though the king said at the same time "all the bishoprics must not be given to chaplains." I hope however, that will not put by poor Dr Garnett'.[46] Robinson was appointed bishop of Killala in January 1752, translated to Ferns and Leighlin in 1759, to Kildare in 1761 and, when the dust settled on his dispute with Bedford, was soon back in favour with the new administration and contender as Stone's successor in Armagh. Nor had

Garnett's career been penalised as feared by Newcastle. In 1752 he was appointed bishop of Ferns and Leighlin and translated to Clogher in 1758.[47]

The last rewards from Bedford's Irish administration were issued in the spring of 1761. In warrants from the treasury on 31 March, Robert Cuninghame and Thomas Adderley were among seven appointments to be commissioners of barracks in Ireland and Lord Newtown to be one of the commissioners of revenue in Ireland in warrants of 8 April.[48] Bedford's last communication to the lords justices was that it was his wish and that of Pitt (the Elder) to hold a general election as soon as possible.[49] A proclamation was issued accordingly for a general election to be held by 19 May 1761.[50]

In March 1761, a nervous Acheson informed Brownlow of rumours undermining their election pact. Brownlow's reply attempted to assuage Acheson's fears. He had investigated reports of a conspiracy by some of Brownlow's freeholders to raise support for Caulfeild and found that five had invited Caulfeild's agent Thomas Verner of Churchhill to a meeting in Lurgan where one had said he preferred Caulfeild as candidate to Acheson, another – awaiting Charlemont's decision to renew a lease in perpetuity – felt tied to Caulfeild and others were related to these by marriage. Brownlow had emphasised to them the advantages of supporting the Brownlow-Acheson election partnership. He reassured Acheson that Caulfeild would win over too few voters to attempt a poll.[51]

Brownlow also assured Acheson that he would share election expenses despite rumours to the contrary and unlike Charlemont's initial proposition to both. He had informed Dean Cope that he would not be treating voters before the poll – his memories of the riotous behaviour of drunken supporters in 1753 were still fresh eight years on – but Acheson could suit himself on that matter. However, he advised Acheson to pre-empt further grumbling by canvassing the Lurgan voters as:

> the people of substance here would to be sure wish to be courted, and to appear of consequence, which they know they cannot be without an opposition, and on that account grumble a little at your going on so smoothly, but I shall take all the care in my power to make that ferment subside, and to strengthen your interest.

Brownlow further advised that a three hour tour of the town by Acheson would be sufficient without treating or providing 'a general entertainment'.[52] Acheson took Brownlow's advice and canvassed Lurgan. The outcome, Brownlow reported, was that all 'persons of consequence' in Lurgan promised their full support for the partnership. He enthused to Acheson: 'I can now wish you joy that there is a certainty of our having no opposition'. The ploy of disarming lingering pockets of opposition by compliance rather than defiance was typical of the election tactics of the Brownlow-Acheson partnership. They had also taken Caulfeild's ground by adopting the patriot programme of parliamentary reform for limiting the duration of parliaments.[53]

In early April, Brownlow and Adderley dined with the Free Citizens of Dublin when Adderley brought peace offerings from Charlemont who, before leaving for England, had directed his brother to visit Brownlow at his Dublin house and tell him 'that no trouble should be given at Armagh'. While Caulfeild had not yet withdrawn from the election, this news was the next best thing for Brownlow, Acheson and the gentry of Armagh who feared a repeat of the violence of 1753. All that was left to do was to wait for the issue of the election writs and fix a date for the election which High Sheriff Kelly had asked the candidates to agree between themselves. The request of the Cavan candidates to hold their election before that in Armagh would have resulted in a late election in Armagh.[54]

The writs for the general election were issued on 10 April.[55] While there is no official record that Caulfeild had withdrawn from the election by then, evidence from contemporary private correspondence refers to his having given up all pretensions of contesting it and to his election advertisements having been dropped that week from the Dublin newspapers. Brownlow told Acheson he reckoned 'it as a certainty that we should have no poll'. Indeed Brownlow's main concern was where to hold the victory dinner and instructed Acheson, who was on the spot, to book McKinstry's hostelry in Armagh rather than Stringer's, as Lurgan voters had bitter memories of a Lurgan man being shot from the latter hotel in 1753. He anticipated the date of the election would be Monday 27 April.[56]

On 27 April 1761 the Armagh election was held – *before* that in Cavan – with Brownlow and Acheson returned without contest as county members. Brownlow and Acheson thanked the Armagh gentlemen, clergy and freeholders for 'unanimously electing' them as parliamentary representatives and promised to 'use our best endeavours to procure a law for limiting the duration of parliaments'.[57] Rigby congratulated Acheson on his election and sympathised with him for the coming task of conducting the Cavan election which promised to be less straightforward.[58]

RELATIONS BETWEEN PATRONS AND PROTÉGÉS
IN BOROUGH ELECTIONS 1761

Francis Caulfeild settled for a Charlemont borough seat. This completed a change of personnel in Charlemont borough with Caulfeild's cousin Henry William Moore of Drumbanagher being nominated for the other seat, keeping both seats in the extended Caulfeild family. Moore (1725–62) was married since 1752 to Anne, daughter of Rev. the Hon. Charles Caulfeild of Castle Stewart, County Tyrone and had a high profile in public service. He had served as high sheriff of County Armagh in 1756 and as a captain in James McCullough's troop of dragoons.[59] Thus two relatively young relations of Charlemont had replaced his aging uncle Hon. John Caulfeild – who died in 1764 – and stepfather Thomas Adderley. Adderley secured one of Francis Bernard's borough seats for Bandon-Bridge – thus moving from the patronage of a stepson to a brother-in-law. It began a new County Cork-based phase in Adderley's parliamentary career, drawing upon the influence of his Bernard in-laws and Lord Shannon connections, also representing the borough of Clonakilty from 1776 until his death in 1791. Charlemont's radical friend Lucas was returned for the City of Dublin after a thirteen days' contest.[60] Henry William Moore served for the first session of parliament only. He died in 1762 and was replaced in 1763 as Charlemont borough representative by his brother-in-law Sir Annesley Stewart, fifth baronet of Fort Stewart, County Donegal who had married Moore's sister Sarah in 1754.[61] That Stewart was a banker undoubtedly influenced Lord Charlemont's decision.

There was also a change of personnel in both seats for Armagh borough. Primate Stone provided a seat for his friend, the ever-ambitious Robert Cuninghame, and the other as insurance cover for his lord justice colleague and political ally, Speaker John Ponsonby. However, when Ponsonby was returned and opted for his native Kilkenny county, Stone could accommodate Barry Maxwell, who had failed to obtain a seat in Cavan where the Butler family dominated the outcome. Maxwell was sworn as member for Armagh borough on 13 November 1761.[62]

HOW THE POLITICS OF PATRONAGE INFLUENCED ARMAGH MEMBERS IN THE 1760s

The machinery of government was kept running smoothly by the politics of patronage which rewarded those who supported the administration. The rapid progress of Robert Cuninghame's military career owed more to the patronage of Primate Stone and Lord George Sackville than to his martial prowess, and he served the Irish establishment as informal go-between for Irish and British officials and supported the government consistently in parliamentary divisions. The initial return of Speaker John Ponsonby for Armagh borough was an example of Stone's putting a seat at the disposal of a key government minister still not returned and a gesture of goodwill to an old political ally. When Ponsonby was found not to need the Armagh seat, Stone's passing it to the Rt Hon. Barry Maxwell was a favour to Maxwell's older brother Robert, Viscount Farnham of the County Cavan family whose career Stone had promoted in the 1750s.

Members returned for Charlemont borough followed the patriot opposition politics of their patron. Lord Charlemont took a Whig-reformist line in politics. His rank and property allowed him to take an independent political stance, untied to the Dublin administration or people. His personal satisfaction derived from the prestige of being the senior peer in the county and its governor. A strong sense of noblesse oblige influenced Charlemont to provide leadership in the county in times of national emergency as during Thurot's invasion in 1760 when he came north to assess the situation and rally the troops. Though not a committed supporter of government, Charlemont was appointed member of the privy council and consulted by government on major issues as in 1754, when he had the lord lieutenant's support in affecting a reconciliation between Stone and Boyle.

But the politics of patronage were not confined to the parliamentary boroughs in County Armagh. County member Acheson was one prepared to court officialdom for self-advancement and personified the politics of favour-bargaining. His overtures typified the post-election surge in such politics by members of parliament determined to obtain some return on their investments in time, effort and expense; and by their followers, at various levels, to profit from their support of those now with favours to bestow. Various examples of favour-hunting and favour-bargaining by Armagh politicians can be identified in contemporary correspondence in the years following the election not least in that of Acheson. In April 1761, he asked Richard Rigby to use his influence to have him appointed to the privy council, echelon of favoured members of the ruling élite. Rigby, acknowledging Acheson's friendship and past support, assured him that he had recommended Acheson and Provost Francis Andrews for appointment to two vacancies on the council, but was unsuccessful in Acheson's case.[63] Even Rigby could not win them all, and in this case his competitor for favours had been the high-profile Henry Fox who had promoted his brother-in-law Thomas Conolly's successful bid for the other vacancy.[64]

Acheson had no compunction at using a strategy of 'a favour for a favour' when dealing with the ruling élite. John Ponsonby sought Acheson's support for his re-election to the speakership in 1761. In the following year Speaker Ponsonby agreed to accompany Primate Stone to a Linen Board meeting with Speaker Ponsonby to support Acheson's business there.[65] At another level, a budding friendship between Acheson and Counsellor Samuel Blacker – frequent visitor to Dublin – was nurtured on an exchange of 'private intelligence' on the latest local gossip and news of the European war. Blacker was quite explicit in seeking more extrinsic reward for his efforts, past and present: '... if places of £500 or £600 a year are flying about at the rising [sic] of the parliament, I hope you will not forget your friends in the country'.[66]

The church was always a fertile ground for the seeds of patronage. One who sought promotion in County Armagh was Dr Benjamin Barrington, rector of Armagh. Barrington built on his service and loyalty to Stone over the years with assiduous cultivation of influential friends such as Acheson, Stewart of Killymoon, Sir Capel Molyneux and Bishop Garnett of Clogher all of whom he invited to dinner at his house in Armagh in 1762.[67]

In April 1763, Acheson asked Rigby – no longer chief secretary but still master of the rolls – to 'put in a word' with the lord lieutenant for his brother-in-law Walter Cope, dean of Dromore, for promotion to the bishopric of that see left vacant by the death of bishop George Marlay. But Cope's hour had not yet come.[68] Rigby explained his failure to oblige Acheson as the post having been filled by Halifax before Rigby received Acheson's letter – the lord lieutenant's final recommendation before he was succeeded by the second duke of Northumberland in April 1763. But Rigby believed his intervention would have made no difference to the appointment in any case, explaining the diminished influence of a former chief secretary.[69]

Acheson continued to avail of all opportunities to extract favours. On a visit to Dublin in early summer 1763, he asked the influential Lord Newtown[70] – to whom Acheson probably had given his Arvagh interest in the general election – to appoint an acquaintance as a 'coast officer' in County Down. No vacancy was available then, but Newtown wrote soon afterwards of a vacancy which had 'fallen in my gift' at Mornington, Drogheda.[71]

Though Brownlow was seen as a government supporter when first elected to parliament in 1753, by 1761 his image was one of an independent country gentleman. His regular attendance, business-like approach to parliamentary affairs and promotion of the economy enhanced his reputation among members and resulted in his being nominated for numerous parliamentary committees. Though not a committed supporter of government, such was the respect Brownlow commanded as parliamentarian that he was appointed to the privy council in 1766.[72]

THE POLITICS OF POPULARITY AND THE CAMPAIGN FOR LIMITED PARLIAMENTS 1761–2

In late 1761, Chief Secretary Hamilton complained of the difficulty of obtaining unequivocal support for the Dublin administration as all members were 'too fond of their popularity'.[73] He was referring mainly to lack of commitment to government policy by too many members who were reluctant to offend the patriot opposition. The compliant policies of the ruling élite in Armagh over the general election which had yielded to popular opposition, maintained good relations between freeholders and landlords and resulted in a peaceful election, were continued subsequently. Peaceful politics were accommodated by an alliance of holders of high electoral interests in the county with a policy of avoiding confrontation where possible.

The continuing deployment of the politics of popularity by the ruling ascendancy was tested by the campaign for limited parliaments and the violent protest against rising cess and small tithes and dues. An on-going dilemma for many members was how to deal with their pre-election pledges to support parliamentary reform limiting the duration of parliament, extracted by the pressure of the patriot movement, but afterwards seen by returned members – particularly county members and undertakers – as contrary to their own interests.

The issue of limiting the duration of the Irish parliament was a running sore to the Dublin administration and an embarrassment to many Irish politicians for seven years following the 1761 election campaign. Politicians could be classified by attitude to the series of septennial bills introduced between 1761 and 1767 in one of three categories: a small group of patriots led by Dr Lucas committed to having the measure enacted; a small group of Castle or court party officials committed to having the measure defeated; and a large group of members who publicly supported the measure but privately hoped it would be defeated. Many in the last group, including some government officers, considered themselves hooked on election pledges and too scared of taking the unpopular line of opposing the campaign for limited parliaments.

Of the Armagh members, patriots like Brownlow, Caulfeild, Moore and his successor, Stewart, were in the first category, Cuninghame in the second. Acheson was probably in the third category suggested by a lack of public criticism from his election partner with whom he had made a joint pledge for shorter parliaments, or lack of censure from Charlemont or Caulfeild who would have welcomed such an excuse to attack him. Thus Acheson probably felt obliged to support a septennial bill publicly. However, his private correspondence would have led him to hope that the septennial bill would not be enacted. Rigby, Dean Walter Cope and Lord Newtown all, in correspondence to Acheson, referred disparagingly to a limitation bill.[74]

But Lucas and his followers among the patriots were determined to remind all members who had given 'previous promises' to support a bill for shorter parliaments and to exert pressure on the administration from the first day of the new session on 22 October 1761 when the radical apothecary was given leave to draft a septennial bill.[75] While this bill was still in draft stage, Lucas, supported by patriots such as Brownlow, Pery and French, vehemently opposed a money bill on 14 November.[76] They were joined in the division on 19 November by Francis Caulfeild and Thomas Adderley but the Money Bill passed easily.[77]

Meanwhile members – including 'many of the known dependents of the primate and Lord Shannon' – afraid of being accused of backsliding on election pledges, were supporting Lucas's septennial bill on a majority of three to one.[78] When the Septennial Bill was passed by 108 votes to 43,[79] Lord Lieutenant Halifax put a brave face on the defeat by claiming that many of those who voted for the bill did not really wish to have it enacted and identified the motivation underpinning their paradoxical voting patterns: ' ... they want to fulfil their engagements by voting for the proposed law, and yet to throw a degree of disrespect on a bill they dislike.'[80] He was probably correct but this was of little consolation when, at the next stage, the privy council also felt obliged to pass the bill on 8 February 1762, albeit by only one vote.[81] Many Irish members, including undertakers, were spared the embarrassment of unwanted legislation proposed by themselves when the bill was dropped in London.

SOCIO-ECONOMIC PROTEST BY THE HEARTS OF OAK, 1763

The effectiveness of the politics of popularity and appeasement in Armagh was put to the test by the outbreak of Oakboy insurrection during the summer of 1763 and the problem of accommodating a limitation bill by the ruling ascendancy temporarily put aside. The proximate cause of this insurrection was an increase in the amount of cess levied in the barony of Oneilland West at the Lenten assizes,[82] and its perceived use for building private roads in the estates of the gentry. Legislation of 1759 enacted that each barony would be charged with the repair of its own public roads.[83] Capital was raised by county cess levied by the county grand jury and collected by the constables in each barony. Tenants protested that such legislation for making 'the king's highways' was abused in 1763.[84]

The first outbreak of disturbances occurred in Armagh in late June 1763 when inhabitants of the barony of West Oneilland combined in protest against presentment grants to William Brownlow for building roads through his own estate.[85] Only £38-7s. was returned out of a warrant for £204-17s.-6d. levied at the Lent assizes for Oneiland West. The protest spread to other baronies and no returns were received from Lower Orior and Upper Fews and very low returns from Upper Orior and Tyranny.[86] Escalation of the protest was facilitated by the dearth of troops – on service in the Seven Years' War, by the absence from the county of the leading politicians and the reluctance of the magistrates to interfere in their absence. Brownlow was in Bath. Charlemont was in Dublin. Acheson had journeyed south in June 1763 to rendezvous with his friend Rigby who was then visiting Ireland. In Brownlow's absence, no-one else was prepared to defend his unpopular road development and a protest which might have been dealt with at source was allowed to develop. People were also sworn not to pay small dues to clergy and attacked tithe gatherers and justices of the peace who had issued warrants against those who refused to pay.[87] In late June, Rigby, on his way home from Ireland, sympathised from Chester with his friend Acheson: 'I hope on your arrival in the county of Armagh you found your neighbours a little returned to their senses, and that you are not likely to be much tormented by their absurd mutiny'.[88] Rigby, briefed at his recent meeting with Acheson, was referring to the growing protest in mid-Armagh against the high levels of cess presented at the grand jury, including a 'visit' to Acheson at Markethill by a protesting crowd in late June.[89]

The need for improved roads and bridges brought on by the expansion of the linen industry had led to presentments for increased county cess to finance such improvements. But some levels of society below gentry resented demands for increased county taxes levied on all tenants and the six days of compulsory unpaid labour maintaining roads from which they perceived themselves less liable to benefit than the coach-travelling gentry. Such perceptions were inflamed at the use of public funds by some landed gentry to construct private roads. While rising cess would seem to have been a key issue in the grievances of the Oakboys, it was not the only one. Other grievances were the lesser tithes levied by clergy of the Established Church on minor farm produce such as cheese and eggs[90] and demanded from tenants of all denominations in their parishes; and the small dues also levied by them as fees for baptisms, marriages and funerals.[91] The anti-tithe part of the Oakboy programme directed against tithe-farmers and Anglican clergy would have had the particular sympathies of Presbyterians and Catholics, both denominations numerically strong in the baronies of Fews, Orior and Tyranny.

As the protest movement grew, huge crowds – reportedly numbering thousands – wearing green oak-boughs in their caps, 'visited' offending leading county figures whom they intimidated into swearing publicly to redress perceived grievances, manhandling – 'hustling' in contemporary jargon – those who hesitated and threatening them with worse, until they co-operated. Most Armagh 'gentlemen' were reported to have co-operated by mid-July after which the momentum moved on to Tyrone, Monaghan, Cavan and Derry. The bishops of Clogher and Kilmore, and some gentry, fled to Dublin to escape these 'visits'.

Perspectives on the composition of the Oakboy movement have varied over the centuries. Nineteenth century historians labelled it a 'Protestant' insurrection.[92] Yet Thomas Waite described the Oakboys: 'By all accounts they consist of people of all religions but are mainly Presbyterians.'[93] Waite's contemporary analysis has been supported by modern research which has emphasised the existence of a cross-denominational composition of Anglicans, Presbyterians and Catholics.[94] A recent reappraisal of the evidence argues that, while all denominations were represented in the movement, it was *Protestant-led*, with Catholics kept to the ranks by arms regulations and a central role for 'Presbyterians, sometimes from the Seceder and Covenanter fringes'.[95] Yet, ironically, the insurrection began in the north of the county where Dissenters were numerically weakest. The Oakboy leaders, it is argued further, were from the level of Irish society just below the landed élite, well-respected in their disciplined military-style organisation and control of Oakboy crowds.[96] The standing of the Oakboy leaders in their communities was probably a factor in the restrained response, generally, of the Armagh ruling élite to the Oakboy insurrection and consistent with its politics of popularity. To attempt to suppress their insurrection by physical force could have brought on a bloody civil war. Other factors contributed to that restraint. Many magistrates who were responsible for maintaining law and order in their own districts, were themselves the target of the Oakboys and felt overwhelmed by the size of the forces opposing them. There were also suspicions that accusations of exploitation of taxes and tithes by gentry and clergy were valid in some cases. Lord Charlemont, who as governor of County Armagh was responsible for maintaining peace and order, was out of immediate touch in Dublin. Deputy governor Acheson was on the spot but had no adequate policing force readily available. The policy of both was to defuse the explosive situation.

The absence of Brownlow avoided initial confrontation. Acheson was left to deal with the problem. He is listed as receiving two payments for road development between Markethill and Dundalk over the period 1762–3.[97] Though the Achesons were a long-standing Church of Ireland family, their seat in Lower Orior was in the heartland of Dissent and Archibald Acheson was reluctant – probably helpless – to oppose the behaviour of a significant number of his tenants in a popular protest and bent under their pressure. The area embracing Markethill and Richhill would seem to have been a centre of Oakboy organisation. A letter from a Markethill resident dated 4 July reported that an Oakboy crowd of four or five hundred had visited 'Sir A[rchibal]d, who readily concurred with our desires, not to demand any of the taxes agreed on at the Assizes'. The Markethill scribe also reported that he had attended an assembly of at least 8, 000 Oakboys in the neighbouring village of Richhill where 'with every person in Markethill, I was engaged to join them', marched from there and extracted promises from two churchmen – probably Rector Benjamin Barrington and Dean Anthony

Cope – to drop demands for small tithes. Cope was another who had received payment, for Kilmacantry Bridge, in 1763. Part of the Richhill crowd marched to visit prominent magistrate, counsellor and land agent Samuel Blacker at Tandragee and forced him to promise not to charge rent for the 'commons' at Tandragee which, hitherto, he had set.[98] Blacker had also received payments in 1762 and 1763 for roadworks in his area.[99]

A further letter from Markethill on 6 July described an armed force of military-style companies, some mounted, some on foot, proceeding from there to the Forkhill home of magistrate Richard Jackson – another recipient of payments for roads and bridges in his area. Jackson, who seemed to have been fore-warned of the Oakboys' visit, welcomed them cordially, co-operated with their 'chiefs' and rode with them to Newry where he publicly 'agreed to their requests'.[100] Individually, magistrates had little option when 'visited' by the Oakboys but to comply with their demands. Collectively, their response was different as in their published 'Terms of Association' dated 4 July by magistrates, freeholders and gentlemen of the grand jury of the county which condemned insurrection and warned of the danger of 'civil war'. But the notice also had conciliatory overtones accepting that mistakes may have been made in the use of cess income and promising that, in future, it would be used for *public* roads and buildings only.[101]

Not all magistrates were prepared to take the insurrection lying down. Ignoring his early promises to the Oakboys extracted under pressure, Samuel Blacker was in touch with Dublin Castle with information and requests for troops. He referred to Acheson's information that the Oakboys were levying the populace of Lower Orior for money to support the movement and demanding a sum of money from a gentleman in the area equivalent to a cess grant he had received for building a bridge.[102] The Oakboys of Richhill reminded Blacker that he had broken his promises to them by asking for the army to be sent in and threatened him with violence if he did not promise in writing to recant.[103] On the 15 July a crowd of seven thousand from Markethill, Clare, Fews and Killylea assembled on the common in Armagh to protest against exorbitant county cess but dispersed without violence.[104] On 17 July, High Sheriff Thomas Rowe of Clonmakate, parish of Tartaraghan, who had imprisoned some Oakboys, received a threatening letter, allegedly from Richhill Oakboys, demanding their release.[105]

The gravity of the situation was brought home to Lord Charlemont when his land agent Thomas Verner, a magistrate and attorney earning £4,000 per annum was alleged to have used cess money to build roads on his own newly acquired estate at Churchhill. He was taken from a corporation meeting he was chairing as portreeve in Charlemont, manhandled and threatened with hanging.[106] Lord Charlemont was torn between a desire not to lose 'the popular interest' of the county by forceful intervention and his responsibility as governor of the county for keeping law and order. Claiming he adopted the principle 'when duty calls, popularity should always be risked',[107] Charlemont came north to Armagh to 'exert himself and animate others' i.e. magistrates whom he found to be intimidated into passivity.[108] The grand jury asked Charlemont to request the lords justices for additional troops and he wrote accordingly to Primate Stone, the only lord justice available in Dublin. Stone replied by express that he had ordered a regiment of four hundred of General Sandford's foot at Galway and two troops of light dragoons at Clonmel to proceed to Armagh.[109] Although Charlemont considered this troop augmentation unnecessary, the news assuaged the fears of Armagh grand jurors and allowed the assizes to proceed.

However, the troops were not allowed by Charlemont to use undue or indiscriminate force in Armagh and, on the advice of Primate Stone – of like mind to Charlemont on this issue – only the leaders were incarcerated to avoid antagonising the populace as a whole. The privy council supported his action by issuing a general admonitory proclamation

> to dehort people from following their wicked leaders, and informing them of the extent and nature of their guilt, which is ordered to be read in all the churches and meetings of Protestant dissenters ... before we proceed towards offering rewards for apprehending particular persons.[110]

Oakboy violence ceased in County Armagh and outbreaks occurred further north and west in Ulster where the army was less gentle in its response.[111]

The longer-term aim was to extend the tenuous peace in Armagh into a lasting, conciliatory settlement. A pointer towards conciliation was the attitude of Dublin Castle officials who believed the initial Oakboy outbreaks had been handled badly. Pervading the Oakboy campaign and its settlement was a feeling that exorbitant levies of cess and its use, in some cases, for private development, had been a breach of the 'moral economy' and betrayal of – in Professor Bartlett's phrase – 'that tacit understanding between governor and governed', a sense of grievance which characterised Irish crowd disturbances pre-1793.[112] Thus influenced in 1763, government officials tended to blame the Armagh gentry for causing the insurrection in the first instance. They also were critical of the magistrates for not resolving the initial protest quickly: 'in the beginning, any justice with two constables could have nipped it in the bud'.[113] High Sheriff Rowe could be included in their criticism as he resided in West Oneilland.

Charlemont's measured approach supported by the privy council's direction to the Presbyterian churches brought a reciprocal response at local level. In late July 1763 a campaign for peace was initiated and many groups in Armagh made public pleas. A published list of Richhill inhabitants condemned the threat made to High Sheriff Rowe and offered a reward for information on the perpetrators.[114] Gentlemen, freeholders and merchants from the barony of Oneilland West in a signed statement, condemned the outrages and appealed for peace. On 19 July, the Presbytery of Armagh issued a 'friendly warning' to its congregation to desist insulting and extracting promises from gentry, magistrates and ministers of the Established Church by force as such deeds produced 'greater evils than they themselves are at present aware of'.[115] Two weeks later the Dissenting Congregation of Markethill, led by its minister George Ferguson and some two hundred members, produced a signed declaration – witnessed by Acheson – which publicly condemned the 'wicked attempts made by a number of our countrymen, of all denominations, to throw this country into anarchy and confusion'[116]

In early August a forgiving – at least partly forgiving! – Thomas Verner gave a lead to other magistrates by urging reconciliation with the Oakboys:

> for they are all conscious of their guilt, but they sincerely repent of their transgressions and seek forgiveness with assurances of good behaviour and obedience to the laws for the future. ... I am using my best endeavours to inform the country that they may all (except a few well known to them) return with security to themselves to their respective homes and employments.[117]

Charlemont returned to Dublin in late August, preening himself that he had settled the insurrection in Armagh 'by an exertion of temperate spirit without bloodshed or any sense of mischief'. His stock was high with the lord lieutenant who promised him an earldom and promotion to trustee of the Linen Board. But Charlemont's persistent obsession with 'popularity' led to a cooling in that relationship. His promised earldom was nearly withdrawn by Northumberland when Charlemont requested that the word 'unsolicited' be included in the inscription on the patent, his 'court favour ... declined' with his increasing display of opposition to government in the house of lords; and his appointment to the Linen Board was postponed.[118]

Local administration of law and order in Armagh county was slowly restored. A meeting of the county grand jury was held on 15 August but many members were still reluctant to attend, decisions on the security situation avoided and the unpopular issue of sentencing Oakboy prisoners ducked.[119] As confidence grew, Samuel Blacker was formally thanked by the Armagh grand jury at a meeting on 5 September for his stand against the Oakboys over the summer.[120] By then the ruling élite was also prepared to be magnanimous and make a conciliatory settlement as evidenced by the paucity and leniency of punishments to perpetrators – most of whom were known to the authorities.[121]

Both sides were glad to see an end to the troubles having given and received lessons. The Oakboys, having made their point to the ascendancy classes in Armagh, were anxious – as were their masters – that they return to the harvest routine and/or other means of livelihood: 'Certain it is that their trades and business are totally neglected and the linen manufacture is very manifestly declining.'[122] The ruling élite in the county had received a short but sharp warning from sections of the electorate that, where rising public taxes and labour services for private estate development were concerned, there was a limit to which tenants would be pushed and, subsequently, avoided unpopularly high presentments. Only half, approximately, of the cess levied in County Armagh in 1763 was collected. Presentments returned to *c.* pre-1763 levels in subsequent years. Ironically, in Oneiland West barony cess continued to rise and was mostly paid – suggesting that the original sense of grievance there was less resentment against the *amount* of cess levied than Brownlow's use of public funds and unpaid tenant labour for development of his own estate.[123]

In 1763, county members Brownlow and Acheson were left to ponder whether they would have been returned as county members of parliament in 1761 had the Oakboy insurrection occurred two years earlier. They were given a reminder on Sunday 16 March 1766 when an anonymous letter was found by the minister under the door of Seagoe Church conveying threats and menaces to William Blacker, a local landlord and justice of the peace, if Blacker should attempt to levy the county cess off parishioners for repairing roads in the parish. In a public notice, High Sheriff Arthur Cope and the county grand jury condemned the threats and offered a reward for information on the letter-writer which seemed to have prevented further incident. But it was another warning that tenants could not be taken for granted.[124]

RESUMPTION OF THE POLITICS OF PATRONAGE
AND THE CAMPAIGN FOR PARLIAMENTARY REFORM, 1764–8

With peace restored to County Armagh in 1764, normal politics resumed as before. Established Church politics came into play in the archdiocese of Armagh. Rector Benjamin Barrington received his long-sought promotion when he was appointed to succeed Dean Anthony Cope who died in late 1763.[125] A year after Barrington's appointment as dean of Armagh, his patron and prominent dispenser of patronage, Archbishop Stone, died in London. Several candidates were proposed for the vacant primatial see. Premier George Grenville favoured English incumbents and the post was offered to Bishop Newton of Bristol and Bishop Edmund Keane of Chester – but declined by both. Lord Granby's nominee, his tutor John Ewer, bishop of Llandaff, Wales, was not acceptable to George III, despite – or perhaps because of – Grenville's support. The duke of Bedford's nominee, Scottish-Hibernian William Carmichael, bishop of Meath was – in Sir Horace Walpole's opinion – 'too wise' to accept the nomination. Carmichael was translated to the archbishopric of Dublin in 1765.[126]

But Richard Robinson, bishop of Kildare, was ambitious to succeed to Armagh. His undistinguished record as churchman in his previous bishoprics would not have made him favourite. But he was well-connected politically. His younger brother, Septimus, was tutor to George III's children. He had the support of Lord Bute and Lord Lieutenant Northumberland – to whom he later built the obelisk in the primate's demesne – suggesting that his appointment was influenced more by political intrigue than merit as churchman. In this respect Robinson's promotion to Armagh was remarkably similar to that of his predecessor and mentor Primate Stone whose brother had been tutor to the Prince of Wales, and older brother confidential secretary to the duke of Newcastle; and Stone had also arrived in Ireland as chaplain to the lord lieutenant – then the duke of Dorset. Robinson was translated from the see of Kildare to Armagh by patent dated 8 February 1765.[127]

Acheson remained in friendly contact with Richard Rigby whom he plied with annual gifts of linen. Rigby in return, was a valued correspondent and advisor who kept Acheson up-dated on political developments in England and in contact with English politicians and absentee Irish landlords. For instance, Lord Sandwich of Hinchingbrooke was glad to hear, through Rigby, of Acheson's 'civil offers relative to his affairs in (your) neighbourhood' – presumably his Clare estate – and promised Acheson all his electoral interest during Acheson's lifetime. In 1766, when Acheson asked Rigby's opinion on whether it was opportune to bid for a peerage, he was advised it was an appropriate time, especially if the Limitation Bill being debated were passed:

> ... if this popular measure of short parliaments, which I think is an absurd one for the people of Ireland themselves, more than for English government, is to take place and if you are to be threatened with opposition in your county for three sessions of parliament ... the house of lords is certainly the quieter and more pleasant situation for a man in your easy and affluent circumstances.[128]

It was a beginning to Acheson's long quest for honour with ease.

Acheson's enquiry about the possibility of elevation to the peerage may have been prompted at this time by a touch of envy at the appointment of Brownlow – temporarily in favour with the Dublin administration – to the privy council in February 1766 by Lord Lieutenant Hertford. In the same dispatch of king's letters to Hertford, Dr Henry Maxwell, bishop of Dromore and former protégé of the late Primate Stone, was translated to Meath to replace Dr Arthur Smith.[129]

The issue of limited parliaments kept reappearing in the second half of the 1760s. During Hertford's viceroyalty a septennial bill passed the Irish house of commons in spring 1766. At the Armagh spring assizes, High Sheriff Cope and the grand jury publicly exhorted Brownlow and Acheson on the issue:

> Heads of a bill for this so constitutional a purpose [to limit the duration of parliaments in Ireland] have lately passed your house and been transmitted to Great Britain ... We have the best assured hopes, that these heads of a bill will be returned to us. We, therefore, request and expect your attendance in parliament on this occasion, and that you will give your utmost assistance to promote the passing into a law these heads of a bill, or of any other which may be offered to your house for limiting the duration of parliaments in this kingdom.

But the 'best assured hopes' of the Armagh grand jurors and freeholders were in vain as this bill suffered a similar fate to that of 1761–2.[130]

Early in the viceroyalty of fourth viscount George Townshend, Dean Walter Cope advised his brother-in-law that 'the frenzy of old Septennial is raging again'. He cited an observer's assessment – which seemed to echo that of Halifax in December 1761 – that '99 out of a 100 who spoke and voted for it were really against it'.[131]

The issue was resolved in early 1768. With some black humour, Lord Newtown advised Acheson that an Octennial Bill was on its way:

> The once desired bill for limiting the duration of parliaments is returned to us with some alterations, to which you can't be a stranger; the most momentous is, putting us to death on the 24th of June next. This bill undoubtedly alters considerably our constitution, I mean our public one, and at the same time proves to me a very strong connection between that and the constitution of individuals, for a very wonderful alteration has appeared within these few days in the faces of several gentlemen, many of them the most sanguine supporters of that bill.[132]

The Limitation (Octennial) Bill passed both houses of the Irish parliament and received the royal assent from the lords justices in mid-February 1768; and notice was given for parliament to be dissolved in May for a general election.[133]

THE 1768 GENERAL ELECTION IN ARMAGH – NEGOTIATIONS AND CANVASS FOR COUNTY SEATS

The general election of 1768 occurred during the terms of office of Lord Lieutenant George Townshend and Chief Secretary Lord Frederick Campbell. By Townshend's arrival in October 1767, executive management of the Irish parliament had deteriorated under previous weak or negligent viceroys[134] and unreliable undertakers such as Speaker John Ponsonby and Lord Shannon who had frequently equivocated on delivery of supply bills. Townshend's instruction from the British ministry – based on a proposal from George III – was to obtain the consent of the Irish parliament to an augmentation of the number of troops paid for by Ireland. But the government was 'routed again' on the augmentation proposals in the Irish house of commons on 2 May 1768 with Ponsonby, Prime Sergeant Hely-Hutchinson and Attorney-General Tisdall in opposition.[135] Five of the six Armagh members also opposed augmentation: both county members Brownlow and Acheson, both Charlemont borough members Caulfeild and Stewart, and Maxwell of Armagh borough. Only Cuninghame of Armagh borough voted for the measure in the division.[136]

Nathaniel Clements, deputy vice-treasurer of Ireland, blamed the coming general election for the defeat: '… if it [augmentation] had been proposed at a time when gentlemen were not afraid to appear for it – on account of the county elections – we should have carried it by a great majority.'[137] Whatever the accuracy of Clements's post-mortem, Townshend was convinced that a complete overhaul of the system of government in Ireland was required. His new management approach was to reside continually in Ireland, appropriate the supply of incentives – pensions, places and peerages – to reward loyal supporters, and thus replace the control of parliament by undertakers with his own direct rule. A major source of undertakers' power was the revenue board which controlled many places and Townshend planned to reform the revenue service and appropriate some of its patronage for his own use.[138]

As Townshend's relationship with the undertakers deteriorated, and patriots such as Lord Charlemont adjudged his policy of direct rule a usurpation of Irish constitutional influence,[139] Townshend would require the support of other unattached members to carry his programme through parliament. It was an ideal opportunity for independent country gentlemen like Acheson with ambitions for hire and attracted by a growing supply of viceregal incentives. Acheson's postal contact, promotion prospector and election broker in Dublin was his brother-in-law Walter Cope, dean of Dromore. Cope affected an early meeting with the lord lieutenant and an invitation to his levee. But Townshend was in such an angry mood with Ponsonby that Cope considered it 'improper' to raise the matter of 'vacancies' for Acheson or himself at that stage and had to be satisfied with leaving such overtures with Lord Campbell who promised Cope an 'audience' with Townshend.[140]

News of the Limitation Act in February 1768 and of a coming general election in June brought a plethora of correspondence between the ruling élite with the usual canvassing and interest-bargaining. Lord Newtown, in Dublin, immediately canvassed Acheson for his Arvagh interest, informing Acheson that he was in conjunction with Barry Maxwell and had the support of Lords Bellomont, Farnham and Tyrone, and a host of landlords in Cavan. Thanking Acheson for his support in the past, he invited Acheson to write to him through Cope if he thought Newtown could give reciprocal help to Acheson in the Armagh election.[141]

Acheson had already signalled his intention to stand again for County Armagh. In an election notice dated 11 February 1768 his supporters were requested 'to keep themselves entirely disengaged till his return from Bath, which … is expected every hour'. In the same edition two other candidates declared themselves candidates viz. William Brownlow and Arthur Cope of Loughgall, both of whom publicly praised the Limitation Act and its implications.[142] One week later Francis Caulfeild declared as a fourth candidate.[143] Richard Rigby, serving Acheson from London in a function similar to Cope's role in Dublin, up-dated Acheson on the passage of the Limitation Bill through the British house of commons and with news of members scurrying out of London to prepare for the British general election. He promised to provide Acheson with 'the earliest intelligence' of developments as possible assistance to him in the Armagh election.[144]

Then in Bath for the health of his sickly children,[145] Acheson did not return immediately as promised in his initial election notice. Instead he wrote from there to a range of friends and landlords – some resident in County Armagh, others not – requesting their support in the coming election. Using Cope as his postal contact in Dublin, Acheson applied to Brownlow, his former election partner, reminding him of the benefits to both of the 1761 conjunction: negligible expense, satisfied constituents and the maintenance of peace in the county. He recommended a repetition in 1768 of that partnership which, he argued, would attract a majority of electoral interests in the event of a contest.[146] Acheson was still in Bath at the end of February when he published a fuller election notice in which he explained his continued absence as family sickness and promised 'to immediately set out for Ireland'. He assured readers that so many had requested him to stand again for election that he was offering himself as candidate. This notice also followed the fashion of praising the Limitation Bill which had been omitted from his first election notice.[147]

A canvass of Wills Hill, earl of Hillsborough, by Acheson brought no success. When he had congratulated Hillsborough on being appointed secretary of state for the American colonies and president of the Board of Trade from 20 January 1768, Acheson had included in his letter a request for any electoral interest held by Hillsborough in County Armagh and the earl's use of influence with south Down landlords Hall and Nedham for their electoral interests west of the Newry River. Hillsborough, tongue-in-cheek, replied he would have given his support to Acheson, Brownlow and Caulfeild – 'if the county of Armagh had the right to send three members to Parliament ...', but regretted he had no electoral interest in County Armagh nor influence with Hall or Nedham.[148]

Acheson had more success with his negotiations – via Rigby – for the former Fane interest at Ballyclare and Tawnavaltiny, having asked for first votes for himself and second votes for Brownlow, his anticipated election partner. But, initially, he found the disposal of the Fane interest beset with complications over reversionary interests. When Charles, second Viscount Fane, died without issue in 1766, the title expired and his Irish estate passed to his two sisters as co-heirs with jointure to his wife. His sisters, Dorothy Fane, wife of John Montague, fourth earl of Sandwich at Hinchingbrooke, County Huntingdon, would inherit the Ballyclare portion, and Mary Fane, wife of Count Jerome de Salis, the portion at Tawnavaltiny. But in 1768, Sandwich claimed that the County Armagh estate was still 'an undivided property between him (Sandwich) and ... Madame de Salis'. Thus Rigby had to approach both families for the electoral interest on Acheson's behalf in 1768.[149] He reported that Lord Sandwich was satisfied to dispose of his interest as he (Rigby) pleased. Rigby also visited Madame de Salis who, though willing to serve Acheson, felt her family's long associations with the Brownlows should entitle William Brownlow to first consideration of estate votes. However, Rigby concluded, any doubt of Acheson receiving de Salis second votes would be resolved by her opposition to Caulfeild.[150]

Rigby's analysis was confirmed in correspondence by Lord Sandwich and Madame de Salis. Sandwich's letter to Acheson referred to his estate as 'an undivided moiety and therefore nothing very effectual can be done without the consent of the other proprietor'. Though Lord Charlemont – a long acquaintance – had asked him for his interest for his brother, Sandwich had sought Madame de Salis's cooperation in putting the entire interest at Acheson's disposal and enclosed her reply with his letter to Acheson.[151] Madame de Salis's letter to her brother-in-law gave her reasons for wishing the Irish estate's first votes to go to Brownlow: she had stayed for long periods with Lady Betty, Brownlow's mother, at the Brownlow house in Lurgan; and her father, first Viscount Charles Fane, had been a close friend of Brownlow's father, as her brother, the second viscount, was to the present William Brownlow. She could only support Acheson in the event of his joining with Brownlow in an election pact.[152]

Other candidates for the Armagh county seat were also making their bids for election partners. As in 1761, Lord Charlemont moved quickly to approach Brownlow, in Dublin, for an election pact with Francis Caulfeild: 'The Limitation Bill was not three hours arrived before Lord Charlemont applied to me for a junction with his brother.' Brownlow's non-committal reply was that he intended to ascertain 'the sense of the county', firstly on his own candidature and then on other candidates, before entering an election partnership with any.[153] The occasion for sounding out opinions on election favourites was the county assizes. A plethora of potential candidates in numerous Ulster counties canvassing for election partners in the 1768 election – four declared in Armagh, five in Cavan, four in Tyrone – planned to ascertain their standing among other gentry with electoral interests in the county at the Lent (spring) assizes scheduled for 6 April 1768, before deciding whether to stand for election and with whom as election partner.[154]

Arthur Cope, son of the late Robert Cope MP and younger brother of the late Dean Anthony Cope, having inherited a large part of the extensive Cope estates, was another taking soundings on whether to stand for a county seat in Armagh. Resident in Loughgall, he was building a reputation as linen entrepreneur in mid-Armagh and, 'at the request of a great number of linen drapers' was promoting a monthly fair in 'the Avenue of Loughgall' since January 1768. In March he offered a reward for information leading to the conviction of culprits who had breached the ramparts of Shaw's Lough, damaging bleach-greens and draining off the water supply on his Mountnorris estate. Cope condemned the vandalism '… every attempt to distress and hurt the linen trade is one of the severest attacks that can be made on the nation, its liberty, and independency.'[155]

Cope visited Brownlow in Dublin and suggested that his considerable electoral interest, combined with that of Brownlow and another, could decide the election of Brownlow plus one other. Initially Cope did not assert that the 'other' should be himself, although he hinted obliquely that he might be a candidate. Later he warmed to that notion and his brother actually spread the rumour that Arthur Cope had joined interests with Brownlow – which was untrue. But Cope received the same response from Brownlow as other applicants. Brownlow was still not ready to decide on his election partner until he had 'received the best information of the sense of the county' at the Lent assizes. He explained to Acheson the motivation underpinning his procrastination: 'My hearty wish is that the county may never again be thrown by a sharp contested election into that state of confusion I have once seen it in.'[156]

Brownlow had little doubt that he would be returned for an Armagh county seat but his return to parliament was guaranteed in any case by an offer of one of the Strabane borough seats controlled by his Hamilton kinsfolk. Before March, the earl of Abercorn had offered Brownlow a seat there. Brownlow, when thanking Abercorn for this insurance, advised the earl to keep his offer secret until after the Armagh county election result so that Abercorn could give the Strabane seat to another friend if not required by Brownlow:

> I really believe I am not in any sort of danger of failing at Armagh myself. ... There are three other candidates who all solicit a junction with me and I only wait to be better acquainted with the general sense of the county to form such a connection as may prevent disturbance. But as the event is in some sort uncertain and as the lower class of weavers may, in case of contest, resent my not bribing them with drink which I am determined on no account ever to do, I shall ... request your recommendation of me at a proper time to the electors of Strabane, which will be a security to me ... for I think I may flatter myself that I shall at the meeting of parliament have an option to make for Armagh.[157]

Acheson, too, had insured his return to parliament by the not uncommon expedient of the 'double return'. He had secured a vacant seat for the rotten borough of Killileagh, County Down, controlled by the Blackwood family.[158] Brownlow's determination to avoid a contested election can be traced to his experience of 1753. That he blamed drunken weavers for part of the violence in that contest was evident in his refusal to treat in the elections of 1761 and 1768. Brownlow found the 1753 contest so abhorrent that he avowed never to pay a similar price for a county seat: 'I have repeatedly declared that I will not put myself to any extraordinary trouble or expense to obtain it (an Armagh county seat).'[159]

A superiority complex and sense of presumption can also be detected in Brownlow's reluctance to canvass electoral interests and votes in 1768. He bared his soul in a strange confession to Acheson of his frustration with the canvassing process:

> For my part I think the trouble of attendance on parliament a sufficient burthen, without the further trouble of soliciting it, and when a man has once taken a part, and proved his principles, he should do no more than offer himself, and never seek to sway or influence votes by means that are in themselves so destructive to the ... welfare of that county he proposes to serve.[160]

Lord Charlemont who did most of the election negotiation for his brother – a captain in Lord Drogheda's regiment – would appear to have concluded from Brownlow's non-committal response and Sandwich's February rejection of his application that Caulfeild had little chance of winning a county seat. Indeed he may not have been confident from the start and unwilling to suffer undue expenses, suggested by the paucity of his election notices in national newspapers. The earl was also probably busy with preparations for his own coming wedding to Mary Hickman on 2 July 1768.[161] Caulfeild's candidature seems to have been withdrawn in early March 1768 and his name is omitted from the list of candidates published in mid-March.[162] Acheson's approach to Charlemont for his electoral interest received the frosty reply that the earl had pledged his Armagh interest to Brownlow and Cope.[163]

Traditionally, Molyneux's electoral support had been for Caulfeild. With Caulfeild's withdrawal, Acheson requested Bishop Garnett to approach his brother-in-law for the Molyneux interest. Molyneux's response, through Garnett, was to withhold any decision on the disposal of his interest until 'a general meeting should be held in the county and the sense of the gentry taken'. Garnett consoled Acheson with his assurance that Acheson would receive the nomination of the Armagh gentry.[164]

Acheson accepted an offer of electoral support from Barry Maxwell of Cavan. Maxwell had applied to Acheson for support against opponent George Montgomery in a possible five-candidate contest in County Cavan, fearing that freehold tenants of non-resident landlords such as Acheson were vulnerable to the approaches of Montgomery. He asked Acheson to press the agent of his Arvagh estate to 'get explicit answers from (your) tenants, and ... let me know the tenants I may depend upon'. As a quid pro quo, Maxwell promised to persuade three or four of his freehold tenants in County Armagh to vote for Acheson – which he did. The threat to Maxwell was eased by the withdrawal of Lord Newtown from the Cavan contest following the death of his father, the earl of Lanesborough, in April 1768 and Newton's resultant succession to the Irish house of lords. But four candidates remained – Maxwell, Montgomery, Pratt and Newburgh – in what promised to be a long and hard-fought contest.

As summer approached, the election campaign intensified and profiles of all Armagh candidates rose. Acheson was elected a trustee of the Inland Navigation Board for Ulster province to replace the late earl of Lanesborough.[165] Some hundred 'linen merchants, drapers and manufacturers' signed and published an address of thanks to Arthur Cope for his promotion of the trade and his offer of reward towards convictions for vandalism to the Shaw's Lough rampart and resultant loss by the linen trade.[166] The inclusion of Mountnorris signatories was a timely public relations exercise on behalf of their landlord Arthur Cope, given the mutiny of Mountnorris tenants against Cope's older brother Dean Anthony Cope and his preferred candidate in 1753.

Brownlow issued a long printed manifesto to his constituents on 9 May 1768.[167] Its tone was one of compliance bordering on humiliating submission, repudiating any hint of the presumption and contempt for the voters in his letter of 5 March to Acheson. It responded to criticisms by the electorate of his earlier disdain for voters on which he may have been too outspoken and/or which may have been leaked to the public. In it Brownlow submitted his public conduct to the scrutiny of the electorate and its approbation. He referred to his record of support for the Limitation Act, for the linen trade, for justice for both rich and poor, his constant attendance in parliament including late sittings which had damaged his health – all to serve the interests of the voters before his own – and submitted his election fate to the judgement of the voters.

The manifesto identified two specific criticisms which Brownlow had heard. The first was that he had not applied to freeholders for their votes, and 'that if a vote was worth giving, it was worth asking' – meaning that he had not personally visited each freeholder to ask for his vote. Brownlow's answer was that he had considered his election address in a variety of newspapers to be an application to each freeholder for his vote and 'supposed further solicitation unnecessary'. He now expressed disappointment if the newspaper addresses carried insufficient currency or had been misinterpreted. But a door-to-door canvass had not been practicable: 'I am not able, gentlemen, as in '53, to ride about the country from house to house and solicit you personally'. He had also believed his record of 'service' to the 'public good' and adherence to 'principle' over the years were sufficient evidence of good faith to freeholders without using 'undue means to continue himself in that station' which was abhorrent to the spirit of the constitutional process.[168]

Brownlow identified the second criticism against him as 'the polling of the grand jury, as it has been called, for members of parliament'. The grand jurors attending the Lent assizes on 12 April had made Brownlow first choice and Acheson second choice as county candidates for the general election. Some freeholders had obviously considered such pre-election selection of candidates as subverting their democratic right to elect parliamentary representatives and resented the intrusion by the grand jury. Brownlow's answer was that the practice introduced at the Armagh assizes was in imitation of many Irish counties and most English counties, had not been proposed by Brownlow, though considered by him to be a useful indication of the choice of the gentry, and not final. Brownlow concluded his letter by reiterating that his only aim was to serve the wishes of the electorate and would stand down if they had another candidate they preferred.[169] Brownlow's letter seemed to have satisfied his resentful freeholders as there is no report of further discord among them.

When High Sheriff Francis Obré appointed Monday 18 July 1768 as opening day of the Armagh election, all three candidates placed new election notices in early July asking freeholders to attend the poll.[170] Candidates began to make arrangements for high profile gentry to be present in support. In response to Acheson's request, William Henry

Fortescue of Reynoldstown, County Louth, explained he would only be there if absolutely necessary as the Louth county election was being held at the same time but named freeholders from his Armagh interest whom he had persuaded to vote for Acheson.[171]

Contemporary correspondence suggests that, until the last moment, candidates anticipated a contest. Brownlow, back at his Lurgan residence, discussed polling arrangements with Acheson. Having enquired about spare accommodation in the primate's Armagh house for key election personnel and discovered that only three beds were available, Brownlow had directed Rev. Henry Leslie of Tandragee[172] to ask Counsellor Samuel Blacker if he required a bed in Armagh. Blacker had requested a bed to be kept for him otherwise he 'must lie in the street'. Brownlow instructed Acheson to ensure that Blacker had a bed there and to arrange 'private lodging at our expense' for Obré, with apologies to the latter that a previous promise for accommodation in the primate's house had been made to Blacker. Brownlow's concern to keep Blacker happy undoubtedly emanated from his memory of the key role of Blacker and the St John tenants in 1753. He informed Acheson that Blacker's son would lead the St John tenants of Ballymore to the poll with 'Parker to bring up the rear'; and he would enquire further of Blacker about arrangements for the St John tenants from the Kernan estate.[173]

The above three candidates remained in the field for the two Armagh county seats until the last moment. On the day of the election, Cope withdrew, thus avoiding a contest. The following notice from him dated 18 July appeared in the *Belfast News-Letter*:

> Mr Cope returns his sincere thanks to the gentlemen, clergy, and freeholders who intended honouring him with their voices on the poll for this county; but finding the major part of the freeholders unable to oppose the authority of landlords, has forced him this day to submit to the necessity of the times, and decline polling.

It was an ironic excuse for withdrawal from one of the larger landlords in the county who, himself, had canvassed conjunction with other landlords, like the rest. The same issue contained a joint statement of thanks from Brownlow and Acheson.[174] Both men could now pass on the safe half of their 'double return' to others. In Brownlow's case, Strabane borough seat went to another Hamilton relation of its patron Lord Abercorn. Acheson's Killileagh borough seat was purchased by rich Down lawyer Arthur Johnson from its patron William Blackwood for £2,000.[175]

Lord Lanesborough congratulated Acheson on his success in Armagh. He also asked Acheson to make every effort to get his Arvagh tenants out in the Cavan election which seemed destined to go to a lengthy poll.[176] A victory 'entertainment' for Brownlow and Acheson attended by many of the county gentry was hosted in Portadown by Acheson's son-in-law, Michael Obins and his freeholders on 1 August.[177] The cautious, slow build-up, consultation with the gentry and painstaking election canvassing tactics and pacts deployed in the Brownlow-Acheson election campaign were shown to be justified, not only by the successful and peaceful outcome in Armagh, but by the contrasting violence of the Cavan election. There a poll, opened on 23 July with four candidates and continuing for sixteen days, was brought to a precipitate close on 11 August by a violent riot of armed men who attempted – unsuccessfully – to destroy the poll-books and the high sheriff felt obliged to declare Barry Maxwell and George Montgomery elected next morning without resumption of the poll.[178]

With the winter of 1768–9 approaching, Acheson and family returned to the south of England and remained there until the following summer. Using Bath and Bristol as his bases, he communicated with his English contacts including Richard Rigby, appointed paymaster of the forces in 1768.[179] During his English sojourn, Acheson seems to have allowed his connections with the Irish opposition to lapse and to have let it be known that he was available to approaches from Townshend's administration.

BOROUGH RETURNS IN 1768

With Archbishop Stone, their former patron, gone, sitting members for Armagh city borough, Colonel Robert Cuninghame and Hon. Barry Maxwell, sought and found seats elsewhere in 1768 – the former for Monaghan borough controlled by his brother-in-law Lord Clermont, the latter for Cavan county, aided by his brother Lord Farnham. Archbishop Robinson had promised nomination of one of the Armagh borough members to the duke of Northumberland in gratitude for his part in Robinson's appointment to the see of Armagh in 1765. In February 1768, Northumberland requested Robinson for the return of Sir George Macartney who was related by marriage to the duke. Macartney and Northumberland's son were married to two daughters of the politically powerful earl of Bute. Macartney used the connection to apply for the Armagh seat and was returned in July.[180]

It is not clear why Macartney desired a seat in the Irish house of commons in the spring of 1768 as he already held a seat in the British house of commons for Cockermouth, Cumberland, courtesy of his wife's brother-in-law Sir James Lowther who was married to another daughter of Lord Bute. And under the terms of the Regency Act of 1707, Macartney would be obliged to relinquish his seat in the British parliament if appointed to any Irish office of profit under the crown.[181] A factor may have been a desire to be closer to his property at Lissanoure, north Antrim, where he was later appointed constable and commander of the fort of Toome on the lower Bann on a pension of £1500 per annum.[182] A more potent reason perhaps was that by 1768 he was being groomed by his father-in-law for a future Irish chief secretaryship as was rumoured in Dublin Castle in early summer: 'Primate Richard Robinson is to make George Macartney an MP for Armagh City at the request of Lord Northumberland. Rumours have Macartney as the next chief secretary, just as soon as Lord Bute chooses a new viceroy.'[183]

Further rumours emerged from St James Street, London, that Macartney would succeed Chief Secretary Campbell who had agreed to exchange his Irish post for a British one.[184] These rumours became reality in autumn 1768 when Campbell succeeded the late Lord Morton as lord register of Scotland and was replaced, officially, in Ireland by Macartney.[185] Macartney, obliged to resign his Westminster seat, was anxious to come to Ireland, but was told by Townshend to wait until the new year when Campbell had finished his business there.[186] And Townshend continued to postpone meeting Macartney until March 1769.[187]

Nominated to the second Armagh borough seat was the Hon. Philip Tisdall, attorney general and former friend of Archbishop Stone, in a 'double return'. But career politician Tisdall was reluctant to be tied to any patron and when returned for his former seat in Dublin University he opted for the relative independence and prestige of the more open university seat. The university seat had an electorate of ninety two – twenty two fellows and seventy scholars. But the provost had wide powers, including those of returning officer at parliamentary elections which usually assured the return of his nominees – if reputable. In 1768 the nominees of Provost Francis Andrews were Tisdall and Sir Capel Molyneux of Castle-Dillon.[188] Tisdall had the requisite credentials: an authority in law, judge of the prerogative court, attorney-general, member of the privy council and king's council. Sir Capel Molyneux, as nephew of the famous William Molyneux, member for Dublin University in the 1690s and cousin of Rt Hon. Samuel Molyneux, university member in the late 1720s, was also an acceptable nominee. The Armagh knight's switch in 1768 from his brother-in-law's Clogher seat to the university constituency was a tactic to facilitate an arrangement by Provost Andrews to introduce his relation William Gamble to parliament without compromising his own position through nepotism. Gamble, who would have been unacceptable to the university electorate as an unknown newcomer and relation of the provost, was placed in the rotten borough seat of Ballyshannon controlled by Thomas Conolly; and Conolly's brother-in-law John Staples was acceptable to Bishop Garnett as nominee for Clogher borough vacated by Molyneux. Thus were patrons, candidates and constituencies all satisfied by the provost's horses-for-courses strategy.[189]

One interested party dissatisfied with the arrangement was the lord lieutenant who had recommended a candidate for Clogher but was refused by Bishop Garnett who had accepted instead Staples and Hon. William Moore – the latter recommended by Lord Bessborough and the duke of Newcastle. Townshend did not forget the snub by Garnett and a year later when the bishop asked his help in finding a seat for his relation G. St George, endorsed his letter: 'which bishop refused a recommendation from me 12 months ago, and brings in 2 members in opposition ... to be shown to the king as an instance of the weakness of the government in this country and the prelates' ingratitude'.[190]

Charles O'Hara, descended from an old County Sligo Gaelic family turned Protestant, had lost out originally to Macartney for nomination to an Armagh borough seat but now replaced Tisdall. Previously, O'Hara had held a vacant 'close' borough seat for Ballynakill, Queen's County, controlled by the Barrington family, attached to Primate Stone and government. Between 1761 and 1768 the Barrington family sold Ballynakill interest to Lord Drogheda.[191] In 1768 the government found another seat for O'Hara in Armagh where he was described as:

> Brought in by the primate who has this borough entirely, a true government man and will go through pitch(?) in hopes of hire. Mema. the two men that represent the primate's constituency are both Deists.[192]

O'Hara's career prospered after 1768 for his loyal service to government as 'a good attender and a sensible man – seldom speaks and ill hear'd (sic).'[193] He voted with government in eight major divisions from 1768 to 1774.[194]

Elections in Charlemont borough in 1768 were less complicated with the return of sitting members Francis Caulfeild and Sir Annesley Stewart. As brother and cousin, respectively, of the borough's patron, both were expected to follow Lord Charlemont's policy of opposition to government. Another in-law of the Caulfeild family, John Moore of the Drumbanagher family, whose mother was a Caulfeild, was introduced to parliament in 1768. Several members of the Moore family had represented the borough of Charlemont in the Irish parliament but when Henry William Moore died in 1763 Charlemont had declined to nominate Henry William's politically inexperienced younger brother John (1726–1809) as replacement. Subsequently John Moore served an apprenticeship in local politics as high sheriff of County Armagh in 1767 and high sheriff of County Down in 1768 before his other kinsman, Lord Drogheda, in 1768 brought him in – in tandem with Drogheda's agent William Montgomery – for Ballynakill borough.[195]

'DISPOSITIONS'[196] OF ARMAGH MPs IN
THE TOWNSHEND VICEROYALTY, 1769-72

The personality and style of Townshend dominated Irish politics in the four years following the 1768 general election. As elsewhere in Ireland, members of parliament representing Armagh constituencies responded in different ways to his leadership. The relationship between Macartney and Townshend, which had started poorly, deteriorated. Under-secretary Thomas Waite observed from Dublin Castle: 'I fancy Sir George is heartily sick of his new master'.[197] Waite himself disliked Townshend's irregular lifestyle and working hours. But both Macartney and Waite worked with second secretary Richard Jackson and John Lees, Townshend's private secretary, in an inner secretariat to identify support among members for Townshend's administration and to rebuild the administration accordingly. After the general election, Jackson's assessment of the anticipated affiliations of members in the coming parliament confirmed that the Ponsonby-Shannon group of undertakers was more intent on rejecting Townshend's programme than delivering it. His report pointed to the necessity of wooing sufficient of the independents – those members attached to neither administration nor to the undertakers – over to the government side to get the business through when parliament met. Many of these independents were country gentlemen such as Acheson and Brownlow.[198]

In 1769, Acheson's disposition was assessed as 'doubtful for [government]' but amenable to approaches from government. His equivocation was recognised in the observations: 'Rather inclined government but courts popularity. Wants to be made a PC. To be spoken to on interesting questions'.[199] Acheson's conversion to government supporter probably dates to this period. In the division of 2 May 1768 he had voted against army augmentation but in divisions over 1771–2 he is listed as voting for government.[200] Brownlow, however, was assessed 'against [government]' and remained firmly in opposition to Townshend's administration.[201]

Francis Caulfeild and Sir Annesley Stewart were both assessed as 'against' and voted consistently against government in divisions during Townshend's viceroyalty.[202] As Lord Charlemont's nominees, neither was independent although Blaquiere's assessment in 1773 suggested that Stewart's professional relationship with the earl gave him some degree of independence: 'Stewart is a banker and my Lord [Charlemont] who is very necessitous owes him a large sum of money which makes Stewart independent.'[203] Stewart was married to Sarah Moore, youngest of eight. Lord Charlemont had chosen Stewart – probably in return for his financial services – to replace the late Henry William Moore in 1763 over Moore's younger brother John, Lord Drogheda's nomination in 1768 who was assessed as a supporter of government. Described by Blaquiere as 'a good honoured [sic] well-meaning man who will go with Lord Drogheda',[204] John Moore repaid his patron's trust by voting constantly with government in divisions during the 1768 parliament. The other Armagh country gentleman serving a constituency borough outside the county, Sir Capel Molyneux of Castle-Dillon, used the relative independence of a Dublin University seat to vote mostly as he pleased, which was frequently against government.[205]

Townshend's strategy of carrot and stick to rally support in parliament rewarded government supporters with favours – to members and/or their relations – at a variety of levels: places, pensions, public offices, posts on revenue board and privy council, army commissions, promotions, command of a regiment, church preferment, promise of a title or step up in the peerage etc. The Townshend viceroyalty was a good time for men of ambition. But the lord lieutenant believed in only rewarding deeds rather than promises of support. Townshend also punished uncooperative members and transgressors both as an example to others and to create vacancies for proven supporters. When parliament rejected the money bill, Townshend angrily prorogued it on 26 December 1769 and kept it in recession for fourteen months. When requesting replacements for three deceased members of the privy council, he also recommended to a hesitant Southern Secretary Lord Weymouth, that lords Shannon and Lanesborough, Ponsonby, and three others be dismissed from the privy council for voting against the money bills. In a 'most secret' dispatch, he described his recommended replacements as 'gentlemen of great property and reputation in the country and have steadily supported government in all the great points of the session'.[206] One was Sir Archibald Acheson. Weymouth approved Townshend's recommendations.[207] Townshend's reply referred to the shock experienced by the former undertakers on hearing of their dismissal. It also requested an early issue of the king's letters as official confirmation of their being struck off the privy council and of their replacement on it by Acheson et al. which were duly issued.[208] By then Townshend was in private correspondence with Acheson who was cultivating a friendship with the lord lieutenant which he would use to seek employment and/or preferment for relations.[209]

In contrast to Acheson's conversion to government supporter, Brownlow was persistent in opposition and perhaps fortunate to escape Townshend's purge of the privy council in early 1770. If the lord lieutenant still had hopes then of winning over Brownlow with Acheson, he was mistaken. This was demonstrated in divisions in the house of commons on all significant measures. When parliament re-assembled on 26 February 1771, the proposal to include an appreciation of Townshend's viceroyalty in an address of thanks to the king was carried by 132 votes to 107, with

Brownlow opposing and Acheson and he on opposite sides for the first time on a major issue since the Money Bill dispute of 1753.[210] Realising the desertion of former members of opposition, such as Acheson, Hely-Hutchinson, et al. to government, Speaker Ponsonby resigned his post on 4 March 1771, rather than deliver the address. In the election of a new speaker on 7 March, Macartney proposed Edmund Sexton Pery – whom Townshend had wooed out of opposition. The opposition proposed Brownlow as rival candidate. It was a measure of the esteem in which Brownlow was held by the house of commons that he pushed the government candidate to a close result, his 114 votes being defeated by Pery's 118.[211]

And Brownlow's opposition to Townshend continued. The lord lieutenant's reports in 1771 to Lord Rochford had several references to Brownlow's opposition to government bills.[212] In November 1771, for instance, Brownlow moved an amendment to shorten the term of a government supply bill to six months but it was rejected by twenty-three votes.[213] He moved further amendments to shorten money bills and opposed Townshend's proposed reforms of the revenue service which, it was argued, would diminish the power of the Irish parliament by transferring future power and influence to the lord lieutenant in appointment of places.[214] In March 1772 when the government moved to extend the Revenue Act until the end of the parliamentary session, Brownlow and Caulfeild voted for limitation to four years, with Acheson, O'Hara, Macartney and John Moore voting 'for perpetuating the act'. The government had a narrow victory by 5 votes.[215]

RETURN OF THE OAKBOY PROTESTS IN 1772

Brownlow's parliamentary activity was interrupted by another outbreak of Oakboy violent protest in Oneilland barony in the spring of 1772. This was an extension into the valleys of the Lagan and Upper Bann of the Steelboy land war of 1767–71 by tenants on the Donegall and Upton estates, County Antrim. It has been argued that a protest triggered off by one grievance arising from cess, tithes or rents, usually generalised to the others.[216] In Armagh the protest began with cess payments being withheld, then spread to the others. The Oneilland Oakboys would seem to have been sympathising with their Antrim neighbours from the beginning as indicated in a letter from a Lurgan resident to his uncle in Strabane: 'For five years and a half, one barony in which Lurgan is situated has paid no county cess, no constable daring to collect it'.[217] The dearth of cess payments paid in Oneilland East mentioned by the Lurgan correspondent is corroborated by the Armagh Presentments book which shows very few returns of cess from the barony between Lent 1766 and summer 1771, and notes there were no collectors for that barony over most of that period. It was not until 1772 that William Hazleton of Lurgan was appointed collector, after the army was moved to Lurgan in March 1772 to quell the insurrection there, and a levy of £210-0s.-5d. was collected subsequently.[218]

Another stimulus to protest in the Lagan and Upper Bann valleys in early 1772 was the economic depression following three poor harvests in succession and a slump in the London linen market 1771–2. The Oakboy campaign intimidated landlords, with threats of arson, to keep down the prices of farm produce on sale and fix leases no higher than twelve shillings per acre.[219] It was a similar situation to 1763 with a restless society defying the law in the absence of a police force and unopposed by sympathetic neighbours or fearful magistrates, until the army arrived.[220] Sir Richard Johnston – high sheriff of County Armagh in 1771[221] – arrested a local Oakboy leader which brought an attempt on 6 March 1772 by his Oakboy associates to rescue him from Johnston's Gilford house. In the fracas, Rev. Samuel Murrell, local Presbyterian Minister, was shot dead. Johnston fled to Dublin to apprise the government and request army assistance.[222] The government, concerned at 'the great deal of disturbance in the north', sent General Gisbourne to quell it.[223]

The lord lieutenant reported to London that the magistrates were afraid to take action at Lurgan – 'the headquarters of the discontented' – where Gisbourne intended to make his headquarters. He also reported that Brownlow was returning to Lurgan to assist him. The army's seizure of leaders and arms in their homes in Lurgan ended the insurrection within days and Gisbourne commended the vigilance and support of magistrates, particularly Brownlow, in the military operation.[224]

Immediate recriminations against the insurrectionists were strong. On 28 March 1772, the lord lieutenant gave assent to legislation for greater punishments for offenders in the counties of Antrim, Down, Armagh and Londonderry – city and county; and Townshend and the Council of Ireland issued a proclamation promising rewards for information against Steelboys who threatened John Blackwood's County Down estate. In late March and April, a plethora of notices in the *Belfast News-Letter*, including that of John Blackhall, agent of the Cope estate at Loughgall, condemned Hearts of Steel and Hearts of Oak. The corporation of Londonderry presented the freedom of the city to Sir Richard Johnston for his efforts to bring Oakboys to book. Some leaders of the Steelboys were tried in Belfast and sentenced to death. Others were to be transported to Dublin for trial.[225]

But Dublin Castle relented after concluding that the 'horrible rumours of trouble in the North [were] exaggerated', with suspicions that protests may have been rooted in a moral economy. The Dublin administration was more concerned at the migration of inhabitants from the north to Scotland and America.[226] By mid-April it was decided that the disturbances were over; and County Armagh grand jury sent Townshend an address of thanks for his support.[227] The severity of sentencing eased. Steelboy leaders were acquitted at their Dublin trial in summer. The northern gentry resented the swing from severity to leniency and similar addresses were sent to Townshend by high sheriffs and grand juries of Armagh and Down from the summer assizes urging the lord lieutenant to continue the earlier suppression of 'the late tumultuous risings in this county'.[228]

The 1772 outbreak of Oakboy protest differed to that of 1763 in that it did not spread significantly southwards through County Armagh. Acheson's estates seem to have escaped the worst effects and his correspondence makes no reference to Oakboy violence. Rather it reveals that while Brownlow was opposing government and Oakboys, Acheson was making overtures to the lord lieutenant and advancing his own claims for a peerage and more favours for his relations. In mid-April he wrote to Townshend about the address of thanks from the Armagh grand jury and transfer of an insurgent to Dublin for trial. Brownlow is listed as foreman of the grand Jury at the 1772 Lent assizes but Acheson is listed as foreman at the summer assizes.[229]

Acheson's high status in Dublin Castle was evidenced in being chosen as one of the two baronets who introduced Macartney to be invested by Townshend with the ensigns of Order of the Bath on 25 June 1772.[230] It was about that time that Acheson was led to believe he was being considered for a peerage as he informed the chief secretary that his choice of title would be 'Baron Gosford'. He also took this opportunity to ask Macartney for employment for his son-in-law, Alexander Macaulay of Glenville, County Antrim.[231]

At the end of June 1772 Acheson wrote to Townshend asking to have a £200 fine imposed on Armagh county by Judge Christopher Robinson reduced to sixpence.[232] There was a delay in response while Townshend considered the case. Acheson wrote again, this time supporting his request with gift of a turtle to the lord lieutenant and an invitation to visit his Markethill seat.[233] The turtle did the trick! Townshend wrote two letters thanking Acheson for the 'bribe', granting the reduction in the fine and explaining the delay in responding, for which he was thanked by Acheson.[234]

Acheson's cultivation of Townshend's friendship was bearing fruit for his extended family. Walter Cope, dean of Dromore from 1759 and rector of Loughgilly since 1771, was appointed bishop of Clonfert and Kilmacduagh in January 1772.[235] Six months later Acheson requested further ecclesiastical preferment for Cope.[236] He probably anticipated a vacancy in the see of Ferns and Leighlin whose bishop, Edward Young was terminally ill. Acheson had ulterior motives for his brother-in-law's translation there, not least his desire to appropriate the seats of the accompanying parliamentary borough for his sons.

In mid-August 1772 Macartney, before leaving for England after a summer sojourn on his Lissanoure estate, replied to Acheson's request in June for a place or pension for the Macaulay family. His letter not only reveals Acheson's privileged relationship with Townshend and Macartney but also provides an insight into government methods of allocating pensions. Macartney had asked John Lees to meet Acheson about the matter as Lees was in contact with Townshend every day. He also observed that the lord lieutenant 'always appeared to me to be perfectly disposed to promote any of your [Acheson's] wishes'. He said there was a 'plan' in Dublin Castle to withdraw a pension from a person – previously impecunious but now wealthy, previously supportive but now opposed to government and daring the government to take the pension from him. The plan was to give it to Mrs Macaulay – Acheson's daughter. Macartney assured Acheson that Thomas Waite was also aware of the plan and would help in Lees's absence.[237]

Longer-term arrangements were disrupted by news in summer 1772 of a change of lord lieutenant and chief secretary – brought on by Townshend's over-spending, his domineering manner and profligate life-style – inducing anxieties in those close to either or both ministers and fresh hopes in those who were not.[238] Acheson conveyed his hopes that Townshend would not be replaced as lord lieutenant and requested last favours – a peerage for himself and the translation of Bishop Walter Cope from Clonfert to Ferns and Leighlin so that Acheson's son might obtain an Old Leighlin borough seat in parliament and serve as a government supporter. His requests were accompanied by a present of venison.[239]

Townshend replied that he had recommended Acheson to George III for a peerage as reward for Acheson's support to government – which he did, on 9 September 1772.[240] However he explained that he was unable to grant Acheson's second request i.e. for Cope's translation, as he had already recommended the merits of another 'old and faithful friend of government ... that I must think myself under an indispensable obligation to promote his family on this occasion'.[241] Thus, on Townshend's recommendation, the Hon. Joseph Bourke, dean of Dromore, was appointed bishop of Ferns and Leighlin in 1772 and Walter Cope remained bishop of Clonfert and Kilmacduagh for a further ten years before he was translated to Ferns and Leighlin.[242] Sir Archibald Acheson's eldest son, Arthur, put his failure to obtain a parliamentary seat in 1772 behind him. He married Millicent Pole in 1774 and lived the good life on the continent[243] until the Old Leighlin seat became available with Bishop Cope's translation there in 1782.

Other disappointments for Sir Archibald Acheson followed in 1772. The best-laid plan of Dublin Castle officials did not produce a pension for the Macaulay family. Acheson, when thanking Townshend for recommending him for a peerage, asked for a pension for Mrs Macaulay.[244] But the lord lieutenant was no more successful in procuring a pension for the Macaulay family than his subordinates. Acheson was finding again that a minister leaving post soon lost power and influence. Lord Simon Harcourt and John Blaquiere replaced Townshend and Macartney at the end of 1772 and Townshend's recommendation that Acheson be made a baron for services to Townshend's administration was put on the long finger by George III.

In spring 1773, with Townshend departed, Acheson plied Richard Rigby at the Pay Office with gifts of linen for news from London of high politics and for advice on whether to pursue Lord Townshend for delayed favours. Rigby reminded Acheson that patronage to Irish supporters was – as always – through the current governor [Harcourt] and 'that the last lord lieutenant's interest upon that score is no better than any of his predecessors who left that kingdom ever so long ago'. Rigby's reference to '... the unpleasant state of your country in point of trade, cash and credit. I hear your treasury is empty', suggested one reason for Townshend's removal. He attempted to console Acheson, however, that a European war had been averted by France's recent assurance to England that it desired disarmament and international peace.[245]

A disgruntled Macartney from Lissanoure, had no better news for Acheson in regard to the delivery of promised favours. He complained that after four years of tough service as chief secretary, he himself had been given 'exactly what the duke of Grafton offered me five years ago on my return from Russia'. He sympathised 'that nothing could be obtained for poor Macaulay' but agreed with Acheson's intention of applying to Lord Harcourt for the favours promised by the previous administration. Lees who was continuing as private secretary, was sufficiently acquainted with the case for Macaulay to brief the new lord lieutenant. Macartney assumed that Acheson's promised peerage would 'lie over till the end of the session.'[246]

DISPOSITIONS OF ARMAGH MPs
IN THE HARCOURT VICEROYALTY, 1772–6

The replacement of Townshend and Macartney with Harcourt and Blaquiere in Dublin Castle was a change of personalities but not of system or policy. Continuity was provided by Waite as under-secretary to Blaquiere and Lees as private secretary to Harcourt, and a good working relationship existed between Harcourt and the efficient Blaquiere. Following his arrival in Dublin, Harcourt reported that he had listened to overtures from

Leinster, Shannon, Ponsonby and Flood but would not rush to meet the price of their support.[247] Nor did Harcourt call the fourth session of parliament until 12 October 1773.[248] Like his predecessor, Harcourt used the interval to investigate causes of discontent and have a survey of affiliations of members undertaken by Blaquiere. In March 1773 he complained to London of 'caballing' against him in the privy council.[249] He also had an audit made of national finances which, he informed Lord North in April, were in a deplorable state; and sent Blaquiere with a plan for financial reform to London for ministerial approval before parliament met.[250]

In summer 1773, Harcourt went to County Armagh to find the underlying causes of the reported heavy emigration from the north of Ireland and of the repeated outbreaks of Oakboy protest. He visited Primate Robinson who, he reported, 'has done more essential services to the crown by paying a proper attention to his duties than any of his predecessors'. Harcourt concluded that emigration from the north was 'considerable' though exaggerated in numbers. He attributed the northern 'disturbances' to the recent 'check on the linen trade on which it almost solely depends', to the absences of nobles and gentry whose incomes were drained from the local economy, and to an unreasonable rise of rents in most places.[251] Inherent in Harcourt's diagnosis of the northern disturbances was some empathy with the insurgents, attributing elements of a 'moral economy' to their protests.

Priorities among Harcourt's instructions from London, were to increase revenue, reduce expenditure and to check the escalation of applications for pensions and peerages under Townshend – of which Acheson's immediate elevation to the baronage was a casualty. At the same time, Harcourt also attempted to allay the resentment of Irish politicians and public opinion antagonised by Townshend. His agreement with Lord North to re-unite the two revenue boards pleased the Irish parliament and brought a saving in salaried posts.[252] But 'private jobs' at the disposal of undertakers were also reduced further making jobbery more the prerogative of the crown than ever before.

Blaquiere's proposed tax on the rents of absentee landlords who spent their Irish income abroad was also popular in Ireland. But the proposal brought opposition from Rockingham Whig landlords with large estates in Ireland and, under pressure from whom, North and Rochford cooled to the measure. Thereafter the Dublin administration adopted a low profile towards an absentee tax and it was left to independent members – and not official spokesman Blaquiere – to introduce the measure in the Irish house of commons where it was left an open issue by government. James Fortescue of County Louth opened the debate for the Absentee Tax in a ways and means committee on 25 November 1773. A motion by Silver

Oliver representing County Limerick, proposed an absentee tax of two shillings in the pound which was followed by an amendment to one shilling. After an eleven hour debate, both the amendment and original motion were narrowly defeated in committee.[253]

Contemporary perspectives saw the Absentee Tax motion as having been defeated at the connivance of Harcourt's inner cabinet. Colonel Robert Cuninghame was critical of Harcourt's volte-face on the motion.[254] More recent analysis, however, having compared the high correlation between voting lists for the Absentee Tax motion of 25 November 1773 and for an amendment vote to omit pamphlets from items to be taxed in the Stamp Duty proposals on 1 December, refutes the conspiracy theory of a complete volte-face on the former by Harcourt's administration, or that Dublin Castle, at the behest of the British ministry, 'had engineered the defeat of a popular tax that it had itself originally devised'. Communications between Harcourt and North indicate an official stance of neutrality which seems to be corroborated by the support for the measure by such as Speaker Pery, Attorney-General Tisdall and Sir Archibald Acheson. The 1988 analysis attributes the debate on the 1773 Absentee Tax proposal as a decisive factor in its defeat.[255]

In the above divisions, Armagh members voted as follows. In addition to Acheson, more predictably, Brownlow, Caulfeild, Stewart and Molyneux voted for the Absentee Tax while Charles O'Hara voted against the measure. Six days later, Brownlow, Caulfeild and Stewart – 'in support of the liberty of the press' – opposed the proposed stamp duty on pamphlets. On the latter occasion the opposition included John Moore, though Molyneux would seem to have abstained. Acheson had switched to the government side and, with Charles O'Hara, was part of an overwhelming division of 107 votes to 47 in favour of the government measure.[256]

Blaquiere's survey of parliament in 1773 observed that while Acheson held a 'very good interest' in County Armagh, he had depended on an electoral partnership with Brownlow to have him returned in 1768. It also noted, however, that Acheson would not be tied to Brownlow in parliament and indicated its confidence that Acheson's 'hopes of being created a peer' would guarantee his support for government. The survey assessed Brownlow as holding the highest political interest in County Armagh. Though adjudged to be generally opposed to government, Brownlow was considered to be a high-principled, sensible man who should be treated with care, especially as he was married – secondly – to a Hall of Narrowwater who was related to the duke of Leinster.[257]

Blaquiere's treatment of both Armagh county members paid dividends. Acheson's allegiance was retained, occasional support from Brownlow gained. This was borne out in a patriot review of the house of commons in 1774 which assessed Acheson 'constantly votes with administration;

divided for the stamp act, but was against the Popery bill'; while Brownlow was described 'has often spoken and voted for the real good of the nation, but divided for Popery and stamps'. In January 1774 Brownlow had joined the government lobby with Acheson, Charles O'Hara – and an impecunious Francis Caulfeild – to vote for another stamp bill which proposed duties on vellum, parchment and paper. The 'Popery bill', proposing that Catholics be granted the legal right to long leases to holdings not exceeding fifty plantation acres, was defeated on 11 February 1774.[258]

In a second survey made in 1775, Blaquiere charted Brownlow's record in parliament, his 'very able' and 'independent' reputation always in opposition during the Townshend viceroyalty, his influence on the voting of Thomas Knox of Dungannon and Colonel Robert Ross of Carlingford and his admiration for the duke of Leinster's politics; then his recent conversion from total opposition to occasional support for government. Blaquiere noted that Brownlow regularly, though not always, supported the Harcourt administration 'upon almost every matter of importance ... and was of the utmost service in carrying through the new taxes'. In reward for Brownlow's support, Harcourt granted a number of places to Brownlow nominees.[259]

A 'favour of very great magnitude' granted by Harcourt was to recommend Brownlow's teenage second son, Lieutenant Charles Brownlow of 8th regiment to be promoted as captain of a company in 57th regiment.[260] The lord lieutenant's letter to London reveals how highly he valued Brownlow senior's support:

> Mr Brownlow was for many years in opposition, but in the course of the last session of parliament no member of the House supported the government with greater zeal or more distinguished abilities; and the countenance of a gentleman so respectable from his character, family, fortune and weight in parliament, was not only in itself extremely honourable to government but of eminent service to promoting the success of His Majesty's measures. The permission for his son to purchase will oblige him very sensibly.[261]

Harcourt's admiration for Brownlow was further evidenced two weeks later when he was considering whether to raise 600 troops – which he had been ordered to recruit for British regiments – in Ulster. Afraid lest this would cause unease among Ulster Protestants, Harcourt decided to consult Brownlow, 'whose opinion will have the greater weight with me as he is a man of a cool and dispassionate judgement and of great integrity'.[262]

Hon. Francis Caulfeild was another traditional opponent of government, especially of Townshend's administration, who was prepared to support some of Harcourt's measures. The patriot review of the Irish house of commons in summer 1774 adjudged Francis Caulfeild: 'He has generally voted for the interest of his country, but it is feared the *Man of Feeling* [Blaquiere] has *felt* for him, as he voted for Stamps, Popery and Tontine'.[263] Blaquiere's 1775 survey assessed him: 'He is very poor and greatly embarrassed in his circumstances', implying that Caulfeild was vulnerable to financial inducement.[264] Whether Caulfeild would have committed himself fully to the government side would remain unanswered when, on 19 October 1775, Caulfeild, wife and infant child were lost in a storm at sea when travelling from Parkgate, England, to Dublin.[265]

A writ was issued for the election of a member for Charlemont borough on 28 November 1775. On 11 December, Lord Charlemont introduced Dublin barrister Henry Grattan, eldest son of James Grattan, late recorder of Dublin, to the Irish house of commons as member for Charlemont borough in replacement for his late brother.[266] Grattan followed his patron's political direction in parliament initially, building a reputation in opposition, but was not accepted as leader of the patriot opposition until late 1779.

The outbreak of war with the North American colonies in 1775 dominated all other issues. Acheson wrote to Rigby at the pay-office in London, seeking the latest news of hostilities, with postscript requesting a post for Macaulay in England. Rigby's reply illustrated the all-pervading effects of the war in the British parliament and on the American economy which still gave hopes of an early settlement. Even Acheson's request for an English post for Macaulay was overtaken by the war. Rigby observed:

> ... you must perceive that in the present state of America all promotion or provision of any kind for any person from this country is entirely at a stop. God knows when that door will be opened again, even after the present disturbances are subsided.[267]

The American Revolution provided a stimulus and focus for the patriot opposition who increasingly sympathised with the American cause to challenge the Castle administration and brought heated debates in the Irish parliament. Again the Armagh parliamentary representatives were divided. On 11 October 1775 Sir Annesley Stewart voted for an unsuccessful pro-American amendment to an address to the throne which was opposed by Acheson. Harcourt emphasised to North the importance of winning this division as the opposition was growing, especially in Ulster where 'the Presbyterians in the north, who in their hearts are Americans, are gaining strength every day' and liaising with the pro-American lobby in England.[268]

Stewart personified northern opposition to the administration which retaliated by attempting, unsuccessfully, to damage the viability of his bank. The patriot review of the Irish house of commons in 1774 lauded him:

This gentleman is a striking instance that a banker may be a patriot. He has been uniform and consistent in his oppositon in support of his country, and took a very distinguished part in favour of the injured Protestant Dissenters. For his conduct in parliament, government has made many attempts to shock the credit of his bank, which have all happily proved ineffectual.[269]

Acheson, on the other hand, campaigned on behalf of government to accommodate George III's desire to withdraw 4,000 troops from Ireland for service in America and replace them with an equal number of Hessian troops to defend Ireland. He moved the king's offer, seconded by Colonel Ross, as a proposal in committee on Saturday 25 November 1775. But the notion of foreign troops defending Ireland was resented by the Irish parliament and, on Monday 27th November, the committee declined the king's offer. Harcourt and Blaquiere, reading the mood of parliament, did not press in further debate for acceptance of foreign troops and on 28 November, Acheson amended his proposal – 'to assure His Majesty of our ready concurrence in granting the 4,000 troops, and that upon mature consideration the house did not think foreign troops to replace them necessary' – which was carried and a committee appointed to prepare an address.[270]

The refusal to accept foreign troops had significant effects. It confirmed a growing patriot national spirit which had withstood government pressure. It led to renewed demands for a national militia which had previously been thwarted by the privy council. It convinced Harcourt and Blaquiere that fresh incentives were urgently required to hold wavering supporters. Blaquiere followed up an earlier letter to John Robinson, secretary of the treasury, with another requesting specified places and pensions for persons and friends who had delivered past services for government and who promised continued support in the next parliament. Some of his requests were to affect satisfaction of unfulfilled promises from Lord Townshend's viceroyalty, especially with a general election pending. Blaquiere further emphasised that a majority for government could only be returned in the coming election with 'the assistance which the expected moves and creations in the peerage will procure'.[271]

Undoubtedly Acheson was one of the persons expecting a long-delayed 'creation' – indeed hoping for a peerage to continue his parliamentary career. For Acheson's amended proposal seemed to have left him a two-way loser. The opposition identified him as a government spokesman while George III was offended that his offer of German troops had been rejected and blamed the Irish ministers for mishandling the situation.[272] Thus Acheson was faced in late 1775 with the very difficult task of re-election for the patriotic Armagh county in the approaching general election. He could only hope that George III's resentment at his spurned offer would not bar the creation of the peerage for which Acheson had been recommended by Lord Townshend in 1772.

CONCLUSION: THE CAMPAIGN FOR LIMITED PARLIAMENTS, PEACEFUL ELECTIONS, OAKBOY PROTEST AND THE AMERICAN WAR, IN THE 1760s

The 1761 general election was transacted according to the wishes of the candidates, gentry and magistrates of the county. Through prior negotiation, a contest was avoided and an outcome reached peaceably. Peaceful politics were accommodated by an alliance of Brownlow and Acheson, the two leading political personalities with high electoral interests in the county and a common policy of avoiding confrontation where possible. Though pressure had been exerted by the patriot interest, the above candidates avoided confrontation and retained the popular vote by publicly declaring their support for shorter parliaments, a pledge perhaps more comfortable with Brownlow than Acheson. The compliant policies of the ruling élite in County Armagh, cautious to avoid weakening the deferential bond between freeholders and landlords and which had resulted in a relatively trouble-free general election, also characterised politics in the county in the years following. Meanwhile the machinery of government was kept running relatively smoothly by the politics of patronage which rewarded those who supported Dublin Castle.

However, the patriot opposition had served notice of its power and intention to press election candidates into supporting a programme of parliamentary reform. Many candidates were pressurised into reluctant promises to support patriot demands for limited parliaments – counter to their own interests in many cases – rather than lose popular support, but subsequently found themselves hooked on those promises and unable to wriggle free of passing the Octennial Act. It was a demonstration of how a determined opposition could manipulate the popular vote in a general election to extract pledges from candidates and ultimately force the government's hand.

An even more painful lesson was given to the Armagh ruling élite among the gentry and Established Church by a discontented tenantry reluctant to pay what was perceived as unfair cess, labour days and tithes. This campaign led to an insurrection which overran the county and beyond for the summer months of 1763 and was only brought under control by a conciliatory approach by both sides. Some nine years later this protest was repeated around Lurgan against a background of economic depression following successive bad harvests and a slump in the London linen market in 1771–2, and triggered off again by the perceived grievance of county cess. These outbreaks of violence were salutary lessons on the dangers of breaching the tacit relationship between rulers and ruled, and a warning to members of parliament in the power of an offended electorate.

The death of Primate Stone, the most political churchman in eighteenth century Ireland, brought other churchmen who, while never reaching the same levels of political influence at national or Armagh county level, were not averse to using political patronage for promotion to or within the archdiocese of Armagh. Stone's successor was one of his protégés, Bishop Richard Robinson whose early progress up the Irish church hierarchy mirrored that of Stone. Traditionally, Robinson's historical image has tended to be that of an apolitical churchman dedicated to church reform and public building – which he was in the period 1765–75 following his appointment to Armagh. More recent research has revealed he was a highly politicised figure during the first phase of his career, from his arrival in Ireland in 1751 until his appointment to Armagh which, itself, was highly political.[273] A key factor in Robinson's diminished involvement in national politics thereafter was undoubtedly the new regime from 1767 of a resident lord lieutenant, George Townshend, who seized the reins of administration from the undertakers leaving less involvement for the three lord justices of whom the primate was one.

The Limitation (Octennial) Act of 1768 introduced the practice of regular elections for parliaments in Ireland. Accompanying the increased incidence of elections and contests were the spectres of high costs haunting candidates and violence haunting magistrates. A poll had been averted in Armagh in 1761 – though only at the eleventh hour – by alignment of the most powerful electoral interests through heavy negotiations of political magnates and canvassing of their freeholders. In 1768 negotiations were held between magnates for alignments as the leading interests took the further step of attempting to reach consensus *between themselves* on the two county candidates – without consultation of freeholders. The occasion and venue for finding this mandate was the county assizes where the arbiters were the grand jurors who represented most of the landed property in the county and were responsible for law and order.

This new development in County Armagh may have seemed a logical and justifiable step to proprietors of the leading electoral interests and had a precedent in English and other Irish counties. But it incurred the wrath of Armagh freeholders who rightly saw it as *selection replacing election* of members of parliament and a subversion of their constitutional right to elect representatives. Significantly, an objection came from the politically conscious freeholders on the estates of Brownlow – who had been nominated as first parliamentary representative at the Lent assizes – illustrating that it was the principle rather than the personality, the process rather than the outcome of the new departure, which concerned freeholders.

The parliament of 1768 began with an opposition majority when leading government managers Ponsonby, Shannon and Hely-Hutchinson withdrew support from Townshend. When the Irish house of commons failed to pass the augmentation programme of 1768 and money bill of 1769, a frustrated Lord Lieutenant Townshend felt obliged to wrest control of the Irish parliament from the unreliable undertakers and set up a new system of direct rule in which he would become his own undertaker, organising a Castle party which he rewarded from his own supply of patronage. His new management approach provided a raison d'être for the opposition who interpreted Townshend's initiative as an attempt by an English overlord to centralise the Whitehall-Castle system into oligarchical government against Irish interests. The opposition responded by highlighting the constitutional conflict between Great Britain and Ireland and revived efforts to promote a cohesive patriot opposition with more sophisticated forms of organisation both inside and outside parliament, leading to new growth of a 'patriot opposition' during the 1770s.

Armagh members were divided over Townshend's approach. When independent country gentlemen members were wooed by government to replace discarded undertakers, Acheson and Brownlow responded differently. Having been electoral partners in two general elections, they parted political company in the 1770s with Acheson succumbing to government enticements while Brownlow remained in the forefront of parliamentary opposition. Acheson attempted to milk the system, shamelessly and relentlessly requesting promotions for himself and his relatives, though he found that favours – or promises thereof – flowed more freely from ministers recently appointed to office than from those leaving it.

The four members – all non-resident – nominated for the two parliamentary borough seats in Armagh county supported or opposed government as directed by their patrons. Stewart and Caulfeild followed Lord Charlemont's patriot opposition as did Grattan, at first, when he replaced Caulfeild in 1775. Initially, however, the opposition to government remained a loose alliance of disparate groups without a consistent leader. Charlemont attempted to rally them in the early 1770s but the defection of their leader Henry Flood to Harcourt's administration in 1773 demoralised the patriots who remained leaderless until Grattan's acceptance as undisputed leader and spokesman in September 1779.[274]

Primate Robinson repaid an old favour to Lord Northumberland by nominating Chief Secretary Macartney parliamentary member for Armagh borough. The other Armagh member, Charles O'Hara, having got a second bite at the cherry when Attorney-General Philip Tisdall opted for the more independent and prestigious seat of Dublin University, was rewarded from a career as government supporter with numerous government places and pensions. Both O'Hara and Macartney retained their seats as Armagh borough members for the duration of the first octennial parliament. However, while the former was a 'good attender', the latter, following the conclusion of his chief secretaryship in November 1772, did not attend the Irish parliament and in 1775 his successor informed the government that Macartney would not be seeking re-election in the next parliament.[275]

And two Armagh residents nominated for borough seats outside the county were on opposite sides in parliamentary divisions. Sir Capel Molyneux of Drumbanagher, as University member, pursued the patriot opposition of his ancestors while John Moore of Drumbanagher, brought into Ballynakill borough by his cousin, Lord Drogheda, followed the government line of his patron.

The Harcourt administration continued Townshend's policy of keeping control of the Irish parliament and patronage in vice-regal hands. Support for the new administration came from unlikely sources when Brownlow and Caulfeild voted with government on some important issues and Brownlow accepted government preferment, places and pensions in the army, church and revenue service for his own family and friends. There is no evidence that Brownlow asked for favours, such as a peerage, for himself; perhaps he wished to avoid compromising his proud reputation as patriot and independent.

The American war polarised relations further between the Dublin administration and the growing parliamentary opposition and highlighted the issue of troops for home defence. As the first octennial parliament drew to a close, the careers of the two Armagh county members had diverged. While Brownlow retained his reputation of independence, voting according to patriot conscience and reasonably assured of being returned as county member, his former partner Acheson, having apostatised to government, had diminishing hopes of being returned as county member. It seemed inevitable that new blood would be infused into the electoral system in County Armagh at the general election of 1776.

Notes

1   Waite to Wilmot (Private) n.d. (PRONI, Wilmot papers, T/3019/3647); Lord Chancellor Bowes to George Dodington, 21 Mar. 1760 (*HMC Eyre-Matcham MSS, Reports on various collections* (London, 1909; hereafter *Eyre-Matcham*), vi, 74.
2   *BNL*, 18 Jan. 1760.
3   Rigby to Robert Wood (under-secretary for state), 19 Jan. 1760. (PRONI, Wilmot papers, T/3019/3681)

4   Rigby to Wilmot, 16 Feb. 1760 (ibid., T/3019/3704).
5   Same to same, 27 Feb. 1760 (ibid., T/3019/3718).
6   *BNL*, 28 Mar. 1760.
7   Rigby to Wilmot, 6 Mar. 1760 (PRONI, Wilmot papers, T/3019/3740).
8   Bedford to the lords justices, 27 Oct. 1760 (ibid., T/3019/3911)
9   Lords justices to Bedford, 7 Nov. 1760 (PRONI, Wilmot papers, T/3019/3922).
10 *BNL*, 17 Feb. 1761.
11 Waite to Wilmot, 22 Feb. 1761 (PRONI, Wilmot papers, T/3019/3998).
12 Same to same, 6 Nov. 1760 (ibid., T/3019/3920).
13 Bowes to Wilmot, 18 Nov. 1760 (ibid., T/3019/3939).
14 Charlemont to Brownlow, 30 Oct. 1760 (*HMC Charlemont*, i, 262).
15 Earl of Kildare to Acheson, 10 Nov. 1760 (PRONI, Gosford papers, D/1606/1/1/30A).
16 Brownlow to Acheson, 4 Nov. 1760 (ibid. D/1606/1/1/28).
17 *BNL*, 21 Nov. 1760.
18 Ibid.
19 Rigby to Acheson, 11 June 1760 (PRONI, Gosford papers, D/1606/1/1/25).
20 Dean Anthony Cope to Acheson, 10 Nov. 1760 (ibid. D/1606/1/1/27).
21 Barry Maxwell to Acheson, 4 Nov. 1760 (ibid. D/1606/1/1/26). 'Lord Newtown' was the title used by Brinsley Butler in the period 1760–8, although styled Lord Newtown-Butler. He served as MP for Co. Cavan 1751–68 until succeeding as earl and viscount of Lanesborough from 1768. See C[okayne] G.E.(ed.) *The Complete Peerage* (6 vols, Gloucester reprint, 1982; hereafter *CP*), iii, 425.
22 Earl of Kildare to Acheson , 10 Nov. 1760 (PRONI, Gosford papers, D/1606/1/1/30A).
23 Brownlow to Acheson, 4 Nov. 1760 (ibid., D/1606/1/1/28).
24 Dean Anthony Cope to Acheson, 4 Nov. 1760 (ibid., D/1606/1/1/27).
25 James Johnston to Acheson, 6 Nov. 1760 (ibid., D/1606/1/1/29).
26 Molyneux (at Clogher) to Acheson, 10 Nov. 1760 (*HMC Charlemont*), i, 264.
27 Molyneux to Bedford, 7 Dec. 1760 (PRONI, Bedford papers, D/2915/10/63).
28 Charlemont to Adderley, 9 Aug. 1760 (RIA, Charlemont correspondence), 12 R9/81.
29 Adderley to Charlemont, 7 Nov. 1760 (*HMC Charlemont*), i, 263–4.
30 Charlemont to Adderley, 11 Nov. 1760 (ibid.), pp 264–5. Footnotes in the text give John Moore as of Drumbanagher and married to Mary Caulfeild , granddaughter of William, second Viscount Charlemont. But as *that* John Moore had died in 1752, the 'uncle John' referred to here was more likely to have been the Hon. John Caulfeild, the other sitting member – with Adderley – for Charlemont borough in 1760. 'Harry Moore' was Henry William Moore of Drumbanagher, the late John Moore's son and Charlemont's cousin.
31 *BNL*, 2 Dec. 1760.
32 *BNL*, 12 Dec. 1760.
33 Sir Richard Cox to Acheson, 17 Oct. 1749 (PRONI, Gosford papers, D/1606/1/1/2). Dr Charles Lucas, Co. Clare-born apothecary, had attacked Dublin corporation politics in the 1740s, denounced Poynings' Law, revived Molyneux's arguments in published addresses, and in 1749, was forced by the Irish house of commons to flee abroad where he studied medicine. He returned in 1761 to contest and win a Dublin seat in parliament, became a leader in the patriot opposition and helped to establish *The Freeman's Journal*. He became personal physician to Lord Charlemont.

34 Lucas to Charlemont, 22 Nov. 1760 (*HMC Charlemont*) i, 265–6. His pamphlet was entitled: *Seasonable advice to the electors of members of parliament in the ensuing general election, addressed to the free and independent electors of Ireland, to those of Dublin in particular.*
35 Rigby to Acheson, 7 Feb. 1761 (PRONI, Gosford papers, D/1606/1/1/31).
36 *BNL*, 17 Feb. 1761.
37 Stone to Bedford, 19 May 1760 (PRONI, Bedford papers, T/2915/9/52). Barrington was appointed dean of Armagh in January 1764; Dean Maxwell was raised to the bishopric of Dromore in March 1765 and in April 1766 translated to Meath; see Henry Cotton (ed.), *Fasti Ecclesiae Hibernicae: the succession of the prelates and members of the cathedral bodies in Ireland* (5 vols, Dublin, 1849; hereafter Cotton *Fasti*), iii, 284.
38 Meredyth to Wilmot, 29 Jan. 1761 (PRONI, Wilmot papers, T/3019/3976).
39 Waite to Wilmot, 3 Mar. 1761 (ibid., T/3019/4010).
40 Rigby to Wilmot, 17 Feb. 1761 (ibid., T/3019/3993).
41 Bishop Richard Robinson to Bedford, 28 Mar. 1761 (PRONI, Bedford papers, T/2915/11/52).
42 Rigby to Bedford, 30 Mar. 1761 (ibid., T/2915/11/54).
43 Bedford to Robinson, 4 April 1761 (ibid., T/2915/11/59).
44 Waite to Wilmot, 20 Mar. 1761 (PRONI, Wilmot papers, T/3019/4026).
45 Rigby to Wilmot, 16 Apr. 1761 (ibid., T/3019/4059).
46 Newcastle to Dorset, 31 Oct. 1751 (*HMC Stopford-Sackville*), i, 177; Christopher Mohan, 'Archbishop Richard Robinson, builder of Armagh', in *Seanchas Ard Mhacha*, vol. 6, no. 1, 1971, p. 96.
47 Cotton, *Fasti*, iv, 76, and ii, 340–1.
48 *Calendar of home office papers of the reign of George III, 1760–75* (4 vols, London, 1878–99; hereafter *Cal. H.O. papers*), i, King's letters, para. 444, p. 135.
49 Bedford to the lords justices, 31 March 1761 (PRONI, Wilmot papers, T/3019/4034).
50 *BNL*, 31 Mar. 1761.
51 Brownlow to Acheson, 21 Mar. 1761 (PRONI, Gosford papers, D/1606/1/1/32).
52 Ibid.
53 Brownlow to Acheson, 4 April 1761 (ibid., D/1606/1/1/33); *BNL*, 5 May 1761.
54 Same to same, 4 Apr. 1761 (PRONI, Gosford papers, D/1606/1/1/33).
55 *BNL*, 10 April 1761.
56 Brownlow to Acheson, 9 Apr. 1761 (PRONI, Gosford papers, D/1606/1/1/34).
57 *BNL*, 5 May 1761.
58 Rigby to Acheson, 30 Apr. 1761 (PRONI, Gosford papers, D/1606/1/1/35A).
59 Drogheda, *Moore*, chart pedigree.
60 *BNL*, 12 May 1761.
61 Drogheda, *Moore*, chart pedigree; Rowley Lascelles (ed.) *Liber munerum publicorum Hiberniae* (2 vols, London, 1824–30; hereafter Lascelles, *Liber munerum*), i, 1, p. 4.
62 *Commons' jn. Ire.* (Bradley), xii, 9.
63 Rigby to Acheson, 30 Apr. 1761 (PRONI, Gosford papers, D/1606/1/1/35A).
64 Henry Fox to Wilmot, 21 Mar. 1761 (PRONI, Wilmot papers, T/3019/4026).
65 Ponsonby to Acheson, 9 May 1761 (PRONI, Gosford papers, D/1606/1/1/35B); Stone to Acheson, 9 Dec. 1762 (ibid., D/1606/1/1/38).
66 Blacker to Acheson, 27 Jan. 1762 (ibid., D/1606/1/1/36).
67 Barrington to Acheson, 6 Nov. 1761 (ibid., D/1606/1/1/37).

68 Cotton, *Fasti*, iii, 289. When Bishop George Marlay of Dromore died on 13 April 1763 he was succeeded by Bishop John Oswald of Clonfert who, within a few months, was translated to Raphoe and Edward Young, dean of Clogher succeeded as bishop of Dromore.
69 Rigby to Acheson, 28 Apr. 1763 (PRONI, Gosford papers, D/1606/1/1/39).
70 Newtown was a commissioner of the revenue in 1761 and member of the privy council from 1756 from which he was removed in 1770 for opposing government but resworn in 1774. See *CP*, iii, 425.
71 Newtown to Acheson, 2 July. 1763 (PRONI, Gosford papers, D/1606/1/1/43).
72 King's letters to Lord Lieutenant Hertford, Feb. 1766, (*Cal. H.O. papers*, ii, 142); Johnston-Liik, *Irish parliament*, iii, 294.
73 Hamilton to Wilmot, 26 Nov. 1761 (PRONI, Wilmot papers, T/3019/4228).
74 Rigby to Acheson, 13 May 1766 (PRONI, Gosford papers, D/1606/1/1/46); Dean Walter Cope to Acheson, 19 Sep. 1767 (ibid., D/1606/1/1/48); Newtown to Acheson, 11 Feb. 1768 (ibid., D/1606/1/1/49).
75 *Commons jn. Ire.* (Bradley), xii, 22; Waite to Wilmot, 22 Oct. 1761 (PRONI, Wilmot papers, T/3019/4204).
76 *Commons' jn. Ire.* (Bradley), xii, 131; Waite to Wilmot, 14 Nov. 1761 (PRONI, Wilmot papers, T/3019/4222).
77 Waite to Wilmot, 19 Nov. 1761 (ibid., T/3019/4226).
78 Lord Chancellor John Bowes to Wilmot, 3 Dec. 1761 (ibid., T/3019/4232).
79 *Commons' jn. Ire.* (Bradley), xii, 159.
80 Halifax to the earl of Egremont, 11 Dec. 1761 (*Cal. H.O. papers*, i, 86).
81 Waite to Wilmot, 8 Feb. 1762 (PRONI, Wilmot papers, T/3019/4285).
82 *Armagh Grand Jury Presentments Book* (PRONI, C & P, ARM/4/1/1A; hereafter *Armagh Presentments Book*). Note: Cess warrants increased in Oneiland West from £155-8s.-8d. in summer 1762 to £204-17s.-6d. at the 1763 Lent assizes, and to £203-7s.-5d. at the 1763 summer assizes.
83 *Irish Statutes*, 33 Geo. (1759), II, C. 8,
84 'A full and circumstantial account of what happened to me on the eighth day of July 1763' by the Rev. Theodorus Martin, rector of Desertlyn, Co. Tyrone (G.M. Stewart Mss., PRONI, T/1442/6), quoted in *Aspects of Irish Social History, 1750–1800*, edit. W.H. Crawford & Brian Trainor, Belfast, 1973; hereafter Crawford & Trainor, *Aspects*, pp 34–6.
85 Waite to Wilmot, 23 July 1763 (PRONI, Wilmot papers, T/3019/4655). This estate was probably Brownlow's Richmond estate in West Oneilland and not Brownlow's-Derry which was in East Oneilland. See also Gillespie, *Brownlow leasebook*, p. xxxi.
86 *Armagh Presentments Book*.
87 Waite to Wilmot, 23 July 1763 (PRONI, Wilmot papers, T/3019/4655).
88 Rigby to Acheson, 30 June 1761 (Gosford papers, D/1606/1/1/41).
89 *BNL*, 12 July 1763.
90 'Tithes' entry in Connolly, *Oxford companion*, p. 543.
91 E.F. Magennis, '"A Presbyterian insurrection"? Reconsidering the Hearts of Oak disturbances of July 1763'; hereafter Magennis, 'A Presbyterian insurrection?' (*IHS*, xxxi, No. 122), p. 167.
92 W.E.H. Lecky, *A History of Ireland in the Eighteenth Century* (London, 1892; hereafter Lecky, *Ireland in the Eighteenth Century*), ii, 41– 50.
93 Waite to Wilmot, 23 July 1763 (PRONI, Wilmot papers, T/3019/4655).
94 J.S. Donnelly, 'Hearts of Oak, Hearts of Steel', *Studia Hibernica* (1981), xxi, 7– 73; see also 'Oakboys' entry in Connolly, *Oxford companion*, p. 397.

95 Magennis, 'A Presbyterian insurrection?' p. 180.
96 Ibid., p. 187; *BNL*, 12 and 15 July 1763.
97 *Armagh Presentments Book.*
98 *BNL*, 12 July 1763. The 'commons' referred to was probably Glen Bogg at Tandragee which had been set annually for summer grazing by Blacker; see *BNL*, 4 Apr. 1755.
99 *Armagh Presentments Book.*
100 *BNL*, 15 July 1763.
101 Ibid.
102 Blacker to Waite, 18 July 1763 (PRONI, Wilmot papers, T/3019/4643).
103 Richhill Oakboys to Blacker, 17 July 1763 (ibid., T/3019/4644).
104 Letter to Waite, 19 July (ibid., T/3019/4642).
105 *BNL*, 5 Aug.1763.
106 Memoirs, July 1763 (*HMC Charlemont*), i, 139.
107 Ibid.
108 Waite to Wilmot, 21 July 1763 (PRONI, Wilmot papers, T/3019/4641).
109 Stone to Charlemont, 28 July 1763 (*HMC Charlemont*), i, 141).
110 Ibid.
111 Charlemont to Marlay, Aug. 1763 (*HMC Charlemont*), i, 275.
112 Thomas Bartlett, 'An End to Moral Economy: The Irish Militia Disturbances of 1793' in *Past and Present*, 99, 1983, p. 42; Eoin Magennis, 'In Search of the "Moral Economy"; Food Scarcity in 1756–7 and the Crowd' in Jupp & Magennis, *Crowds in Ireland.*
113 Waite to Wilmot, 23 July 1763 (PRONI, Wilmot papers, T/3019/4655).
114 *BNL*, 5 Aug. 1763.
115 *BNL*, 2 Aug. 1763.
116 *BNL*, 9 Aug. 1763.
117 Verner to Charlemont, 5 Aug. 1763 (*HMC Charlemont*), i, 274.
118 Memoirs (*HMC Charlemont*), i, 142– 3.
119 Molyneux to Charlemont, 24 Aug. 1763 (ibid.), i, 274.
120 *BNL*, 13 Sept. 1763.
121 Magennis, 'A Presbyterian insurrection?' pp 182– 3.
122 Verner to Charlemont, 5 Aug. 1763 (*HMC Charlemont*, i, 274).
123 *Armagh Presentments Book*. In 1762 the total cess levied in the Lent assizes warrants was £692-13s.-7d, all of which was collected; and the summer assizes warrants levied £619-5s.-4d. of which £602-4s.-5d. was collected. In 1763 the total in Lent assizes warrants increased to £803-6s.-7d. of which only £326 - 6s.-10d. was paid; and when the summer assizes warrants levied £1,092, only £665-13s.-5d. was paid. In 1764, the Lent assizes levied £700-0s.-8d. of which £674-13s.-10d. was collected; and the summer assizes levied £737-13s.-9d. all of which was paid. Cess warrants for Oneiland West *rose* in 1764 to £209 at Lent and £373-4s.-7d. in summer and were paid except for a small shortfall of £4-14s.-6d.
124 *BNL*, 20 May 1766.
125 Memorandum in Wilmot's hand, Jan. 1764 (PRONI, Wilmot papers, T/3019/4785).
126 Archbishop G.O. Simms, 'Archbishop Robinson', a 1971 lecture printed in (*Armagh: history & society*, ed. Hughes and Nolan), p. 574; W.S. Lewis ed., *Sir Horace Walpole's Correspondence with Sir Horace Mann* (Yale and London, 1960), xxii, 269 and 275– 6; Richard Pares, *George III and the politicians* (Oxford, 1953), p. 145, note 1.

127 *Dictionary of National Biography*, ed. Sidney Lee (London, 1897), xlix, 39–40; Cotton, *Fasti*, iii, 26; Malcomson, *Agar*, pp 437–41.
128 Rigby to Acheson, 13 May 1766 (PRONI, Gosford papers, D/1606/1/1/46).
129 King's letters to Hertford, Feb. 1766 (*Cal. H.O. papers*, ii, 142).
130 *BNL*, 9 and 13 May 1766.
131 Dean Walter Cope to Acheson, 19 Sept. 1767 (PRONI, Gosford papers, D/1606/1/1/48).
132 Newtown to Acheson, 11 Feb. 1768 (ibid., D/1606/1/1/49).
133 Waite to Wilmot, 16 Feb. 1768 (PRONI, Wilmot papers, T/3019/5694, 5695).
134 Thomas Thynne, third viscount Weymouth, never visited Ireland during his viceroyalty in 1765, yet pocketed the annual salary of £16,000 plus £3,000 allowance for equipage; George William Hervey, second earl of Bristol, appointed on 6 October 1766 with specific instructions to reside in Ireland, drew similar remuneration though resigning without having set foot in Ireland – nor having called the Irish parliament even once during his ten months term of office. See *Eighteenth Century Irish Official papers in Great Britain. Private collections, vol. 2*, compiled A.P.W. Malcomson (Belfast, 1990; hereafter Malcomson, *Irish Official papers in G.B.*), ii, 270.
135 Waite to Wilmot, 3 May 1768 (PRONI, Wilmot papers, T/3019/5742).
136 Division list on the augmentation vote (ibid., T/3019/5745).
137 Clements to Wilmot, 7 May 1768 (ibid., T/3019/5751).
138 Thomas Bartlett, 'The Townshend viceroyalty, 1767– 72', in Bartlett & Hayton, *Penal Era and Golden Age*, pp 88–94.
139 Memoirs (*HMC Charlemont*), i, 28– 31, 39.
140 Dean Walter Cope to Acheson, 19 Sept. 1767 (PRONI, Gosford papers, D/1606/1/1/48).
141 Lord Newtown to Acheson, 11 Feb. 1768 (ibid., D/1606/1/1/49).
142 *BNL*, 16 Feb. 1768.
143 Ibid, 23 Feb. 1768.
144 Rigby to Acheson, 16 Feb. 1768 (PRONI, Gosford papers, D/1606/1/1/50).
145 Lodge, *The peerage of Ireland* (1789), vi, 83– 4, lists two of Acheson's children who died young.
146 Acheson to Brownlow, 19 Feb. 1768 (PRONI, Gosford papers, D/1606/1/1/51).
147 *BNL*, 11 Mar, 1768.
148 Lord Hillsborough to Acheson, 25 Feb. 1768 (PRONI, Gosford papers, D/1606/1/1/52).
149 Rigby to Acheson, 27 Feb. 1768 (ibid., D/1606/1/1/53).
150 Ibid.
151 Lord Sandwich to Acheson, 7 Mar. 1768 (ibid., D/1606/1/1/56).
152 M. de Salis to 'My Lord' (Sandwich), 29 Feb. 1768 (ibid., D/1606/1/1/54).
153 Brownlow to Acheson, 5 Mar. 1768 (ibid., D/1606/1/1/55).
154 Brownlow to the earl of Abercorn, 3 Mar.1768 (PRONI, Abercorn papers, T/2541/1A1/8/30 & 41)
155 *BNL*, 12 Feb., 1 Mar., 8 April 1768.
156 Brownlow to Acheson, 5 Mar. 1768 (PRONI, Gosford papers, D/1606/1/1/55).
157 Brownlow to the earl of Abercorn, 3 Mar.1768 (PRONI, Abercorn papers, T/2541/1A1/8/30).
158 David Large, 'Select documents: XIX 'The Irish house of commons in 1769' (*IHS*, Mar. 1958; hereafter Jackson's 1769 parliamentary list), xi, 43.
159 Brownlow to the earl of Abercorn, 3 Mar.1768 (PRONI, Abercorn papers, T/2541/1A1/8/30 & 41)

160 Brownlow to Acheson, 5 Mar. 1768 (PRONI, Gosford papers, D/1606/1/1/55).
161 *CP*, i, para. 137.
162 *BNL*, 15 Mar. 1768.
163 Charlemont to Acheson, 22 Mar. 1768 (PRONI, Gosford papers, D/1606/1/1/57).
164 Bishop Garnett to Acheson, 26 Mar. 1768 (ibid., D/1606/1/1/59).
165 *BNL*, 17 May 1768.
166 Ibid., 7 June 1768.
167 Brownlow's printed election manifesto, 9 May 1768 (PRONI, Gosford papers, D/1606/1/1/62).
168 Ibid.
169 Ibid.
170 *BNL*, 8, 12 July 1768.
171 Fortescue to Acheson, 5 July 1768 (PRONI, Gosford papers, D/1606/1/1/63); *CP*, i, 1982 gives Fortescue as sitting member for County Louth 1761– 8, post-master general 1764– 84, created Viscount Clermont in 1776 and earl in 1777.
172 Leslie, *Armagh clergy*, p. 67, gives Henry Leslie as prebendary of Ballymore 1759– 1803.
173 Brownlow to Acheson, 13 July 1768 (PRONI, Gosford papers, D/1606/1/1/64).
174 *BNL*, 22 July 1764.
175 M. Bodkin, 'Notes on the Irish parliament in 1773' (*RIA Proc*, 1942– 3; hereafter Blaquiere's 1773 parliamentary list), xlviii, C, 189, 216.
176 Lanesborough to Acheson, 23 July 1768 (PRONI, Gosford papers, D/1606/1/1/65).
177 *BNL*, 9 Aug. 1764.
178 Lanesborough to Acheson, 13 Aug. 1768 (PRONI, Gosford papers, D/1606/1/1/66).
179 Rigby to Acheson, undated (ibid., D/1606/1/1/68).
180 *BNL*, 29 July 1764.
181 Thomas Bartlett, *Macartney in Ireland 1768– 72. A calendar of the chief secretaryship papers of Sir George Macartney* (PRONI, 1978), Intoduction, x– xi.
182 King's letters of appointment to Lord Lieutenant Harcourt, 7, 10 Oct. 1774 (*Cal. H.O. papers*, iv, 305, 308).
183 Waite to Wilmot, 9 June 1768 (PRONI, Wilmot papers, D/3019/5769).
184 Wilmot to Waite, 25 June 1768 (ibid., D/3019/5773); same to same, 12 July 1768 (ibid., T/3019/5779).
185 Rigby to Wilmot, 14 Oct. 1768 (ibid., D/3019/5822).
186 Waite to Wilmot, 11 Dec. 1768 (ibid., D/3019/5853).
187 Wilmot to Waite, 28 Mar. 1769 (ibid., D/3019/5912).
188 Blaquiere's 1773 parliamentary list, p. 191.
189 Ibid.; Johnston, *G.B. & Ire.*, p. 156
190 Bishop Garnett's letter to Townshend, 15 Nov. 1769 (PRONI, Townshend's letter-book, T/3590).
191 Johnston-Liik, *Irish parliament*, v, 395–6; Jackson's 1769 parliamentary list, p. 40; A.P.W. Malcomson, "The parliamentary traffic of this country" in Bartlett & Hayton, *Penal Era and Golden Age*, p. 50, note 35.
192 Blaquiere's 1773 parliamentary list, p. 177.
193 William Hunt, ed. *The Irish parliament 1775* (Dublin, 1907; hereafter Blaquiere's 1775 parliamentary list), pp 39– 40.
194 Johnston-Liik, *Irish parliament*, v, 396.

195 Drogheda, *Moore*, chart pedigree.
196 Jackson's 1769 parliamentary list used the contemporary term 'how disposed' (i.e. for or against government), when categorising members.
197 Waite to Wilmot, Nov. 1769 (PRONI, Wilmot papers, D/3019/5985).
198 Jackson's 1769 parliamentary list, p. 26.
199 Ibid., p. 28.
200 Johnston-Liik, *Irish parliament*, iii, 50.
201 Jackson's 1769 parliamentary list, p. 30; Johnston-Liik, *Irish parliament*, iii, 295.
202 Ibid., p. 31 and p. 40; Johnston-Liik, *Irish parliament*, iii, 387 and vi, 334.
203 Blaquiere's 1773 parliamentary list, p. 177.
204 Ibid., p. 210.
205 Johnston-Liik, *Irish parliament*, v, 263 and 300.
206 Townshend to Weymouth, 23 Dec.1769 (PRONI, Macartney papers, D/572/7/9); *Cal. H.O. papers*, ii, 548.
207 Weymouth to Townshend, 22 Feb.1770 (ibid., D/572/7/14); King's letters to Townshend re. appointments, 20 Mar. 1770 (*Cal. H.O. papers*, iii, 175).
208 Townshend to Weymouth, 7 Mar. 1770, (PRONI, Macartney papers, D/572/7/14); King's letters re. appointments, 20 Mar. 1770 (Cal. H.O. papers), iii, 175.
209 Townshend to Acheson, 28 Feb. 1770 (PRONI, Gosford papers, D/1606/1/1/71D).
210 *Commons' jn. Ire.* (Bradley), xiv, 752.
211 Ibid., xiv, 762– 3.
212 The earl of Rochford had replaced Weymouth as southern secretary of state on 19 Dec. 1770.
213 Townshend to Rochford, 26 Nov. 1771 (*Cal. H.O. papers*), iii, 329.
214 Same to same, 11 Dec. 1771 (ibid.), iii, 337. Waite to Wilmot, 12 Dec. 1771 (PRONI, Wilmot papers, T/3019/6254).
215 *The Public Register or Freeman's Journal*, 17– 19 Mar. 1772; hereafter *FJ*.
216 Crawford & Trainor, *Aspects*, p. 42.
217 A nephew, Armagh, to Mr. Barclay, 8 Mar. 1772 (PRONI, Abercorn papers, T/2541/1A1/10).
218 *Armagh Presentments Book*, cess levies and returns 1766–72 (PRONI, ARM/4/1/1A).
219 A nephew, to Mr. Barclay, Strabane, 8 Mar. 1772 (PRONI, Abercorn papers, T/2541/1A1/10).
220 Crawford & Trainor, *Aspects*, p. 42.
221 Thomas Clarke of Summer Island was Johnston's successor as high sheriff for 1772. See *BNL*, 24 Jan. 1772.
222 *BNL*, 13 Mar. and 17 Mar. 1772.
223 Macartney to Wilmot, 17 Mar. 1772 (PRONI, Wilmot papers, T/3019/6283).
224 Townshend to Rochford, 18 and 23 Mar. 1772 (*Cal. H.O. papers*), iii, 456 and 463.
225 *BNL*, 3, 4, 28 Apr., 5 May 1772.
226 Waite to Wilmot, 13 Apr. 1772 (PRONI, Wilmot papers, T/3019/6289).
227 Macartney to Wilmot, 19 Apr. 1772 (ibid., T/3019/6291).
228 *BNL*, 22 Sep. 1772.
229 Acheson to Townshend (NAI, Townshend papers, M.648); *Corporation Book of Armagh* (PRONI, T/636) pp 85– 112.
230 *BNL*, 3 July 1772.
231 Acheson to Macartney, 24 June 1772 (NAI, Townshend papers, M.649); Lodge, *The Peerage of Ireland*, 1789, vi, 84 gives Acheson's third daughter,

Julia-Henrietta married to Alexander Macaulay of Glenville, Co. Antrim, in 1766, a barrister and son of the late Alexander Macaulay MP for Thomastown.
232 Acheson to Townshend, 30 June 1772 (NAI, Townshend papers, M.650).
233 Same to same, 19 July 1772 (ibid., M.651).
234 Townshend to Acheson, 21, 29 July 1772 (PRONI, Gosford papers, D/1606/1/1/74 A, 74B); Acheson to Townshend, 29 July 1772 (NAI, Townshend papers, M.653).
235 King's letters to Townshend re appointments, 27 Jan. 1772 (*Cal. H.O. papers*), iii, 635.
236 Acheson to Townshend, 24 July 1772, (NAI, Townshend papers, M.652).
237 Macartney, Lissanoure, to Acheson, 16 Aug. 1772 (PRONI, Gosford papers, D/1606/1/1/75A).
238 Wilmot to Macartney, 9 June 1772 (PRONI, Wilmot papers, T/3019/6323).
239 Acheson to Townshend, 26 Aug. and 2 Sep.1772 (NAI, Townshend papers, M.654, 655); Townshend to Acheson, 7 Sep.1772 (PRONI, Gosford papers, D/1606/1/1/75B).
240 Townshend to Rochford, 9 Sep. 1772 (*Cal. H.O. papers*), iii, 542.
241 Townshend to Acheson, 7 Sep.1772 (PRONI, Gosford papers, D/1606/1/1/75B). 'The old and faithful friend' was John Bourke, MP for Naas and consistent supporter of Townshend's government whose son was appointed bishop of Ferns and Leighlin in 1772.
242 Cotton, *Fasti*, ii, 342.
243 *BNL*, 23 Jan. 1807.
244 Acheson to Townshend, 21 Sep.1772, (NAI, Townshend papers, M. 657).
245 Rigby to Acheson, 6 May.1773 (PRONI, Gosford papers, D/1606/1/1/76).
246 Macartney to Acheson, 23 July 1773 (ibid., D/1606/1/1/77).
247 Harcourt to Rochford, 8 Dec. 1772 (Dublin City Library and Archive – hereafter DCLA – Harcourt correspondence, MS. 93, ff. 2– 5).
248 *Commons' jn. Ire.* (Bradley), xvi, 9.
249 Harcourt to Rochford, 28 Mar.1773 (*Cal. H.O. papers*), iv, 33.
250 Harcourt to Lord North, 24 Apr. 1773 (DCLA, Harcourt correspondence, MS. 93, ff. 25– 6).
251 Harcourt to Rochford, 18 July 1773 (*Cal. H.O. papers*), iv, 67.
252 Harcourt to North, 30 Sep. 1773 (DCLA, Harcourt correspondence, MS. 93, ff. 28– 9).
253 Same to same, 9, 22, 26 Nov. 1773 (ibid., ff. 37– 8, 50– 1, 53– 6).
254 Hunt, *The Irish Parliament, 1775*, Introduction, pp xxiii– iv.
255 'Two voting lists for the Irish house of commons in 1773', Peter D.G. Thomas in *Parliamentary History*, vii, part 2 (1988) 313– 27; hereafter Thomas, 'Two voting lists, 1773'.
256 *London Evening Post*, 9– 11, 28– 30 Dec, 1773; Thomas, 'Two voting lists, 1773', pp 320– 6; *FJ*, 2– 4 Dec. 1773.
257 Blaquiere's 1773 parliamentary list, pp 176–7.
258 *FJ*, 2– 5 July 1774; ibid., 5– 8 Feb., 12– 15 Feb., 1774.
259 Blaquiere's 1775 parliamentary list, p. 8. Places included: a clergyman nominated by Brownlow to a 'living of £120' and later promoted to one of £300; the switch of Brownlow's old friend Meredyth Workman of Portadown from Collector of Dundalk to a post in the stamps office worth *c*. £300; a clerkship worth £60 granted to a Brownlow friend; and 'three boatmen and one tide waiter to his recommendation'.
260 Ibid.

261 Harcourt to Rochford, 14 Jan. 1775 (*Cal. H.O. papers*), iv, 315– 6.
262 Same to same, 2 Mar. 1775 (DCLA, Harcourt correspondence, MS. 93, ff.164–5).
263 *FJ*, 30 July to 2 Aug. 1774.
264 Blaquiere's 1775 parliamentary list, p. 12.
265 *BNL*, 1–5 Dec. 1775.
266 Ibid.; Memoirs (*HMC Charlemont*), i, 41.
267 Rigby to Acheson, 24 Nov. 1775 (PRONI, Gosford papers, D/1606/1/1/79).
268 *FJ*, 17–19 Oct. 1775; Harcourt to North, 11 Oct. 1775 (DCLA, Harcourt correspondence, MS. 93, ff. 259– 60).
269 *FJ*, 20–23 Aug. 1774.
270 Harcourt to North, 26 Nov. 1775 (DCLA, Harcourt correspondence, MS. 93, ff. 292– 4); *BNL*, 28 Nov.–1 Dec. 1775, 1–5 Dec.1775.
271 Blaquiere to John Robinson, secretary of the treasury, 2 Nov. 1775 (DCLA, Harcourt correspondence, MS. 93, ff. 275–7); same to same, 15 Dec. 1775 (*State Papers Ireland*, 444, f. 292) cited in Hunt, *Irish Parliament*, pp 86– 91.
272 Hunt, *Irish Parliament*, pp 85– 6.
273 Malcomson, *Agar*, pp 440–1.
274 David Lammey, 'The growth of the "patriot opposition" in Ireland during the 1770s' in *Parliamentary History*, vii, pt. 2 (1988; hereafter Lammey, 'Patriot opposition'), pp 256– 81.
275 Blaquiere's 1775 parliamentary list, pp 33, 40.

4

The general election of 1776; dispositions of Armagh MPs 1777–8; Volunteer politics 1778–83

INTRODUCTION: GOVERNMENT APPREHENSION, NEW CANDIDATES DECLARE FOR THE 1776 GENERAL ELECTION

Attitudes to the scheduled general election differed. The Dublin Castle administration awaited it with apprehension. In October 1775, a frustrated Chief Secretary Blaquiere reported to Secretary of State Lord Rochford difficulties in the Irish parliament resulting from pro-American factions in England stirring up 'the natural fanaticism of the northern province' and from rows with disappointed 'outs' and 'jobbing ins'. He referred to his dread at being forced into a general election in such times: 'at the approach of a dissolution, the Octennial Bill, God forgive us, is our curse and may God forgive those who advised the assent to it'. Three weeks later Blaquiere wrote to Secretary of the Treasury John Robinson, asking for additional emoluments of £9,000 per annum for thirty to forty government supporters who needed financial assistance to be re-elected. Many, he argued, were on small pensions of £200–300 per annum which required raising to afford purchase of seats costing up to £2,500. Others were waiting for promotions since Lord Townshend's viceroyalty.[1]

By early 1776, Lord Lieutenant Harcourt was battle-weary from being caught in the crossfire between London and Dublin over changed money bills, the raising of troops for America and their replacement with foreign troops, and feeling insulted by proposals to give the commander-in-chief powers that were once the preserve of the lord lieutenant. He let it be known he wished to be recalled to avoid the anticipated contest for the speaker's chair and another parliamentary session, to retire from such activity at sixty-three and see his family more often. But his sense of duty to the king made Harcourt remain for the general election. He prorogued the first octennial parliament by proclamation on 4 April 1776 and dissolved it on 30 April.[2]

In County Armagh, by 1776 the successful partnership over two general elections of sitting county members William Brownlow and Archibald Acheson had dissolved. Brownlow, a veteran county representative since his election in 1753, stood again. But Acheson decided to retire from the electoral arena. Growing opinion by independent interests against conjunctions of political magnates may well have influenced him to save himself the bother and expense of running in a crowded field with the distinct possibility of ignominious defeat by a well-supported dark horse. In a county where political opinion was overwhelmingly patriot, Acheson may have considered that his pro-government record would have caused his defeat at a poll in 1776. He may also have been informed that the peerage he had first requested in 1766 and expected for services to government since 1769 but denied to him on Lord Townshend's departure in 1772, was now imminent.[3] Whatever Acheson's reasons for not defending his county seat, his decision meant that at least one new face would be representing Armagh county after fifteen years.

Acheson found there were further strings attached to a move from the house of commons to the house of lords. The recommendations by the Harcourt administration for the creation of peers were not made to overcome a majority in the Irish house of lords but to secure a government majority in the house of commons by gratifying influential politicians and rewarding faithful government supporters. Indeed it has been argued that members of the house of commons were not promoted until arrangements had been made for their seats to be filled by supporters of government.[4] Such a condition would have presented the huge problem for Acheson of finding a credible pro-government candidate in a county imbued with patriot fervour. He would seem to have supported Sir Capel Molyneux as his successor in the preliminary negotiations between landlords at the turn of the year.[5] A rumour in the county also referred to an attempted alliance between Acheson, Lord Charlemont and Arthur Cope of Loughgall to return Molyneux. But any possibility of such a coalition was removed with Cope's own declaration as candidate in December 1775.[6]

Lord Harcourt's main achievement had been to win a majority in the Irish parliament in support of the British government's policy against the American revolution. But the relationship between the executive and legislative was weakened by a significant patriot lobby supporting the Americans and the growing preference for local forces to defend Ireland against threatened invasion by a foreign power. The latter issue, arising in late 1775, promoted the concept of 'Volunteer politics' in County Armagh and influenced the selection and election of candidates. The idea of a voluntary defence force, the 'independent' interest, 'popular' issues, public service and ability of candidates all emerged as significant factors in the course and outcome of the 1776 general election.

FIVE CANDIDATES AND AN 'INDEPENDENT' FACTOR
IN THE QUEST FOR ARMAGH COUNTY SEATS IN 1776

The 1776 general election promised to be very exciting in County Armagh with no fewer than five candidates in the field. Brownlow, in Europe, had left his election address with the *Belfast News-Letter* where it appeared alongside those of Arthur Cope, Sir Capel Molyneux and William Richardson in the issue of 29 December 1775, and that of Thomas Dawson a week later.[7] Only Cope of Loughgall Manor claimed to reside on a full-time basis in the county. Having withdrawn to avoid a contest in 1768, Cope decided to try again in 1776. His election communication refuted a rumour that he had joined with the political interests of Charlemont and Acheson to return Molyneux. In deference to his declaration of 1768, Cope avowed his opposition to all combinations of political interests which he believed subverted the constitution by undermining freedom of individual voting rights. He also attacked the undue influence of the house of lords in elections through 'venal' jobbery and declared his election manifesto was to represent the individual rights of voters against all interests and 'unconstitutional combinations'. Such comment may have reflected public displeasure at the strategy of the Harcourt administration to have former members promoted from the house of commons to lords build a dynasty of pro-government replacements in the lower house.[8]

Molyneux (1717–97), third baronet of the famous patriot family, had inherited the Castle-Dillon estate but gave his residence as Clare Street, Dublin, in his election notice. Experienced in local and parliamentary politics, Molyneux was keen to win the accolade of a county seat in Armagh. In early January 1776, both Molyneux and Richardson applied to the absentee Lord Sandwich for the interest of the Fane estate. Oxford-trained lawyer Richardson (1748–1822) of the Legacorry family but with residence given as Gardiner's Row, Dublin, had been a minor when his father, sitting county member for nineteen years, died in 1758. His father's old seat had been filled in the previous two parliaments by Archibald Acheson, Richardson's brother-in-law. With Acheson not running in 1776, Richardson decided to enter.[9]

Fifth candidate Thomas Dawson (c.1744–1812) also gave his address as Dublin.[10] Dawson was the eldest son of Walter Dawson of Clare Castle near Tandragee, poorer relations of Lord Cremorne and the earls of Dartry of Dawson's Grove, County Monaghan who leased extensive landholdings from the primate around Armagh city and Blackwatertown.[11] He had followed a professional career, being educated at Queen's College Oxford in 1761, Middle Temple in 1762 and TCD in 1763.[12] This rising young professional was chosen as high sheriff of County Armagh in 1770 when his residence was given as Clare-Castle which he seems to have regarded as his home despite his father's acquisition of his first wife's Charlesfort estate in County Wexford.[13]

But Thomas Dawson's candidature for a parliamentary seat in Armagh county elections was surprising given his immediate family's lack of landed property in County Armagh. He was a tenant of Clare-Castle on the estate of the late Viscount Charles Fane inherited jointly by Fane's daughters – the absentee Lady Dorothy Sandwich and Madame Mary de Salis – and his widow the Dowager Lady Susanna Fane. Thus Dawson owned little or no freehold land in Armagh, had an insignificant number of freehold votes and would be almost totally dependent on the political interests of others.

Yet Thomas Dawson had influential political connections, a tradition of public service in the family and able political advisors. In addition to affluent Dawson kinsfolk in counties Monaghan, Armagh, Louth and Wexford, the service of his Dawson ancestors in Armagh and his own service as high sheriff of the county, provided Thomas with a political pedigree, if narrow electoral base from which to fight an election.[14] His main electoral strength emanated from his mentors and strategists, his younger brother James and Francis Dobbs – a formidable election campaign team. James Dawson, born *c.* 1745, was described as 'assistant barrister, County Armagh' with a residence at Forkhill where he was agent and legal advisor to the Jackson estate.[15] Francis Dobbs (1750–1811) was son of a clergyman of the Established Church from County Antrim who combined an army career and the law. In the early 1770s he purchased an ensigncy in the sixty-third regiment, progressing to lieutenant and adjutant by 1773. A student in TCD, he entered Middle Temple in 1773 and was called to the Irish bar in 1775, where, Barrington reported, Dobbs 'acquired some reputation as a constitutional lawyer', describing him as 'a gentleman of respectable family but moderate fortune'. In July 1773 Dobbs married Jane, daughter of Alexander Stewart of Acton estate, where he settled as Stewart's agent and neighbour of the Dawson family at Clare-Castle.[16]

Thomas Dawson was described variously as the representative of the 'popular interest' and 'independent interest' and opposed to government.[17] It has been observed that the terms 'independent' and 'popular' were often used as synonyms to describe the electoral interests espousing popular political causes and outside the control of leading political magnates in a county.[18] Dr Malcomson's observation would seem appropriate to Dawson's candidature in the Armagh county election of 1776 which seems to have been encouraged from an early stage by unattached voters independent of the magnates' control of traditional mainstream political interests in the county. In his election address dated 22 December 1775, he claimed to have 'received a most flattering and honorable invitation from the independent electors of the county of Armagh to stand'.[19]

William Richardson was soon to withdraw his candidature. In a letter dated 17 January 1776, he commented, that while his aim had been:

> ... to promote that independent interest which I could wish to see flourish in your's and every other county; as I find that that interest can more effectually (sic) be supported in the person of another gentleman, I shall upon this occasion ... resign my pretensions ... and shall most heartily co-operate with the independent gentlemen in supporting that candidate who is so deservedly the object of their wishes.[20]

The 'independent gentleman' he had in mind would seem to have been Dawson though all candidates would have claimed to be 'independent'– a very fashionable word in eighteenth century politics and a sine qua non for success in Armagh county elections.

'Independent' meant different things to different candidates. Long-established patriots, Brownlow and Molyneux, had traditionally interpreted it as the freedom to vote independently on parliamentary issues – usually in opposition to government. Neither intended freeholders to be free to vote independently of their landlord's wishes. Indeed Brownlow, in 1768, considered it reasonable for the electorate to return him, as sitting member, without the bother of contesting further county elections. Both candidates had favoured selection of parliamentary representatives by grand jurors in 1768.[21] And, like most eighteenth century parliamentary candidates, they had followed the practice of negotiating election pacts to affect their return without contest, if possible.

In 1776, however, new electoral standards seemed to have pervaded the politically conscious constituencies of Armagh. Large election interests controlled by political magnates – and especially the election strategy of conjunctions of these – seemed to have been frowned upon as almost corrupt and a subversion of the contemporary constitutional process of electing representatives. Such standards were exemplified in Arthur Cope's election manifesto. Undoubtedly, like other candidates, however, the freedom he advocated for the 'free and independent electors' to return to parliament 'men of their own choice' was not intended to be extended to freeholders on his own estate.[22]

Veteran campaigner Brownlow also seemed to have been caught up in the new dispositions. Weather-bound in the French Alps, his letter to Charlemont suggests that a number of candidates had previously agreed not to enter into conjunctions in the Armagh county election. Brownlow confirmed that he, too, would stand alone in 1776 and felt honour bound to continue so as his correspondence had confirmed that other candidates remained 'unconnected':

> ... circumstanced as I was, the most sensible and respectful part I could act was to throw myself on the favour of the county and interfere no further ... so that if the candidates remain unconnected I shall observe the strictest neutrality.

Thus, while Molyneux and Dawson had both promised him electoral support, Brownlow had repeated to them his 'determination' – presumably to remain free of election conjunctions. Brownlow's personal large interest and record of parliamentary service allowed him more security to remain 'unconnected' than others. However, even he acknowledged the danger of going it alone:

> We who are practised in elections, know the difficulty of collecting a straggling, and what is called an independent interest, and ... the risk of standing single upon a double election is obvious.[23]

So obvious was the risk, that Brownlow did not consider it necessary to elaborate on the pit-falls in the double-voting system for a candidate eschewing a conjunction in a general election. The single candidate faced with opponents in conjunction carried multiple handicaps: not only was he denied the second votes of a potential running partner but could not ensure that all the votes of his own freeholders would be 'plumpers' i.e. that their votes would not be 'split', with second votes going to opponents. In such circumstances the single candidate usually set up a 'running horse' to draw his own second votes and stray second votes of others away from opponents. Professor Jupp cites an example of a 'running horse' in the Down county election of 1790.[24] The absence of apparent conjunctions in the five-candidate Armagh field of 1776 suggests that conjunctions were opposed by freeholders and that there was tacit agreement in advance among candidates to exclude them. But the uncanvassed support of Charlemont, Molyneux and Dawson when added to his own significant interest, seemed to guarantee the return of Brownlow for the fourth time, without conjunctions.[25]

In May, Arthur Cope found that his adopted white knight role as opponent of electoral corruption – denouncing 'ruinous, unconstitutional combinations' – was insufficient to draw sufficient electoral support from interests outside his own and estimated that the election arithmetic was going against him. His immediate election ambitions ended on 18 May with his withdrawal.[26]

The second Armagh county seat now rested between Molyneux and Dawson. Molyneux's chances had seemed bright in late winter and spring of 1776, prompting Brownlow to observe: 'From the strong support Sir Capel [Molyneux] receives there seems to be little doubt of his success'.[27] Molyneux had the support of Lord Charlemont. His hopes were further

James Caulfeild, 1st Earl of Charlemont, b. 1728–d. 1799.
Armcm.84.1937 © National Museums Northern Ireland 2011.
Collection Armagh County Museum

Rt Hon. William Brownlow, MP for Co. Armagh 1753–94.
Armcm.T098.32 © National Museums Northern Ireland 2011.
Collection Armagh County Museum

Primate George Stone, Archbishop of Armagh, 1747–64.
Reproduced from an original portrait of *c.* 1750.
By permission of the Governing Body of Christ Church, Oxford

Rt Hon. Sir Capel Molyneux MP.
Armcm.T098.34 © National Museums Northern Ireland 2011.
Collection Armagh County Museum

Rt Hon. Henry Grattan, MP for Charlemont Borough 1775–90.
Armcm.47.1936 © National Museums Northern Ireland 2011.
Collection Armagh County Museum

Rt Hon. Sir Isaac Corry, MP for Newry, 1776–1800, 1802–06.
Armcm.T098.2 © National Museums Northern Ireland 2011.
Collection Armagh County Museum

Richhill Castle, seat of the Richardson family, MPs for Co. Armagh in the late-seventeenth and eighteenth centuries. Pencil drawing by Raymond Piper, 1940. Armcm.139.1981 © National Museums Northern Ireland 2011. Collection Armagh County Museum

Narrow Water, 1787, near residence of Roger Hall MP. Water-colour by John Nixon. Armcm.96.1980 © National Museums Northern Ireland 2011. Collection Armagh County Museum

Primate Richard Robinson, Archbishop of Armagh 1765–94.
Painting by Angelica Kaufmann. Reproduced by kind permission
of the Governors and Guardians of Armagh Public Library

The Primate's Palace, built 1770–1 for Archbishop Robinson.
Reproduced from *Historical Memoirs of the City of Armagh* (1819), by James Stuart

Hugh Hamilton, Dean of Armagh 1768–96.
Armcm.T098.35 © National Museums Northern Ireland 2011.
Collection Armagh County Museum

Francis Dobbs, MP for Charlemont Borough 1798–1800.
Armcm.T626.1 © National Museums Northern Ireland 2011.
Collection Armagh County Museum

Rt Hon. Francis William Caulfeild, 2nd Earl of Charlemont, MP for Co. Armagh 1797–9.
Armcm.T625.1 © National Museums Northern Ireland 2011.
Collection Armagh County Museum

Arms of the Caulfeild family, taken from the same portrait of Francis William Caulfeild

Rt Hon. Thomas Pelham, MP for Armagh Borough 1797–9.
Armcm.1.1954 © National Museums Northern Ireland 2011.
Collection Armagh County Museum

Market Street, Armagh, pencil drawing by Cornelius Varley c. 1810.
Armcm.8.1973 © National Museums Northern Ireland 2011. Collection Armagh County Museum

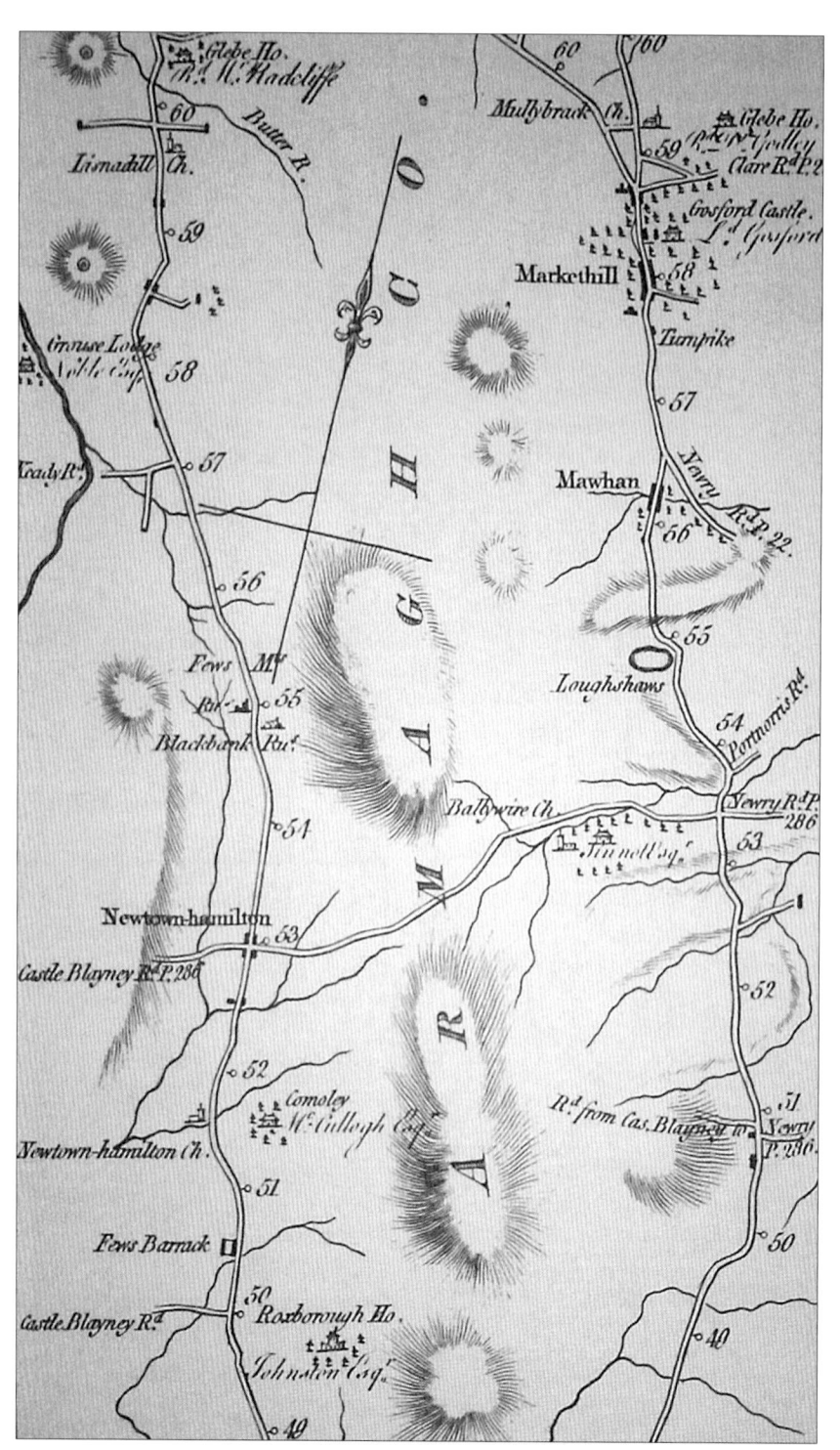

Portrush by [via] Charlemont, reproduced from Taylor and Skinner's
Maps of the Roads of Ireland, surveyed 1777

boosted by the support of Acheson and the government. When applying in early January to Lord Sandwich for the Fane interest, Molyneux had used Acheson's name as reference and Sandwich had checked out Molyneux's credentials with Richard Rigby. Acheson's name was sufficient testimony for Rigby to recommend Molyneux to Sandwich.[28]

However, joint ownership of the former Fane estate between Lady Sandwich, Madame de Salis and Dowager Lady Fane was still causing complications in directing its electoral interest. In early March 1776 Acheson wrote to Lady Fane recommending Molyneux but found that she had already promised her part of the electoral interest to Dawson, one of her tenants at Clare-Castle. The dowager confessed to being 'unacquainted' with the Armagh candidates and, though acknowledging the weight of Acheson's recommendation, felt obliged to honour her previous pledge to Dawson.[29]

Acheson's request to Lord Sandwich on Molyneux's behalf would also seem to have been in vain. Sandwich later apologised that while he had wished to support Acheson's interest, his influence on his Armagh estate had been fruitless on this occasion. His explanation illustrates how the allocation of an electoral interest by an absentee landlord might be constrained by multiple factors and occasionally fall outside his control:

> ... but as I am circumstanced with an undivided moiety, myself unknown and unknowing of the state of things in the place, and the steward who is resident and whose family have long had the management of the estate lately removed and acting against me, it is not to be expected that at this time I could carry much interest for any candidate.[30]

Molyneux remained in the election arena until the eve of the poll, set to begin on Monday 3 June. But with the tide of public opinion in the county flowing with Dawson for the second county seat, Molyneux withdrew at the beginning of June – excusing himself that he wished to avoid potential disorder from an election contest.[31]

In a sense, Thomas Dawson was probably the truest 'independent' candidate in 1776, as he had no significant electoral interest of his own or second votes to trade and thus had to win votes on his own merits as champion of the popular political issues of the day. His success depended upon the strength of popular support for his political cause and the efficiency of his election campaign in harnessing that support in an election. At the end of 1775, the topical political issues were support for or opposition to the American revolution and how to replace – for home defence – the Irish troops sent to fight in the American war i.e. whether to accept George III's offer of Hessian troops or raise local voluntary militias. A local defence force was the popular option but the voluntary principle was suspected by government as having the potential to undermine its control. The professional backgrounds of Dawson and Dobbs made them ideal leaders in the event of local defence militias being raised.

Dawson would seem to have received support from the interests of Brownlow, Fane, Richardson and others, although the full range of interests supporting him is conjectural. He could retain good relations with all candidates as he had no significant interest of his own to commit.[32] A tacit arrangement not to have conjunctions would also have suited Dawson. While candidates with significant personal interests probably regarded opponents with suspicion, Dawson was an obvious catch-all candidate for second votes. And Dawson's professional competence, record of service to the county community, independence of political thought and enthusiastic support of the American cause, all made him an attractive candidate to the independent interest in the county.

Brownlow and Dawson were returned without a poll in the 1776 general election when the other candidates withdrew. Eight years previously, veteran patriot Brownlow would have thought this no less than his due. But Dawson's election was a phenomenon. He was the only landless candidate to be returned for Armagh county in the eighteenth century, and one of the few elected largely by the independent interest on a popular issue. Both factors were noted in Castle circles: '… his property it is said very inconsiderable'.[33] Heron described him as: 'a man of no property set up and elected by the independent interest'.[34] Another report for Lord Lieutenant Temple referred to him as: 'a man of no property – elected by the popular interests'.[35]

Dawson was one of many lawyers who entered parliament to further a career in public life and enhance opportunities for preferment. It has been estimated that between forty and fifty professional lawyers were returned as members to the parliament of 1776.[36] Although Dawson was returned on the popular vote by the independent lobby, perceptive Dublin Castle analysts detected early a weakness which could be exploited to win him over to the government side with the appropriate career incentive. Sir Michael Cromie observed that Dawson; 'wants something – has no for[tune]'.[37]

While three candidates were withdrawing from the general election, Acheson, having initially declined to defend his Armagh county seat, was drawn back into the election to help the government. His long-awaited peerage had been finally confirmed in writing in early May.[38] But, three weeks later, Acheson was asked by Harcourt to do the government a final favour by having his peerage postponed in order to take, temporarily, a house of commons seat for Enniskillen borough. Government supporter Lord Mountflorence controlled that borough but a person intended by him for a seat had been found less reliable than expected and Harcourt turned to Acheson to fill the breach at this crucial period until another placeman, suitably loyal to government, could be procured.[39]

The occasion of the lord lieutenant's anxiety and Acheson's call to service in a house of commons division in the Castle cause, was the re-election of Edmund Sexton Pery as speaker – regarded as an important trial of strength for the government following the assembling of the new Irish parliament in June 1776.[40] With John Ponsonby's attempt to oust Pery thwarted by 43 votes, Acheson was finally raised to the Irish house of lords when created Baron Gosford in early July 1776.[41]

RETURNS FOR PARLIAMENTARY BOROUGHS IN 1776

The death of Charles O'Hara, and departure of Lord Macartney, meant that both members of parliament for Armagh borough in the first octennial parliament would be replaced in the second.[42] Primate Robinson brought in his agent Henry Meredyth (c.1709–89), veteran administrative official of Armagh archbishops and Dublin Castle. Meredyth had been Primate Stone's secretary and agent when summoned as a witness to give evidence at the parliamentary hearing of the Armagh by-election petition in 1753. In the same period he was first clerk to the chief secretary, later served as deputy auditor-general and secretary to the master-general in the civil branch of the ordnance, and in 1758 was awarded a salary of £500 per annum when military fees were replaced by fixed salaries.[43] Meredyth continued as part of the Dublin Castle secretariat until 1775 when he retired on a pension of £500 per annum and, when elected in 1776, was described as 'a secretary lately, now pensioned'.[44] His secretarial experience resulted in his being called out of retirement later in 1776 to act as second secretary to Richard Heron at the beginning of the Buckinghamshire administration which he served for another two years.[45]

Attorney-General Philip Tisdall was brought in for Armagh borough in 1776 when he was forced out of the University seat by his old adversary, the grasping John Hely-Hutchinson who had been appointed provost of TCD following Francis Andrews's death in 1774. Primate Robinson rescued an ailing Tisdall as an ally against the provost, and the Buckinghamshire administration valued Tisdall's advice in the selection of officers until his death in September 1777.[46] The primate replaced Tisdall with George Rawson, a professional soldier from County Wicklow hoping to make a career in politics and potential government supporter.[47]

Lord Charlemont returned both sitting members for Charlemont borough in 1776. By then Sir Annesley Stewart would seem to have severed his banking partnership with Sir George Colebrook. It was noted that Lord

Townshend had obtained a vacant cornetcy for him; but that Stewart 'has always been' and had remained 'in constant opposition'. Barrister Henry Grattan was described as 'a capital speaker' brought in by Lord Charlemont to oppose government who 'has hitherto acted in strict conformity to the conduct of his patron by opposing most strenuously every measure of government'.[48]

When Sir Capel Molyneux withdrew from the contest for the Armagh county seats he was facing the prospect of losing his parliamentary seat. He, like Tisdall, had been a sitting member omitted by Hely-Hutchinson from the 1776 nominations for the University of Dublin seat. With a grudging blessing from government – who, in 1775, had considered his support 'always very doubtful' – Molyneux was returned for his old seat of Clogher borough, by his brother-in-law, Bishop Garnett.[49] He received a further consolation prize a month later when appointed to the Irish privy council. Both appointments were probably reward for undertaking a temporary pro-government role as Acheson's replacement candidate – sufficient reason to turn independent voters in Armagh to Dawson and Brownlow.[50]

Two Armagh gentry were returned for parliamentary constituencies outside the county. The young Isaac Corry (1755–1813), from a Newry merchant family with residence at Derrymore, succeeded his father Edward as member for the pot-walloping borough of Newry in 1776. Corry junior, was agent to William Nedham, a large but absentee landowner with land round Newry in counties Down and Armagh although his main interest was in English politics. Corry was returned in tandem with Nedham for Newry after a hard-fought contest and duel with his opponent Sir Richard Johnston.[51] John Moore senior was returned by the earl of Drogheda for a second term for the borough of Ballynakill.[52]

DISPOSITIONS OF ARMAGH MPs
IN PARLIAMENTARY DIVISIONS, 1777–8

Following the general election of 1776, Harcourt and Blaquiere were replaced at the end of the year by the aristocratic John Hobart, second earl of Buckinghamshire and Sir Richard Heron from a middle-class background as his chief secretary. Neither was a strong manager but Buckinghamshire's connection by marriage to the two leading Irish aristocrats Thomas Conolly and the duke of Leinster and the friendly dispositions of Buckinghamshire and Heron, enabled the latter pair to form a working relationship with some patriots. Their chief advisors were Speaker Pery, Attorney-General Scott and Prime Sergeant Hussey Burgh, until his defection.[53]

Armagh members were divided in their attitudes to Buckinghamshire's new administration. Brownlow and Dawson opposed it. Brownlow was annoyed at the new lord lieutenant's refusal to recommend his son Charles to the king for a company in the army over the heads of lieutenants. Meredyth, Rawson, Corry and Moore supported, Grattan and Stewart opposed.[54] In 1777, Grattan had not yet been accepted as undisputed leader of the opposition members despite his attacks on the government. When he moved in November 1777 'that the expenses of government ought to be seriously retrenched', Hussey Burgh countered with an amendment postponing Grattan's motion. Brownlow, Dawson, and Stewart voted with Grattan. Meredyth and Isaac Corry supported the government amendment which had a comfortable victory on 17 November 1777.[55]

Grattan and the patriots attacked the government's embargo since February 1776 on the export of Irish provisions to France, Spain and America as illegal and unnecessary. They demanded an official enquiry into alleged malpractice by Robert Gordon, commissary for the purchase of provisions for the armed forces, forcing a division on 16 December 1777. The motion was supported by Brownlow, Dawson, Grattan and Stewart. Though the administration succeeded in having the motion defeated, there were defections in the government ranks suggesting some substance to the patriots' accusation.[56] One year later the embargo was lifted. Against a background of bankruptcies, redundancies in manufacturing, poverty and riots by the unemployed in Dublin over the winter, the patriots maintained pressure on an administration struggling to raise troops for the American war and desperately seeking loans in London to replenish a near empty treasury but finding money difficult to obtain due to falling stocks in the city occasioned through fear of a French war.[57] On 6 February 1778, Grattan's motion for retrenchment was defeated by 145 votes to 68. Grattan was supported by Brownlow, Dawson, Stewart, and Molyneux.[58]

The need for augmentation of troops for abroad and ensuring wartime security at home made it expedient to recruit Catholics for the army and to conciliate them in case of invasion by alleviating some of their grievances under the Penal Laws. In May 1778, the British government, opened the way by passing two Whig bills: a relief act for English Catholics and the repeal of statutes from Queen Anne's reign prohibiting Catholics from buying forfeited Irish estates. Speaker Pery returned from London on 30 April to inform Buckinghamshire that George III was keen to see a relief act for Irish Catholics during the current session. But Buckinghamshire was apprehensive about which concessions would satisfy the Catholics without antagonising Irish Protestants.[59] Thus, while the Catholic Relief Bill of 1778 was not a government measure, it was supported openly by Dublin Castle. Buckinghamshire was encouraged by the primate's 'liberal and temperate' comments on the measure, a reversal of the latter's opposition to proposed legislation for Catholic relief between 1772–4. Recent research suggests Robinson's conversion in 1778 was in part due to his efforts to win Buckinghamshire as an ally in the primate's power-struggles with Archbishop Charles Agar and with Hely-Hutchinson over TCD.[60]

Luke Gardiner's heads of a bill on 23 May 1778 proposing that Catholics be given the right to buy land in fee simple and that the hated gavelkind and conforming clauses be repealed, had the support of government but split the patriot opposition. The proposed controversial right of Catholics being allowed to purchase land in freehold or outright ownership was circumvented by a new proposal confining them to longer leases for up to 999 years. In the ensuing debate, a frequent argument by supporters of the bill was that affluent Catholic merchants would emigrate to England with their wealth if legal rights to acquire land continued to be denied them in Ireland.[61] Sir Edward Newenham's amendment to the heads which added repeal of the Sacramental Test for Dissenters, burdened Gardiner's measure and may have been intended by opponents to bring about the whole bill's rejection by London. But the British cabinet excised the amendment and returned to the Dublin parliament the original bill – which would permit Catholics to lease beyond thirty one years, inherit and bequeath land, and would remove the gavelkind and conforming clauses.

The main opposition to the returned Relief Bill in the Irish house of commons came from the patriots. The only patriots to support it were Gardiner, Conolly, the duke of Leinster and Yelverton, and the measure owed its passing narrowly by 114 votes to 103 on 3 August 1778 mainly to the administration led by Speaker Pery. Grattan – ironically a future champion of Catholic rights in the Irish parliament – opposed the measure vigorously in 1778 in deference to his patron's views; and was supported in the parliamentary division by Stewart and Dawson. Meredyth and Rawson, influenced by the primate, and Corry and Moore, following the direction of their respective patrons, supported the measure. Conspicuous by their absence from the division list were the names of Brownlow and Molyneux who seem to have ducked this controversial issue.[62]

The measure also passed a divided Irish house of lords. In the division of 10 August, Primate Robinson, Lord Chancellor Lifford and the duke of Leinster led the support for the bill while the earls of Charlemont, Shannon and Moira led the opposition. Like his Armagh neighbours Brownlow and Molyneux, Lord Gosford's absence from the division suggested he was not prepared to commit himself to Catholic relief.[63]

SEVEN PHASES OF ARMAGH VOLUNTEER POLITICS, 1778–83

In Armagh, as elsewhere, the belief that the American war would lead to European war, invasion and the necessity of home defence caused foreboding. A Richhill resident wrote to Lord Gosford's son, Arthur: 'A war has damped our spirits here, nothing else is talked of but an invasion'. Lord Southwell informed Gosford that speculation in Dublin was of 'a French war' and that France and Spain were 'arming fast'.[64] The French treaty of friendship with the Americans in March 1778 soon brought the inevitable war against an alliance of France, Spain and America. The inhabitants of Belfast in March 1778 formed the Belfast Volunteer Company as a voluntary force to defend the city from possible attack by foreign shipping when Buckinghamshire's administration could not provide regular troops nor afford to raise a militia.[65] Other areas emulated Belfast, and Volunteer companies were formed independently over Ireland during 1778. The raising and development of the Volunteers in County Armagh may be considered over seven distinct phases.

Phase 1: Emergence of Volunteers for home defence amid official suspicions from September 1778 to April 1779

The initial phase was in late 1778 and early 1779. First Armagh Company was raised in the city on 1 December 1778 with county governor, Lord Charlemont, appointed its captain on 13 January 1779.[66] Charlemont's negotiations with government for a loan of militia arms stored in Charlemont Fort since 1760 – until the Volunteers could procure their own – was initially unsuccessful and delayed formation. Since only men of substance could afford the sustained costs of membership of a voluntary force, the original Volunteer companies emanated from the more prosperous levels of society – in Grattan's phrase 'the armed property of the nation.'

As companies sprung up over the county during 1779, both upper class landed gentry and middle class professional/commercial personnel were represented in the officer command, though in varying proportions of each category from area to area. The latter category predominated in urban areas. Thus, in Armagh First Company, while Lord Charlemont was captain; surgeon Samuel Maxwell was first lieutenant and second-in-command, a second surgeon, Samuel Carson held the post of surgeon in the company; Thomas Prentice, second lieutenant, was from an established Armagh city seed imports and grocery business family; Lee McKinstry, third lieutenant, was an elected freeman of Armagh City in 1766; Adjutant Andrew Boyd later took service with the East India Company. Captain of Armagh First Artillery Company was Robert Jackson, a well-known linen merchant in Armagh City and a trustee of Armagh Presbyterian Church.[67]

Most of the Armagh gentry held commanding roles in the Volunteers. A notable exception was Lord Gosford who, as committed government supporter, remained aloof from the movement and, with his son Arthur abroad, the Acheson family was not represented in the Volunteers, and Markethill was one of the few towns in the county without a company. In the first phase, the Volunteers did not have a political agenda, being formed out of perceived need for home defence. But those early self-embodied companies of armed men outside government control created an uneasy public conscience, doubts and dilatory recruitment.

Phase 2: Official acceptance of Volunteers for defence from April 1779
When it became obvious by 1779 that Buckinghamshire's government could not afford to raise a militia and would not suppress the Volunteers, the latter became 'respectable' and recruitment flourished. Thus, in April 1779, when Heron – seeking subventions in London for the Irish administration – reported suggestions for calling the Irish parliament to pass a militia act to regulate the increasing 'self-created corps' of independent companies, the lord lieutenant informed his chief secretary: 'The possibility of very disagreeable inconvenience arising from them [Volunteers] is very evident, but not more than the very great utility which has been derived from them'. Buckinghamshire reminded Heron that a militia would have the same composition as the Volunteers and require money which the administration did not have; and to stand down the Volunteers would cause resentments at a time when they were providing efficient local defence.[68]

The acceptability of the Volunteers in official circles received further boosts in the second half of 1779. In late summer the Irish privy council authorised county governors to distribute stored militia arms to Volunteer companies. When Lord Charlemont applied again at Brownlow's request, permission was granted in September to issue 500 stands of militia arms from Charlemont store.[69] This was followed on 14 October 1779 by the Irish Parliament's vote of thanks for Volunteer services. In Armagh, as elsewhere, morale and recruitment flourished in the Volunteer movement as a result – to such an extent that there were insufficient supplies of weapons in storage to meet the increased demands.[70]

Phase 3: Volunteer involvement in free trade politics, autumn 1779
The Volunteer movement's entry into national politics from October 1779 was facilitated by the composition of its membership and leadership, and by structural changes. Membership of the Volunteers was from the

politically conscious section of Irish society, providing potential and leadership for political activism. Links between Volunteering and politics were reinforced by the fact that many Volunteer leaders were also members of parliament. One estimate gives twenty-three members at least from Ulster in the house of commons in 1782 who were Volunteers and about a dozen in the lords.[71]

At least eight MPs with County Armagh connections – residential and/or political – became high-profile Volunteers. Brownlow was captain of the Lurgan company of Volunteers and lieutenant-colonel of the Armagh Northern Battalion of the First Ulster Regiment. Dawson was captain of Clare Company and lieutenant colonel of the Southern Battalion of the First Ulster Regiment of Volunteers. Molyneux was captain of Castle-Dillon Volunteers, John Moore captain of the Drumbanagher Volunteers and Isaac Corry of Derrymore, captain commandant of the First Newry Company of Volunteers.[72] Lord Charlemont gave a lead to his political protégés. As well as being chosen captain of the influential First Armagh Company of the City of Armagh Volunteers, he was also appointed colonel of the Southern Battalion of the First Ulster Regiment and commander-in-chief of the Irish Volunteers, surmounting problems of ill-health and lack of professional military training for the Volunteer posts. Stewart was lieutenant colonel of the Donegal Volunteers, Grattan colonel of Independent Dublin Volunteers.[73]

In September 1779 Grattan emerged as undisputed leader of and spokesman for the parliamentary opposition. On 12 October 1779, his speech in the house of commons appealed to extra-parliamentary support: 'we must therefore support ourselves!' The duke of Leinster's Dublin Volunteers responded by organising a demonstration for free trade on 4 November in College Green threatening 'short money bill – a free trade – or else!!!!!' (sic). On 10 November Grattan warned the house of commons that associations all over the country had decided that parliamentary representatives must oppose further taxes until free trade had been conceded – 'commands' which an MP, 'as the servant of his constituents', was 'bound to obey'.[74]

Grattan's exhortation to extra-parliamentary intervention in parliamentary affairs caused unease among patriots like Brownlow who condemned Grattan's 'associations formed to frighten the members of that house, to vote contrary to their judgments ... such as the dignity of parliament should spurn at'. Brownlow argued that constituents could 'advise' but not 'compel' their members of parliament who were 'trustees', not 'slaves', of the electorate and should retain their freedom of decision-making – a relationship consistent with his views of 1768. But many associations in towns and counties were already pressurising their local members with 'instructions', including those in County Armagh.[75]

County Armagh played a leading part in the co-ordination of Volunteers for political purposes with the Dawson brothers and Francis Dobbs champions of the new initiative. Charlemont and his supporters by-passed Armagh City and district – where attitudes to the Volunteers were divided – and chose the Ballymore area in Lower Orior, east Armagh, as centre for development. A number of reasons influenced their choice. Despite Charlemont's own First Company being formed in Armagh city, the influence of Primate Richard Robinson and Lord Gosford on the 'minor gentlemen' had diluted support for the Volunteers in the area. Established local gentry like Molyneux and Richardson were by-passed as leaders of the new initiative in favour of the Ballymore radicals. Tandragee was targeted as epicentre for political agitation. This was partly because of the number and activism of Volunteer units in the area and partly because of the ability and commitment of an emerging group of professional political activists including the Dawsons of Clare-Castle and Dobbs of Acton – the latter beginning to make a name for himself as political letter-writer – and local leaders such as Nicholas Johnston of Tandragee Castle.[76]

In October 1779, Dobbs persuaded freeholders to make application to High Sheriff Thomas Morres Jones to call an early county meeting to draw up 'instructions' for members of parliament. The 1,000-strong meeting in Armagh city on 4 November was divided between moderates and radicals. William Richardson and John Blackhall, Arthur Cope's agent, seem to have opposed holding the meeting. They may have considered the proposals too radical, perhaps still smarting over the rejection of Richardson and Cope at the general election and/or being by-passed in the current initiative. Representatives of the Established Church, Dean Hugh Hamilton, Rev. Dr Arthur Grueber, master of Armagh Royal School and Rev. Dr Charles Woodward, Loughgall, prebendary of Armagh, were critical of procedures.[77]

However, the meeting accepted the proposal of Rev. William Campbell, chaplain of Armagh First Company of Volunteers and minister of the Presbyterian congregation in the City, and other dissenting clergy, that Sheriff Jones nominate a committee to draw up an address and 'instructions', firstly, to be distributed for signatures though Robert Livingstone – Charlemont's estate agent and captain lieutenant of Charlemont Volunteers – then to be presented to Brownlow and Dawson.[78] Only the two county members were lobbied. Presumably it was taken for granted that Grattan and Stewart would support the address and that Meredyth and Rawson, would not. The county electorate may also have regarded as pointless any attempt to 'instruct' members they did not elect.

The published address to the two county MPs had the signatures of 1,033 freeholders. It included the following resolutions: support for free trade, an absentee tax, measures of economical reform such as greater scrutiny of public accounts, public expenditure, opposition to placemen, sinecures, undeserved pensions, and opposition to money bills exceeding six months. Dawson accepted all the radical demands of the Armagh address without reservation. Brownlow's independence made him less subservient. While prepared to support the campaign for economical reform, he was unwilling to concede to constituents the absolute right of deciding how he would vote. His qualified and carefully worded reply informed them that he was always happy to receive their advice and 'particularly happy when I can frame my conduct to coincide with [your] wishes'.[79]

Within parliament, a parallel wildfire of support for free trade, sparked off by Grattan's fiery speeches, was sweeping all before it including many from the government side. On the 25 November 1779, during the debate on limiting the money bill for supplies to six months, Prime Sergeant Burgh's angry allusion to the Cadmus legend of 'dragon's teeth ... sprung up in armed men' was an ominous reminder of Volunteer guns in Irish politics.[80] On the same day, Burgh voted against the government which was defeated by 138 votes to 100 in a division on the opposition's six months money bill which was supported by Brownlow, Dawson, Grattan, Stewart, Molyneux and Corry. Meredyth, Rawson and Moore took the government side and opposed the bill.[81]

It was the combination of pressures from Volunteer public demonstrations and county meetings outside, and patriot demands inside the Irish parliament which forced through the shorter money bill and free trade concessions from Lord North and the British parliament. In County Armagh news of trade concessions by the British legislature was celebrated by Volunteer parades, volleys and bonfires including those in Lurgan on 25 December, Armagh market-place on 30 December and Tandragee on 3 January 1780. Local companies in Armagh had assumed the trappings of an army, becoming the 'Volunteer army of Ireland', as in north west Ulster where their 'getting-up' activities have been re-assessed as a manifestation of national identity.[82]

Phase 4: Volunteer agitation for legislative independence, 1780–81

Many Volunteers revelled in the praise from politicians for their political contribution to the campaign for free trade and by the end of 1779 some units were moving to a fourth political phase. In late December 1779, Newry Volunteers called for legislative independence to protect commercial concessions – '[the way of guaranteeing] the commercial ... is to obtain the political freedom of this kingdom'.[83] In 1780, the three-fold strategy of the radical wing of the patriots for the removal of the constitutional supremacy of Britain over the Irish Parliament was: to introduce a resolution that only the king, lords and commons of Ireland could legislate for Ireland; to be followed by a bill partially repealing Poynings's Law; and an Irish mutiny bill invalidating the current British Mutiny Act which controlled the armed forces in Ireland.[84]

In County Armagh this strategy would be facilitated by a re-structuring of Volunteer organisation into larger units. Company officers met at Clare on 27 December 1779 and at Tandragee on 10 January 1780 to discuss the formation of battalions and artillery companies and the appointment of commanding officers. The Lower Orior influence on these developments is apparent. In addition to the venues chosen, officer appointments had a strong Orior representation. At the 10 January meeting, two battalions were formed for the county with Thomas Dawson and Francis Dobbs appointed commander and major respectively of a Southern Battalion. Dobbs was captain of Tyrone Ditches and Acton Company whose influence in the Volunteers was second only to Armagh First Company. Brownlow was chosen as commander of a Northern Battalion with William Richardson his major.[85]

Dobbs articulated the demand for legislative independence in a radical pamphlet, published on 1 January 1780, addressed to Lord North:

> When the parliament of Ireland addressed their king, and told him that nothing but a free trade could save their country, they could not, I am persuaded they did not, forget why Ireland had not a free trade; they could not forget that Ireland was bound by British acts of parliament.[86]

The pamphlet threatened England with physical force if legislative independence was not granted 'because Great Britain has exerted an arbitrary power to which she was not entitled, Great Britain must either relinquish such an invasion of our rights, or support it, as she made it – *by power*'. Dobbs's pamphlet brought public addresses of thanks and support from Volunteer companies.[87]

Volunteer agitation was supported by eighteen county meetings. The gentlemen and freeholders of County Armagh requested High Sheriff Maxwell Close to call a county meeting to prepare a motion of legislative independence and 'instructions' for their MPs. At the meeting in Armagh courthouse on 23 February Brownlow and Dawson were instructed as follows:

> We acknowledge no authority on earth, but that of the king, lords and commons of Ireland ... Thus determined, we publicly call upon you, our representatives, to exert your utmost efforts to establish the independence of the king, lords and commons of Ireland; and we also deem it indispensably necessary to repeal such parts of Poynings's laws, to give a power to the king and privy council,

unknown to our ancient constitution, and subversive of our rights.[88]

Both Brownlow and Dawson publicly acknowledged the communications from the Armagh county meeting. Significantly, while Dawson called them 'instructions', Brownlow referred to them as 'your petition against superfluous places and pensions' and advised that while 'constitutional liberty has ever been with me a favourite object ... let us act with prudence and moderation'. On 15 April Brownlow presented a petition in the house of commons signed by 1,800 Armagh freeholders requesting retrenchment in public expenses which was referred to parliamentary committee.[89]

The campaign for legislative independence in 1780 was less successful than that for free trade in 1779. As divisions appeared in the movement both inside and outside the Irish Parliament, the government began to regain control. On 19 April, despite Grattan's eloquence, his Declaration of Right that only the king, lords and commons of Ireland could legislate for Ireland was negatived by government amendments.[90] A week later, Yelverton's motion for a partial repeal of Poynings's Law was defeated by 130 to 105. In the division on 26 April 1780, Brownlow, Dawson, Stewart and Corry supported the motion while Meredyth, Rawson and Moore opposed. Molyneux is not listed among those who voted.[91]

Numerous Volunteer companies thanked Grattan and Yelverton for their patriot zeal in parliament. The Southern Battalion of the Armagh Volunteers at a meeting chaired by James Dawson on the 22 May 1780 thanked both for their motions on 19th and 26th April and also praised 'the upright and spirited conduct' of county members Brownlow and Dawson in resolutions.[92] But the movement for constitutional change had lost much of the support enjoyed by that for free trade.

In spring, the patriots attempted to have the Irish parliament pass its own Mutiny Bill, which would, implicitly, have negated the validity of the British Mutiny Act in Ireland. But the Irish administration outflanked Gervaise Bushe's heads of an Irish Mutiny Bill with John Foster's amendment on 29 May 1780 which placed the army in Ireland solely under the king. Foster's amendment was carried by 117 votes to 80.[93] When the Mutiny Bill returned from London on 11 August, it had been further altered to a perpetual one giving the king the right to maintain an army in Ireland forever. Though Grattan, Brownlow and others fulminated against the changes, so divided were the patriots that their proposal on 16 August to remove the offending perpetual clause was easily defeated by 114 votes to 62. Brownlow, Dawson, Stewart and Grattan voted against the Perpetual Mutiny Bill while Meredyth, Rawson, Moore and erstwhile patriot Molyneux voted for the measure.[94]

Explanations have varied for the diminution in radicalism, divisions among patriots and regain of control of parliament by Buckinghamshire's Irish administration in 1780. A traditional view attributed recovery of control to bribery of pro-government majorities.[95] More recent analysis, however, has ascribed the weakening of the radical campaign to a growing consciousness among the landed ruling classes that the free trade agitation was developing into a challenge by the middle classes for a share of political power; and has argued that leaders of the landed gentry such as Conolly and Lords Leinster and Shannon distanced themselves from the radical movement which government outmanoeuvred with popular legislation. Conversely, the constancy of Charlemont's patriotism was rewarded by his being confirmed as national leader of the Volunteers.[96]

Legislation by the Irish administration in the summer of 1780 took the patriots' ground and weaned sections of the radical middle classes out of opposition. A Combinations Act preventing militant journeymen from organising workmen against masters won over middle class manufacturing employers. Aggrieved lower artisans who had comprised the 'mob' element of 1779 protests in Dublin and the larger towns became disillusioned by the lack of opposition to the measure by patriots and extra-parliamentary associations and were less eager to man Volunteer barricades in 1780.

More widespread abandonment of radical opposition and widening of divisions among patriots accompanied the Tenantry Bill to establish in law the Irish custom whereby leases for lives would be renewed on expiry of a life by substitution of another life and payment of a fine to the lessor/head landlord. This custom had enabled lessees retain their holdings in perpetuity. The increase in population and land values in the second half of the eighteenth century had made head landlords desirous of recovering possession of their estates. Their hopes were raised when the legalities of the above custom were questioned in court cases between 1775 and 1779. The Murray v. Bateman case of 1775–6 ruled in favour of the lessor. On appeal to the Irish chancellor's court, Lord Chancellor Lifford reversed the ruling. Following further appeal to the British house of lords, Lord Mansfield restored judgement to the lessor. The impasse was resolved in favour of Irish lessees by Attorney-General Scott's Tenantry Act in 1779–80 which restored 'the old Irish equity'. Tens of thousands of Irish leaseholders and their undertenants sought the protection of Scott's popular measure, while lessors sulked in unpopular opposition.[97]

Patriots, comprising both lessors and lessees, in both houses of parliament, were split according to vested interest on the Tenantry Bill. A group of County Armagh inhabitants requested High Sheriff Maxwell Close to call a county meeting on 18 July 1780 to form an address requesting their MPs to support the Tenantry Bill.[98] But extensive landowner Brownlow seems to have ignored the meeting. In the house of commons debate, crown servants were joined by some patriots such as Grattan, Burgh and Bushe in support of the measure. But other prominent patriots, like Brownlow and Yelverton, were conspicuous by their silence. In the parliamentary division on 11 August 1780 Meredyth and Rawson were joined by Grattan and Dawson in voting for the Tenantry Bill; but Corry and Moore voted against, while Brownlow and Stewart abstained. Many patriot peers opposed the measure in the upper house on 18 and 19 August but it scraped through.[99]

When parliament was prorogued in September 1780 and the exhausted Buckinghamshire and Heron replaced by Carlisle and Eden as lord lieutenant and chief secretary respectively in late November, the Volunteer influence on patriot politics had already diminished significantly. Only Grattan and a small minority of patriot members continued to condone Volunteer interference in parliamentary matters. Others, however, like Burgh, now repudiated political interference from armed Volunteers.

In County Armagh, Brownlow strove to retain the confidence of the patriot electorate against a campaign of political disinformation intended to smear him. In a notice in early 1781 he refuted a rumour that he was about to receive a peerage. Certainly a year earlier Brownlow's political support had been sufficiently in demand by Buckinghamshire as to reverse the lord lieutenant's earlier decision and recommend young Charles Brownlow to the king for promotion, over Commander-in-Chief Sir John Irwin's choice; and Brownlow had been close enough to Buckinghamshire's administration as to have been consulted by the lord lieutenant on the viability of a Test Bill.[100] The content of Brownlow's notice in February 1781 re-affirmed his pride of political independence and appealed to the patriot tradition in the county:

> ... and further, that I never at any period of my life solicited, or looked for a peerage, that probably I never shall, and that if there was one now at my option to accept, unsolicited and unconditioned, so little am I ambitious of that species of honour, that I should respectfully decline it. Feb. 13th, 1781.[101]

That Brownlow's political integrity had been impugned – but restored – was indicated in a toast at the annual general meeting of County Down freeholders at Dundonald in June 1781 where he was described as 'one who preferred being an honest man to a peer'.[102]

In December 1781 Brownlow hinted again at a conspiracy to undermine his relationship with the county electorate when his reply to 'instructions' from Armagh freeholders received on 13 November was not published. Thomas Dawson assured the Armagh freeholders that he felt bound by their 'address of instructions ... to support the collective voice of his constituents' and apologised for his delay in replying publicly due to his absence in England on business.[103] However, both the spirit of Volunteering and opposition to the Dublin administration flourished in County Armagh, though Brownlow's restrained approach was, perhaps, closer to Conolly's model in Derry than the more expansive approach of Dawson and Dobbs.

While Brownlow strove to defend his patriot reputation, Charlemont, Dawson and Dobbs continued throughout 1781 to enhance their reputations through organisation of Volunteer military reviews. The latter two assisted in the planning of a huge review of officers and deputies in Belfast from 18 to 20 July which was reviewed by 'Reviewing-General' Charlemont with Colonel Dawson in the chair and Major Dobbs as exercising officer. Subsequent reports in the press contained resolutions of thanks bordering on a mutual admiration exercise between the leaders of the Armagh Southern Battalion. Charlemont served as general for several reviews including Newry on 20 and 21 August where Dawson, Dobbs, Brownlow and Richardson played prominent roles.[104]

Public offers of service from lists of Volunteer associations, however, following the annual invasion-scare in summer 1781 suggested that the Volunteers had forsaken politics for their original aim of providing voluntary emergency defence; while Carlisle's expression of satisfaction with Volunteer offers of help, indicated the movement's reputation in official circles had been rehabilitated.[105] But when parliament returned in October, the patriot opposition found itself powerless from divisions within its own ranks and lack of extra-parliamentary political pressure from the Volunteer movement. Grattan's motion on 13 November 1781 to have the perpetual Mutiny Act amended was defeated by 133 votes to 77.[106] And the opposition led by Grattan and Brownlow to Yelverton's address of loyalty against the enemies of the British Empire on 4 December, was even less successful when Yelverton's notion was victorious by 167 votes to 37.[107]

Phase 5: Armagh Volunteers reactive agitation for legislative independence, December 1781 to April 1782

The fuse of extra-parliamentary political agitation was re-lighted in County Armagh – or, more specifically, in Lower Orior – when Dawson and Dobbs persuaded the officers of the Southern Battalion of Volunteers to exhort the Volunteer movement to resume political activism.[108] The officers and delegates of eleven companies comprising the Southern Battalion of Charlemont's First Ulster Regiment met at Markethill on 10 December 1781 with James Dawson in the chair and passed an address of thanks to all members of parliament who voted for a limitation of the Mutiny Law. The fusion of Volunteering and high politics was emphasised:

> We therefore, as freeholders and Volunteers, return you our warmest thanks for your spirited efforts to procure a limitation of the Mutiny Bill, a law which, in its present form, we must ever behold with a jealous eye, and consider as unconstitutional, being enacted in direct opposition to the foundation of our constitution, on which alone we conceive the representatives of this free kingdom, as part of the British empire, can claim any power to constitute a law.[109]

A further meeting of the same body at Armagh on 28 December 1781, on this occasion chaired by Francis Evans of Orior, passed resolutions and called on all Volunteer companies in Ulster to send elected delegates to a meeting in Dungannon, County Tyrone on 15 February 1782 to discuss them.[110] Brownlow was not consulted; nor is it clear how far Charlemont was party to the above initiative. The idea seems to have been that of Dawson and Dobbs.[111] Charlemont, though commander of the Southern Battalion, only seems to have become involved when Dobbs travelled to Dublin after the meeting in Armagh and liaised with Charlemont, Grattan, Flood and James Stewart (MP for County Tyrone) in Charlemont's house in drawing up resolutions to be put to the Dungannon Convention.[112]

Representatives of 143 Volunteer corps – less than half of those then existent in Ulster – attended the Dungannon convention. The influence of Lower Orior Volunteer personnel was considerable. James Dawson was secretary. On the committee of thirty six comprised of four representatives from each Ulster county, Armagh representatives were Francis Dobbs, Francis Evans, James Dawson and John Cope. The nine members on a sub-committee to liaise with Volunteer associations in the other provinces on constitutional means of putting the convention's resolutions into operation, included Dobbs, Dawson and Evans.[113] Resolutions – with a few dissenting voices – called for legislative independence, amendment of the perpetual Mutiny Act and appointment of independent and impartial judges. Also passed – with eleven dissentients – was a resolution that support at elections be given only to candidates who promoted these measures.[114]

The Irish parliament did not respond immediately or directly to the measures proposed by the Dungannon Convention. Grattan's motion on 22 February 1782, seconded by Brownlow, which challenged parliament to state its constitutional rights, was deflected by Attorney-General Scott's amendment to adjourn by an overwhelming 137 votes to 68. Flood's motion of 25 February suffered a similar fate by 132 to 76 votes.[115] Parliament was forced to take notice in the weeks ahead, however, when county grand juries and meetings of freeholders all over the country adopted the Dungannon resolutions and threatened electoral revenge on members who rejected them.

In Armagh, at a 'numerous' county meeting of freeholders on 4 April

1782 convened by High Sheriff Henry Harden of Harrybrook, Tandragee and chaired by William Richardson, the Dungannon resolutions were read and adopted. The meeting also agreed an address for presentation to parliamentary representatives Brownlow and Dawson, amounting to an ultimatum: 'The Dungannon resolutions are by adoption ours – support them'; and directed the two members to publish their answer in the press. Richardson, Thomas Townly Dawson and Dobbs were thanked by the meeting for efficient organisation. The Armagh county freeholder meeting was followed in April 1782 by local Volunteer meetings supporting the growing campaign for constitutional reform: at Richhill chaired by Richardson, at Loughgall with Arthur Graham and Joshua McGeough sharing the chair, and at Mountnorris convened by John Blackhall and co-chaired by John McCamon and Captain John Ingram.[116]

Brownlow and Dawson published prompt replies to the ultimatum presented by the county meeting. Both approved of the sentiments of the Armagh freeholders and affirmed their support for the resolutions. Dawson assured them 'your resolutions shall have my warmest support'. Brownlow claimed 'I have anticipated your commands'. He correctly identified the key to obtaining constitutional change: 'The united voice of the people ... such union and firmness must prevail, and the happy era cannot be remote'.[117]

The 'happy era' was close at hand. Constitutional change in Ireland was facilitated by the fall of Lord North's government in March 1782, its replacement by a Whig ministry under the marquis of Rockingham and the replacement in Ireland of Carlisle and Eden by William Henry Cavendish-Bentinck, third duke of Portland and Richard Fitzpatrick on 8 April. The union of parliamentary and extra-parliamentary voices, as in 1779, had pressurised the British parliament to accede to Irish demands and, over April–May 1782, grant the measures comprising the Constitution of 1782. Leadership from County Armagh had played a leading part in initiating that union and maintaining political pressure.

Phase 6: Armagh Volunteer politics and the national issue of renunciation, June to December 1782

The second half of 1782 brought further involvement by Armagh Volunteers in national divisions over the renunciation dispute and the raising of fencible regiments. In the former, Armagh politicians were largely united behind Grattan's support for the duke of Portland's Whig administration in accepting its promise to repeal the Sixth of George I as sufficient guarantee. Lord Charlemont, in the uniform of the Armagh Southern Battalion, accompanied the duke of Portland to parliament on his arrival. Brownlow seconded Grattan's welcoming speech on 27 May 1782 which 'expatiated on the present happy situation of this country, protected in her commerce, secured in her constitution' and which promised to propose later that parliament grant £100,000 to raise 20,000 seamen for the navy of the empire. On the same day, the Dungannon resolutions and address of the 15 February were approved at a meeting of the Portadown Volunteers, signed by chairman Captain Hamlet Obins.[118]

In late May 1782, Dobbs, on behalf of the Ulster Committee of Nine, invited the Volunteer corps of Ulster to send delegates to a meeting at Dungannon to express loyalty to king, Britain and the Whig administrations in Ireland and England. And a notice from Captain James Dawson, 'secretary to the Ulster Association of Volunteers', requested 'such corps who approved the resolutions and address of the 15th February last' to enrol in the Ulster Association. Delegates of the 306 Ulster companies at Dungannon on 21 June carried unanimously the recommendation of Charlemont and Grattan for raising 20,000 seamen. Four of a group of five chosen to present a eulogistic address to the king at St James's Palace in full Volunteer uniform, had Armagh connections viz Dobbs, Evans, James Dawson and Thomas Morres Jones.[119]

In the leadership struggle between Grattan and Flood in the renunciation dispute, most Ulster Volunteer companies initially followed Grattan's government stance, though some Belfast companies later supported Flood's 'declarative renunciation' demands. Charlemont's address to the Leinster Volunteer delegates on 22 June 1782 considered 'simple repeal ... satisfactory'. An Armagh meeting of 'nobility, gentry and clergy' co-chaired by High Sheriff Harden and Lord Gosford, supported Under-secretary Sackville Hamilton's letter proposing – and one from Charlemont approving – the raising of 20,000 men for the navy.[120]

Francis Dobbs was prominent among Ulster delegates in the Grattanite National Committee accused by Belfast Companies of attempting to stage-manage consensus that 'simple repeal' of the Sixth of George I was sufficient safeguard of the Constitution of 1782. It has been argued that paucity of consultation caused the resentment and division in Volunteer ranks as much as any major concern about lack of guarantees to secure the newly-won constitution. An affronted Dobbs cited 'the great and virtuous Charlemont, and the truly amiable and respectable Grattan' as testimony to his actions and argued that 'the majority of them (the twenty five thousand Volunteers he represented) cannot be capable of nice discussions'. The angry public exchanges which followed were ironic, considering the profuse thanks of the Belfast companies to Dobbs for his services as exercising officer to the Belfast military reviews of 1781 and to the review near Belfast of sixty five corps on 31 July, 1 and 2 August 1782.[121]

A significant part of Grattan's strength had been the support of

Charlemont who, initially, interpreted and resented Flood's attacks and smears as jealousy of Grattan's national leadership.[122] After their quarrel, however, Charlemont's loyalty to Grattan gradually diminished until, in December 1782, he, too, had changed sides.[123] And Flood's vindication and ascendancy temporarily soared with the British cabinet's Renunciation Act in January 1783.[124]

Phase 7: Divisions in Armagh over fencible regiments, 1782–83

The friendship between the Grattanites and the Portland administration was put to the test by plans in the summer of 1782 to raise an Irish militia of provincial regiments called fencibles. These were to be deployed for home service only during the American war, to be commanded by local gentry on commissions from the government and paid out of the public purse. The practice was not new as the English parliament in the eighteenth century raised fencible regiments for service within the British Isles.[125]

But raising fencible regiments in Ireland was motivated by ulterior motives in 1782 when Portland desired to bring the existing Volunteer movement and its commanders under direct government control:

> The idea of provincial regiments was first suggested to me by a consideration of the various possible means of accomplishing the wishes I entertained in common with the king's ministers of restoring to the crown the sole exercise of the sword, and this was the only one which occurred to me that wore any semblance of probability. When this country had consented to part with 5,000 men, and when it was determined to remove them all to England, the defenceless state of this kingdom appeared so striking that ideas of safety united themselves to those of policy.[126]

The '5,000 men' referred to those in Luke Gardiner's bill proposing further Irish troops for the American war, a proposal supported by Brownlow on the grounds that opposition could be construed as cowardice by Irishmen and lack of confidence in the current protection afforded by the Volunteers.[127]

Using James Cuffe as intermediary, Portland offered Charlemont the position of major general of the proposed fencible regiments; but a wary Charlemont, on Grattan's advice, declined the offer and warned Portland against the plan: 'Every man who leaves the Volunteers for this new service will become odious, and the plan itself will be detested as the cause of such desertion'.[128] Portland was not deflected from his fencibles plan by Charlemont's refusal or dire prophecies and by late summer, structures were in place for raising six such regiments – four representing the four provinces, and Ulster and Munster each getting an additional regiment. Six colonels were appointed with commissions to recruit 577 men for each regiment.[129] It probably seemed an attractive proposition for recruits, offering a career, regular army pay and conditions without the danger. Weapons and equipment were to be supplied from regular army ordnance stocks. Paid commissions and high ranks were particularly seductive incentives to would-be commanders and commissioned officers. Colonels, in turn, appointed their own officers though they had an initial expense of having to provide uniform and kit for their men from their commission allowance. Not all Volunteer officers followed Charlemont's principled refusal and some, together with retired army officers and MPs, competed keenly for fencible commissions. Lord Gosford requested a commission for a 'Mr. Obins' but was informed by Portland that appointment of officers was the prerogative of fencible commanders.[130]

A double prize for Portland was the recruitment of Thomas Dawson to commander of the Royal Ulster Fencibles who brought Dobbs with him as his major. It must have seemed an attractive career move for both men who owned little or no land or property. Both were very high-profile Volunteer leaders who had initiated and led the Volunteers back into politics at the beginning of 1782; so their defection in the latter half of the year was all the more bitterly felt by many Volunteers. It was particularly ironic that the Lower Orior leadership who had been in the vanguard of Volunteer revival in County Armagh should have been among the first to defect.

The anti-fencible lobby in the Volunteer movement, aware of the government's ulterior motives, reacted with fury to protect their continued existence. Notices appeared in the press from late August exhorting Volunteer personnel to follow Charlemont's example of remaining faithful to Volunteer companies and condemning Volunteers who were deemed to have been bought over to the fencibles. Volunteer corps were exhorted and warned to 'be so tenacious of their independency and honour as to reprobate every attempt to seduce them to become mercenaries'. Invective in the press dubbed recruiting agents 'kidnappers of Volunteers', threatened that rival agencies would be formed to identify Volunteers 'who shall quit the free and independent standard of their country for the hire of a slave', and used gibes such as "that's a fensible (sic) Volunteer – a mercenary Volunteer – a ministerial Volunteer ... mercenary apostates'.[131]

The arrival of new lord lieutenant, George Nugent-Temple-Grenville, third Earl Temple and his chief secretary, William Wyndham Grenville, in September 1782 brought no change in policy by the Dublin administration. Portland's sentiments of 18 July were echoed in Temple's letter to Lord Townshend, home secretary of state: 'the sword of the Volunteers has made them masters of the country. The crown has been forced too frequently to yield to it ... and nothing can restore us to that power but the disunion of this army'.[132]

The speed at which the administration moved in forming fencible regiments over the autumn took many by surprise. Charlemont's prophecies to Portland were fulfilled and written criticisms of the fencibles and their indiscipline pervaded Dublin Castle and the press. Invective turned to violence on occasion, as on 20–21 October 1782 when Richard Talbot's undisciplined Royal Leinster Fencibles clashed with local Volunteers at Drogheda, lasting two days and resulting in deaths and wounded. A showpiece public military review was organised as a public relations exercise in Phoenix Park in November where fencible regiments were reviewed by General Burgh and Lord Charlemont. In this instance Charlemont's personal opposition to fencible regiments would seem to have been overcome by his sense of duty as privy councillor and admiration for Earl Temple.[133]

It is unclear how many Armagh Volunteers defected to Dawson's Royal Ulster Fencibles. If the three members from one company, Keady Volunteers, who followed Dawson were representative, a significant number of recruits from County Armagh joined the fencibles. That the Royal Ulster Fencibles Regiment warranted the sustained campaign by Volunteer companies and a section of freeholders in the county, to thwart enlistment in its ranks over the year of its existence and that it was only one of two fencible regiments to survive until disbandment on 1 October 1783, suggests a substantial recruitment.[134]

Yet, while concerns about the fencible proposals were expressed from early September 1782 by Volunteer companies in Belfast, Lisburn and Comber, no protest meetings were called by Volunteers in Armagh until some weeks later. Charlemont's fence-sitting and old loyalties in the Volunteer movement to Dawson and Dobbs and their efforts to justify their actions, undoubtedly influenced the delayed protest in Armagh. Dobbs published a letter on 11 August addressed to the Dungannon Volunteers of 28 June meeting defending the 'principle' behind the formation of fencible regiments and his own acceptance of a commission in Colonel Dawson's Ulster Fencibles Regiment. When First Armagh Company eventually met on 27 September to address the problem, it confessed that it would have expressed its opposition to fencible regiments much sooner: 'but for our connections with *the once-spirited southern battalion* as they have postponed their determinations through a mistaken delicacy for their lieutenant colonel and major'. Indeed, initially, delegates of the Southern Battalion of County Armagh First Ulster Regiment would seem to have condoned the actions of Dawson and Dobbs at an unpublicised meeting at Markethill on 23 September as a battalion meeting a month later was critical of earlier misrepresentation by 'previous delegated power'.[135]

The first concerns in Armagh about the raising of the fencible regiments were expressed, not by Volunteer companies, but by the freeholders in the county who met with the two-fold purpose of deciding how far the current constitutional guarantees were sufficient; and secondly, to decide how far the raising of fencible regiments was 'proper or constitutional'. A large crowd of gentry, clergy and freeholders attending the meeting in Armagh sessions-house chaired by High Sheriff Harden on 20 September seemed to have equivocated on the issue of sufficient guarantees for the 1782 constitution. While, following the Grattan-Charlemont-Dobbs line, it was unanimously resolved that the repeal of the Sixth of George I 'is a sufficient apology ... [and] satisfactory', the meeting also agreed – with two dissenting voices – that a bill of rights passed by the Irish parliament and assented to by the king should now be sought as 'solemn security and record'.

The meeting was less equivocal on the issue of fencible regiments. Having approved and justified parliament's granting 5,000 additional Irish troops for America on the grounds that 'this country was, is, and will be sufficiently protected by the spirit, number of discipline of its Volunteer army', the government's fencible proposals were roundly condemned. The meeting – again with two dissenting voices – considered 'the raising of fencible regiments as totally unnecessary for the protection of this country' and attributed the proposals 'as an insidious attempt, for private ends, to disunite and weaken the volunteer army, and to create particular influence'.[136]

The county meeting of freeholders was followed by a series of Volunteer meetings. A joint meeting of First Armagh Volunteers and Armagh Volunteer Artillery on 27 September declared fencible regiments 'totally unnecessary' and denounced defecting Volunteers as 'deserters ... deserving our severest censure'.[137] On Monday 7 October 1782 Armagh Light Dragoons adopted the resolutions of Galway Volunteers demanding a bill of rights and denouncing the 'offenceable (sic) regiments'. On the previous Thursday an address by Teemore and Johnstown Volunteers under Captain Benjamin Bell had praised Brownlow for his efforts in achieving commercial and legislative independence, expressed their detestation against fencibles and urging him to advise the Dublin administration to disband them. Brownlow concurred with their sentiments. The other county member, Thomas Dawson, who had accepted his fencible commission was censured by omission as offending defectors were not yet being publicly named.[138]

Such sensibilities were soon to be discarded with attacks on fencibles becoming personalised. A meeting of the local company of Volunteers at Keady on 27 October 1782 resolved not to continue under the command of government-controlled officers and refused to serve under Thomas Dawson and Francis Dobbs. They further deposed their own company captain, James Black for accepting a fencible commission and expelled two colleagues, William Taylor and Robert Lawson, for enlisting in the fencible regiment. All five defectors were publicly named and denounced in secretary Hamilton McCall's press report.[139]

Resentment against perceived misrepresentations condoning the proposed fencible regiments by delegates of the Southern Battalion in September 1782 resulted in an advertisement signed by two hundred and fifteen members of the Southern Battalion of First Ulster Regiment of Volunteers calling upon the battalion's officers and privates 'to a man' to meet at Markethill to voice, unequivocally, 'your own genuine opinions'.[140] Francis Evans chaired the Markethill meeting of the Southern Battalion with Samuel Cuming of Keady who had succeeded James Black as captain of Keady Company, as secretary. The ghosts of 'previous delegated power' were laid at Markethill on 22 November when the proceedings of the 23 September meeting there were expunged from the battalion's books. Fencible regiments were formally opposed, members of the battalion who had accepted fencible commissions or enlisted as privates were expelled, and corps delegates invited to attend a further meeting at Markethill on 15 February 1783 to elect a lieutenant colonel and major to replace Thomas Dawson and Francis Dobbs. One optimistic aspect for the Southern Battalion leadership was that Captain James Dawson, younger brother of Thomas, had declined a fencible post of major – for which he was thanked by the meeting.[141]

Loughgall Volunteers, under Captain John Blackhall, resolved on 29 November that fencible regiments were 'totally unnecessary' and barred Loughgall Volunteer officers and privates from enlisting as fencibles. The meeting also resolved that simple repeal of the Sixth of George I, was inadequate to safeguard recently won legislative independence without an express renunciation of the previous claim.[142] These resolutions indicated that political demands for renunciation and disbandment of fencible regiments had grown more radical in County Armagh.

CONCLUSION: NEW ISSUES IN THE 1776 GENERAL ELECTION
AND THE CAMPAIGN FOR THE CONSTITUTION OF 1782

While rivalries between leading interests continued as a key dynamic in the electioneering process and outcome of the 1776 general election for Armagh county seats, undercurrents of public opinion and freeholder power also influenced the electoral statements and decisions of candidates and potential candidates. Most candidates had learned from the elections of 1753 and the 1760s the importance of respecting the power of the electorate and public opinion. Sitting county member Brownlow would seem to have appeased his freeholders sufficiently to be able to remain abroad for most of the election period. In 1768 he had been forced by his freeholders to reject the attempt by county grand jurors to decide the county MPs. Eight years on, he bowed to pressure to avoid landlord conjunctions as a means of deciding MPs, deemed as undermining the power of a freeholder electorate. But the anti-conjunction campaign and a growing anti-government undercurrent of public opinion in the county had convinced Brownlow's former election partner, Archibald Acheson, not to make a second defence of the county seat he had first won in 1761.

With Acheson's withdrawal from the electoral arena, four new candidates – some unfamiliar to absentee landlords – replaced him. Candidates Cope, Richardson and Molyneux had ancestors who had held parliamentary seats. But newcomer Thomas Dawson had neither land nor property to provide an electoral base of freeholders, nor fortune to purchase a seat, and depended for electoral support on what was referred to as the 'popular' and/or 'independent' interest in the county. The popular/independent interest played a significant part in the 1776 election with a wave of public opinion pressurising candidates to eschew the traditional election strategy of conjunctions. The anti-conjunction campaign was promoted by candidate Arthur Cope mindful that a pact – of Brownlow and Acheson – had deprived him of a county seat in 1768. Cope's tactic of going it alone – and attempting to pressurise others to do the same – depended largely on his own large personal interest. Though Cope's campaign failed to win him a seat, it did whip up temporary opposition by freeholders to landlord conjunctions in 1776 and probably adversely affected the chances of Richardson and Molyneux who required conjunctions to succeed. The prevalence of anti-government feeling, 'independent' interests and anti-conjunction spirit in 1776 benefited Brownlow, who had the largest personal interest and mutual respect of freeholders, and the independent Dawson who had no interest of his own to trade. Both were returned without contest when Richardson, Cope and Molyneux, probably with memories of 1753, all declined a poll.

Though Molyneux's opportunism in deserting the family tradition of patriotism to run as pro-government replacement for Acheson had failed to win him an Armagh county seat, he was rewarded by government for his service with a seat on the privy council. Acheson's long service to government was also finally rewarded with a baronage in 1776, though not before a final favour to government was extracted by his briefly accepting an Enniskillen borough seat to augment voting power in the house of commons to re-elect Pery as speaker. Predictably, both sitting members, Henry Grattan and Sir Annesley Stewart were returned for Charlemont borough under the patronage of Lord Charlemont. But both members for Armagh city borough were replaced by Henry Meredyth and Philip Tisdall, servants of the primate and government.

The importance of Volunteering in the growth of a patriot opposition has been emphasised in modern research.[143] The influence of Volunteering on Armagh society progressed through several phases: initial unofficial voluntary home defence against threat of foreign invasion at the turn of 1778, official acceptance of that service in summer 1779, entry into the national free trade political campaign in late 1779, progression to agitation for legislative independence 1780–1, its key role in reactivating the campaign for the new constitution of 1782, initial solidarity with Grattan on the national issue of renunciation and in divisions over the raising of fencible regiments. As well as extending County Armagh's role in national politics, the Volunteer 'army' brought a new dimension to Armagh politics by introducing the gun into extra-parliamentary pressure to parliamentary decision-making. Armagh Volunteers, led by gentry and professional and merchant middle classes, were to the forefront in issuing 'instructions' to its county members to support free trade legislation in 1779. Brownlow resented such direction but Dawson accepted it without objection.

As elsewhere, opinion in Armagh county in late 1781 was divided between moderate and radical on how far Volunteer associations should be involved in influencing parliamentary decisions. When the fire of Volunteer politics seemed to be dying, the flames were re-kindled in east Armagh mainly through the efforts of the Dawson brothers and Francis Dobbs, resulting in the Dungannon Convention and the eventual parliamentary measure of the constitution of 1782 granted by the Whig government. On the major political issues of 1782, Armagh politicians initially tended to follow Grattan's moderate approach to 'simple appeal' of the 6 George I, though by 1783 many had switched allegiance to support Flood's demand for 'declarative renunciation'. But the crucial issue which divided Armagh Volunteers was not renunciation but fencible regiments.

In 1782, the decision of Portland and his successor, Temple, to raise government-controlled fencible regiments in Ireland in order to undermine the influence of the Volunteers was rigorously opposed by the latter and made Irish Whigs suspicious of the English Whig administration. Charlemont's wariness kept him aloof and a cautious Brownlow retained a silent independence.[144] But the impetuous Dawson and Dobbs accepted commissions in the fencible regiments without hesitation, evidence that the government scheme had found the political weakness in non-propertied Volunteers. The fencibles issue caused bitter divisions in Armagh society and politics. Families, such as the Dawsons of Clare-Castle were split over the issue. In late 1782, defectors to the fencibles – including Thomas Dawson and Dobbs – were deposed by rank and file members from their Volunteer commands. Dawson was now faced with the loss of a significant part of his electoral support for the coming general election.

Notes

1. Sir John Blaquiere to Lord Rochford, 12 Oct. 1775 (DCLA, Harcourt correspondence, MS 93, ff 261–3); Blaquiere to John Robinson, secretary of the treasury 1770–82, 2 Nov. 1775 (ibid., MS 93, ff 275–9); Lammey, 'Patriot opposition', pp 257–81.
2. Harcourt to North, 29 Mar. 1776 (DCLA, Harcourt correspondence, MS 93, ff 369–70); same to same, 6 Apr. 1776 (ibid., ff 373–4); *Commons' jn. Ire.* (Bradley), xvii, 348; ibid., xviii, 5.
3. Richard Rigby to Sir Archibald Acheso'sn, 13 May 1766 (PRONI, Gosford papers, D/1606/1/1/46).
4. Blaquiere's 1775 parliamentary list, p. 90.
5. Rigby to Acheson, 21 Jan. 1776 (PRONI, Gosford papers, D/1606/1/1/81).
6. *BNL*, 29 Dec. 1775–2 Jan. 1776.
7. *BNL*, 29 Dec. 1775–2 Jan. 1776, 9–12 Jan. 1776.
8. *BNL*, 29 Dec. 1775–2 Jan. 1776.
9. Rigby to Acheson, 21 Jan. 1776 (PRONI, Gosford papers, D/1606/1/1/81).
10. *BNL*, 9–12 Jan. 1776.
11. Lodge, *Peerage of Ireland*, vi, 78–9; A.P. Burke (ed.), *History of the landed gentry of Ireland by Sir Bernard Burke* (London, 1904; hereafter Burke, *Landed gentry*), p. 137; Collins, *County Monaghan sources*, p. 40.
12. Johnston-Liik, *Irish parliament*, iv, 31.
13. List of High Sheriffs of Co. Armagh (PRONI, T/2704/1–2); *BNL*, 6 Feb. 1770. Burke's *Landed gentry*, p. 137 gives Walter Dawson (1700–56) as having married three times: to Elizabeth Newton in 1731 – an heiress of estates in Charlesfort, Co. Wexford; to Katherine Grattan in 1741 and thirdly to widow Elizabeth Bennett by whom he had three sons, Thomas, James and Walter junior.
14. Burke, *Landed gentry*, p. 137; Collins, *County Monaghan sources*, p. 40.
15. Burke, *Landed gentry*, p. 137.
16. Johnston-Liik, *Irish parliament*, iv, 67; T.G.F. Paterson, 'The County Armagh Volunteers of 1778–93' in *UJA* (3rd series, 1941–3; hereafter Paterson, 'Armagh Volunteers'), vi, 104–5; Jonah Barrington, *Rise and fall of the Irish nation* (Dublin, 1843; hereafter Barrington, *Irish nation*), pp 144–5.
17. Parliamentary list, 1776–7, for Lord Lieutenant Harcourt, 'The parliament of Ireland, house of commons, 1776–7' (DCLA, Harcourt correspondence, MS 94, ff 227–314; hereafter Harcourt's 1776–7 parliamentary list); two parliamentary lists for Chief Secretary Sir Richard Heron, 'Irish house of commons after 1776 election' (NLI, MSS 3532, 5168, PRONI, MIC 243; hereafter Heron's 1776–7 parliamentary lists); parliamentary list for Earl Temple in G.O. Sayles, 'Sketches of the members of the Irish parliament in 1782', *RIA Proc.*, lvi (1954; hereafter Temple's 1782 parliamentary list), sect C, p. 235.
18. Malcomson, *Foster*, pp 116–7.
19. *BNL*, 9–12 Jan. 1776.
20. *BNL*, 26–30 Jan. 1776.
21. Brownlow to Acheson, 5 Mar. 1768 (PRONI, Gosford papers, D/1606/1/1/55); Bishop Garnett of Clogher to Acheson, 26 Mar. 1768 (ibid., D/1606/1/1/59).
22. *BNL*, 29 Dec. 1775–2 Jan. 1776.
23. Brownlow in Mountpellier to Charlemont, 8 Mar. 1776 (*HMC Charlemont*), i, 333–4.
24. Malcomson, *Foster*, pp 294–5; Jupp, 'County Down elections, 1783–1831', p. 183.

25 Brownlow to Charlemont, 8 Mar. 1776 (*HMC Charlemont*), i, 333–4.
26 *BNL*, 21–24 May 1776.
27 Brownlow to Charlemont, 8 Mar. 1776 (*HMC Charlemont*), i, 333.
28 Ibid., p. 124; Rigby to Acheson, 21 Jan. 1776 (PRONI, Gosford papers, D/1606/1/1/81).
29 Lady Fane to Acheson, 10 Mar. 1776 (ibid., D/1606/1/1/82).
30 Lord Sandwich to Gosford, 17 Sept. 1776 (ibid., D/1606/1/1/86B).
31 *BNL*, 4–7, 14–18 June 1776.
32 Brownlow to Charlemont, 8 Mar. 1776 (*HMC Charlemont*), i, 333–4.
33 Harcourt's 1776–7 parliamentary list.
34 Heron's 1776–7 parliamentary list.
35 Temple's 1782 parliamentary list, p. 235.
36 Johnston, *G.B. & Ire.* p. 236.
37 Parliamentary list for Sir Michael Cromie, 10 July 1777 and revised 1779–82 (Pelham papers, PRONI, T/2876/1; hereafter Cromie's 1777 parliamentary list).
38 Blaquiere to Acheson, 6 May 1776 (PRONI, Gosford papers, D/1606/1/1/83).
39 Harcourt to Acheson, 29 May 1776 (ibid., D/1606/1/1/85); *Commons' jn. Ire.* (Bradley), xviii, 8.
40 James Kelly, *Prelude to Union: Anglo-Irish politics in the 1780s* (Cork, 1992; hereafter Kelly, *Prelude to Union*), p. 202.
41 *HMC Emly*, p. 195; Blaquiere to Gosford, 4 July 1776 (PRONI, Gosford papers, D/1606/1/1/86A).
42 Harcourt 1776–7 parliamentary list; Blaquiere's 1775 parliamentary list, pp 33, 40; Peter Roebuck (ed.), *Public service and private fortune: life of Lord Macartney, 1737–1806* (Belfast, 1983), pp 89–90.
43 Thomas Waite to Robert Wilmot, 8 Dec. 1753 (PRONI, Wilmot papers, T/3019/2219); Rigby, Dublin Castle, to Wilmot, 15 and 19 Jan. 1758, (ibid., T/3019/3306, 3308).
44 Cromie's 1777 parliamentary list.
45 Johnston-Liik, *Irish parliament*, v, 246.
46 Johnston, *G.B. & Ire.*, pp 158–9; Malcomson, *Foster*, p. 34.
47 Cromie's 1777 parliamentary list.
48 Blaquiere's 1775 parliamentary list, p. 48; Harcourt's 1776–7 parliamentary list; Cromie's 1777 parliamentary list.
49 *Commons' jn. Ire.* (Bradley), xviii, 10.
50 *BNL*, 9-12 July 1776.
51 Malcomson, *Isaac Corry*, p. 5.
52 Cromie's 1777 parliamentary list.
53 Thomas Conolly to Buckinghamshire, 27 Nov. 1776 (NLI, Heron MS 13035/2); Buckinghamshire to Lord Suffolk, northern secretary of state, 20 Feb. 1777 (ibid., MS 13035/3); Speaker Pery to Heron, 11 Sept. 1777 (ibid., MS 13035/10); Buckinghamshire to Germain, secretary of state for the colonies, 20 Sept. 1777 (ibid., MS 13035/11).
54 Cromie's 1777 parliamentary list.
55 *FJ*, 18–20 Nov. 1777.
56 *FJ*, 18–20 Dec. 1777; Heron to John Robinson, 17 Dec. 1777 (NLI, Heron MS 13034/15).
57 Heron to Buckinghamshire, 7 Jan. 1778 (NLI, Heron MS 13036/2).
58 *FJ*, 7–10 Feb. 1778.
59 Buckinghamshire to Weymouth, southern secretary of state, early May 1778 (NLI, Heron MS 13036/8).

60 Buckinghamshire to Germain, 5 May 1778 (ibid.); Malcomson, *Agar*, p. 446.
61 Buckinghamshire to Germain, 27 May 1778 and Germain to Buckinghamshire, 30 May 1778 (NLI, Heron MS 13036/10).
62 Division list on the 1778 Relief Bill in the Irish house of commons, 3 Aug. 1778 (NLI, Heron MS 13060/2).
63 Division list on the 1778 Relief Bill in the Irish house of lords, 10 Aug. 1778 (ibid.). This became the Catholic Relief Act of 1778 i.e. 17 and 18 George III (1777–8) C. 49.
64 Thomas Kelly to Hon. Arthur Acheson, 28 Nov. 1776, (PRONI, Gosford papers, D/1606/1/1/87); Lord Southwell to Gosford, 2 Dec. 1776 (ibid., D/1606/1/1/88).
65 The militia was the official civilian army, trained and paid by the government when called to act as reserve to the regular army in emergency.
66 *BNL*, 2–5 Nov. 1779.
67 Paterson, 'Armagh Volunteers' vols iv–vii; Benjamin Bell to Charlemont, 12 Jan. 1780 (ibid.), vii, 82–3.
68 Heron to Buckinghamshire, 2 Apr. 1779, and Buckinghamshire to Heron, 8 Apr. 1779 (NLI, Heron MS 13037/ 7, 8).
69 P.D.H. Smyth, 'The Volunteers and Parliament, 1779–84' (hereafter Smyth, 'Volunteers') in Bartlett & Hayton, *Penal Era and Golden Age*, p. 116; Charlemont to Brownlow, Aug. 1779 (*HMC Charlemont*), i, 353; Heron to Charlemont, 21 Sept. 1779 (ibid.), i, 355.
70 *BNL*, 15–19 Oct. 1779; Brownlow to Charlemont, 18, 23 Oct. 1779 (*HMC Charlemont*), i, 355–67.
71 Smyth, 'Volunteers', p. 113.
72 Paterson, ' Armagh Volunteers', vi, 77; *BNL*, 4–18 Jan. 1780, 9–12 Sept., 23–6 Dec. 1783; T.G.F. Paterson, Derrymore, County Armagh, (Belfast, 1963), p. 5.
73 Paterson, 'Armagh Volunteers', iv, 103; M.R. O'Connell, *Irish politics and social conflict in the age of the American Revolution* (Philadelphia, 1965; hereafter O'Connell, *Irish politics*), p. 292; Charlemont to Thomas Dawson, June 1779 (*HMC Charlemont*), i, 350; Dobbs to Charlemont, 18, 27 Mar. 1780 (ibid.), i, 371–2.
74 *BNL*, 15–19 Oct., 5–9 Nov. 1779.
75 *BNL*, 12–16 Nov. 1779.
76 Brownlow to Charlemont, 23 Oct. 1779 (*HMC Charlemont*), i, 361–2; Samuel Maxwell to Charlemont, 30 Oct. 1779 (ibid.), i, 363–40.
77 Maxwell to Charlemont, 30 Oct. 1779 (ibid), i, 363; High sheriffs of County Armagh, 1593–1969 (PRONI, T/2704/1–2); grand jurors of County Armagh in Corporation Book of Armagh (PRONI, T/636/ pp 96–7); *BNL*, 29 Oct.–2 Nov., 12–16 Nov. 1779.
78 Robert Livingstone to Charlemont, 6 Nov. 1779 (*HMC Charlemont*), i, 365–6.
79 *BNL*, 12–16 Nov., 16–19 Nov. 1779.
80 Henry Grattan, junior, (ed.) *Memoirs of the life and times of the Rt. Hon. Henry Grattan by his son, Henry Grattan esq., MP* (new ed. 5 vols, London, 1849; hereafter *Grattan's Memoirs*), i, 403.
81 *BNL*, 3–7 Dec. 1779; *FJ*, 7–9 Dec. 1779.
82 *BNL*, 31 Dec. 1779–4 Jan. 1780, 7–11 Jan. 1780; Breandan Mac Suibhne, 'Whiskey, potatoes and Paddies: Volunteering and the construction of the Irish nation in North West Ulster, 1778–9' in Jupp and Magennis (eds.) *Crowds in Ireland*, p. 68.

83 *BNL*, 28–31 Dec. 1779.
84 O'Connell, *Irish politics*, pp 215–6.
85 *BNL*, 28–31 Dec., 14–18 Jan. 1780.
86 Francis Dobbs, *A letter to the Right Honourable Lord North, on his propositions in favour of Ireland* (pamphlet, Dublin, Jan. 1780).
87 *BNL*, 4–8, 11–15 Feb. 1780.
88 *BNL*, 15–18 Feb, 25–28 Apr. 1780.
89 *BNL*, 18–21, 21–25 Apr. 1780.
90 Buckinghamshire to Lord Hillsborough, 20 Apr. 1780, *Grattan's Memoirs*, ii, 51–2; *BNL*, 21–25 Apr. 1780.
91 *BNL*, 9–12 May 1780; *FJ*, 4–6 May 1780.
92 *BNL*, 26–30 May 1780.
93 *DEP*, 30 May 1780; *HJ*, 29–31 May 1780.
94 *BNL*, 25–29 Aug. 1780; *FJ*, 22–24 Aug. 1780.
95 W.E.H. Lecky, *A history of Ireland in the eighteenth century* (new impression, London, 1908; hereafter Lecky, *History*), ii, 261.
96 O'Connell, *Irish politics*, pp 258–96.
97 Ibid., pp 260–81; J.C.W. Wylie, *Irish land law* (2nd ed. Abingdon, 1986) pp 244–5; *Irish Statutes*, 19 & 20 Geo III (1779–80), C. 30.
98 *BNL*, 11–14 July 1780.
99 O'Connell, *Irish politics*, pp 275–6; *FJ*, 15–17 Aug. 1780.
100 Johnston, *G.B. & Ire.* p. 54; Buckinghamshire to Heron, 4 Jan. 1780 (NLI, Heron MS 13039/1).
101 *BNL*, 13–16 Feb. 1781.
102 *BNL*, 22–26 June 1781.
103 *BNL*, 4–7, 11–14 Dec. 1781.
104 *BNL*, 11–15 May; 20–24, 24–27, 27–31 July; 24–28, 28–31 Aug. 1781.
105 *BNL*, 14–18, 18–21, 21–25 Sept.; 28 Sept.–2 Oct. 1781; Carlisle to Hillsborough, 24 Sept. 1781, cited in O'Connell, *Irish politics*, p. 307.
106 *BNL*, 16–20 Nov. 1781.
107 *BNL*, 7–11 Dec. 1781.
108 Francis Dobbs, *A history of Irish affairs from the 12 October 1779 to the 15th September 1782* (Dublin, 1782; hereafter Dobbs, *A history*), pp 50–1.
109 *BNL*, 11–14 Dec. 1781.
110 Dobbs, *A history*, pp 47–8; *BNL*, 8–11 Jan. 1782.
111 Unaddressed letters from Charlemont, 3, 25 Jan.1782 (*HMC Charlemont*), i, 391–2, 395–6; *Grattan's Memoirs*, ii, 204.
112 *Grattan's Memoirs*, ii, 204–6; Dobbs, *A history*, pp 51–2.
113 Dobbs, *A history*, p. 53; Paterson, 'Armagh Volunteers', v, 116; *BNL*, 22–26 Feb. 1782.
114 *BNL*, 15–19 Feb. 1782; Dobbs, *A history*, pp 54–5.
115 *Commons' jn. Ire.* (Bradley), xx, 311–3; *FJ*, 23–26 Feb. 1782.
116 *BNL*, 5–9, 16–19 Apr., 30 Apr.–3 May 1782.
117 *BNL*, 12–16 Apr. 1782.
118 *BNL*, 28–31 May 1782; 7–11 June 1782.
119 *BNL*, 25–28 June 1782.
120 *BNL*, 25–28 June, 12–16, 26–30 July 1782.
121 Smyth, ' Volunteers', pp 125–6; *BNL*, 25–28 June, 28 June–2 July 1782; William Drennan to William Bruce, 6 July 1782 (PRONI, Drennan-Bruce papers, D/553/1); *BNL*, 2–5, 16–19, 19–23 July, 6–9 Aug. 1782.
122 Memoirs (*HMC Charlemont*), i, 65.

123 Charlemont to Flood, 28 Dec. 1782 (*HMC Charlemont*), i, 423–4.
124 James Kelly, *Henry Flood, patriots and politics in eighteenth century Ireland* (Dublin, 1998; hereafter Kelly, *Flood*), pp 336–8.
125 Heron to Buckinghamshire, June 1779 (NLI, Heron MS 13038/1); Connolly, *Oxford companion*, p. 189.
126 Lord Lieutenant Portland to Thomas Townshend (created Lord Sydney in 1783), secretary of state for home affairs, 18 July 1782 (H.O. 100/2, PRONI, MIC/224/2, Ireland, civil correspondence).
127 Memoirs (*HMC Charlemont*), i, 70; *Commons' jn. Ire.* (Bradley), xx, 420–1; *BNL*, 20–24 Sept. 1782.
128 Memoirs (*HMC Charlemont*), i, 71–3; *BNL*, 20–24 Sept. 1782.
129 *BNL*, 30 Aug.–3 Sept. 1782.
130 Portland to Gosford, 6 Sept. 1782 (PRONI, Gosford papers, D/1606/1/1/96B). This 'Mr Obins' may have been Gosford's son-in-law Michael Obins or, more likely, Michael's younger brother Hamlet Obins.
131 *BNL*, 27–30 Aug., 30 Aug.–3 Sept. 1782.
132 Earl Temple to Lord Townshend, 21 Sept. 1782 (PRONI, Stowe Collection, Grenville papers, ST 17, ii, cited in PRONI, ENV/5/HP/2/3).
133 *BNL*, 22–25 Oct. 1782; E.A. Coyle, 'Talbot's fencibles and the Drogheda mutiny', in *Journal of the County Louth archaeological and historical society*, xxiv (1997), pp 39, 47–9; Temple, Dublin Castle, to W.W. Grenville, 21 Dec. 1782 (*HMC, Fortescue MSS, 13th Report on the manuscripts of J.B. Fortescue, appendix 3* (London, 1892; hereafter *HMC Fortescue*)), i, 172.
134 *BNL*, 8–12 Nov. 1782, 3–7 Oct. 1783.
135 *BNL*, 3–6, 6–10, 10–13, 13–17 Sept., 27 Sept.–1 Oct., 22–26 Nov. 1782.
136 *BNL*, 20–24 Sept. 1782.
137 *BNL*, 27 Sept.–1 Oct. 1782.
138 *BNL*, 8–11, 18–22 Oct. 1782.
139 *BNL*, 8–12 Nov. 1782.
140 *BNL*, 15–19 Nov. 1782.
141 *BNL*, 22–26 Nov. 1782.
142 *BNL*, 29 Nov.–3 Dec. 1782.
143 Lammey, 'Patriot opposition', pp 276–8.
144 Kelly, *Prelude to Union*, p. 62.

5

The 1783 general election contest; Armagh MPs in parliamentary issues; the Armagh 'disturbances' 1783–90

INTRODUCTION: A NEW ADMINISTRATION, 1783

Preparations for the general election of 1783 began against a background of recovery from harvest failure in 1782.[1] Resultant rising food prices and hardship for the poor over the winter were alleviated by subscriptions from Armagh gentry to buy food. Voluntary relief was subsidised by government grant-aid following the successful bid of Armagh county MPs, Brownlow and Dawson, to new Lord Lieutenant, third Earl Temple and his brother Chief Secretary William Wyndham Grenville.[2]

In high politics, there was division on the national issues of renunciation and the government's scheme to raise fencible regiments which threatened the continuance of the Volunteers and bitterly divided Armagh politicians. The fencible proposals had been inherited from Lord Lieutenant Portland by his successor. Temple's administrative approach in high politics displayed the same pragmatism he had shown in his programme of famine relief. He bowed to demands of Irish politicians for a renunciation bill, pushed London for answers and energetically reduced waste and corruption in government departments. He was respected by Volunteer leaders – despite his efforts to undermine their influence with fencible commissions. Lord Charlemont assessed him 'the best-fitted of any [viceroy] I ever knew for the conduct of Irish affairs' – though later reduced his initial high rating during Temple's second viceroyalty from 1787 to 1789.[3]

Temple's administration was terminated in April 1783 with the formation of the Fox-North Coalition when the Irish lord lieutenant was removed to create a vacancy for the nominee of the new government. A county meeting of gentlemen, clergy and freeholders in Armagh on 2 May 1783 moved an address through High Sheriff Sir Walter Synnot praising Temple for his reform of abuses in government departments.[4] Fox's friend Robert Henley, second earl of Northington, was appointed on 3 May and sworn on 3 June. W.W. Grenville remained as chief secretary until the end of August along with Under-secretary Sackville Hamilton during the general election held over the summer months. Before then, preliminary canvassing was well underway in County Armagh.

THE 1783 CONTEST FOR ARMAGH COUNTY SEATS

In mid-October 1782 an unsigned press advertisement had advised the County Armagh electorate of an imminent requisition for a meeting to choose candidates for the general election and requesting 'as you value the independence of your county, to hold yourselves disengaged until the sense of that meeting be taken'. This notice was quickly followed by an address from the Teemore and Johnstown Volunteers to William Brownlow, extolling his record on political and constitutional achievements and requesting him to advise the Dublin administration against fencibles. The omission of any mention of the other sitting county member, their close neighbour Thomas Dawson, had an ominous message for him.[5]

Dawson was not prepared to surrender his seat without a fight. He was first candidate to press with his election notice from Clare-Castle dated 10 December 1782 – within three weeks of his dismissal as leader of the Southern Battalion of Volunteers – appealing for electoral support on his record of political service and justifying his haste to press by the necessity to refute a smear he alleged was being circulated against him by the anti-fencible lobby:

> I feel most sensibly, the impropriety of so early an address to you, but I trust that the active canvass now making to supplant me, and the reports industriously propagated that I shall not again offer myself to represent you in parliament, will plead my excuse.[6]

With political society divided on the issues of renunciation, an Irish bill of rights and fencible regiments, Dawson had cause for concern, as the politically-conscious wing of the anti-fencible and pro-renunciation wing of the Volunteers dominated press coverage while government supporters remained mostly silent. Yet the election prospects of pro-government candidates in open constituencies were not as hopeless as the impression conveyed in the press campaign. Indeed, whether Volunteers should use their organisation for electioneering was being debated in spring 1783 when some Volunteer companies argued that Volunteers, per se, should remain aloof from politics. A meeting of Monaghan Rangers on 31 March argued that publication of resolutions on political subjects was 'unbecoming the dignity of Volunteers' and resolved that 'the interference of Volunteers, as such, in electioneering matters is unconstitutional ... *freeholders*, not men in arms, should settle the business of elections'.[7] But, on the evidence of press notices, apolitical Volunteer corps would seem to have been in a small minority.

With Brownlow an established incumbent and reasonably assured of being returned, competition for the second Armagh county seat would be between Dawson and challenger William Richardson of Richhill. Both had obviously decided early to contest the 1783 election. One week after publication of Dawson's early election address, Richardson published his election intentions, apologising, like Dawson, for a 'premature' address but excusing it because of pressure from similar declarations. Richardson cited the long parliamentary service of his late father when appealing for electoral support.[8]

Following his early withdrawal as candidate from the 1776 general election in the face of the phenomenal swing of the popular vote to Dawson, professional lawyer Richardson had bided his time for an opportunity to follow the family tradition into parliamentary politics. He sought to build a reputation and political base at local level, moving from Dublin to Richhill, serving as high sheriff of County Armagh 1777–8 and as member of the county grand jury from Lent 1779 to Lent 1783. He was elected captain of Richhill Company of Volunteers and major in Brownlow's battalion.[9]

Richardson was also earning goodwill and a reputation as tolerant benefactor in his local community and beyond. In 1782, James Todd, local Dissenting minister publicly thanked Richardson for donating a rent-free site on perpetual lease in Richhill and a 'bountiful subscription, not solicited'; and praised his record as a generous landlord and promoter of civil and religious liberties. It was a timely tribute to Richardson as a general election approached. When Dawson was dismissed from the Volunteers, Richardson seized the opportunity and followed Dawson's election notice with his own on 23 December 1782.[10]

In late 1782, Volunteer companies in Armagh pressed for a renunciation act and disbandment of fencible regiments.[11] The issue of British renunciation was removed from the electoral agenda by British Home Secretary Thomas Townshend's motion, seconded by Irish Chief Secretary Grenville and carried in Westminster on 22 January 1783.[12] Election issues in press correspondence thereafter concentrated on the issues of fencibles and parliamentary reform. Demands for parliamentary reform were raised at a meeting of the Clogher Volunteers on 15 February 1783.[13] A meeting of Munster Volunteer delegates in Cork on 1 March proposed measures for both economical and parliamentary reform and resolved that election candidates should sign a pledge to obey the instructions of constituents and reject all influence, bribery and corruption.[14]

Similar criteria for 'an honourable discharge of parliamentary duty' were recommended by the Constitution Club of Lisburn and adopted by the inhabitants of Lisburn at a meeting on 26 March when nominating local Volunteer leaders Lieutenant Colonel William Sharman of Moira-Castle and Captain William Todd Jones of Lambeg as candidates to oppose Lord Hertford's nominees for the two seats of Lisburn pot-walloping borough situated on the Hertford estate. Obedience to constituents and avoidance of 'the paths of venality' were promised to the Lisburn electorate in the public acceptance of nomination by Sharman and Jones.[15] The rhetoric of Belfast Society on 16 April 1783 – with toasts such as 'May Ireland never want hemp to exalt all fencible commanders who deserve it … May no fencible ever enjoy a fair bedfellow' and to 'the free and independent electors of the County Armagh' – was a signal to Volunteers everywhere in the approaching general election to reject sitting MPs who had accepted commissions in fencible regiments.[16] Thus was targeted Thomas Dawson.

Armagh county, whose independent politics had found favour with the Belfast Society, also had a direct connection with the Lisburn election when John Moore junior, of Drumbanagher was nominated by the first marquess of Hertford as a candidate for a Lisburn borough seat – to be opposed by the two independent candidates for Lisburn extolled in the Belfast Society's toast. Moore's connection with Hertford was through the sixth earl of Drogheda – Moore's kinsman – who was married to Hertford's daughter. Hertford 'donated' one Lisburn borough seat to his son-in-law, Drogheda, who passed it to Moore. The gift turned into a hot potato for Moore in 1783 when Sharman and Jones contested the proprietorial rights of Hertford to Lisburn borough, reminding the 'independent electors' of Lisburn that 'times are gloriously changed'.[17]

Over the summer of 1783, the Volunteer movement accelerated the campaign for parliamentary reform and for radical candidates who supported it. Reviews of Ulster Volunteer corps at Belfast, Lisburn and Broughshane called for 'a more equal representation of the people in parliament', a tax on absentees and an Irish bill of rights. A 'committee of correspondence' was formed at Lisburn to co-ordinate communication. Prominent among Volunteer leaders present were Lord Charlemont and Armagh High Sheriff Synnot whose Volunteer profile had risen since his appointment as lieutenant colonel of the Southern Battalion of Volunteers in succession to the deposed Thomas Dawson and use of his own company, the Armagh Rangers, as a law-enforcing agency in south Armagh.[18]

Delegates were instructed to attend a further meeting at Dungannon on 8 September with written declarations as to whether their companies supported parliamentary reform.[19]

With Volunteer companies across the country becoming more involved in parliamentary politics and elections, freeholder organisations had taken a back seat. However, the absence of Volunteer military reviews in Armagh in summer 1783 afforded opportunity for freeholders to become involved in general election publicity. A published eulogy to sitting member Brownlow from 'a freeholder' chided electors for their silence to date and appealed to them to request a requisition for a meeting to give public thanks to Brownlow for his service and to formally nominate him as their representative. The hitherto silent Brownlow – perhaps assuming his high Volunteer profile was sufficient publicity – responded by publishing his first election manifesto addressed to his 'old friends' the freeholders of the county of Armagh confirming his candidature.[20]

Further press coverage of events in Armagh followed a meeting of Loughgall parishioners who published thanks to the county gentry for subscriptions to buy food for the poor during the high prices following the harvest failure of 1782. Particular gratitude was expressed to the lord lieutenant for his aid following representations from county members Brownlow and Dawson to whom a special address was directed. Both MPs returned thanks. Dawson, target of anti-fencible attacks, had the more reason to be thankful for public recognition of his services. William Richardson – of Loughgall parish but excluded from those Armagh gentry thanked for contributions – was stung by the above address, and by the issue of the writs for the election on 26 July 1783, into up-dating his election manifesto on 28 July 1783.[21]

Meanwhile, two of the Armagh gentry were enjoying mixed fortunes in election contests outside the county. Isaac Corry of Derrymore, popular Newry Volunteer leader, government opponent, supporter of parliamentary reform and then friend of Charlemont and Grattan, topped the poll of four candidates in the pot-walloping borough of Newry on 11 August. Sitting members Corry, with the blessing of the absentee Nedham family, and Colonel Robert Ross of Rostrevor, protégé of Lord Hillsborough and government supporter, obtained 335 and 332 votes respectively to defeat Alexander Stewart, younger brother of Robert Stewart, sitting member for Down county, and John McClintock of Drumcar, County Louth.[22]

John Moore junior was intimidated into defeat in a contest for the Lisburn borough seat he had believed was in the gift of Lord Hertford.[23] Moore, still searching for his maiden seat, turned again to Lord Drogheda who provided him with another of his borough seats. Moore's father-in-law, Sir Annesley Stewart of County Donegal, having initially taken Lord Drogheda's borough seat at Ballynakill, Queen's County, elected to switch to Charlemont borough controlled by another in-law, Lord Charlemont, to accommodate Moore with a Ballynakill seat. It was the seat 'given' to John Moore senior for the 1768 parliament following the purchase of Ballynakill by Lord Drogheda from the Barrington family.[24]

The influence of radical Volunteer politics was not a definitive predictor of success in Ulster elections during August 1783. The victory of Sharman and Jones – with intimidatory supporters from Belfast – was the first occasion that Hertford's political bastion in Lisburn had been stormed. High-ranking Volunteer officers Hercules Rowley and John O'Neill were returned for County Antrim. But not all Volunteers were successful. In a three-cornered contest for the two Down county seats, popular Volunteer Colonel Robert Stewart lost his seat to Edward Ward – raising some doubt on the invincibility of high-profile Volunteer candidates. In Fermanagh, sitting member Mervyn Archdall was returned for the county despite his acceptance of a fencible commission.[25] The stormy and highly publicised Lisburn poll may have influenced Armagh gentry and freeholders to requisition High Sheriff Synnot who called a county meeting on 9 August in Armagh courthouse to nominate their representatives in the next parliament and thus avoid a poll.[26]

Of the three Armagh candidates, Brownlow was favourite for re-election due to his status as elder statesman, respected country gentleman, captain of the Lurgan company of Volunteers and lieutenant colonel of the Armagh Northern Battalion of First Ulster Regiment.[27] Quintessential patriot and spokesman in the house of commons, he was now facing his fifth election in thirty years. While Rev. Todd's letter reminded Presbyterians that they owed Richardson a favour for his gift of a rent-free site in Richhill on freehold lease, a published letter from Dissenter James Birch of Dromara suggested that Brownlow was also winning support from Dissenter congregations in County Armagh opposed to him in 1753.[28]

The other sitting member, Dawson, was being pushed strongly by Richardson for the second seat. As Richardson's ancestors had been involved in Armagh local and parliamentary politics for over a hundred years and had developed a significant political interest, Richardson might well have considered an Armagh county seat as part of his birthright. His growing status, residence in Armagh and development of the family political interest, put him in a stronger position than in 1776 to challenge Dawson's more vulnerable position in the county and re-gain the seat for the Richardsons. Castle circles tipped Richardson to take the seat from Dawson.[29]

The political future of Thomas Dawson was in a precarious position in 1783. His dismissal as Volunteer leader by grass-roots Volunteer members in late 1782 had been a huge blow to his chances of being returned given his dependence on popular political support as he remained 'a man of no property' with little or no estate in the county and few freehold votes of his own.[30] His strengths were his organisational skills and cool-headed leadership which had underpinned his rise in the Volunteer ranks from relative obscurity and been admired by Lord Charlemont, and had so impressed government interests as to be offered a fencible regiment. Charlemont praised Dawson's contribution to the Volunteer movement even after the latter's dismissal from it 'having been one of my principal and most trusty agents in quelling the more violent, and in securing moderate measures ... he was to me and to the country an irreparable loss'. Charlemont considered Dawson's acceptance of a fencible regiment as insufficient reason for voting against him in the coming election and, magnanimously, decided to now give Dawson his own interest – which he had refused him in 1776.[31]

Dawson's prestige remained sufficiently high within the county to co-chair with Synnot a meeting of freeholders in Armagh courthouse on 20 May 1783 called to vote on an address of thanks to George III for 'the late Irish Legislation Bill passed in England', i.e. the British Renunciation Act of January 1783.[32] In July, Dawson's stock was still high in Loughgall for his negotiation of government relief for the poor.[33] Another factor in Thomas Dawson's favour was the secretarial skills and prestige of his younger brother, James, barrister and secretary of a group of independent freeholders in the county chosen to support Dawson and Brownlow in the coming election. James Dawson's continuing high profile in the Volunteer movement – he would serve as secretary at the Dungannon meeting on 8 September 1783 – may have mitigated his older brother's fall from grace in the movement and retained some Volunteer support for Thomas in the election.[34]

The major factor in Dawson's bid to retain his seat would be how much ground he had lost among the main political interests by his defection to the fencibles. It was an issue obviously engaging the minds of those Armagh freeholders who met on 9 August to consider 'the merits of the several candidates, and putting into nomination such gentlemen as they may think proper persons to represent them in the next parliament'.[35] The outcome of this meeting did not remove the necessity of a poll. Subsequent press notices suggested that all three candidates received significant support at the meeting. Richardson was selected as a candidate, in his words, 'by a considerable majority of independent freeholders'.

However, a notice from 'the independent freeholders of the county of Armagh' thanked Dawson for his 'open, candid, and unsolicited declaration of his principles at the county meeting' and pledged their support at the coming poll for 'him and his worthy colleague [Brownlow], who have been faithful in the discharge of their duty in parliament'. The notice added a significant rider 'and to convince every candidate that they will, on every future occasion, expect a declaration of the principles of an untried man, and be happy to receive a renewal of profession, even from an approved man'. The implication was that Richardson had not made such a declaration at the county meeting and he was stung into responding through his counsellor John McKinstry attesting to Richardson's sworn declaration to take direction from constituents and to support constitutional reform for their enhanced representation.[36] The above group of 'independent freeholders' was probably the same as that chaired by John Blackhall who supported the Dawson-Brownlow pairing as candidates and, in a very unusual resolution, proposed to set up a committee to collect private subscriptions to defray the election expenses of Thomas Dawson and Brownlow.[37] Such financial assistance would have been particularly appreciated by the impecunious Dawson.

As the county meeting called by Synnot on 9 August did not specify which political interests supported which candidate, the sources of votes for each candidate are conjectural. Brownlow's political interest, prestige and long parliamentary service would undoubtedly guarantee his return. Richardson could hope for second votes from Brownlow, his commander in the northern Battalion of the Volunteers, and from Lord Gosford, his brother-in-law. Gosford, as a government supporter, may have had mixed feelings over his political affiliations on this occasion, but seems to have supported Richardson despite the latter's patriot affiliations. In May the absentee Lord Sandwich had replied to Gosford that he would instruct his agent Sweetman to direct his Armagh interest to Richardson.[38] The problem of canvassing joint family interests became evident some six weeks later when Sandwich chided Gosford for omitting to ask Madame de Salis for the Tawnavaltiny interest and Lady Fane for her Clare-Castle interest through jointure, informing Gosford that the 'piqued' ladies would support Dawson. Sandwich had requested the influential Sweetman to follow Gosford's wishes and the agent would probably advise Sandwich's freeholders at Ballyclare to vote for Richardson.[39]

The sources of Dawson's votes remain largely conjectural. He would appear to have received the interests of Lady Fane on the Clare estate where he lived and those of the neighbouring Tawnavaltiny estate of Madame de Salis. He probably received a large block of votes from the Cope estate at Loughgall who had commended his service in July and whose agent John Blackhall had chaired the group of independent freeholders backing the sitting members. He undoubtedly received the electoral support promised him by those 'independent freeholders' based on old friendships and his past record. He also probably received the promised interest of Lord Charlemont.[40]

Synnot opened the County Armagh poll on Thursday 28 August 1783. For the first week Brownlow led, with Dawson second and Richardson a close third. By close of poll on Saturday evening, 30th August, Brownlow had polled 409 votes, Dawson 235 and Richardson 221. By close on Wednesday 3 September, the poll stood at: Brownlow 1,010, Dawson 567, Richardson 546. Thereafter, Richardson began to overhaul Dawson. The poll continued until Saturday morning 6 September when Dawson notified Synnot that he was withdrawing. The poll continued for about an hour until Synnot declared Brownlow and Richardson elected.[41] Figures given for the final poll were: Brownlow, 1,414; Richardson, 800; and Dawson, 755.[42]

Supporters of Richardson attempted to play down the closeness of his victory over Dawson, claiming that Richardson had more votes to come and had 'above four hundred freeholders unbroken, to support him, if he had thought it needful to resort to his own, and other estates in said county'.[43] While such brinkmanship now seems unusual by a candidate fighting for his maiden seat and running last for the first seven days of polling, an election strategy deployed at eighteenth century polls was to withhold an assured interest until a critical phase of the poll when its deployment would discourage further opposition from potential voters of wavering opponents.

After the 1783 election, Thomas Dawson disappeared from the Armagh political scene. His military career seems to have ended when the Royal Ulster Provincial Regiment of fencibles was discharged at Armagh on 1 October 1783. The de-commissioning of the fencibles and loss of income left many of its former officers – some of whom had incurred personal expense in raising the regiments – financially embarrassed. Francis Dobbs, for example, found himself in financial difficulties at this time. Dawson continued residence in Clare-Castle after 1783 but now reduced to a lodger of new occupant, Lee, until the great house was totally destroyed by an accidental fire in October 1785.[44] The impoverished Dawson sought recompense from the government for his thwarted political career and expenses incurred on the short-lived fencible regiments and was rewarded when returned as a government nominee for Sligo borough.[45]

RETURN OF ARMAGH MPs FOR BOROUGH SEATS IN 1783

Sitting members were returned for both parliamentary boroughs on 4 August 1783. Contemporary surveys for the administration confirmed the primate's control of Armagh borough and the continuing allegiance of its parliamentary members – Robinson's ageing agent Henry Meredyth and George Rawson – to government, and updated information on the primate-borough's incumbent members.[46] Sir Annesley Stewart, and Rt Hon. Henry Grattan were returned for Charlemont borough.[47] In 1783, retired banker Stewart, as in-law of Lord Charlemont and the Moore families of Drumbanagher and Drogheda, had the option of Charlemont and Ballynakill borough seats. He chose the former which he had served for twenty years, allowing his nephew and son-in-law, John Moore junior, to succeeed John Moore senior in Ballynakill.[48] The government surveys of 1782 and 1783 confirmed Stewart's continuing opposition to the government. They updated Grattan's political record as having led the opposition in the last session of Earl Temple's administration but having supported that of Portland. The Castle parliamentary list in 1783 predicted that Grattan would 'probably oppose' Northington's administration.[49]

Other aspiring members of parliament who resided in County Armagh had mixed fortunes in 1783. Following the death in March 1782 of his brother-in-law and patron John Garnett, bishop of Clogher, Sir Capel Molyneux, having served as member of parliament for twenty two years, was not returned for the Clogher borough seat by Garnett's successor Bishop John Hotham. Sir Capel, who had ambitions to promote his sons' careers, had some consolation when his second son George William Molyneux, a lawyer, succeeded in purchasing a Granard borough seat and entered parliament 'in opposition'.[50]

The Acheson family of Markethill also had ambitions to update the family tradition of having a member in the house of commons, a tradition broken since Sir Archibald Acheson's elevation to the peerage in 1776. Sir Archibald's attempt to earmark a seat for his son Arthur as far back as 1772 – when he had asked Lord Lieutenant Townshend to translate his brother-in-law Walter Cope, bishop of Clonfert to the vacant bishopric of Ferns which had parliamentary borough seats for disposal by the incumbent bishop – came to nothing then when Cope was not transferred.[51] The Acheson family had to wait a further ten years, until 9 August 1782, before Bishop Walter Cope was translated from Clonfert to the sees of Ferns and Leighlin.[52]

Arthur Acheson and family, having lived for 'many years' on the continent, returned to Dublin with fortune depleted. In September 1782, with a general election approaching, Arthur approached Dublin Castle. Chief Secretary Fitzpatrick, in the process of leaving post, passed Acheson's request to his successor W.W. Grenville.[53] The thirty seven year old Acheson, outside mainstream politics for upward of ten years and – whether desiring to remain independent of family ties or considering himself to be estranged from both his father and uncle – had written also for support from former acquaintance Lord Edward Bentinck, brother of the outgoing Lord Lieutenant Portland. Bentinck advised Acheson:

> ... my brother [Portland] tells me he understood the first condition your father made was that you should live with him. He has all the

reason to believe your uncle [Bishop Walter Cope] is your sincere friend and will do (if he has not done) all he can with your father in your favour. One thing he desires me to set you right in, as to what regards the condition for the boroughs. My brother has no recommendation to give, as he transacted the business as lord lieutenant and it consequently belongs to the present lord lieutenant [Temple] to recommend or to whomsoever may be the lord lieutenant at the time of the dissolution of the parliament, the condition being made for government ... .[54]

Acheson pursued correspondence with the Bentinck family and new Lord Lieutenant Northington over the summer of 1783.[55] He submitted his candidature for Old Leighlin borough, County Carlow for which he was returned in August 'by the recommendation of my good friend Lord Northington' as a supporter of the latter's administration.[56] Undoubtedly the services of Lord Gosford and Bishop Walter Cope to government were a factor in Acheson's return. Gosford was a valued, experienced advisor to government. In November 1782 Lord Lieutenant Temple had requested his attendance at an emergency privy council meeting in Dublin to deal with a food shortage following failure of the harvest.[57] In summer 1783, Edmund Sexton Pery, speaker of the house of commons since 1772, requested and was promised Gosford's support in the approaching election for the chair.[58] Gosford's on-going support for successive administrations was recognised in 1785 when Northington apologised for omitting to remind his successor, the duke of Rutland, that he had promised advancement in the peerage to Gosford for supporting the administration. Northington also supported Gosford's case for promotion by reference to his brother-in-law, Bishop Cope of Ferns, being the only bishop out of the four holding parliamentary boroughs who gave both seats to government nominees.[59] Baron Gosford was raised to the viscountcy on 20 June 1785.[60]

But Arthur Acheson's support of government was less constant to the new administration as that of his father, and Arthur was not prepared to donate his vote freely to his friend Northington's Pittite successor, Rutland. The price of Acheson's vote was reckoned to be a 'place or pension' in April 1784 when he was assessed by Orde as 'contra' to government. With Buckingham's return as lord lieutenant in 1787, however, Acheson was reckoned to have softened to 'doubtful' and as being prepared to give provisional support to government.[61]

INVOLVEMENT OF ARMAGH MPs IN KEY NATIONAL ISSUES, 1783–90:
VOLUNTEERS; CATHOLICS AND PARLIAMENTARY REFORM, 1783–5

The period 1783–90 brought a host of perceived constitutional, social and economic grievances before the Irish parliament and pressures upon the administration of the day, often impinging upon the Anglo-Irish relationship. Armagh politicians played significant roles in all these. Lord Northington's short administration from May to December 1783 faced demands for parliamentary reform and was concerned at attempts to mobilise support for the campaign from extra-parliamentary forces such as the Volunteers and Catholics.[62] The political vacuum left after the successful renunciation agitation by the Volunteers to 22 January 1783 was filled by a campaign for parliamentary reform thereafter. Whether Catholic suffrage should be part of the programme of parliamentary reform proved to be a divisive issue.[63]

While Frederick Hervey, earl-bishop of Derry and the liberal William Todd Jones of Moira were committed to the enfranchisement of Irish Catholics, most Irish reformers did not wish the issue raised at all, lest it divide the wider reform movement. Thus the support for Catholic relief displayed in 1782 and early 1783 had evaporated by the end of 1783 when politicians were faced with the real possibility of having to share political power. This was observed to be the case in Armagh by the Rev. William Campbell, Presbyterian minister there 1764–89. Politicians such as Charlemont, Brownlow and Grattan side-stepped the issue at every turn fearing that enfranchisement of Catholics would lead to a transfer of political power from Protestant to Catholic hands. Nor were Catholics encouraged to become activists in the parliamentary reform movement by a conservative Catholic hierarchy led by John Thomas Troy, archbishop of Dublin, suspicious of Hervey's promotion of Gallicanism and satisfied to leave further Catholic relief to the goodwill of the government; nor by the Catholic Committee still dominated until 1792 by the conservative Catholic aristocracy of Lords Kenmare, Fingall and Gormanston. Both bodies advocated a policy of non-intervention by Catholics in the movement for parliamentary reform.[64] And thus the main extra-parliamentary force for reform came from the Volunteers.

It has been argued that the Volunteer-led agitation for parliamentary reform in 1783 was the first campaign led by middle-class members – rather than by moderate patriots from the gentry – with the objective of broadening parliamentary representation to reflect their own aspirations.[65] Agitation intensified over autumn 1783, building up pressure on the new house of commons due to assemble in October 1783 to reform the electoral process. The campaign was strongest in Ulster. In late summer, a 'specific plan of reform' was formulated for approval by an Ulster assembly of

Volunteer delegates scheduled for 8 September 1783 in Dungannon.[66] Its content was influenced by contemporary English radical reformers and the Lisburn Corresponding Society led by Sharman and Jones to include demands for parliamentary sessions, election by ballot, disfranchisement of rotten boroughs and extension of the elective franchise to persons of all religions.

Armagh Volunteer leaders were deeply involved in the new campaign. Captain James Dawson, secretary to the Ulster Association of Volunteers summoned Ulster companies to the Dungannon rally. Other delegates from Armagh were Lord Charlemont, Lieutenant Colonel Brownlow, Lieutenant Colonel Synnot and Sir Capel Molyneux.[67] But all was not well with the new Volunteer initiative as their former unity was fragmenting. The Dungannon meeting was attended by delegates from only 272 companies. This significant decrease from the number of companies represented at the Dungannon Convention in February 1782 reflected a growing unease among Volunteer companies and probable diminution in membership. It has been estimated that Armagh's 23 companies represented were less than half the county's total strength.[68]

The decrease in 1783 resulted from multiple factors: the bitter divisions in the county over the fencible regiments, the confrontational stance of some corps over renunciation, the county election contest, government peace overtures to America, unease over the programme of parliamentary reform – particularly proposals for Catholic suffrage – and the method of procedure which appeared to trespass upon parliament's legislative authority. To avoid further divisions at Dungannon, resolutions based on 'the specific plan of parliamentary reform' were referred to a National Convention of Volunteers in Dublin in November with little debate on the controversial issue of Catholic relief. Sir Capel Molyneux was appointed Armagh Volunteer representative to attend the National Convention.[69]

Supporters of parliamentary reform in County Armagh attempted to whip up support. At a meeting of the Armagh grand jury on 20 September 1783 fifteen members adopted the Dungannon resolutions.[70] A few days later Sheriff Synnot was requested by freeholders to call a county meeting for 7 October in Armagh courthouse to instruct its representatives on the 'great national question, a reform in the representation of the people'. Among resolutions passed on the 7 October were:

> That every representative is bound in duty to obey the instructions of his constituents, and that when he ceases to speak their sentiments in parliament, he ceases to be a constitutional representative. ... That we consider a reform in the representation of this country a measure of the highest moment and consequence, and in which the rights and liberties of freemen are particularly interested.[71]

Synnot's published address to Brownlow and Richardson conveyed the instructions from the meeting. Brownlow gave a public assurance that he had always promoted parliamentary reform, opposed corruption and would zealously continue to do so; though his old resentment at being told what to do by constituents would seem to have been reactivated in his comment 'I am sensible that your instructing your representatives on this occasion does not arise from doubt, but only to show your earnestness in the great cause Ireland is now engaged in'. Richardson showed no such sensitivity in giving an unqualified pledge of compliance with his constituents' wishes.[72]

Over autumn 1783, doubts and divisions emerged both in the Volunteer movement and among patriot members of parliament. Grattan confounded Castle predictions by joining Northington's broad-bottom administration and the rivalry between Flood and he flared up again during the debate on 3 November in the house of commons on the old issue of augmentation of Irish military forces. When Flood moved that the termination of the American War provided an excellent opportunity of reducing the number of Irish soldiers from 15,000 to 12,000, Grattan countered with the argument that the augmented Irish army was Ireland's contribution to the defence of the empire and a return for Ireland's protection by the British navy. Flood was supported in debate by Isaac Corry and George William Molyneux. The motion was defeated by 132 votes to 58. Grattan's speech and vote against Flood's motion was seen as a betrayal of his former patriot principles and, in the division, Stewart, his colleague for Charlemont borough, voted against him.[73]

Grattan's support for the Northington administration also caused an irreparable breach with Lord Charlemont in opposition. The latter, who tended to personalise political quarrels, regarded Grattan's flirtation with Northington as a betrayal which he never fully forgave despite Grattan's expressions of contrition and attempts at restitution. When Grattan offered not to attend meetings at Dublin Castle unless Charlemont was also invited, his offer was 'received with coldness'. When he offered to finance the introduction to parliament of any nominee by Charlemont to offset his own apostasy as perceived by Charlemont, the latter refused to nominate anyone. And when Grattan paid £2,000 for an Enniskillen borough seat for James Stewart, son of Sir Annesley, to support Charlemont's policies, Charlemont stubbornly insisted: 'He is your friend in parliament, and there only ceases to be mine' – despite the fact that Stewart was an in-law of Charlemont and opposed Grattan on the augmentation issue.[74]

In the weeks following the Dungannon meeting the ranks of the Volunteers also continued to divide into a group led by Hervey seeking a radical franchise – including Catholic suffrage in the programme of parliamentary reform – and a group led by the cautious Charlemont who was uneasy about parliament's growing resentment at what was perceived as a self-destructive programme of change and at an armed extra-parliamentary force's attempt to intimidate parliament into passing it. While political leaders in Armagh, generally, opposed radical measures such as Catholic relief, divisions in the Volunteer ranks would seem to have been concealed as far as possible and when Hervey made his dramatic three days journey from Derry to Dublin in early November, a report described his triumphant reception in Armagh 'amid the exclamations and benedictions of several thousands ... and [Volunteer companies] showed him every respect which his patriotic behaviour hitherto deserves'. And, despite the rivalry between the two peers for leadership of the Volunteer movement in 1783, Charlemont observed the normal courtesies when Hervey arrived at his house in Palace Street, Dublin at noon on Friday 7 November by entertaining the earl-bishop to breakfast.[75]

Protestant fears of a Catholic take-over of Irish politics at the National Convention led to Catholic suffrage being dropped from the programme of parliamentary reform forwarded to parliament thus allowing the Armagh members to support it; and when Henry Flood moved to bring in a bill 'for the more equal representation for the people in parliament' on 29 November 1783 it was seconded by Brownlow. But Chief Secretary Pelham had whipped up the fears of government that an armed assembly was attempting to impose its will on parliament.[76] Attorney-general Yelverton immediately opposed Flood's motion on the grounds 'If this bill, as it is notorious it does, originates from an armed body of men, I reject it. Shall we sit here to be dictated to by the point of the bayonet?' Brownlow responded: 'I am surprised to see an opposition to this bill on the principles I hear; the phantom of armed men adduced as argument to preclude the discussion of a measure which almost every gentleman approves'. Molyneux attacked opponents of Flood's motion for 'such illiberal reflections' on the Volunteers whom he described as 'saviours of their country'.[77]

Flood's motion was rejected by an emphatic 157 votes to 77. Brownlow, Richardson, Grattan, Stewart, Molyneux and Corry were in the minority who supported the motion. Among those opposing it were: Meredyth, Rawson, Moore and Arthur Acheson, the latter still in support of government.[78] This crushing defeat was a serious setback for the Volunteers and parliamentary reform and brought confusion among reformers as to the best way forward. The attack by the house of commons upon the Volunteers left some reformers wondering if Volunteer muscle on that occasion had been counter-productive and whether future rallies for reform should be left to freeholder meetings rather than Volunteer assemblies. However, the Volunteers embarked on a campaign of petitions to parliament over the winter and spring of 1783–4, moderated by Lord Charlemont and following established constitutional procedures which they hoped might bring a more favourable response from parliament.

Freeholders also began to organise petitions for parliamentary reform. County Armagh freeholders claimed to be the first to call for a meeting after the rejection of Flood's bill. Within days of the defeat Armagh freeholders requisitioned Sheriff Synnot to call a county meeting. Synnot fixed a county meeting for 23 December 1783 in Armagh court-house to consider a petition to parliament for better representation and to instruct members of parliament.[79]

Not to be outdone, a 'full meeting of the Lurgan Company of Volunteers on parade' on 18 December passed an address of thanks to Brownlow, their captain, for his efforts to have parliament reformed. Brownlow published his appreciation, suggesting it had been 'ill-founded jealousy' and a misrepresentation by the house of commons – that the National Assembly was using the Volunteers to intimidate parliament – that had resulted in refusal of parliamentary reform. He urged a constitutional way forward:

> If the united voice of the nation shall persist in calling for a reform, and proceed with firmness and temper in that pursuit, sooner or later it must prevail. I shall be ever ready to cooperate with you in every constitutional means of establishing and maintaining the rights of the people.

Two days later, two hundred freeholders from the manor of Brownlow's-Derry met in Lurgan on 20 December 1783 with Adam Cuppage in the chair to prepare for the Armagh meeting. They approved the Plan of Reform of the National Assembly and appointed freeholder delegates to present it at the coming county meeting of freeholders in Armagh, recommending its adoption for presentation to parliament by Brownlow and Richardson supported by a petition. Thanks were passed to Lord Charlemont and other members of the National Convention who were exhorted to persist in their efforts for parliamentary reform.[80]

The county meeting of freeholders in Armagh on 23 December chaired by Synnot appointed a sub-committee who prepared resolutions adopting the National Convention's Plan of Reform as the programme to be supported by county petition and presented to parliament by Brownlow and Richardson. A committee of Synnot, Brownlow, Richardson, Sir Capel Molyneux senior, Capel Molyneux junior, John Blackhall, James Johnston, Robert Jackson, Dr Samuel Maxwell, Adam Cuppage, Thomas Prentice and John Marshall was appointed to identify decayed parliamentary boroughs in the county to be disenfranchised and those areas to be enfranchised as replacements – in accordance with the Plan of Reform. Returns were to be made to Captain James Dawson, Armagh, or J.T. Ashenhurst, Dublin.[81]

Again the Armagh Volunteers were determined not to be omitted from the campaign. On 23 February 1784, at a meeting of the Northern

Battalion of the Ulster Regiment at Armagh chaired by Captain Blackhall of Loughgall Company, resolutions were passed adopting the National Assembly's Plan of Reform to be presented to parliament on behalf of Volunteers. Addresses of support were made to Charlemont and Brownlow, both of whom published replies.[82]

The struggle for control of the reform movement between the radical wing, led by Hervey and Jones and backed by radical middle-class Volunteers, and moderate patriot reformers led by Charlemont and Brownlow continued into 1784. Casualties of the struggle were the Volunteer movement itself and Catholic relief as part of the reform agenda. Despite defiant addresses by Hervey – such as his answer on 13 December 1783 to an Armagh address[83] – the radical Volunteer wing was losing ground. The Volunteers attempted to rebuild through broadening the membership base by inviting recruits from all classes and religions. This initiative brought temporary numerical strength but a diminution in influence and support from the patriot gentry, many of whom left the Volunteer movement as the lower orders joined.[84]

It also brought sharpened opposition from a new Irish administration appointed by Pitt which was not prepared to brook rival organisations of authority. With the fall of the Fox-North Coalition, an affronted Northington was replaced by the Pittite fourth duke of Rutland as lord lieutenant in February 1784. Rutland was advised that vexatious issues included the Volunteers and the National Assembly's campaign for parliamentary reform led by Brownlow, Charlemont, Lord Bristol and Sir Edward Newenham. On arrival, Rutland ordered his Chief Secretary Thomas Orde to investigate and quantify the Volunteer organisation with a view to removing its influence as a force in domestic politics; and during 1784 floated his idea of a new Protestant militia to replace them.[85]

When Brownlow presented the County Armagh petition to the house of commons on 1 March 1784, government supporter Sir Richard Johnson of Gilford questioned whether signatories were genuine freeholders and was informed by Brownlow that 'near five thousand had signed it'. Johnson commented that the total number of freeholders in Armagh county was not much more than two thousand. Brownlow responded that 1,440 signatories were by freeholders but that 'the petition was signed by 6,146 persons, all of whom were persons of property, and ought to have votes'. Two days later, when the mostly non-resident Chancellor of the Exchequer, W.G. 'Single-speech' Hamilton – who had occupied the post as a sinecure for twenty years – was granted an annuity of £2,500 to vacate the post for John Foster, Molyneux, supported by Brownlow, proposed that the next chancellor of the exchequer of Ireland 'ought to be resident in this kingdom'.[86]

Meanwhile Rutland was keeping Home Secretary Lord Sydney briefed on the activities of the parliamentary reformers, such as Brownlow's arranged meeting at Charlemont's house on 7 March 1784 attended by about forty supporters who planned the re-introduction of the reform bill as framed in the plan of the National Convention 'but that all allusion to that assembly be studiously avoided in the introduction'. Rutland's plan was to admit the bill on this occasion, then defeat it heavily in debate. He was also monitoring Hervey's activities carefully.[87]

Flood moved his second reform bill on 20 March 1784 with many petitions from counties and towns supporting and only two opposing. In debate, Brownlow argued that the excuse of Volunteer intimidation to reject Flood's first reform bill was now removed 'as the freeholders of Ireland had now adopted it as their own, and earnestly recommended it to parliament' and 'that persons of the highest rank and property had signed these petitions'. Molyneux and Grattan also spoke in favour of the bill. But the bill was again rejected by a decisive 159 to 85 votes. In the division, Brownlow, Richardson, Stewart, Grattan, Corry and Molyneux voted for the motion. Meredyth, Rawson, Moore and Thomas Dawson voted against. Acheson was not included in the published voting lists and it was about this time he was reckoned by Orde to be withholding his vote for reward.[88]

The emphatic defeat of Flood's second reform bill was another serious setback for the reform movement. The radicals attempted to revitalise the latter in early summer by recruiting Catholics into the ranks of parliamentary reformers and the Volunteers. In late May 1784, the *Belfast News-Letter* asserted:

> The Machiavelian doctrine of every enemy of Ireland, in order to destroy our hopes by encouraging dissension among the inhabitants, would be divide and govern. But the sound doctrine of every true Irishman, be he of the Church of Ireland, of the Dissenting Church, or the Catholic – must ever be *unite and conquer*!

The newspaper then described how, on the previous Sunday, the Belfast First Company and Belfast Volunteer Company had marched in full dress to Mass to hear a sermon by Rev. Hugh O'Donnell and a 'handsome collection made to aid in defraying the expense of erecting the new 'Masshouse'. Great numbers of other Protestant inhabitants also attended'.[89] In County Armagh, a similar initiative by the Loughgall Volunteers passed resolutions: 'We most cordially invite the Roman Catholics of the manor of Derrycrew and Drumilly and its vicinity to flock to the standard and strengthen the ranks of the Loughgall Volunteers'.[90] Behind the Loughgall initiative was John Blackhall, agent of the Cope estates, magistrate, independent thinker and outspoken reformer and captain of Loughgall Volunteer Company.

But the Loughgall notice has given a misleading impression that recruitment of Catholics into County Armagh companies was on a similar scale to that in Belfast and elsewhere. Orde's return of the Volunteers in 1784 asserted that in Connacht, Munster and Leinster, significant numbers of Catholics had joined the ranks; but in Ulster, statistics for Catholic recruits were influenced by local attitudes and personalities and varied from area to area. It concluded that Donegal, Derry and Tyrone, influenced by Hervey, did have substantial recruitment of Catholics, that Antrim, Down, Cavan and Monaghan had some, but that Armagh had no Catholic recruits, noting:

> No Roman Catholics were ever admitted into the corps of this county [Armagh]–neither have there been any new corps lately established. It is generally allowed that the spirit of Volunteering has been long on the decline in many of the northern counties particularly in this. And that the late Belfast resolutions in favour of Roman Catholics have contributed to its almost total extinction.[91]

Orde's conclusion that no Catholics had ever been admitted to Volunteer corps in Armagh would seem to have been an overstatement and was at variance with contemporary and later reports. A chaplain to the Southern Battalion of the Armagh Regiment complained: 'The battalion, at their meeting in Markethill in June last [1784], decided to receive into their ranks a description of men who, in their religious exercises, make use of a variety of thumpings, crossings, and gesticulations'.[92] Some thirty-five years later Stuart asserted that Roman Catholics were admitted into the City of Armagh Cavalry Corps founded April 1782 and into the Second Company of Armagh Volunteers.[93] A mid-twentieth century survey also found evidence of Catholics serving in the Volunteers of Loughgall and Tyrone's Ditches, though none at officer rank.[94]

However, Catholic recruits to Armagh Volunteer companies were few. While Orde's conclusion on Armagh may not have been strictly accurate, his remark reflected the comprehensive opposition of Armagh gentry and Protestant clergy – such as Hugh Hamilton, Anglican Dean of Armagh, Primate Richard Robinson and William Campbell, Presbyterian minister there – to Catholics having legal right to the franchise, firearms or membership of Volunteer companies; and was evidence of the success of Armagh political leaders at keeping the radical reformers at bay and the Volunteers an essentially Protestant force in the county. Rev. Campbell agreed with Charlemont's description of the radicals in his own flock as 'wild heads' and reported to Charlemont on his efforts to keep their activities in check.[95]

Undoubtedly Blackhall's initiative caused consternation in Armagh. Dean Hamilton reported to Dublin Castle via his brother Chief Baron Hamilton of Hampton Hall, Balbriggan, that Blackhall had broken ranks from his fellow Volunteer leaders in the county. He railed against Blackhall: 'He, a justice of the peace went publicly to Mass, armed and drilled several Papists, led them to Armagh to the review in July last'. According to Hamilton, the parading careers of Loughgall Catholics as Volunteers were short-lived:

> This gave universal offence. The others declared he [Blackhall] should not drill with them and were going to have him ducked. He was obliged to dismiss his Papists and get himself out of the scrape as well as he could.[96]

Dean Hamilton's letter, with its recommendation to take instant punitive action against Blackhall and his armed Catholics, revealed the alarm of the Church of Ireland in Armagh at the possibility of Catholics bearing firearms. His brother conveyed the news to Thomas Orde of 'Blackhall's dangerous activities' but advised the chief secretary 'to hold fire for the moment ... as the danger is over', but, if repeated, an example should be made of Blackhall. Orde took the chief baron's advice of festina lente and, although also concerned at the perceived danger, advised waiting for the appropriate opportunity for action.[97] Primate Robinson, by the 1780s domiciled in Bath, held similar fears of Ireland becoming a Catholic-controlled country.[98]

Despite pressures from Armagh ruling élite, Blackhall's company still contained Catholic recruits one year later. Loughgall had been part of Brownlow's Northern Battalion and an embarrassed Brownlow had tried to pressurise Blackhall into dismissing his Catholic Volunteers, but had to admit to Charlemont in 1785: 'I can do no more than I did before, to request that he should leave his four Roman Catholics at home if the company comes to Newry.' The quarrel between Brownlow and Blackhall in 1784–5 had resulted, to Brownlow's chagrin, in the Loughgall company seceding from the Northern Battalion, withdrawing from the Newry review and attending the Belfast review.[99]

Charlemont and Brownlow extended their efforts to suppress radical demands and to control the Volunteers beyond Armagh county. Radicals were out-manoeuvred at a Volunteer review in Belfast on 12 July 1784 when Charlemont rejected an address by Todd Jones which had included support for extending the franchise to Catholics. At the Newry review of 16 and 17 July, a motion to adopt Jones's address was replaced by a moderate Charlemont-influenced one.[100] Charlemont even bearded Hervey in his own den when he imposed his brand of moderation on the Londonderry review of 21 July 1784. He boasted later: 'At the meeting the Catholic question was proposed, and, after a long debate, withdrawn, so that old Latimer's bishop was routed, horse and foot, even in his own metropolis'.[101] In 1784–5, the Armagh political leaders had seized the initiative from radical reformers across the north of Ireland. At the end of 1784 Rev. William Campbell assured Charlemont that the campaign for parliamentary reform continued but without demands for Catholic suffrage.[102]

A group of 105 Armagh freeholders bypassed High Sheriff Thomas Verner and appealed directly to all Armagh freeholders to meet in Armagh city on 18 January 1785 with the objective of appointing five county delegates to liaise with delegates from other counties to a National Assembly in Dublin on 20 January. None of the 105 signatories was a member of the Lenten grand jury of 1785. This initiative would seem to have originated in the Cope estates as Arthur Cope and John Blackhall were among the first signatories, with many linen merchants from Loughgall and Mountnorris.[103]

The Armagh meeting was chaired by the radical Alexander Thomas Stewart of Acton, supported by Blackhall, and the five delegates appointed were: Stewart, Sir Capel Molyneux and his son Capel junior, Arthur Cope and William Brownlow junior. Whether the Armagh county members of parliament had declined an invitation to be delegates is unclear. Brownlow senior, was opposed to the new initiative for which there seems to have been little enthusiasm in the county. William Campbell commented to Charlemont: 'There has been no call of our county to send delegates to congress, and it is thought there will be none. Mr Brownlow, it is said, has declared against it, and there are many in the county who join with him'. A newspaper report from the National Congress informed readers that twenty four counties and twelve towns were represented and that 'the Roman Catholic Question, it seems to me, will not be entertained at all – in this place'.[104]

By 1785, the Volunteers were also being shorn of political influence. In the house of commons on 21 January 1785, Grattan attributed their political demise to their transformation from the 'armed property' to the 'armed beggary' of Ireland.[105] Charlemont, urged surgeon Samuel Maxwell, his second in command of Armagh First Company, to keep the Volunteers out of politics at this time: 'Let the Volunteers be quiet – let no resolutions be entered into – a paper war with parliament is unjustifiable in itself', and, like Grattan, denounced the trends in recruitment: 'The Catholic business and the augmenting our corps with the dregs of the people have been measures disgraceful and ruinous'.[106]

The political impotence of the Volunteers was revealed during the debate on Luke Gardiner's proposal that £20,000 be voted towards raising a new national militia to replace the Volunteers which was accepted in committee by 139 to 63 votes on 14 February 1785. Gardiner had argued that 'their [Volunteers] existence now was unconstitutional, and not of the least use to support the civil power and keep the peace'. Even the wording of

Brownlow's motion of thanks four days later: 'that the Volunteers of Ireland have been eminently useful to their country', seemed to concede that the Volunteers were yesterday's men. And Gardiner's amendment that 'this house highly approves of the conduct of those [Volunteers] who, since the conclusion of the war, have retired to cultivate the blessings of peace' – was a contemptuous dismissal.[107] Perhaps the most telling evidence of the demise of the Volunteers was that Rutland no longer considered it necessary to raise a militia to replace them in 1785 and a new militia act was not passed until 1793.

Occasional motions in parliament attempted to keep the issue of parliamentary reform alive. Such a motion by Flood and Forbes on 12 May 1785 which was defeated by 112 votes to 60, received the support of Armagh representatives Grattan, Stewart, Brownlow, Richardson, and new recruit Arthur Acheson, now firmly in the opposition camp.[108] By 1785, Acheson would also seem to have taken Lord Edward Bentinck's advice to heart and was spending more time in Markethill, serving as foreman of the Armagh grand jury at the summer assizes in 1785 whose political lead he was then following.[109]

But the Irish parliament remained unreformed. The Dublin administration and its supporters concluded that it was easier to control parliament the way it was. With parliamentary reform off the agenda, Pitt and Orde attempted to solve the on-going thorny problem of commercial relations between Ireland and England emanating from the Navigation Laws. In the petitioning drive against Orde's commercial propositions, the Volunteers were only minimally involved.

ARMAGH MPs AND THE COMMERCIAL PROPOSITIONS, 1785

In the parliamentary negotiations over the commercial propositions in 1785, all Armagh MPs made some contribution and Corry, Grattan and Brownlow played key roles. Corry was a constant opponent of the proposals. When the measure was presented in parliament by Thomas Orde on 7 February 1785, Brownlow led a ferocious attack on the clause that Ireland should make an annual financial contribution for the defence of the empire in return for trade concessions. Brownlow accused Orde of making 'a proposition in this house that we should become a tributary nation' for which, in a less civilised country, 'he would not have lived to carry back an answer', though later apologised for his violent language.[110] Despite some adverse petitions from merchants and chambers of commerce, Orde's proposals passed easily through the Irish parliament and on to Westminster.

However, the Commercial Propositions met fierce opposition in the British parliament. Pitt, in the face of opposition from the Foxite Whigs inside parliament and petitions from manufacturing centres outside, devised in May a revised list of twenty propositions which satisfied neither the English nor Irish opposition. Rutland anticipated that the deviations from the original propositions in the English house of commons would 'afford to discontent and faction an instrument to work much mischief ... and open a field of difficulty and embarrassments which it will require all my exertions to overcome'.[111]

Rutland's observation was prophetic. Early opposition in Ireland from spring 1785, led at first by Flood and Corry – the 'zealous watchman' of Irish interests – received little support. Moderate patriots such as Grattan and Brownlow held fire and the Volunteers refrained from political agitation on the direction of Charlemont who hoped that their silence would earn a reprieve from government plans for their abolition and replacement by a government-controlled militia. However, the inactivity of the Volunteers was balanced by the popular press's hostile political mood to the reconstituted commercial arrangement which was perceived as an assault on Ireland's legislative independence. This perception influenced Grattan to declare his opposition to it in June, and Brownlow and other leading patriots followed; and when the British parliamentary opposition actively participated, a nationwide campaign of opposition took off. Grattan and Corry were prominent in opposition in the Irish house of commons during June and July 1785.[112]

Renewed calls were made in June 1785 for nationwide petitions to parliament against the revised British propositions. Armagh was one of the first northern counties to circulate a requisition for a county meeting. However, the county would seem to have been divided over taking that route as evidenced by High Sheriff John Maxwell's refusal to convene the county meeting requested by 74 freeholders. The latter proceeded to call the meeting at Armagh courthouse on 5 July without Maxwell's co-operation.[113] Brownlow reported to Charlemont that the Armagh meeting was small – due to the absence of linen drapers in Dublin and a fair at Tandragee – but had agreed unanimously to have a petition to parliament against the twenty British propositions. Tenants of Brownlow and Cope had dominated attendance and John Blackhall had given a lengthy oration attacking the obnoxious fourth proposition which was perceived as making Irish legislation subservient to British regulations.[114]

The Commercial Bill was presented in the Irish house of commons by Orde on 12 August 1785. Grattan's categorical reprobation of the bill was the high point of the debate which continued overnight. In the division lobby on Saturday 13 August the opposition was only narrowly defeated by 127 votes to 110 (129 to 112 including tellers). Members who had voted with Grattan against the bill included Brownlow, Richardson, Stewart, Corry and Arthur Acheson, the latter encouraged by his friend, Lord

Northington. Acheson's defection from the administration lobby was offset by the recruitment to the government ranks of G.W. Molyneux who voted for the Commercial Bill in hope of a peerage for his father and a government post for himself. Meredyth, Rawson, Moore and Dawson also supported the administration vote.[115]

The humiliatingly narrow victory for the bloodied Dublin administration resulted in Orde's decision to leave the Commercial Bill to another day. Charlemont wrote triumphantly to Dr Haliday: 'I have barely time to tell you we have been victorious. ... Yesterday the secretary ... declared that he should proceed no farther this session'. On his return to Lurgan, Brownlow was hailed as a hero with bonfires and illuminations by the inhabitants and victory volleys by his Volunteer company which – against his earlier inclinations – he treated to beer.[116]

But the opposition was also reluctant to push the matter further. Armagh county's division over Orde's proposals was a microcosm of national indecision. At the summer assizes of 1785, it was resolved that Arthur Acheson, foreman of Armagh grand jury, on behalf of fifteen members, publicly thank the 'one hundred and ten worthy members of the house of commons', and Armagh county representatives for their 'patriotic conduct' in rescuing the country from the Commercial Bill.[117] Acheson's new involvement in Armagh local politics and flirtation with the independent faction on the grand jury suggested he had designs on a future Armagh county seat. While he partially owed his Old Leighlin borough seat to previous Lord Lieutenant Northington, he felt less obliged to support Rutland and sought the popularity of an opposition stance within his own county.

However, a significant minority of Armagh grand jurors did favour Orde's bill. Sheriff Maxwell and seven like-minded jurors felt obliged to publicly dissent from the vote of thanks, claiming that they believed a revised commercial system between the two kingdoms was necessary. It was an unusual but determined declaration by a group of grand jurors in the face of the popular opposition of fifteen of their colleagues and such high-profile representatives as Brownlow, Richardson, Grattan and Stewart.[118]

But these eight 'dissentient' Armagh gentry – five of whom served as high sheriffs in the 1780s – represented the thinking of many northern merchants, particularly those involved in the linen trade which had much to gain from a new commercial arrangement. Brownlow, who saw their point, was convinced that opposition to the bill in Armagh had been essentially on constitutional rather than commercial grounds:

> ... in this county we are not to expect total unanimity ... the grand jury were averse to condemn the commercial part of the bill ... It is certain that the northern counties, where the linen manufacture prevails, have less reason to be dissatisfied with the bill than other part of Ireland, as that trade might benefit by it, and could not suffer.

Thus Brownlow was persuaded, initially, that having given the sharp rebuke to Dublin Castle and Westminster, 'it is better to let it rest and proceed no further'.[119]

Dublin Castle soon retrieved the political initiative. At the end of the parliamentary session, the addresses to the king and lord lieutenant, having been pushed into a division, were overwhelmingly carried by 130 votes to 13, encouraging the administration to believe there was hope for the Commercial Bill in the 1786 session.[120] Uneasy at the government's comeback, Charlemont, Brownlow and Corry countered with resolutions against the Bill and exhorted high-profile patriot figures such as the duke of Leinster, Brownlow, Annesley Stewart and James Stewart to call county meetings in Kildare, Armagh, Donegal and Tyrone to adopt them. Brownlow and Richardson set an example by requisitioning Sheriff Maxwell to call a county meeting. Brownlow confessed he had considered by-passing Maxwell but had been persuaded by Richardson to follow protocol. Maxwell called a meeting for 21 November 1785. Brownlow also acknowledged that Blackhall was the obvious choice to propose Charlemont's resolutions at the meeting but was reluctant to ask him due to their contretemps over Loughgall Volunteers' withdrawal from the Northern Battalion.[121]

Charlemont urged Dr Haliday in Belfast to have his resolutions adopted quickly by meetings of freeholders there, even before Armagh. He gave the rationale for the campaign against the revised Commercial Bill:

> We have scotch'd the snake, not killed it, but it will be our own fault if we should remain in danger of her former tooth. If the people will but unanimously declare their disapprobation, I will venture to say that no further attack will be hazarded.[122]

The renewed campaign of opposition was sufficient to convince an uncertain Dublin Castle and British government to shelve the Commercial Bill in the 1786 session and, encouraged by Pitt, to disarm resistance by adopting a more conciliatory strategy. When a new British Navigation Bill was rejected in Ireland in 1786, it was withdrawn to avoid friction. Subsequently, its provisions were so relaxed and further amended from the 1660 Act in Ireland's favour, that it passed easily through the Irish parliament on 26 March 1787 when a divided opposition could only muster 52 votes for Grattan's amendment against the government's 127. Richardson, Stewart, and Corry voted with Grattan, with the absent Brownlow denoted as 'sick' – and probably anxious to avoid offending the linen interest. The vote was evidence that the Irish administration was back in control of Anglo-Irish affairs.[123]

ARMAGH MPs AND THE ELECTION OF A NEW SPEAKER IN 1785

An earlier indication that the Irish administration had regained control was seen in the election of a new speaker to replace Edmund Sexton Pery in 1785. The administration seems to have been unprepared for Pery's resignation in the immediate aftermath of the debacle of the Commercial Bill in August 1785 and was concerned at the possibility of another embarrassment when its candidate for the speakership, John Foster, was challenged, at the last moment, by William Brabazon Ponsonby. Foster had been identified with strong advocacy of the Commercial Bill, Ponsonby associated with opposition to it; and the government feared that a similar swing of votes to Ponsonby supported by the substantial Ponsonby borough interest might capture the chair for Ponsonby. Both camps canvassed vigorously for support.

On the day following Pery's resignation, Foster canvassed Arthur Acheson who promised him his vote. In this instance Foster had beaten Ponsonby to the punch. Acheson's friendship with Fox and Lord Northington who supported Ponsonby, made him feel obliged to apologise to Northington, explaining that Pery had informed him over the winter of his intention of retiring, he had understood John Foster was the only candidate when George Ogle withdrew, was unaware of Ponsonby's candidature and had pledged his vote to Foster accordingly. Northington, in Paris, requested Acheson right up to the eleventh hour of the election to support Ponsonby. Acheson's father had also been requested by Orde to support Foster, no doubt expecting political return on Lord Gosford's recent advancement to viscount.[124]

On this occasion the government's campaign was successful, though not solely for that reason. Multiple factors contributed to the change around. Foster was not only the government candidate, but also the popular candidate with the independent country members. His country gentleman ethos and superior ability made him a respected and outstanding candidate and the country members – the great majority of whom had opposed the unpopular Commercial Bill on 12/13 August – now swung behind the popular candidate on an issue in which there had been a tradition of independent voting.[125]

Brownlow resisted the rhyming couplet of one correspondent, 'Let Brownlow take the chair / nor quit it till he leaves his equal there', to join with Richardson and other northern county members backing Foster from an early stage.[126] Acheson withstood pressure from Lord Northington and honoured his pledge to Foster. Grattan also promised support. Charlemont's Whig principles would not permit him to support Foster but he, too, soon conceded, in consultation with the Ponsonby faction, that William Ponsonby could not muster sufficient votes in an election.

Ponsonby retired from the contest and, on 5 September Foster was elected speaker unopposed.[127] The election of Foster regained the initiative for the administration. The temporary patriot/Whig alliance of 12–13 August had been broken, to the disappointment of Charlemont and Corry. Until 1789, the administration controlled the business of parliament, easily defeating a series of bills introduced by the opposition.

In 1785, the chief secretary thanked Gosford for his support in Foster's election.[128] Reciprocal favours between Gosford and Dublin Castle followed over the winter of 1785–6. When Gosford requested the appointment of a Mr. Johnston as County Keeper of Armagh, Orde recommended the appointment to the lord lieutenant and, in turn, called upon Gosford's attendance for the opening of the new session of parliament on 19 January 1786. While Gosford asked to be excused attendance – 'till business of consequence makes it absolutely necessary' – on the grounds of being in his sixty-eighth year, unwell and the severity of the weather, he re-affirmed his consistent political allegiance to the king's business:

> No man has been more uniformly a friend to the king's government here than I have been and shall remain during my life, unconnected with any party but such as support the real interest of my king and country; unplaced, unpensioned and determined (from my first coming into parliament which was in 1741) never to accept of either, are in as few words as I can express them, my real political sentiment.[129]

Arthur Acheson had also been requested by Orde to attend on 19 January and Gosford urged his son repeatedly to 'attend the first day that you may show your respect to the lord lieutenant by being upon the spot when the addresses are going through your house of parliament'.[130] By then Acheson was holding out for offers before committing himself to government or opposition, prompting the government to rate him 'doubtful' in early 1788 and to refer to him as 'strangely uncertain'.[131]

ARMAGH VOTES IN PARLIAMENTARY DIVISIONS 1786–90

From 1785, Grattan led the opposition to the government but the administration withstood a series of opposition bills introduced by John Forbes over the following three years. On 6 March 1786, Grattan, Brownlow, Richardson, Sir Annesley Stewart and Corry supported Forbes's motion for retrenchment through reform of the civil list but it was defeated. The last four had some small success in a vote on the same day to protect the rights of grand juries, when Beresford agreed to meet the wishes of the country gentlemen and omit an obnoxious clause. One year later, the same group, minus an indisposed Brownlow, voted, in vain, for Forbes's revived bill to limit pensions on 12 March 1787.[132]

Two further opposition bills met a similar fate in February 1788 when Travers Hartley's motion that the service provided by the Dublin police was insufficient return for the public cost and Forbes's revived motion for limiting pensions, were supported by Brownlow, Grattan, Corry, Sir Annesley Stewart and son James.[133] In 1788, too, Grattan after two years of research into the causes of the distress of clergy and people over tithes, introduced his Tithe Bill, seconded by Lord Kingsborough and supported by Brownlow. But the government defeated his motion by 121 votes to 49.

In early 1789 the most serious challenge since 1785 to the Dublin and London administrations arose out of the mental incapacity of George III since autumn 1788. The Foxite Whig opposition in England wished to have the Prince of Wales installed as regent. While the English parliament debated the issue, Irish members led by Grattan and influenced largely by the English Whigs, brought a motion by Thomas Conolly, seconded by George Ponsonby on 11 February 1789 inviting the prince to assume the regency of Ireland. The motion attracted majority support from many quarters. With Grattan as teller, usual opposition stalwarts Brownlow, Richardson, Sir Annesley and James Stewart, and Corry were joined by fence-sitters such as Acheson and by erstwhile supporters of the administration – now split on the regency issue – such as John Moore and Thomas Dawson. Moore seems to have ignored the wishes of his patron Lord Drogheda while Dawson, though now 'in office', took his lead from the Ponsonby lobby, in voting for a regency. Armagh peers Charlemont and Gosford supported the motion in the house of lords. George Rawson remained steadfastly in the government lobby, though his aged political colleague Meredyth seems to have been unable to attend for the division. Molyneux, still pursuing the elusive peerage for his father, spoke against the address and voted with government.[134] His loyalty was rewarded with his appointment to the post of comptroller of stamp duties though his father never did receive a peerage.[135]

When motions for a regent were carried in both houses of the Irish parliament, an angry Lord Lieutenant Buckingham[136] took the strong step of refusing to transmit the addresses to the Prince of Wales and commissioners were appointed by both Irish houses to present them in person. But by the time the Irish delegation arrived in London, the king had recovered. The bid for power taken by Grattan and his followers had foundered on the vagaries of the health of George III. Perhaps the main benefit for the Grattanites of the regency episode was its bonding effect as evidenced by the formation in June 1789 of a new Irish Whig Club and a political party by Grattan, Charlemont et al.

The independence of Armagh MPs reached its zenith in opposition to the administration on the regency crisis division on 11 February 1789. Buckingham attempted to reduce the growing number of Armagh members opposing government. Isaac Corry, whose talents had been admired for some time by government which noted in early 1788 that he 'speaks frequently, has parliamentary talents, and [is] perhaps among the first in opposition', was recruited to the administration by Buckingham.[137] By 1789 Acheson, too, had communicated his political allegiance to Home Secretary Portland and Pelham in London and was re-negotiating his Old Leighlin seat.[138]

At the beginning of Lord Lieutenant Westmorland's administration and conclusion of the parliament in 1790, the number of Armagh members voting against government had been reduced to the Whig group supporting economical reform. Heavily defeated motions by Grattan and Curran in early February 1790 against creation of new offices and pensions increasing the influence of the crown, were supported by Brownlow, Richardson and Sir Annesley Stewart. George Ponsonby's motion on 3 March censuring the practice of judges issuing fiats for large sums of money in actions of slander was supported by Brownlow, Richardson, Grattan and Stewart, and opposed by Rawson, Duquery (who had replaced Meredyth for Armagh borough), Molyneux, Moore and Dawson.[139]

POLITICS IN THE ARMAGH DISTURBANCES OF 1784–90

Armagh was not the only county in Ireland to experience violent disturbances in the 1780s but was unique in the duration, intensity and sectarian nature of the violence and in the special circumstances which precipitated it. Contemporary accounts varied as to the origins, causes and perpetrators of the sectarian disturbances in County Armagh society between 1784 and 1791. Primate Robinson and Dean Hugh Hamilton over the winter of 1784–5 attributed the Armagh disturbances to high politics and warned the Dublin administration against a political coup by armed Catholics.[140] However, an account by an inhabitant of Armagh town, signing himself J. Byrne, attributed the outbreak in 1784 to a drunken brawl between two Protestant neighbours which escalated into faction fights in the mid-county parishes of Mullaghbrack and Loughgilly. The composition of these earliest area gangs calling themselves 'fleets' soon became sectarian, with Protestant gangs referred to as Peep O'Day Boys and Catholic gangs as Defenders. The number of gangs and disturbances spread north and south across the county and, by 1792, into County Down.[141]

Parts of Byrne's account are corroborated by other contemporary records. In 1785, a concerned Lord Gosford requested Lord Lieutenant Rutland to appoint a county keeper to assist in 'the safety and tranquillity' of County

Armagh.[142] In early 1787, John Moore of Drumbanagher reported to Gosford that he had been threatened by Peep O'Day Boys.[143] In late summer, Gosford referred to five 'fleet boys' in Markethill jail and 'bills [of indictment] found against twenty eight or thirty more'.[144] Rev. Dr. Richard Allott's report from Armagh to Dublin Castle blaming the 'immoderate consumption of spirituous liquor' in unlicensed houses in the countryside 'where mischief is hatched' also corroborated Byrne's references to the influence of shebeens as venues for Peep O'Day activities.[145]

Armagh would seem to have been an exceptional trouble spot in the northern province. In early August 1787, Rutland reported to Whitehall that Ulster generally was quiet and the 'spirit of Volunteering ... nearly extinguished'.[146] By summer 1787, however, the Dublin administration was receiving detailed reports of the Armagh disturbances from trusted residents in the county. Allott's appraisal of the state of Armagh county for Orde, identified the centre of disturbance as around Newtownhamilton, and described an offensive by magistrates Synnot and Thomas McCann, in leading an army party to arrest local Peep O'Day ringleaders. But his report also referred to other magistrates being intimidated against serving bills of indictment on local terrorists: '[When] Lord Gosford was asked publicly [at a county meeting of magistrates] whether he believed he could execute his warrant in the town of Markethill (his own place of residence) against one of these Peep O'Day Boys, his answer was he could not'. Allott also observed that, despite such intimidation, magistrates opposed a Magistrates' Act fearing the expense of appointing additional constables who, to compound the problem, were 'to a man, offenders themselves'.[147]

By early 1788, rumours were rife in Dublin that order and control had broken down in County Armagh. Gosford communicated with Dublin Castle through his son Arthur. His report for Buckingham also placed the Armagh disturbances around Newtownhamilton and identified the perpetrators:

> In the southern parts of the county it [rioting] still prevails, with great terror to the well disposed of every denomination and these acts are perpetrated by a low set of fellows, who call themselves Protestant Dissenters and who with guns and bayonets and other weapons break open the houses of the Roman Catholics and, as I am informed, treat many of them with cruelty and take from them such eatables and drink as they find and this under the pretence of searching for arms. Several of the rioters to a large number have had indictments heard against them and five have been several months in jail who must be tried for their lives next assizes.[148]

Gosford's location of Dissenter involvement in Armagh agreed with the distribution of denominations in the county with Presbyterians strongest in the middle third.[149] Gosford refuted rumours that Catholics were importing arms. He recommended severe measures to be taken by juries against the ringleaders – deportation to Botany Bay and hanging for those involved in murder. But he recommended avoidance of an over-military response to the Armagh disturbances and advised that a single army company of foot stationed at Newtownhamilton – fodder was too scarce after a bad harvest for a troop of dragoons – would be sufficient support for Synnot to enforce law and order in that area.[150]

Presbyterian minister Campbell was less willing to condemn members of his own flock. When letters from Chief Secretary Alleyne Fitzherbert to Campbell and to the sovereign of Armagh city and from County Governor Charlemont to Campbell, sought details of reported riots and sectarian outrages in Armagh, Campbell conceded that Peep O'Day Boys had taken the law into their own hands in attempting to disarm Catholics; but he was prepared to excuse their illegalities because of Protestant fears of Catholics possessing firearms. Campbell strove to convince Charlemont that many reports were exaggerated, though he conceded there had been disturbances in mid-Armagh. However, he believed that a more active magistracy could maintain order and control – perhaps with help from Volunteer companies – but without interference from the army or other proposed police force. He attributed the worst reports of violence to rumour mongers with an agenda of 'introducing the odious establishment of the police in our county'.[151]

But Campbell's attempts to minimise the Armagh disturbances were given the lie in spring 1788. Disturbances spread northwards in the county; magistrates, grand juries and petty juries – as in 1763 and 1772 – were all encountering difficulties in keeping law and order, and Richard Power, baron of the exchequer and John Toler, Irish attorney-general, had threatened to impose martial law on Armagh county and to recommend the appointment of the unwanted police-force. Charlemont, who was being pressurised, as governor, to visit Armagh to deal with the situation, came north in July on the occasion of a Volunteer review and expressed his disgust at the sectarian disturbances he found in the county including those among his own tenants. He observed ruefully:

> A few years ago, I was compelled to hazard all my popularity to prevent the Protestants from ruining themselves and their country by giving up all to the Papists; and now I am forced to [risk] the same popularity, to prevent them from cutting each others throats.[152]

Riots, raids and recriminations escalated in late 1788 and 1789. Rev. Campbell alleged the Presbyterians were being smeared and blamed Catholics for the troubles. The intervention of Volunteers made matters worse.[153] Violence spread southwards. John Moore of Drumbanagher asked Charlemont for help and informed him: 'This whole country for ten mile round is in absolute rebellion and confusion'.[154] Rev. Edward Hudson, Rector of Forkhill, reported that Defenders controlled south Armagh, south Down and north Louth.[155] Some six weeks later Hudson conveyed his fears that a contested election would exacerbate the violence in the county and appealed to Charlemont to use his influence to pressurise potential candidates to withdraw from the general election in 1790 for which they were already canvassing support.[156]

CONCLUSION: THE ELECTION CONTEST OF 1783, FENCIBLES, VOLUNTEERS, CATHOLICS AND PARLIAMENTARY REFORM IN THE 1780s

National issues dominated the general election of 1783 in County Armagh and brought a poll for the first time in thirty years. The issues of British renunciation and fencible commissions had led to divisions in the politically-conscious population of Armagh. The concession of renunciation by the British parliament in January 1783 removed the former issue from the electoral agenda. As the general election approached, the Armagh electorate was divided between supporters of the government's commissioning of fencible regiments in Ireland and the anti-fencible Volunteer lobby which adopted the further electoral issue of parliamentary reform.

At the 1783 Armagh poll, sitting member of an Armagh county seat, Thomas Dawson, who had been elected in 1776 on the popular vote and adopted as a key organiser and leader of the Volunteer movement, was ousted when a significant number of Volunteers turned against him for accepting a government fencible commission in 1782. Despite a spirited defence, Dawson lost his seat to William Richardson who was returned with veteran patriot and Volunteer Commander William Brownlow, thus continuing the Armagh county tradition of patriot opposition.

The commissioning of Irish fencible regiments had been introduced by the Portland administration in 1782 to break the influence of the Volunteer movement in Irish politics, and although the fencible regiments were decommissioned again in late 1783, their brief existence caused a split in the Volunteers, a debilitating weakness and decline in their political power over the following ten years. Following the rebuff by parliament of their support for the first reform bill in November 1783, the Volunteers played a diminishing role in the constitutional battles ahead such as the later campaign for parliamentary reform, the commercial propositions, the regency crisis etc. And after Pittite Lord Lieutenant Rutland threatened to disband them in 1784, the ever-cautious Charlemont strove to keep the

Volunteers out of politics thus facilitating their survival into the 1790s.

In 1783, Volunteer organisation and issues had superseded Armagh freeholder electoral initiatives and concerns of 1776 – such as landlord conjunctions. But some freeholders were anxious that they should not be diminished as a significant political group. In the absence of Volunteer reviews in Armagh in July 1783, freeholders made their presence felt by an appeal to electors to support Brownlow. In August, a group of 'independent freeholders' rallied behind Brownlow and Dawson with promises of financial assistance and demands that all candidates submit their political principles to freeholders for approval – which Richardson had not then done. But most freeholders would seem to have followed their landlords' lead in voting for or against the Volunteer ethic of Richardson or the government fencible ethic of Dawson. As the majority of Armagh freeholders favoured the former, only a significant personal following for Dawson and the professionalism of his election team facilitated Dawson's bid.

One can only speculate at the size of the Armagh electorate in 1783. The 2,969 poll in 1783 represented at least 1,485 voters and the electorate was probably nearer to 2,000, a significant increase on the 1753 poll of 1,180. Following the election, Armagh freeholders met in October to remind Brownlow and Richardson of continuing freeholder power, stating they regarded MPs as bound by the instructions of their constituents and duly instructing them to support measures to reform parliamentary representation.

The 1783 election resulted in status quo for the sitting members of Armagh parliamentary boroughs, with all four re-elected. Henry Meredyth and George Rawson, as nominees of Primate Robinson for Armagh cathedral borough, continued to support the administration. Henry Grattan and Sir Annesley Stewart were returned again for Charlemont. Stewart was found consistently in opposition lobbies for the duration of the parliament but Grattan's occasional flirtation with government so displeased his patron that relations between Charlemont and he were damaged irreconcilably.

There were mixed fortunes in 1783 for Armagh resident gentry holding seats for boroughs outside the county. Following the politically untimely death of his brother-in-law and patron Bishop Garnett in 1782, Sir Capel Molyneux of Castle-Dillon was not returned for the cathedral borough of Clogher and was without a seat for the first time in twenty two years. However, his second son George William purchased a seat for Granard. Molyneux junior, having begun his parliamentary career in the family tradition of active opponent of the administration, succumbed to a combination of eighteenth century venality and careerism and was entering the government lobby by 1785 for which he was rewarded with a government post in 1789. His political volte-face prompted the contemporary conclusion:

> In his parliamentary voyage, he set out with a violence of opposition that surprised even the violent; but extremes are seldom lasting, and, long since, the strong gale of court influence has filled the sails of his little barque, before which it scuds rapidly away into the gulf of oblivion.[157]

Volunteer Isaac Corry of Derrymore, Bessbrook, was returned for Newry pot-walloping borough as a reformer in 1783 and was a consistent anti-government spokesman for reform until appointed to government office by Buckingham in 1788. But the attempt by John Moore junior of Drumbanagher to win his maiden seat for Lisburn pot-walloping borough fell foul of the south Antrim Volunteer campaign for parliamentary reform in a bitter contest and he was forced to settle for the Ballynakill borough seat belonging to his kinsman Lord Drogheda and previously held by Moore's father. In accordance with his patron's wishes, Moore junior supported the Dublin administration for a few years but voted more independently in divisions towards the end of the 1783–90 parliament.

In 1783 Arthur Acheson renewed the family representation in the Irish house of commons, missing since his father was elevated to the upper house in 1776. With the help of his uncle Bishop Walter Cope's timely translation to Ferns in 1782 and approval of his Foxite friend Lord Lieutenant Northington, Acheson was returned for the cathedral borough of Old Leighlin. For a while, his parliamentary allegiance took an opposite direction to that of George Molyneux, beginning as government supporter but becoming less supportive of the Rutland viceroyalty and joining the opposition lobby as the life of that parliament progressed. But as the 1990 general election approached, Acheson was back in contact with his Portland friends in England.

Armagh members played leading roles in key parliamentary issues in the period 1783–90. Because of the heavy involvement of Armagh gentry in the Volunteer movement, it was inevitable that Armagh politicians would be drawn into their campaign for parliamentary reform in 1783. As government supporters, Meredyth, Rawson, Acheson and Moore were tied to opposing reform. Most other Armagh politicians favoured moderate reform but were uneasy with the inclusion of Catholic suffrage as part of the package. Charlemont and Brownlow used their influence within and without the county to prevent addresses advocating Catholic suffrage by Volunteer companies, thus outflanking earl-bishop Hervey, Todd Jones and other radicals. Their efforts were also influential in having Catholic suffrage omitted from the programme forwarded to parliament by the National Convention in November 1783, thus enabling Flood's motion there to be supported by Brownlow, Richardson, Grattan, Stewart, Corry and Molyneux.

The emphatic rejection of Flood's bill by parliament sounded the death-knell for Volunteer political power. Most reformist politicians turned to the use of organised petitions from county freeholders – Armagh freeholders among the first to do so in December 1783 – as more constitutionally acceptable. But a stiffened resolve against reform by Pitt's new Irish administration headed by Rutland and Orde – described as Whigs in England but Tories in Ireland[158] – kept the would-be reformers at bay, defeating easily a series of motions by the opposition. Armagh members contributed to breaching the government's defences on two occasions when – with the possibility of Pitt's government falling in England – the Irish patriots and English Whig opposition teamed up in attack. When Pitt's attempt in 1785 to solve the commercial differences between England and Ireland fell foul of the English parliament's changes to the Commercial Bill which had passed the Irish parliament, opposition rallied in Ireland abetted by the English Whigs, and the revised measure only scraped a Pyrrhic victory for government in the Irish parliament. The division was regarded as a moral victory for the opposition forcing Orde to shelve the measure. Grattan, back leading the opposition, had received vigorous support from Corry, Brownlow, Richardson and Stewart while Acheson had been enticed to absent himself from the government lobby.

Armagh's significant political opposition to Orde's Commercial Propositions had been mainly on constitutional grounds and the county was divided on the economic merits of the measure to such an extent that the high sheriff and seven like-minded grand jurors advertised their support for a commercial scheme which they perceived would benefit the Irish linen industry. When Pitt adopted a more conciliatory approach to Irish constitutional sensibilities, his revised Navigation Act was passed with an overwhelming majority by the Irish parliament in 1787. By then the Dublin administration had regained control of parliament as evidenced in the 1785 campaign to appoint a new speaker when Armagh members were prominent among northern county members who supported government candidate, John Foster.

The effective alliance of Irish and English Whig opposition in storming the Irish administration on a sensitive constitutional issue recurred in the regency crisis of 1789 when Grattan, supported by English Whigs, persuaded the Irish parliament to invite the Prince of Wales to assume the regency of Ireland. The initiative was thwarted by George III's recovery to health, but led to the formation of an Irish Whig Club and more formal ties with the English Whigs. In 1789 most Armagh members defied Buckingham and voted for a regency.

Armagh was unique among Irish counties in the duration and intensity of sectarian violence in the closing decades of the eighteenth century. At the height of the Armagh outrages in 1787, Rutland was reporting to Whitehall that Ulster, elsewhere, was at peace. Many contemporary observers attributed the Armagh disturbances to political factors. Growing suspicions and fears in the Protestant ruling élite that Catholics had designs on a political take-over through inclusion of Catholic suffrage in the programme of parliamentary reform were expressed by Primate Robinson – albeit from distant Bath, by Dean Hamilton and other Armagh clergy such as Presbyterian minister William Campbell. Armagh Protestant clergy served as the eyes and ears of the ruling élite in their communities and constantly communicated their fears to the Dublin administration. Moderate reformers such as Lord Charlemont and Brownlow – already opposed to Catholic suffrage – were also wary of any Catholic social advance and condemned the efforts of more radical Loughgall agent John Blackhall to enlist Catholics in his Volunteer company which would have given them access to firearms. Blackhall's ecumenical efforts were exceptional in County Armagh and minimal in results.

Government supporter Lord Gosford, was less inclined to blame Catholic political aspirations for the Armagh disturbances but pointed to the depredations of the Peep O'Day Boys – whom he identified as mainly 'Dissenter' in denomination – and reprisals from the Catholic Defenders. Gosford's report was corroborated by reports from Rev. Dr. Allott, precentor of Armagh, and local textile dyer John Byrne. Social and economic rivalry has been posited as reason for the Armagh disturbances by Crawford and Miller. By the 1780s Protestants felt increasingly threatened by the entry of Catholics into the commercial aspects of linen manufacture previously controlled by Protestants. Those Catholics who had become more affluent through linen production and marketing were better able to compete for the growing number of subdivided holdings coming on market, compounding the resentment of Protestants.[159]

With the downgrading in political and social status of the Volunteers, many lent assistance to the Peep O'Day Boys and, with grand jurors reluctant to support legislation for, or expense of, a new constabulary, the magistrates were finding it difficult to maintain order and control. This degenerating situation continued despite a visit to the county by Governor Lord Charlemont to deal with the situation. It was in such an atmosphere that the Armagh ruling élite prepared for the 1790 general election.

Notes

1. Chief Secretary W.W. Grenville to Lord Gosford, 9 Nov. 1982 (PRONI, Gosford papers, D/1606/1/1/98).
2. *BNL*, 25–29 July 1783.
3. Memoirs (*HMC Charlemont*), i, 81–2, 159, note 1.
4. *BNL*,16–20 May 1783.
5. *BNL*, 11–15, 18–22 Oct. 1782.
6. *BNL*, 13–17 Dec. 1782.
7. *BNL*, 4–8 Apr. 1783.
8. *BNL*, 20–24 Dec. 1782.
9. 'High sheriffs of Co. Armagh 1593–1969', (PRONI, T/2704/1–2); 'Grand juries of County Armagh 1735–75' in Corporation Book of Armagh, (PRONI, T/636; hereafter 'Armagh grand juries'); Paterson, 'Armagh Volunteers', vi , 94–6.
10. *BNL*, 22–26 Mar., 20–24 Dec. 1782. Presbyterian Historical Society of Ireland (ed.), *A history of congregations in the Presbyterian Church of Ireland 1610–1982* (Belfast, 1982; hereafter Presbyterian Historical Society, *A history of congregations*), p. 735, gives Richhill congregation as initially an outpost of Vinecash, and occasional services were conducted by Rev. James Todd on the Richhill site donated in 1782 by Richardson.
11. *BNL*, 31 Dec. 1782–3 Jan. 1783, 10–14 Jan. 1783.
12. *BNL*, 28–31 Jan. 1783.
13. *BNL*, 7–11 Mar. 1783.
14. *BNL*,18–21 Mar. 1783.
15. *BNL*, 25–28 Mar, 28 Mar.–1 Apr. 1783.
16. *BNL*, 22–25 Apr. 1783.
17. *BNL*, 3–6 June 1783.
18. *BNL*, 9–13 May, 10–13 June, 1–4 July 1783.
19. *BNL*, 11–15, 22–25 July 1783.
20. *BNL*, 22–25, 25–29 July 1783.
21. *BNL*, 25–29 July, 29 July–1 Aug. 1783.
22. *BNL*, 12–15 Aug. 1783.
23. *BNL*, 8–12, 12–15, 15–19 Aug. 1783.
24. *Commons' jn. Ire.* (Bradley), xiv, 580; ibid., xxi, 9, 187; A.P.W. Malcomson, 'The parliamentary traffic of this country' in Bartlett and Hayton, *Penal Era and Golden Age*, p. 150.
25. *BNL*,15–19 Aug., 5–9 Sept. 1783; A 1783 Dublin Castle list of the house of commons, before and after the general election (PRONI, T/3035/1; hereafter Dublin Castle 1783 parliamentary list).
26. *BNL*, 1–5 Aug. 1783.
27. Paterson, 'Armagh Volunteers', vi, 77.
28. *BNL*, 22–6 Aug. 1783.
29. Dublin Castle 1783 parliamentary list.
30. Temple's 1782 parliamentary list, p. 235.
31. Memoirs (*HMC Charlemont*), i, 150; Charlemont to ?, 9 Aug. 1783 (RIA, Charlemont correspondence, ii, MS 104).
32. *BNL*, 23–27 May 1783.
33. *BNL*, 25–29 July 1783.
34. *BNL*, 26–9 Aug., 12–16 Sept. 1783.
35. *BNL*, 15 Aug. 1783.
36. *BNL*, 15–19, 19–22 Aug., 29 Aug.–2 Sept. 1783.

37 *BNL*, 26–29 Aug. 1783.
38 Lord Sandwich to Lord Gosford, 19 May 1783 (PRONI, Gosford papers, D/1606/1/1/102A).
39 Same to same, 1 July 1783 (ibid., D/1606/1/1/102B).
40 Memoirs (*HMC Charlemont*), i, 150; Charlemont to ?, 9 Aug. 1783 (RIA, Charlemont correspondence, ii, MS 104).
41 *BNL*, 29 Aug.–2 Sept., 2–5 Sept., 5–9 Sept. 1783.
42 'Figures for contested election in Co. Armagh, 1783–1826' (NLI, 'County Armagh Townlands', MS 2716, on fly-leaf).
43 *BNL*, 4 –9 Sept. 1783.
44 *BNL*, 3–7, 17–21 Oct., 28 Oct.–1 Nov. 1783.
45 Orde's 1784 parliamentary list (PRONI, Ashbourne papers, T/2955/F1/1; here after Orde's 1784 parliamentary list); Orde's parliamentary lists for 1784 –7 (NLI, Bolton MSS 15,917, 15,918, 15,919; hereafter Orde's parliamentary lists for 1784–7). Sligo parliamentary borough was controlled by Rt Hon. Owen Wynne who took one seat for himself and sold the other to Peter Metge – a baron of the exchequer – for use by the government to bring in Dawson 1783–90. Dawson was not returned in 1790.
46 Temple's 1782 parliamentary list, p. 235; Dublin Castle 1783 parliamentary list. Meredyth's annual pension of £500 had been supplemented with a sinecure of £100 per annum as secretary to the master of ordnance and, in December 1780, his nieces had been granted a pension of £200 per annum for Meredyth's services in the war department. Former army lieutenant colonel, Rawson, described as 'of small fortune', was reported as having been strongly recommended for office by his relative and patron, Lord Chief Justice Paterson, and being a loyal supporter of government.
47 *BNL*, 8–12 Aug. 1783.
48 *Commons' jn. Ire.* xxi, 9, 187; Drogheda, *Moore*, pedigree chart. Sir Annesley Stewart was married to Sarah Moore, sister of John Moore senior. Their only daughter was married to John Moore junior.
49 Temple's 1782 parliamentary list, p. 235; Dublin Castle 1783 parliamentary list.
50 Orde's parliamentary lists for 1784–7.
51 Lord Townshend to Sir Archibald Acheson, 7 Sept. 1772 (PRONI., Gosford papers, D/1606/1/1/75B).
52 Cotton, *Fasti*, ii, 342.
53 *BNL*, 23 Jan. 1807; Fitzpatrick to Arthur Acheson, Sept. 1782 (PRONI, Gosford papers, D/1606/1/1/96, 97).
54 Lord Edward Bentinck to [Acheson], 28 Feb. 1783 (PRONI, Gosford papers, D/1606/1/1/101).
55 Same to same, 5 Aug. 1783 (ibid., D/1606/1/1/106).
56 B. Hobart, portreeve of Carlow, to Arthur Acheson, 30 July 1783 (ibid., D/1606/1/1/104). Following the Shelburne ministry's expulsion from office in April 1783, the duke of Portland had succeeded as figure-head premier of the Fox-North Coalition and, on 3 May, a Portland Whig, Robert Henley, second earl of Northington, was appointed successor to Lord Temple as lord lieutenant of Ireland.
57 W.W. Grenville to Lord Gosford, 9 Nov. 1782 (ibid., D/1606/1/1/98).
58 Speaker Pery to Gosford, 20 July, 2, 4 Aug. 1783 (ibid., D/1606/1/1/103,105).
59 Earl of Northington to the duke of Rutland, 27 Feb. 1785, *HMC, 14th report, appendix, pt.1. The manuscripts of his grace the duke of Rutland, KG, preserved at Belvoir Castle* (4 vols, London, 1894; hereafter, *HMC Rutland*), iii, 76.

60 *CP*, ii, para. 31.
61 Orde's parliamentary lists for 1784–7. Earl Temple had been created marquess of Buckingham in 1784.
62 Connolly's usage is followed i.e. 'Catholic' is used for the contemporary 'Roman Catholic', 'Papist' or 'Romanist'; 'Anglican' or 'Established Church of Ireland' for the contemporary 'Protestant'; 'Presbyterian' for 'Dissenter'. 'Protestant' is used as an umbrella term denoting adherents of the Established Church of Ireland and Presbyterian/Dissenters; see Connolly, *Religion, law and power*, references page.
63 An English Catholic Relief Act in 1778 was followed by Luke Gardiner's measure for Ireland (*Irish Statutes*, 17 & 18 Geo. III, C. 49) which removed restraints against Catholics receiving and granting leases for years and disposing of their estates. Support for further relaxation of penal legislation against Catholics at the Dungannon Convention in February 1782 led to a second relief act by Gardiner in 1782 (21 &22 Geo. III, C. 24) granting Catholics the legal right to lease freehold – the same as Protestants, to practise their religion and to found educational institutions. But political rights were still denied to Catholics and advocates of parliamentary reform in Ireland were divided in 1783 on Catholic suffrage.
64 James Kelly, 'The parliamentary reform movement of the 1780s and the Catholic question' in *Archivium Hibernicum*, xliii (1988; hereafter, Kelly, 'Parliamentary reform movement'), pp 95–117; William Campbell, D.D. to Charlemont, 9 Oct. 1784 (*HMC Charlemont*), ii, 7–8; Lord Sydney to Rutland, 14 May 1784 (*HMC Rutland*), iii, 94.
65 'Select documents XLIII: A secret return of the Volunteers of Ireland in 1784', James Kelly (ed.) in *IHS*, xxvi (May 1989; hereafter Kelly, 'A secret return of the Volunteers, 1784'), p. 270.
66 *BNL*, 8–12 Aug., 19–23 Sept. 1783.
67 *BNL*, 29 Aug.–2 Sept., 12–16 Sept. 1783.
68 P.D.H. Smyth, 'The Volunteers and parliament, 1779–84', in (Bartlett & Hayton, *Penal Era and Golden Age*; hereafter, Smyth, 'Volunteers') p. 131.
69 *BNL*, 12–16 Sept., 11–14 Nov. 1783.
70 *BNL*, 23–26 Sept. 1783. The fifteen members – foreman William Richardson and jurors John Moore, John Blackhall, Alex T Stewart, James Dawson, Francis Tipping, James Johnston, Thomas McCann, Jacob Turner, Joseph McGeough, Robert Jackson, David Bell, Thomas Clarke, Samuel Falkner and James Eastwood – published a resolution 'to give them every support which the great importance of the object demands from all friends of constitutional liberty, and the unalienable rights of mankind'.
71 *BNL*, 26–30 Sept., 10–14 Oct. 1783.
72 *BNL*, 10–14, 17–21, 21–24 Oct. 1783.
73 *BNL*, 4–7 Nov. 1783.
74 Charlemont to Grattan, 9, 14 Feb. 1784 (*Grattan's Memoirs*), iii, 192–195; memoirs (*HMC Charlemont*), i, 105–7; Johnston-Liik, *Irish parliament*, vi, 342.
75 *BNL*, 4–7, 7–11 Nov. 1783.
76 Pelham to Portland, 30 Nov. 1783 (Pelham papers, British Museum, Additional MSS 33100; PRONI, T/755/1, p. 427).
77 'Irish Parliamentary Debates', p. 2 in *BNL*, 2–5 Dec. 1783.
78 *BNL*, 2–5 Dec. 1783.
79 *BNL*, 5–9 Dec. 1783.
80 *BNL*, 23–26 Dec. 1783.
81 *BNL*, 23–26 Dec. 1783.
82 *BNL*, 2–5 Mar. 1784.

83   *BNL*, 9–13 Jan. 1784.
84   Patrick Rogers, *The Irish Volunteers and Catholic Emancipation 1778–1793* (London, 1934), pp 144–56; Smyth, 'Volunteers', pp 134–5.
85   Northington to Rutland, 29 Feb. 1784, and Home Secretary Lord Sydney, Whitehall, to Rutland, 3 Mar., 17 Oct. 1784 (*HMC Rutland*), iii, 77–8, 143–4. Charles Manners, duke of Rutland, a follower of Chatham and his son, was appointed lord privy seal in Pitt's first administration in December 1783; then almost immediately was transferred to lord lieutenant of Ireland, much to Northington's disappointment. Rutland's policies to deal firmly with the Volunteers, parliamentary reformers and demands for Catholic suffrage had the approval of George III.
86   *BNL*, 2–5, 5–9 Mar. 1784. Sir Richard Johnston was a government pension-holder brought in by Lord Hillsborough.
87   Rutland to Sydney, 10 Mar. 1784 (*HMC Rutland*), iii, 79–80.
88   *BNL*, 19–23, 23–26, 26–30 Mar. 1784; Orde's 1784 parliamentary list.
89   *BNL*, 28 May–1 June 1784. The 'new Mass-house' was probably St. Mary's Catholic Church, Belfast, erected in 1784, see Ambrose Macaulay, *William Crolly, archbishop of Armagh* (Dublin, 1984), p. 10.
90   *BNL*, 8–11 June 1784.
91   'Returns of the Volunteer voluntary corps with private observations' (NLI, Bolton papers, MS 15,891/3).
92   *Belfast Mercury or Freeman's Chronicle*, 18 Mar. 1785 (Linen Hall Library, Belfast).
93   Stuart, *Armagh*, p. 560.
94   Paterson, 'Armagh Volunteers', v, 48.
95   William Campbell to Charlemont, 9 Oct.1784 (*HMC Charlemont*), ii, 7; Sydney to Rutland, 26 Sept. 1784 (*HMC Rutland*), iii, 140.
96   Dean Hamilton to Chief Baron Hamilton, 20 Oct. 1784 (NLI, Bolton papers, MS 16350/47).
97   Baron George Hamilton to Thomas Orde, 22 Oct. 1784, and Orde's reply (ibid., MSS 16350/48, 49).
98   Primate Robinson to Orde, 18 Jan. 1785 (ibid., MS 16350/71).
99   Brownlow to Charlemont, 6 July 1785 (*HMC Charlemont*), ii, 21; same to same, 5 Nov. 1785 (ibid.), ii, 28.
100   *BNL*, 20–23, 23–27 July 1784; William Drennan to Mrs McTier, July 1784 (PRONI, Drennan papers, T/765/2/1, letters 152, 158).
101   Charlemont to Haliday, 27 Aug.1784 (*HMC Charlemont*), ii, 6; *BNL*, 30 July–3 Aug. 1784.
102   Campbell to Charlemont, 24 Dec. 1784 (*HMC Charlemont*), ii, 16.
103   *BNL*, 11–14 Jan. 1785; 'Armagh grand juries'.
104   *BNL*, 18–21, 21–25 Jan. 1785; Campbell to Charlemont, 25 Dec. 1784 (*HMC Charlemont*), ii, 16.
105   *BNL*, 25–28 Jan. 1785.
106   Charlemont to Maxwell, 22 Feb. 1785 (*HMC Charlemont*), ii, 17.
107   *BNL*, 15–18, 18–22 Feb. 1785; *Grattan's Memoirs*, iii, 226–7.
108   *BNL*, 13–17 May 1785.
109   *BNL*, 30 Sept.–4 Oct. 1785.
110   *BNL*, 8–11 Feb. 1785; Rutland to Pitt, 6 Feb. 1785 (*HMC Rutland*), iii, 175–6.
111   Rutland to Sydney, 20 May 1785 (*HMC Rutland*), iii, 207.
112   Kelly, *Prelude to Union*, pp 131–69.
113   *BNL*, 21–24, 24–28 June 1785.

114 Brownlow to Charlemont, 6 July 1785 (*HMC Charlemont*), ii, 21; *BNL*, 8–12 July 1785.
115 *BNL*, 16–19 Aug. 1785; *Grattan's Memoirs*, iii, App. iv, 493.
116 Charlemont to Haliday, 16 Aug. 1785 (*HMC Charlemont*), ii, 22–3; *BNL*, 19–23 Aug. 1785.
117 *BNL*, 30 Sept.–4 Oct. 1785.
118 Ibid.
119 Brownlow to Charlemont 15 Oct. 1785 (*HMC Charlemont*), ii, 25–6.
120 Earl of Mornington to W.W. Grenville, 30 Nov. 1783 (*HMC Fortescue*), i, 225.
121 Charlemont to James Stewart, 17 Sept. 1785 (PRONI, Stewart papers, D/3167/1/20, MIC/509/1); Brownlow to Charlemont, 5 Nov. 1785 (*HMC Charlemont*), ii, 27–8; *BNL*, 8–11, 11–15 Nov. 1785.
122 Charlemont to Haliday, 7 Nov. 1785 (*HMC Charlemont*), ii, 28–9.
123 *DEP*, 27 Mar. 1787 (DCLA, newspaper collection).
124 Acheson to Lord Northington 23 Aug., Orde to Gosford 24 Aug., Northington to Acheson, 3 Sept. 1785 (PRONI, Gosford papers, D/1606/1/1/109B, 109C, 109D).
125 Malcomson, *Foster*, pp 60–1.
126 *DEP*, 23 Aug. 1785.
127 Orde to Pery, 24 Aug. 1785 (PRONI, Emly papers, T/3052/198); Charlemont to James Stewart, 31 Aug. 1785 (PRONI, Stewart papers, D/3167/1/19, MIC 509/1); Sydney to Rutland, 8 Sept. 1785 (*HMC Rutland*), iii, 240.
128 Orde to Gosford, 24 Aug. 1785 (PRONI, Gosford papers, D/1606/1/1/109C).
129 Same to same, 31 Dec. 1785 and Gosford's reply on 5 Jan. 1786, (ibid., D/1606/1/1/112).
130 Gosford to Acheson, 7, 9 Jan. 1786 (ibid., D/1606/1/1/113A, 113B).
131 Hobart's 1788 parliamentary list (PRONI, Hobart papers, T/2627/1/1/1; hereafter, Hobart's 1788 parliamentary list).
132 *DEP*, 7, 9 Mar. 1786, 13 Mar. 1787.
133 *DEP*, 26 Feb., 1 Mar. 1788.
134 *DEP*, 17 Feb. 1789; Orde's parliamentary lists for 1784–7; *FJ*, 10–12 Feb. 1789.
135 *Grattan's Memoirs*, iii, 390.
136 The marquess of Buckingham's second term as viceroy which followed the duke of Rutland's death at Phoenix Lodge on 24 October 1787, lasted for two years. Buckingham's chief secretaries were Alleyne Fitzherbert, until April 1789, followed by Robert Hobart. When the unpopular Buckingham was recalled in October 1789, Hobart continued as chief secretary to Buckingham's successor, John Fane, tenth earl of Westmorland; see *CP*, i, para. 407; v, para. 271.
137 Hobart's 1788 parliamentary list; Malcomson, *Isaac Corry*, p. 6 gives Corry as having accepted the semi-sinecure office of surveyor-general of the ordnance during 1788.
138 Lord John Townshend to Acheson, 27 Feb. 1789 (PRONI, Gosford papers, D/1606/1/1/136).
139 *DEP*, 2, 6 Feb., 6 Mar. 1790; *BNL*, 5–9, 9–12 Feb. 1790; *FJ*, 4–6 Feb. 1790.
140 Dean Hamilton to Chief Baron Hamilton, 20 Oct. 1784, and Primate Robinson to Orde, 18 Jan. 1785 (NLI, Bolton MSS 16350/47, 71); Sydney to Rutland, 1 Feb. 1785 (*HMC Rutland*), iii, 174.
141 Pamphlet, *An impartial account of the late disturbances in the county of Armagh … by an inhabitant of the town of Armagh*, signed J. Byrne (Dublin, 1792, PRONI, T/3575/1); T.G.F. Paterson's transcript copy of 'An impartial account of

the late disturbances in the county of Armagh' (Armagh County Museum and PRONI, T/1722/1–100, with Paterson's notes).
142 Orde to Gosford, 31 Dec. 1785 (PRONI, Gosford papers D/1606/1/1/112).
143 Moore to Gosford, 25 Feb. 1787 (RIA, Charlemont Correspondence, iii, MSS 84, 85); D.W. Miller (ed.), *Peep O'Day Boys and Defenders: selected documents on the County Armagh disturbances 1784–96* (Belfast, PRONI, 1990; hereafter, Miller, *Peep O'Day Boys*), pp 42–3. This John Moore was probably John Moore senior, then c. 61 years old.
144 Gosford to Arthur Acheson, 25 Aug. 1787 (PRONI, Gosford papers, D/1606/1/1/120).
145 [Rev.] Allott, Armagh, to Orde, 23 Aug. 1787 (NLI, Bolton papers. MS 16350/94). Leslie gives Dr Richard Allott as precentor of Armagh 1775–95 and dean of Raphoe 1796–1832 where he died 1832; see Leslie, *Armagh clergy*, p. 35.
146 Rutland to Sydney, 5 Aug. 1787 (*HMC Rutland*), iii, 403.
147 Allott to Orde, 23 Aug. 1787 (NLI, Bolton papers, MS 16350/94). Sir Walter Synnot lived at Ballymoyer, near Newtownhamilton, and in 1787 was magistrate and lieutenant colonel of the Southern Battalion of Volunteers; Thomas McCann was captain of Armagh Second Company of Volunteers and had served numerous spells as sovereign of Armagh city.
148 Gosford to Arthur Acheson, 8 Feb. 1788 (PRONI, Gosford papers D/1606/1/1/125B, 125C).
149 '1766 religious census' (PRONI, T/808).
150 Gosford to Arthur Acheson, 8 Feb. 1788 (PRONI, Gosford papers D/1606/1/1/125B, 125C).
151 Campbell to Charlemont, 9 Feb. 1788 (*HMC Charlemont*), ii, 68–70.
152 Enclosure in Haliday to Charlemont, 2 Apr. 1788 (*HMC Charlemont*), ii, 74; Charlemont to Haliday, 1 Aug. 1788 (ibid.), ii, 76; *BNL*, 22–25 July 1788; Charlemont to ? (RIA Charlemont Correspondence, x, MS 109).
153 [Rev.] Campbell to Charlemont, 26 Nov. 1788 (*HMC Charlemont*), ii, 78–9.
154 Moore to Charlemont, 15 July 1789 (RIA Charlemont Correspondence, iv, MS 56).
155 [Rev.] Edward Hudson to Charlemont, 11 July 1789 (*HMC Charlemont*), ii, 102–3.
156 Same to same, 26 Aug. 1789 (RIA Charlemont Correspondence, iv, MS 61).
157 Falkland [Rev. J.R. Scott], *A review of the principal characters of the Irish house of commons* (Dublin, 1789), p. 40.
158 Haliday to Charlemont, 10 Apr. 1785 (RIA Charlemont Correspondence, iii, MS 29).
159 W.H. Crawford, 'The Linen Triangle in the 1790s', in *ULS*, xviii, no. 2 (1997) pp 43–51; Miller, *Peep O'Day Boys*, p. 4.

6

The 1790 general election poll; the struggle for political control of County Armagh 1790–6

INTRODUCTION: PRE-ELECTION CONCERNS

The Dublin administration of Lord Lieutenant Westmorland and Chief Secretary Robert Hobart had cause to view the approaching 1790 general election in County Armagh with some apprehension. Opposition politics remained in the ascendancy in what was regarded as one of the leading 'independent' counties where county members William Brownlow and William Richardson and Lord Charlemont's nominees Henry Grattan and Sir Annesley Stewart all adhered to Whig liberal politics of campaigning for economical reform. All four had consistently opposed government measures for additional posts, pensions and places in the parliament of 1783–90.

Charlemont, Grattan and Stewart were founder members of the Whig Club of Ireland in June 1789, Brownlow, Francis Dobbs and Charlemont original members of the Northern Whig Club founded by Charlemont's friend Dr Alexander Haliday in Belfast in February 1790. The Whig clubs comprised liberal peers, radicals, independent country gentlemen and businessmen and could muster about ninety members of parliament in a division. Their parliamentary programme advocated such measures as a place bill, a pension bill, a bill for the disenfranchisement of revenue officers, a responsibility bill limiting signatures of approval for public expenditure to officials permanently resident in Ireland, and reform of the costly and ineffective Dublin City police.[1] But while Armagh opposition members followed Irish Whig political principles of economical reform, they had tended to avoid, as far as possible, two contemporary major issues in Irish politics i.e. parliamentary reform and Catholic suffrage. In 1790, a challenge still facing the Dublin administration was how to break down the political traditions of independence and opposition in Armagh.

An internal problem for the Armagh ruling élite on the eve of the general election was the persistent climate of fear in the county as sectarian disturbances continued. Competition within the linen industry continued to breed mutual distrust between Protestants and Catholics and attacks upon each other's homes. Many Protestants also feared a political take-over by the Catholics and were particularly alarmed that the latter might acquire firearms. The Volunteers, whose numbers, status and political influence had diminished by 1790, were distrusted by many Catholics and only exacerbated the sectarian violence where they became embroiled, as at Blackwatertown in 1788.[2]

Some Volunteer companies were also used as private armies by the gentry. Rev. Edward Hudson, rector of Forkhill, accused John Moore's Volunteers of being the cause of the riot and bloodshed of unarmed Catholics assembled to celebrate the feast of St. John's Eve on 23 June 1789 near Drumbanagher.[3] In late summer, Hudson was urging Lord Charlemont to use his influence on aspiring candidates to withdraw in order to prevent a general election contest in such troubled times.[4] On 19 December 1789, the violence was brought home to Hudson when his horse was shot beneath him when riding on the high road near Forkhill.[5] A local leader of a band of Peep O'Day Boys was charged with his attempted murder but released on probation.[6]

The ruling élite in County Armagh in 1789–90, always concerned since 1753 about the potential for violence at a contested county election, was particularly worried about the coming election amid sectarian tensions and violence. This was evident in the reluctance of gentry Francis Tipping of Mounthill, Thomas Ball of Cullyhanna, Savage Hall of Mount Hall and Mullaghglass and James Harden of Clare-Castle, to accept appointment to sheriff in election year. An alarmed Harden appealed to Lord Gosford to use his influence to have him excused from the onerous post. None of the above was chosen and James Johnston of Knappagh was appointed sheriff for 1790.[7] But despite expressed concerns that an election contest would increase violence in the county, at least two new potential candidates were considering their chances of ousting the sitting county members. Arthur Acheson and John Moore junior, eldest sons of resident gentry in the county and sitting members for borough seats outside the county were, in 1789, exploring the possibility of winning Armagh county seats.

PRELIMINARY NEGOTIATIONS, JANUARY 1789 TO MAY 1790, IN THE CONTEST FOR ARMAGH COUNTY SEATS

As early as January 1789, Arthur Acheson had approached absentee landlord William Nedham for his Armagh electoral interest west of Newry but had been refused by Nedham on the grounds that Nedham had hitherto supported Brownlow and Richardson and felt obliged to continue to do so.[8] About the same time, Acheson, on the advice of his father, also wrote to Richard 'Dick' Dawson asking for his interest in Armagh.[9] Dawson's reply was little more promising – that he had received a similar application from Richardson in the same post and was hoping the two applicants could come to some arrangement before the election to spare him 'the necessity of disobliging one of two friends.'[10]

In February 1789, Acheson would seem to have been keeping his options open when he renewed communications with Portland and Pelham to reassure them of his loyalty to the English connection and offering his services to the administration rumoured to be succeeding that of Buckingham.[11] Acheson's profession of loyalty must have been very welcome to Whitehall in a period when the Irish opposition had hardened against the arrogant Buckingham, though the latter's administration survived for another eight months. The Whitehall reception of his communication was sufficiently warm to encourage Acheson to re-open negotiations for the Old Leighlin borough seat which he currently held but had been no longer sure of retaining since the death of his uncle, Bishop Walter Cope, in 1787.

It was about this time that Acheson would seem to have abandoned his campaign for an Armagh county seat. In summer 1789, his friend 'R. Johnston, inspector of ports in Ulster', based in Newry, who was canvassing there on Acheson's behalf, reported hearing rumours that Acheson was considering withdrawing as candidate for the county. Johnston, as one of absentee landlord Nedham's Armagh tenants around Newry, confirmed that while Nedham had given his interest to Brownlow, all was not lost for Acheson, as most of Nedham's tenants were in a similar situation to himself i.e. 'neither known to him [Nedham], courts his smiles, or fears his frowns' – and presumably vulnerable to a canvass by the Acheson camp.[12]

An important document emerging from the Acheson-Johnston correspondence of mid-1789 was a list of some twenty two County Armagh holdings with estimated numbers of freeholders on each. The figures, rounded to the nearest ten, totalled 2,540 freeholders, and provide a useful approximation of the County Armagh electorate pre the 1793 Catholic Relief Act.[13] These pre-election calculations in the June 1789 list would seem to have convinced Acheson to abandon plans to contest a county seat. After Johnston's letter, there are no further references to Acheson as county candidate in contemporary correspondence. Instead, the challenge to the Armagh sitting county members was taken up by John Moore junior of Drumbanagher who revealed his determination to make the break-through into northern politics by standing as candidate for the constituencies of Lisburn borough and Armagh county.

In 1790, Lord Drogheda persuaded his father-in-law Lord Hertford to nominate John Moore junior again as candidate in the Lisburn borough election – this time as running partner with George Hatton, Hertford's son-in-law. Their opponents were sitting member, old Volunteer and economical reformist Todd Jones – 'unbought and unacquainted with the minister of corruption' – and Richard Griffiths who were supported by the toasts of the Northern Whig Club. But with Volunteerism in terminal decline, Moore and Hatton were easy winners. At the termination of poll on 26 April 1790, Hatton had polled 288 votes and Moore 286 votes against the 109 and 108 votes of Jones and Griffiths respectively. A disappointed Jones and Griffiths petitioned against the winners 'on the grounds of every species of undue influence having been made use of by their opponents'.[14]

With the Lisburn poll result in abeyance, Moore turned to his second option as candidate for Armagh county. His opponents were sitting members Brownlow and Richardson who, at County Armagh Lenten Assizes, had been invited to continue as MPs by the county grand jury chaired by Alexander Thomas Stewart of Acton. However, an unsigned newspaper notice dated 29 March 1790 asked Armagh voters to 'hold themselves disengaged' until a *meeting of freeholders* had been convened to choose suitable candidates for parliament. Moore was probably the author, exploiting old divisions between freeholders and the grand jury over the right to choose county MPs, as a means of challenging the Brownlow-Richardson tenure of county seats.[15]

Publicity for the general election escalated in April 1790. A newspaper notice at the beginning of April emphasised the importance of the electorate setting a 'test' for potential general election candidates. The Northern Whig Club at its meeting in Belfast on 16 April promoted the tactic of extracting pledges from would-be candidates in support of economical reform and issued a set of questions to be put by electors to candidates.[16] Early April brought a burst of canvassing from candidates and their supporters. From Dublin, Brownlow – who had not considered it necessary to canvass other interests in the previous two elections – was now sufficiently concerned to request Lord Gosford for his interest in County Armagh.[17] In the following week, parliament was dissolved and writs issued for the Armagh election.[18]

William Richardson's election strategy was to discourage Moore by canvassing heavily those estates surrounding Moore's estate. Moore's earlier reference to a conspiracy against him by avoidance of a poll, was confirmed in Richardson's letter to Lord Gosford in Dublin asking Gosford to nominate a local guide to accompany him on his election tour of the Gosford estates:

> My Lord, In order if possible to prevent a poll at the ensuing election, it will be absolutely necessary for me to go through all the estates that surround Drumbanagher – Your lordship seemed to be entirely of that opinion, and that it might be prudent also to visit yours, though it was not likely he [Moore] could make any impression there – your lordship was good enough to say you would leave sufficient directions for communicating your wishes to your tenantry, before you went to Dublin.[19]

The hopes of the ruling élite avoiding a contest in Armagh county were thwarted by a group determined to stir up opposition to the sitting members. Brownlow found himself victim of a resurrected smear campaign branding him pro-Catholic, similar to the smear he had suffered in his first contest thirty six years earlier when his ancestors had been dubbed crypto-Catholics, dating to his grandfather's attendance in James II's parliament of 1689. With some breast-beating, Charlemont confirmed to Dr Haliday in Belfast 'the contagion has spread itself even among some of my tenantry'. The earl avoided mentioning that the same 'contagion' had pervaded the Charlemont tenantry in 1753 when his younger brother Francis Caulfeild had challenged Brownlow for the county seat. While agreeing with Haliday that Brownlow's record had earned the support of Armagh freeholders, he claimed he was reluctant to attempt forcing his tenantry to vote for Brownlow and sufficed with a suggestion to his friend that a refutal of the smear by the Northern Whig Club would help Brownlow's cause.[20]

The smear campaign against Brownlow forced him into election activity he had not anticipated necessary. Now sixty four years of age and living in Dublin, he was not prepared to undertake an election tour of County Armagh. Instead, he published an extended election manifesto on 17 April 1790, reminding constituents of his thirty six years of selfless public service, that he was no longer fit enough for the physical efforts of a tour – and if he was really serving his own interests should be retiring – and that his candidature rested on his political record. He invited them to review his promotion of key patriotic issues as their representative over the years: 'the freeing of her constitution from the dependence in which it was so long held – shortening the duration of parliaments, which is a proper check on the conduct of the representative, extending the freedom of trade, and encouraging the linen in every branch'. Thus Brownlow rested his case for re-election, saying he would he would never resort to 'any of the arts too frequent at elections.'[21]

It is not clear how far Moore was party to the smear campaign against Brownlow. His own election image was that of saviour of the people as enforcer of law and order – in Brownlow's sarcastic description, 'the man of the people and protector of his country'.[22] The Drumbanagher Volunteers had been deployed as a vigilante company by the Moore family who persisted with this out-of-fashion paramilitary image in 1790 when the Volunteer ethos was jaded.

THE POLL FOR ARMAGH COUNTY SEATS, 5–14 MAY 1790

Moore junior attempted to cut a military dash when the Armagh poll opened on Wednesday 5 May 1790 by entering the arena escorted by a 'grand cavalcade and band of music', and accompanied with his followers and freeholders. However, his lack of electoral nous was soon evident. When Sir Capel Molyneux proposed Moore and a Captain McCullough, 'an American loyalist of very indifferent character' for his running partner, McCullough did not receive a seconder, leaving Moore without a running partner and his second votes 'all sunk'. In contrast, Brownlow and Richardson arrived quietly without escort – perhaps with the objectives of avoiding fuss and violence in the sensitive atmosphere. They also won the best position on the court and first tally. Moore was represented legally by George William Molyneux, Francis Dobbs – Stewart's land agent, admired by Brownlow – and a Mr. Hawkshaw. Brownlow and Richardson were represented by Counsellor Pollock of Newry. The size of crowd and general disorganisation allowed few votes to be polled for each candidate on the opening day before the court adjourned – Brownlow wrote that ten votes had been cast for each.[23] The *Belfast News-Letter* reported that only five votes had been cast for each.[24]

The second day of the poll provided extraordinary public gimmickry and verbal exchanges between the contestants and legal advisors. George Molyneux would seem to have made a number of tactical errors. After a few votes were polled on 6 May, he dramatically produced a 'test' pledging attendance at parliament and obedience to his constituents which his client Moore publicly signed. Brownlow and Richardson responded with enhanced flourish by not only pledging themselves publicly to Molyneux's test but to 'a much fuller and explicit one', whereupon their supporters reaffirmed their confidence in Brownlow and Richardson. When Molyneux attacked Brownlow's conduct in parliament, Brownlow refuted the attack and, in turn, attacked the records of both Moore and Molyneux there reminding them they had mostly opposed the patriotic stance of Richardson and himself. Molyneux erred further when he agreed to the first twenty votes polled being 'ten pounders'. While Brownlow and Richardson polled theirs, Moore could only produce the single £10 freeholder vote of Sir Capel Molyneux, indicating that the wealthier freeholders were mostly in the Brownlow-Richardson camp.[25]

Despite initial tactical errors by his advisors at the poll, Moore was still well placed to win a seat as voting neared completion. At the close of poll on Tuesday 11 May, the state of the Armagh poll was as follows: Brownlow led with 414 votes, Moore was second with 406 votes and Richardson third with 402 votes.[26] On Thursday, 13 May, Moore was narrowly leading the poll with 586 votes to Brownlow's 585 and Richardson's 574.[27]

Contemporary correspondence and the election calculations of 1789 allow an estimate and identification of most of the election interests controlling those who voted for each candidate at the Armagh county poll of 1790. The mutual pact between Brownlow and Richardson seemed to assure the Armagh interests of Gosford, Nedham and Dick Dawson. The combined total of these five interests by Arthur Acheson's election calculations, if maximised, was 860 freeholder votes for each candidate. Charlemont had also promised Brownlow his personal support but it is unclear how many of his tenants followed him.

Moore had the support of Sir Capel Molyneux and his close neighbour Alexander Thomas Stewart – who, ironically, had chaired the Armagh grand jurors proposing Brownlow and Richardson for re-election at the Lenten assizes. These three interests would have totalled 280 votes and Moore would probably have expected some votes from Charlemont's tenants. However, there would have been little point in Moore going to the poll with so few votes and it is likely he had been promised one of the bigger interests. That was probably the Cope interest of Loughgall Manor, largest of the 1789 calculations at 450 freeholders. Arthur Cope's ambitions for a county seat having been thwarted by Brownlow and the Armagh ruling élite in 1768 and 1776, the widespread Cope interest may well have been directed against them in 1790. By the 1789 estimates, the combined maximum support from Cope, Molyneux and Stewart, with his own interest, would have produced 730 votes, and given Moore a chance of taking a county seat, depending on the direction of votes by the absentee landlords and smaller interests.

Moore's election ambitions for an Armagh county seat were not to be realised. About mid-day on Friday 14 May, while Brownlow and Richardson continued to poll their freeholder supporters, Moore was unable to find further voters within the time allowed and was obliged to concede the contest and rest his hopes for a return to parliament on the outcome of the suspended Lisburn borough election. Brownlow and Richardson had polled 820 votes each and Moore, 619 votes. When High Sheriff Johnston declared Brownlow and Richardson elected, a musical band paraded the pair around Armagh city. Their camp boasted: 'Had it been thought necessary to continue the poll, there were at least 800 more freeholders would have polled for the successful candidates'.[28] As the 1789 election calculations had estimated an Armagh county electorate of 2,540 freeholders and – assuming split-voting between Brownlow and Richardson – approximately 1,440 had voted, their boast may not have been idle.

BOROUGH RETURNS IN 1790

At the 1790 general election, George Rawson was returned again for Armagh borough by Primate Robinson on behalf of the Dublin administration. By then, he had been rewarded with appointment to commissioner of stamps on £500 per annum for consistent support of government in parliamentary divisions since 1777.[29] His sitting partner, the long-serving Henry Meredyth had died on 10 December 1789 and been replaced by serving government officer Henry Duquery who was sworn for Armagh borough on 1 February 1790.[30] However, Duquery only served in his maiden seat from then until dissolution on 8 April 1790. He purchased his own seat in the new parliament for Rathcormack, a close borough in County Cork, the property of Lord Riversdale, a minor. Duquery had not changed seats on political grounds since he continued as supporter of Westmorland's administration for which service he was promoted to second sergeant in 1791. Later, however, Duquery used his new-found independence to oppose the Convention Bill of 1793 and to support the Short Money Bill of 1795.[31]

Duquery's replacement in the Armagh borough seat at the general election by the primate was Chief Secretary Major Robert Hobart. Hobart had come to Ireland with his uncle Lord Lieutenant Buckinghamshire in 1777, served as aide-de-camp to the duke of Rutland and been brought in by the government as member for Portarlington, Queen's County, 1784–90 – re-paying the favour by supporting the Commercial Propositions in 1785 and opposing a regency in 1789. He was appointed chief secretary to Lord Lieutenant Buckingham, at the latter's request, as replacement for the unsuitable Alleyne Fitzherbert on 6 April 1789 and continued in post from 24 October 1789 to December 1793 under Buckingham's successor, Westmorland. Hobart represented Armagh borough from 1790 to 1797. Though personally opposed to Catholic relief, Hobart faithfully followed instructions from the British government and steered the Catholic Enfranchisement Bill through a reluctant Irish parliament from its introduction on 4 February to the royal assent on 9 April 1793.[32] Aware that war with France was imminent, the British government had defied the wishes of the Irish administration to force through Catholic Relief, to prevent Irish Catholics supporting United Irish assistance to France.

There was also one change to the representation for Charlemont borough in 1790. The sixty five year old Sir Annesley Stewart who had represented Charlemont since 1763 and who, in the previous parliaments had consistently voted Charlemont's opposition-reformist line, was nominated again by Lord Charlemont. But Grattan's support for the Northington administration in 1783, for the augmentation of the regular army and restoration of its dominance over the Volunteers, had angered Charlemont who tended to regard political differences as personal and unpardonable. As the 1790 general election approached, Grattan looked elsewhere for a return to parliament. In March he accepted an invitation from '1,500 of the free and independent electors of the city of Dublin' and, in a contest, was returned with Lord Henry Fitzgerald to the Dublin City seat held by his father in 1761–6.[33]

Charlemont had researched carefully for a person of suitable political principles to replace Grattan as Sir Annesley Stewart's parliamentary partner. Possible candidates of Whig persuasion included: Stewart's son James – for whom Grattan had purchased an Enniskillen borough seat in the previous parliament; Richard Mountney Jephson, a young lawyer due to be called to the Irish bar; and Richard Sheridan, a namesake and cousin of the dramatist, a lawyer from Quilca, County Cavan, barrister since 1774 and, by 1790, king's counsel and circuit judge.[34] In mid-April 1790, Charlemont's literary acquaintance Edmond Malone recommended the son of their mutual friend Jephson 'your thoughts might perhaps lean to Richard Jephson, the second son of our old friend ... a thorough Whig'.[35] But Malone's recommendation was too late. Following the issue of the writs, Charlemont had offered Sheridan the Charlemont borough seat outlining his own political 'creed' as patriot first – 'wishing to act, at all times and upon every occasion, in the manner which I may deem most essentially advantageous to her [Ireland]' – and Whig second – 'a Whig, almost by nature ... But I was an Irishman before I was a party man'.[36] Sheridan accepted Charlemont's terms and, in his three years in parliament, faithfully followed his patron's patriot/Whig policy. Jephson's turn would come when Sheridan died in December 1793. Brought in for Charlemont borough in January 1794, he also faithfully voted Charlemont's opposition line.

By April 1790, Arthur Acheson believed that he was now well enough ensconced in the government camp to ask for a government post for his brother-in-law, Alexander Macaulay, though, again, such a request on Macaulay's behalf by the Acheson family was unsuccessful.[37] Acheson was more successful with his own application for the Old Leighlin borough seat he had held since 1783. In early May, he was informed by Rev. Nicholas Forster that he had been unanimously elected with Edward Cooke, election expenses costing £30.7s.6d.[38]

Isaac Corry of Derrymore, recently promoted from surveyor-general of the ordnance to commissioner of the revenue, was returned with his sitting partner Colonel Robert Ross after a contest for the potwalloping borough of Newry. Corry topped the poll, followed by Ross and easily defeated Messrs Camac and Gordon. Corry's services for government in the revenue board and in parliamentary debate would bring his honorary promotion to privy councillor in 1795.[39] Following his defeat in the Armagh county election, John Moore had to suffer the additional indignity of being adjudged 'not duly elected' in Lisburn borough, was only returned after a re-election and not sworn until 28 March 1791. In the 1790 parliament Moore followed the disposition of his patron Lord Drogheda and supported government.[40]

THE STRUGGLE FOR POLITICAL CONTROL OF COUNTY ARMAGH: DISPOSITIONS OF ARMAGH MPS IN PARLIAMENTARY DIVISIONS, 1790–6

The predilection of Armagh MPs in the speakership election of 2 July 1790 seemed propitious for Westmorland's new administration. When John Foster retained the speakership by 145 votes to 105 in the face of William Brabazon Ponsonby's Whig challenge, of the Armagh MPs, only Lord Charlemont's protégés Stewart and Sheridan – and former Charlemont member Grattan – voted for Ponsonby. In addition to the expected support of Armagh borough members George Rawson and Chief Secretary Hobart and that of Isaac Corry, Foster secured the vote of Armagh county member William Richardson while Brownlow and Acheson, seem to have ducked a decision by absenting themselves from the vote.[41]

But, as Malcomson has pointed out, Foster's position was exceptional in that his acknowledged ability as speaker and his country-gentleman ethos continued in 1790 to win him the support of members 'not normally amenable to government influence'.[42] Voting patterns of the Armagh county members reverted to patriot type subsequently. In 1791, Richardson, Stewart and Sheridan supported Curran's resolution for an enquiry into the sale of peerages, Grattan's motion for the exercise of free trade – both in February – and Grattan's resolution on 4 March 1791 that the police system established for Dublin city had not justified its expense and should be changed. Brownlow missed the first two divisions but voted for abolition of the Dublin police establishment. John Moore voted for enquiry into peerages and abolition of the Dublin police.[43]

Over the following years most Armagh members avoided major parliamentary divisions. When Grattan moved to postpone the government's Convention Bill on 17 July 1793, the only Armagh member to support him was Stewart, while Corry and Hobart voted with government. No Armagh member voted in the division on the short money bill on 3 March 1795.[44]

The Armagh politicians were determined to keep the divisive issue of 'complete' Catholic Emancipation at a distance. Though the British government had forced the 1793 Catholic Relief Act through the Irish parliament, the attempts of others to pass 'complete' Emancipation at that time were defeated. All Armagh MPs were absent from the division on 25 February 1793 on George Knox's motion to enable Catholics 'to sit and vote in parliament'.[45] In the division on Grattan's Catholic Bill on 7 May 1795, when most county members from Ulster, including Armagh's William Brownlow junior and William Richardson, voted with government against complete Emancipation, all other Armagh members absented themselves from the vote.[46]

And the trend of abstention by Armagh members continued, with Jephson, who had replaced Sheridan in 1794, the only Armagh MP publicly reported as supporting Grattan's 21 January 1796 amendment motion for equality of trade with Great Britain and W.B. Ponsonby's motion for parliamentary reform on 15 May 1797.[47] Thus, in the parliament of 1790, four of the six members returned for Armagh seats were 'independent'. Their political dispositions were part of the Armagh political tradition which, in the 1790s, the Dublin administration sought to change.

DEVELOPING A PRO-GOVERNMENT CAUCUS IN ARMAGH IN THE 1790s

The Dublin administration sought to establish a pro-government caucus in the 1790s to challenge the patriot/Whig opposition and eradicate any resurgence of Volunteerism. Leaders of this government interest in the north eastern counties were John Foster in County Louth, the marquis of Downshire in County Down and Arthur Acheson – soon to succeed as second Viscount Gosford – in County Armagh.[48] Acheson's pre-election offer to support government had paid further dividends when he was chosen as new leader of the government party in his native county following his father's unexpected death in September 1790 and his inheritance of the Gosford title and seat in the house of lords.[49]

Arthur, Lord Gosford had a rapid rise to prominence in his new role. Following his succession, he moved residence from 88 Sackville Street, Dublin – retained by the Gosfords as a city house until 1808 – to the family home at Markethill.[50] His move may have been prompted by Dublin Castle which, on 5 October 1790, appointed him joint-governor of the county with Lord Charlemont.[51] While the appointment of a resident governor could be seen as sensible strategy in a county torn with recurring internal strife, Charlemont, who had been sole governor since 1749 and claimed to have only heard of the new arrangement some four months after its occurrence from a friend who had read of it in the *Gazette*, took Gosford's joint appointment as a personal insult by government. If the appointment was a calculated insult by government, it had the desired result. Charlemont flounced out of post on 7 February 1791, leaving Gosford as sole governor and better positioned to challenge the monopoly control by Whig opposition.[52]

Another step was taken with the official suppression of the Volunteers and their replacement with a national militia to oppose the threat of the United Irish Society which was publicly reporting meetings in Armagh. Masonic lodges in the county were similarly demanding 'radical and impartial reform of the constitution'.[53] Westmorland's proclamation – signed by the Irish privy council, including Lord Gosford – banned armed assemblies in Dublin county and city in late 1792 and in the Belfast area on 11 March 1793. This was followed by acts of parliament prohibiting all unlawful assemblies and re-constituting a national militia under the crown.[54] Some of the more radical ex-Volunteers, like Dr William Drennan of Belfast and Alexander Thomas Stewart of Acton, joined the United Irishmen. More conservative ex-Volunteers changed their uniforms for the red coat of the new militia, continuing the original Volunteer ethos of middle and upper-class respectability in a military force commanded by men of property, to protect security and the constitution of the Irish kingdom.

The Militia Act of April 1793 authorised a militia force in each Irish county as reserve to the regular army during the war with France. Militia officers – unlike the Volunteers – held their commissions from the crown, and, when on duty, militiamen received the same rate of pay as that of the regular army. Lord Arthur Gosford was appointed colonel of the Armagh militia on 25 April 1793. It was a post with vast political and symbolic significance and extensive patronage.[55] The colonel selected the regiment's officers and non-commissioned officers to be retained in peacetime. To ensure an ethos of wealth in the command structure, the colonel was required to possess a personal income of £2,000 or to be heir to £3,000 per annum, and his officers to be propertied e.g. his lieutenant colonel to possess £1,200 or be heir to £1,800 per annum, his major £300 or heir to £600 per annum. The colonel also controlled the clothing account estimated as being worth £1,000 profit per annum.[56]

But Gosford faced practical difficulties in raising the Armagh militia. Membership of full-time militia corps, conscripted for four years and garrisoned away from home, was less socially convenient than part-time, locally based Volunteering. Apart from a minority professional officer class, the gentry and propertied middle classes were reluctant to absent themselves from their estates and/or businesses, and many, caught by conscription ballot, availed of a loophole to subsidise substitutes from the 'lower orders' for military service. Thus, while the government order for Armagh militia was issued on 3 May 1793, the force was not actually embodied until 16 September; and only 362 rank and file recruited out of its quota of 420 by 31 March 1794.[57]

Further, the command structure was disrupted when William Richardson resigned his commission as lieutenant colonel and Gosford's deputy following a bitter quarrel with Gosford in April 1794.[58] Richardson's successor in the militia was Gosford's political protégé, Robert Camden Cope who would frequently deputise for Gosford as colonel in the years ahead. William Brownlow junior, a major in the new militia, would also leave the regiment over political differences with Gosford in the county by-election of 1794.

THE ARMAGH BY-ELECTION CONTEST OF 1794–5: A TEST OF POLITICAL STRENGTH

When William Brownlow senior died on 28 October 1794, his eldest son requested Gosford's support for his candidature for his father's county seat.[59] On the same day, William junior made a proposition to Lord Charlemont: that, in deference to his late father's wishes, he would support the earl's son, Lord Francis William Caulfeild, if the latter intended standing as candidate; otherwise he (Brownlow junior) would be a candidate now and stand down in favour of Caulfeild next time.[60] Brownlow junior was probably aware that neither Gosford nor Charlemont had a son of age to sit in parliament in 1794–5. His offer to stand down for young Caulfeild in future may have reflected his desperation for the Charlemont interest on this occasion, or recognition that Caulfeild, strengthened by the potential emergence of a new Catholic freeholder vote on the Charlemont estates in south Armagh, was the future heir to Whig patriotism and a county seat. In the event, Charlemont accepted Brownlow's promise of support for Caulfeild in the general election of 1797 in return for his support for Brownlow's election now as locum tenens; and both peers decided to use the 1795 by-election as a dry run to test their electoral strength for the coming general election.[61]

The by-election was also an opportunity for the government to challenge the traditional political monopoly of Armagh county seats held by the Whig opposition interests of Brownlow, Richardson and Caulfeild. A rival candidate was available in Robert Camden Cope, son of Arthur Cope of Loughgall, backed by a group of Armagh professional advisors. One such advisor in Dublin canvassed Gosford's support with the offer that a

Gosford-Cope alliance should succeed, and if it did not, Gosford would have the Cope electoral interest at his future disposal.[62] Other holders of political interests willed Gosford to take up the challenge and support Cope against Brownlow.[63]

The Armagh 1795 by-election had a significance beyond its immediate outcome. Political observers in Armagh considered it a rehearsal for the general election – 'a trial of strength, and like a field day preparatory to a general review'. Like Charlemont, Gosford was advised that he should only promise his electoral interest on condition that it would be reciprocated at the 1797 general election when his son Archibald could be a candidate. He was also advised to remain with his regiment in Mayo for the duration of the election to avoid 'expense and trouble', the latter a reference to fears that an election contest would further enflame the already disturbed state of the county.[64]

When Gosford was drawn into the contest, the 1795 election took on another dimension as a struggle for political control of Armagh county between Lord Charlemont's Whig opposition caucus and Lord Gosford's new pro-government group. Writing to Gosford, Cope's election agent James Dawson regarded it 'as the grandest struggle that can be made for power, weight and consequence in the county, your lordship at the head of one party, Lord Charlemont heading the other', and urged Gosford to return to the county for the canvass. In a bid to have Cope adopted as the government candidate, Dawson had visited Lord Lieutenant Westmorland and now asked Gosford to seek Westmorland's backing for Cope.[65]

In a further letter on the following day, Dawson informed Gosford that Westmorland had promised to advise absentee Lord Sandwich that 'Lord Gosford, a very good friend of government' favoured Cope, if Gosford would confirm (to Westmorland) that that was his position. Influenced by Dawson's re-affirmation that 'Cope ... is fighting your lordship's battle for power, influence and consequence in the county',[66] Gosford wrote accordingly to Westmorland who promised to persuade Lord Sandwich to direct his Clare estate votes to Gosford's choice of candidate in the by-election.[67] Gosford had also written to absentee landlord Peter, Count de Salis who replied that, as both parties had approached him for his Tawnavaltiny estate interest, he was still undecided about the coming by-election, but promised to support Gosford's son if Archibald stood at the next general election.[68]

While the direction of all electoral interests is not given in contemporary correspondence, those of Richardson in north Armagh and those of Hall, Seaver, Nedham, McGeough in south Armagh were expected to go to the Charlemont-Brownlow camp, and those of Moore, Sandwich, Pringle and Alexander in mid-Armagh to the Gosford-Cope camp.[69] It was recognised that the poll would be close with every opportunity explored for additional votes. When it was discovered that an oath of identification would not be administered at this poll, John Moore was prepared to send prosperous-looking acquaintances from Dublin who would pass for £100 freeholders.[70] And Dawson paid a Dublin specialist to visit the Gosford estate and advise on how to create additional freehold votes through lease-splitting and preparation of new freehold for registration.[71] It was an opportune time for such practice given the passing of the Catholic Relief Act of 1793.

The poll lasted 31 days with Brownlow winning narrowly. Sources differ on poll figures. The Charlemont camp gave the result as 1,336 votes to Brownlow against Cope's 1,254.[72] A later source reported 1,356 votes to Brownlow and 1,274 to Cope, a voterate of 2,630.[73] The 1795 poll had exceeded that of 1790 by 371 votes which, allowing for split-voting in 1790, may have represented an increase of almost 1,000 freeholders in the voterate.

The electoral arithmetic of the 1795 poll raises the issues of why the voterate had increased and why the result was so close. There are multiple reasons for the increased turnout at the 1795 poll. One explanation was that the 1790 poll had been low – the Brownlow-Richardson camp had claimed they were holding 800 votes in reserve which were not required. Another reason for the increase was the wider range of constituencies or interests involved in 1795: Gosford's pro-government caucus, the Brownlow-Charlemont Whig opposition group, the anti-Whig radicals, and the recently enfranchised Catholics. Probably the greatest single factor was the rapid increase in freehold registration after the Catholic Relief Act of 1793.[74] Gosford, Charlemont and Cope, all with estates in mid-south Armagh, would have benefited from the new Catholic vote.

The reasons for a hitherto safe Brownlow seat becoming at risk are also complex. By the mid-1790s the political dominance of the moderate Whig opposition was being challenged, both by Gosford's new government interest and by the radicals, spurred on by the secret United Irish Society, and encouraged by overt radical freemason lodges particularly numerous round Loughgall.[75] Also, the ageing Charlemont and ageing and ailing Brownlow had lost their appeal for many radicals by 1794 and the low-profile Brownlow junior lacked the charisma and dynamism to regain it in 1795. The situation was ripe for new young faces like those of Francis William Caulfeild and Archibald Acheson. Though still too young in 1795, their political futures seemed bright as a significant part of their family estates were situated in the predominantly Catholic south Armagh with potential to develop family political interests there. The fact that Brownlow held the county seat in 1795 says much for the strength of traditional independency of the Whig patriot interest in the county which his father had personified.

While there can be little doubt about the importance of the 1794–5 by-election as a determined attempt to win a seat held in unbroken Brownlow tenure since 1753, the political composition of the forces behind that attempt is less clear. Professor Cullen has attributed the dynamic to an incongruous misalliance of radicals disillusioned by too-moderate Brownlows, and Lord Gosford – anxious to secure a future seat for his underage son – cobbled together by the opportunist and erstwhile radical Cope 'as a test of strength of county radicalism'.[76] Cullen's hypothesis perhaps over-rates the radicalism of Robert Camden Cope, and under-rates the commitment of Gosford to the government interest and the involvement of Westmorland. Cope's use of the *Northern Star* to promote his election campaign was perhaps more due to his opportunism than his radicalism, and the election campaign more a test of the relative strengths of Whig opposition and the government interest than that of radicalism which never fully took hold in Armagh. Whatever the competing ideologies in 1795, the outcome meant the previously solid independent opposition in Armagh was now split into a fractured polity of freeholders, leaving both county seats vulnerable at the general election.

THE POLITICS OF LAW AND ORDER, 1794–6

Modern commentary has differed in emphasis on the factors which triggered the resumption of sectarian disturbances – perpetrated by growing numbers of Peep O'Day Boys, Defenders and new Boyne Societies – in County Armagh in 1794 on a greater scale than ever before. Systematic attacks on the Catholic tenantry of mid-Ulster in late 1795 and 1796 forced thousands to flee to Connacht, the majority as refugees to County Mayo.[77] A letter from the Markethill area to America describing the disturbances and expulsion of Catholics from north Armagh in 1796 asserted that 'the Orange Boys have not left a Papist family in all the lower [northern] part of the county from Richhill downward [northward] but they have driven away'.[78]

Crawford and Miller have attributed the atrocities to socio-economic rivalries and suspicions between Catholics and Protestants within 'the linen triangle'. It is argued that demands by Catholics to have their social status recognised included their right to carry arms, prompting Protestants to insist on reinforcement of the law forbidding that, and serving as excuse for Peep O'Day raids on Catholic homes. However, Crawford's reference to 'the rise of a new political force among the farmer-weavers' in both denominations also recognises the presence of political forces at work.[79]

Cullen and Bartlett have emphasised political factors underpinning unrest in Armagh. The former argues that unrest in County Armagh in the 1790s emanated from Dublin Castle's policy of undermining Armagh's traditional political independence through creation of a hard-line government caucus under Lord Gosford – in the process provoking the Protestant and Catholic lower orders and radical liberal political opinion.[80] The suppression of the Volunteers had left Protestant landlords and lower orders alike feeling powerless. The resultant vacuum was filled by popular secret societies such as the Orange Society which attracted both, as landlords were reluctant to alienate themselves from the Orange Society to which their Protestant tenants were flocking. Catholic tenants, in turn, joined the Defenders for protection. At the same time, the United Irish Society was also recruiting former Volunteers.

Bartlett attributes the destabilisation of Armagh society to 'an envenomed ... sectarianised atmosphere' of growing alarm among Protestants resulting from the 1793 Catholic Relief Act, plans for total Catholic emancipation by the earl of Fitzwilliam, the impetuous Whig lord lieutenant replacing Westmorland in December 1794, and spread of Defenderism. He argues that societal breakdown in the county was allowed to develop as a result of ineffectual measures to enforce the law by inept army commander Dalrymple, and a partial Armagh magistracy lacking the will to convict offenders.[81]

Initially, a concerned Lord Gosford used an even-handed approach in his attempts as governor to keep the peace. In November 1795, he requested additional troops from Lord Lieutenant Camden who promised to direct the commander-in-chief to station cavalry where Gosford had indicated.[82] On 28 December 1795, Gosford addressed the county magistrates and strongly denounced the sectarian outrages perpetrated on Catholics.[83] The Armagh magistrates responded with resolutions to administer the law impartially. But when these had little effect and disturbances continued into 1796, a desperate Gosford was considering the possibility of placing troops in Catholic homes for their protection, and even providing arms for Catholics to defend themselves.[84] Gosford's report to the chief secretary in February 1796 had no better news and blamed the absence of gentry for the continuing sectarian outrages in the county.[85]

The government, fearing that the sectarian outrages which continued into the summer of 1796 were being used as recruitment propaganda by the United Irish movement to enlist Catholics, asked Gosford for a report on Orange atrocities and on proposed Orange marches in the county.[86] Gosford's reports to Dublin Castle on the general security situation, and on the Orange march from Portadown through Loughgall and Richhill to Markethill when he had permitted 1,500 Orangemen to parade through his own demesne on 12 July 1796, played down the incidence and significance of Orange atrocities and seem like an apologia for his weakness in the face of Orange pressure. His apparent tolerance of Orange assemblies in July 1796 was contrary to official policy and a contradiction of Gosford's own denunciation of Orangeism on 28 December 1795.[87]

Modern commentary offers different interpretations of Lord Gosford's volte-face on 12 July 1796 and his relationship with the Orange Order subsequently. Bartlett suggests that Gosford rejected Cooke's direction to stop the parade because, in union with other Protestant gentry in south and mid-Ulster, he had already 'thrown in his lot with the new Orange Society'.[88] Blackstock argues that Gosford was intimidated into compliance by the size, trappings and organisation of the parade with its intimidatory overtones intended as a display of Protestant power to counter the current United Irish – Defender coalition.[89] Senior hypothesises that Gosford intended to win the support of the Orangemen as a future local defence force committed to national security, though the Acheson family distanced itself from closer liaison with the Order.[90] Crawford and Trainor assert: 'At no time in his career did he [Gosford] ever support the Orange Order', and that he had been given insufficient notice to stop the parade by a government dithering over General Dalrymple's intelligence reports. They argue that by July 1796, Dublin Castle may have been considering using 'loyal' associations as security alternative to the militia which was suspected of having been infiltrated by United Irishmen. Further, Gosford's permission to Orangemen to parade through his demesne on this occasion, may have been an attempt to bolster moderate Orange leadership against rank and file 'wreckers' who had defied the leaders and moved into west Down.[91]

It may be concluded that Lord Gosford's confrontation with Orangeism forced him to address overtly a latent personal conflict between ideological and pragmatic considerations. The Acheson family had traditionally eschewed popular local unauthorised movements such as the Volunteers, Peep O'Day Boys and Defenders in the 1780s, and those like the United Irish Society and Orange Order in the 1790s. The key to Gosford's softer approach to Orangeism in summer 1796 would seem to lie in the deteriorating security situation since late 1795 in the face of a dual threat of insurrection and invasion. The growing militarisation of the United Irish movement, its alignment with Defenderism, its spread into Tyrone and Derry and approaches to Orangeism over that period, plus growing public distrust of visiting southern militia corps whose rank and file were mainly Catholic, had persuaded the government to consider a range of options for forming yeomanry-type units for local law and order duties.[92] These included proposals from Dungannon magistrate and Tyrone county MP Thomas Knox and Rev. William Richardson, rector of Clonfeacle, for organising local peacekeeping associations under the magistrates which had been submitted to and received guarded approval from Camden in June 1796.[93]

It was in such changing circumstances that Gosford took a pragmatic decision to allow the Orange parade through his demesne rather than alienate a prospective ally and counter-insurgency force. In justifying his decision to Camden and Cooke, he was at pains to emphasise Orange professions of loyalty to the crown in their demonstration. Gosford's reversal of policy on Orangeism would seem to have been based on the new priority that in times of national emergency, Orange loyalty took precedence over Orange sectarianism. Gosford's decision on 12 July 1796 – like his earlier successful appeal for Orangeman William Tremble's life – was a pragmatic quid pro quo for future Orange support as part of a locally based security force against United Irishmen and Defenders.

Gosford's change of stance may also have been motivated by a desire to steal a march on his rival Charlemont. The earl's former Volunteer companies would seem to have been the preferred option of Camden for the new yeomanry. Gosford hoped to curry favour with the lord lieutenant through promotion of Knox's proposals.

THE POLITICS OF NATIONAL SECURITY, 1796

Weaknesses in security became apparent as the twin threats grew in 1796 of invasion by the French and insurrection by the United Irishmen. In the event of invasion, the regular army and militia corps would be drawn to key coastal regions, leaving inland counties exposed to insurrection. Gentry and other committed loyal interests pressed the government to authorise local yeomanry units based on Thomas Knox's scheme. Gosford canvassed support for its proposal by Armagh county grand jury, though Isaac Corry was not convinced that Knox's model was the answer.[94]

Camden also had reservations about the Dungannon proposal. He feared that Knox's Orange connections would dominate membership of local yeomanry corps, thus driving alienated Catholics into the United Irish movement. Camden's patrician background also inclined him towards a yeoman cavalry on the English model which was not wholly practical in Ireland because of insufficient horse-ownership at local level.[95] Preferring the wider experience and influence of Lord Charlemont as ex-commander-in-chief of the Volunteers and his acceptability with Protestant gentry and Catholics, to Knox's narrower support base, Camden accepted Charlemont's advice to compromise on the composition of yeomanry units allowing infantry in the north and in southern towns and cities where cavalry was unavailable. Thus the origins of the Irish yeomanry in late 1796 owed more to the old Volunteer movement than to the newer Orange Society. And in the on-going rivalry for political control in Armagh county, Lord Charlemont had made a brief comeback to his former influence, while Governor Gosford appeared to have been snubbed by the lord lieutenant.[96]

The essential difference between the yeomanry and Volunteers was that the hundred-strong territorial units of the former were government-controlled. Differences between the yeomanry and the militia were in the former's localised service and in its personnel of gentry and middle classes, while the militia, whose rank and file tended to be from the peasantry and 'lower orders', was stationed outside its own county of recruitment.[97] The predominantly religious persuasion of yeomanry units varied from county to county. In southern counties like Kerry, yeomanry was mainly Catholic while the Armagh yeomanry was mainly Protestant, many recruited from the Orange Society.[98] So great was the response in Armagh that Dublin Castle closed further recruitment of yeomanry corps in early December 1796.[99] Locally recruited, locally led and operating locally, the yeomanry would prove an effective counter-insurgency force in its familiarity with the local area and knowledge of potential United Irish supporters in it; and was particularly effective in keeping them at bay in County Armagh.

Lord Gosford had supported the concept of yeomanry units from an early stage and, as governor, was the key figure in Armagh recommending commissions. He set an example by raising a yeomanry cavalry corps at Markethill where Gosford reported that after initial difficulties in convincing his 'stiff dissenters' to join, there was enthusiastic recruitment under his eldest son Archibald, brought home from Oxford, to lead it.[100] Most Armagh gentry responded by raising and commanding yeomanry corps designated as cavalry or infantry, including cavalry corps by Lord Charlemont at Armagh, Lord Caulfeild at Keady, Brownlow at Lurgan and Richardson at Richhill. So enthusiastic was the response that Gosford told Camden of his disappointment at receiving Pelham's letter closing recruitment in the county.[101]

In the interests of national security, there was a truce in the political rivalry between Gosford and Charlemont. But in the late autumn and winter of 1796, Gosford and Charlemont would clash again on the application of proclamation. Escalating sectarian unrest and militarisation of the United Irishmen had brought extreme repressive measures from government. Following sectarian disturbances along the border between north east Armagh and west Down, seven parishes were proclaimed under the Insurrection Act.[102] When Gosford recommended that Armagh city should also be proclaimed as a means of dissuading United Irishmen meeting there, Charlemont advised Camden it should not. Camden informed Gosford: 'I was aware of your lordship and Lord C[harlemont] being at the head of different parties in Armagh', but that Pelham and he agreed with Charlemont that Armagh city should be excluded from proclamation.[103]

Gosford resented Camden's decision again to accept Charlemont's advice and reminded the lord lieutenant that Rev. William Bissett and the magistrates supported his (Gosford's) view on republican infiltration of the city and were keen on stronger policing there.[104] Smarting at Camden's references to Charlemont's concern about proclaiming Armagh city, Gosford criticised the absence of Lords Charlemont and Caulfeild from recent important meetings on security in the county. However, he promised to persuade magistrates to use an alternative plan to proclamation for security in the city and to forward it to Dublin with Bissett.[105] When Gosford reported at Christmas that the county was quieter and recommended the lifting of the autumn proclamation on Lower Orior, Camden – to rub salt into the wounds – advised an extension.[106]

By the beginning of 1797 constitutional politics had been relegated from the priorities of the ruling élite in Armagh, as elsewhere, by those of national security. In election year it was not clear when or whether a general election could be held.

CONCLUSION: ELECTION CONTESTS AND POLITICAL CONTROL, 1790–6

The 1790 general election provides evidence of the complex relationships involving Armagh landlords and freeholders. Arthur Acheson's 1789 calculations were based on the premise that election outcomes were still decided by conjunctions of landlord interests. This was corroborated by Richardson's request to his brother-in-law Lord Gosford for permission to canvass his estates. However, the necessity of Richardson to tour Gosford's estates also suggested that Gosford's direction to his freeholders on whom to vote for was insufficient in itself, insinuated freeholder expectations to be canvassed by candidates, and implied freeholder rights to dispose freely of their votes. This episode indicated not only a protocol between landlords on territorial rights over the franchise of freeholders on each estate but also implied that such rights were based on mutual respect between landlord and freeholders out of which the latter expected to be asked for their votes by both landlord and candidate. If such courtesies were honoured, freeholders, normally, would accommodate their landlord's wishes at the polls.

The importance of not taking the votes of freeholders for granted is also illustrated in Brownlow's anxiety to canvass his estates. This sitting MP who had actively represented the county continuously since 1753, considered it necessary to apologise to freeholders at being too infirm to tour his estates on this occasion and to issue a lengthy manifesto outlining his patriot record on political issues and promotion of the linen industry. Brownlow had been pushed into this address by the resurrection of the old smear labelling him a Catholic-phile. This smear was particularly influential on the Charlemont estates – as it had been in 1753 – causing Lord

Charlemont to claim it undermined his influence over his freeholders at the polls. It illustrated how an effective election campaign – based on emotional issues such as denominational sympathies – could be whipped up to influence freeholders to defy the wishes of their landlords in elections.

The three-way contest for the Armagh county seats in the 1790 general election resulted in the return of sitting members, Brownlow and Richardson who disposed of John Moore junior's challenge. Despite – or perhaps because of – fears of violence in the background of unrest leading up to the election, the canvass and poll were undertaken without reported serious incident. The tradition in the county of independent Whig/patriot politics had been maintained and reinforced by Lord Charlemont's protégés, Sir Annesley Stewart and newcomer Richard Sheridan, both committed Whigs and patriots.

Thus in parliamentary divisions, four of the six members for Armagh constituencies usually opposed government except on such occasions as the 7 May 1795 division on Grattan's Catholic Emancipation Bill when county members Brownlow and Richardson voted with government to defeat it. Only the on-going resistance of these Armagh members to Catholic Emancipation, over-rode their usual opposition to government.

The determination of the Dublin administration in the 1790s to break the solidarity of Armagh independence and build a pro-government caucus in the county brought Lord Arthur Gosford's appointment in 1790 as joint-governor of the county with the ageing Lord Charlemont, formerly sole holder of the post. The resignation of an aggrieved Charlemont left government protégé Gosford in control of local government in the county and in favourite position for appointment to other key posts.

In 1793, Charlemont received a further blow when the independent Volunteers, whom he had commanded and striven to retain for over fourteen years, were officially disbanded and replaced by national militia corps under the crown, recruited on a county basis. Gosford was appointed colonel of the Armagh militia and stationed in Mayo. But enforced militia duty outside the county was not popular with gentry and middle classes who resented time spent away from their estates and/or business interests, and from security of their homes. Recruitment was slow; and the strength of the Armagh militia was further weakened by political differences which influenced the resignations of William Richardson, Gosford's deputy in the militia and of Major William Brownlow junior.

The relative strengths of Gosford's government party and that of the Whig/patriot interest of Charlemont, Brownlow and Richardson were put to the test in the by-election of 1795 following Brownlow senior's death in 1794. Robert Camden Cope of Loughgall Manor, backed by an incongruous coalition of Gosford's government caucus and disparate radicals disillusioned with too-moderate Whigs, contested the seat with

Brownlow junior backed by Charlemont, Richardson, and supporters of his father's memory. Following a thirty-one day contest Brownlow was successful but the solidarity of the traditional Whig party in the county had been severely fractured and made vulnerable at the next general election.

But Gosford's efforts to break the monopoly of patriot/Whig control in Armagh and win political control there for the government interest were frustrated by the polarisation of communities through the sectarian violence of popular societies such as the Orange Society and Catholic Defenders, and the militarisation of the United Irish Society. The vacuum left by the disbandment of the Volunteers was filled by the Orange Society, formed as a result of Protestant feelings of vulnerability by the enforced external service of county militia corps and suspicions that visiting militia corps were infiltrated by United Irishmen, reinforced with feelings of betrayal by the Catholic Relief Act and Lord Lieutenant Fitzwilliam's pro-Catholic policy, and fears of attack from a coalition of Defenders and United Irishmen.

Gosford's conversion to acceptance of the Orange Society and his support for the formation of local yeomanry units stemmed from his concern over national security against rebellion and French invasion. But he felt snubbed by Lord Camden's decision to use Lord Charlemont's Volunteer model for yeomanry corps and his advice on security measures for Armagh county, though Camden's choice of Charlemont as consultant may have been as much an attempt to keep the Volunteer earl's followers out of the United Irish camp as the value of his security advice. While Gosford had made inroads into Whig/patriot control of Armagh county, wider political interests strove for the hearts and minds of Armagh political interests at the beginning of 1797 general election year.

Notes

1. R.B. McDowell, 'Parliamentary independence, 1782–9' in T.W. Moody and W.E. Vaughan (ed.), *A new history of Ireland. IV: eighteenth century Ireland, 1691–1800* (Oxford, 1986), p. 286.
2. Thomas Prentice to Charlemont, 28 Nov. 1788 (*HMC Charlemont*), ii, 79–80.
3. Hudson to Charlemont, 11 July 1789 (RIA Charlemont correspondence, iv, MS 54).
4. Same to same, 26 Aug. 1789 (ibid., iv, MS 61).
5. *BNL*, 1 Jan. 1790.
6. *FJ*, 14–17 Aug. 1790.
7. Lord Gosford to Arthur Acheson 25 Jan. 1790 (PRONI, Gosford papers, D/1606/1/1/140).
8. W. Nedham (to Arthur Acheson), 22 Jan. 1789 (ibid., D/1606/1/1/133). 'Nedham' is also spelt 'Needham' in the documents. For consistency, the form 'Nedham' is retained here.

9 Richard 'Dick' Dawson was a nephew and representative of the childless and absentee first Viscount Cremorne of Dawson Grove, County Monaghan who held extensive property around Armagh and Blackwatertown, see Collins, *County Monaghan sources*, pp 38, 40, 43.
10 Richard Dawson to Arthur Acheson, 31 Jan. 1789 (PRONI, Gosford papers, D/1606/1/1/135).
11 Lord John Townshend to Arthur Acheson, 27 Feb. 1789 (ibid., D/1606/1/1/136).
12 R. Johnston to Arthur Acheson, 27 Feb. 1789 (ibid., D/1606/1/1/139A).
13 Acheson's reply to Johnston, with enclosed list of freeholders, 19 June 1789 (ibid., D/1606/1/1/139A).
14 *BNL*, 19–23 Mar. 1790. Richard Griffiths, 1752–1820, had made a fortune in the East Indies before settling in Naas, Co. Kildare. He served as an opposition MP for Askeaton borough, Co. Kerry 1783–90, see J.S. Crone, *A concise dictionary of Irish biography* (Dublin, 1928) p. 83; *BNL*, 27–30 Apr. 1790.
15 *BNL*, 6–9, 9–13 Apr. 1790.
16 *BNL*, 2–6, 16–20 Apr. 1790.
17 Brownlow to Gosford, 6 Apr. 1790 (PRONI, Gosford papers, D/1606/1/1/141).
18 *BNL*, 9–13 Apr. 1790.
19 Richardson to Gosford, 12 Apr. [1790] (PRONI, Gosford papers, D/1606/1/1/177).
20 Charlemont to Haliday, 29 Apr. 1790 (*HMC Charlemont*), ii, 125.
21 *BNL*, 23–27 Apr. 1790.
22 Brownlow to Charlemont, [5 May 1790] (RIA Charlemont correspondence, x, MS 166).
23 Ibid. This Counsellor Pollock was probably Joseph Pollock, a prominent Newry barrister, see Dr William Drennan to Mrs M. McTier, spring 1783–5, D.A. Chart (ed.), *The Drennan letters* (Belfast, 1931), p. 27.
24 *BNL*, 11–14 May 1790.
25 Ibid.
26 Ibid.
27 *FJ*, 15–18 May 1790.
28 'Figures for contested elections in Co. Armagh 1783–1826' (NLI, County Armagh townlands, MS 2716); *BNL*, 14–18 May 1790. Election figures for the 1790 poll are similar in both sources.
29 Thomas Knox's parliamentary list for Lord Abercorn, 1791, E.M. Johnston, 'The state of the Irish house of commons in 1791', *RIA Proc.*, lix (1957; hereafter, Knox's 1791 parliamentary list), sect. C, 18.
30 *BNL*, 11–15 Dec. 1789; Johnston-Liik, *Irish parliament*, iv, 94; ibid., v, 245–6. Duquery was a fifty year old Dublin lawyer who had been appointed surveyor of the Custom House Quay in 1770 on the recommendation of John Hely-Hutchinson, his brother-in-law, and from the 1780s had advanced his legal career as king's counsellor and judge, serving as third sergeant when selected to replace Meredyth in parliament.
31 Knox's 1791 parliamentary list', pp 23–4; *The Northern Star* (hereafter, *NS*), 17–20 July 1793, 5–9 Mar. 1795.
32 *Commons' jn. Ire.* (Grierson), xv, 141, 167, 177, 184, 189; *Irish Statutes*, 33 Geo. III (1793) C. 21; Johnston-Liik, *Irish parliament*, iv, 430–1.
33 *BNL*, 16–19 Mar. 1790; *FJ*, 11–13 May 1790.
34 Charlemont to ? Stewart, 8 Apr.1790 (*HMC Charlemont*), ii, 122; Johnston-Liik, *Irish parliament*, vi, 270–1, 342.

35 Malone to Charlemont, 15 Apr. 1790 (*HMC Charlemont*), ii, 123.
36 Charlemont to Sheridan, 10 Apr. 1790 (ibid.), ii, 122–3.
37 Major R. Hobart to Arthur Acheson, 20 Apr. 1790 (PRONI, Gosford papers, D/1606/1/1/144).
38 Rev. Nich. Forster to Arthur Acheson, 4 May 1790 (ibid., D/1606/1/1/145, 146A, 146B).
39 *BNL*, 14–17 July 1789, 30 Apr.–4 May 1790; Malcomson, *Isaac Corry*, p.10.
40 Knox's 1791 parliamentary list', pp 17–18.
41 *DEP*, 8 July 1790.
42 Malcomson, *Foster*, p. 61.
43 *BNL*, 15–18 Feb. 1791; *HJ*, 7 Mar. 1791.
44 *NS*, 17–20 July 1793, 5–9 Mar. 1795.
45 *DEP*, 2 Mar. 1793. In the debate following the second reading of Hobart's Catholic Relief Bill to allow Catholics the franchise, Knox's motion for an additional clause to enable Catholics to sit and vote in both houses of the Irish parliament was defeated by 103 votes to 69; see *Commons' jn. Ire.* (Grierson), xv, 167.
46 *NS*, 4–7, 7–11, 11–14 May 1795; *FJ*, 7, 9 May 1795.
47 Johnston-Liik, *Irish parliament*, iv, 483; *DEP*, 18 May 1797.
48 L.M. Cullen, 'The United Irishmen: problems and issues of the 1790s' in *ULS*, xviii, no. 2 (Spring, 1997; hereafter, Cullen, 'United Irishmen') pp 14–5.
49 Lord Bective to Arthur Lord Gosford, 14 Sept. 1790 (PRONI, Gosford papers, D/1606/1/ 1/149).
50 'Old Dublin Mansion Houses' in *The Irish Builder*, 1 June 1894 (DCLA, newspaper collection).
51 *Commons' jn. Ire.* (Grierson), xv, 378.
52 Charlemont to Thomas Prentice, 8 Feb. 1791 (*HMC Charlemont*), ii, 133–4.
53 *BNL*, 25–29 Jan. 1793.
54 *BNL*, 12–15 Mar. 1793; *NS*, 13–16 Mar. 1793; *Irish Statutes*, 33 Geo. III (1793), C. 22.
55 I.F. Nelson, 'The Irish Militia, 1793–1802' (Ph.D. thesis, QUB, 2001; hereafter Nelson, 'Irish Militia') pp 25, 105–6, 115; Malcomson, *Foster*, p. 252.
56 Sir Henry McAnally, *The Irish militia 1793–1816: a social and military study* (Dublin, 1949; hereafter McAnally, *Irish militia*), pp 169, 249; *Irish Statutes*, 33 Geo. III (1793) C. 22; Lord Waterford to Lord Gosford, 23 June 1793 (PRONI, Gosford papers, D/1606/1/1/157C); Francis Tipping to Colonel Ogle, summer 1793 (ibid., D/1606/1/1/157D).
57 *DEP*, 10 Dec. 1793, 7 Jan. 1794; Lord Gosford's notice in January 1794 confirmed that an advertisement in December by his deputy, William Richardson, for thirty men and a drum-major, was filled; McAnally, *Irish militia*, pp 47–8; Nelson, 'Irish Militia', pp 70–9.
58 Correspondence between Gosford and Richardson, 17–28 Apr. 1794 (PRONI, Gosford papers, D/1606/1/1/159B, 159C, 159D, 159E, 160A, 160B).
59 William Brownlow junior to Lord Gosford, 31 Oct. 1794 (ibid. D/1606/1/1/164).
60 Brownlow to Lord Charlemont, 31 Oct. 1794 (RIA Charlemont correspondence, MS 12, R.18, vii, No.37).
61 Charlemont to Brownlow, 1 Nov. 1794 (ibid. MS 12, R.18, vii, No.38).
62 J. Turner to Lord Gosford in Castlebar [the Armagh militia was stationed there], 5 Nov. 1794 (PRONI, Gosford papers, D/1606/1/1/165). 'J. Turner' was probably Jacob Turner, an Armagh grand juror 1779–97.

63   Captain John Pringle to Lord [Gosford], 12 Nov. 1794 (ibid. D/1606/1/1/166); Lord Gosford to Major Brownlow, 15 Nov. 1794 (ibid., D/1606/1/1/168). Pringle, of Limepark Lodge, was Lord Caledon's estate agent, served as high sheriff of Armagh in 1793 and as grand juror in 1794.
64   John Godley to Gosford, 15 Nov. 1794 (ibid. D/1606/1/1/167). John Godley was second son of Rev. William Godley, former prebendary of Mullabrack parish. John served as Armagh grand juror 1786–96.
65   James Dawson to Gosford, 27 Nov. 1794, (ibid., D/1606/1/1/172). James Dawson was second son of Walter Dawson, Clare Castle and brother of Thomas Dawson MP. He was a barrister, Armagh grand juror 1773–83, secretary to the Ulster Association of Volunteers, and agent to the Jackson estate at Forkhill.
66   Dawson to Gosford, 28 Nov. 1794 (ibid. D/1606/1/1/173).
67   Earl of Westmorland to Gosford, 1 Dec. 1794 (ibid. D/1606/1/1/174B).
68   P[eter Count] de Salis to Gosford, 1 Dec. 1794 (ibid. D/1606/1/1/174C).
69   Dawson to Gosford, 27 Nov.1794 (ibid. D/1606/1/1/172).
70   John Moore to Gosford, 19 Jan. 1795 (ibid. D/1606/1/1/175).
71   Thomas D. Logan to Gosford, 3 Feb. 1795 (ibid. D/1606/1/1/176).
72   Thomas Prentice to Charlemont, 31 Jan. 1795, (RIA Charlemont correspondence, MS.12, R.18, vii, No. 62).
73   'Figures for contested elections in Co. Armagh 1783–1826' (NLI, County Armagh townlands, MS 2716). 'Voterate' is used here to denote the total number of voters who cast their votes.
74   Peter Jupp, 'Irish parliamentary elections and the influence of the Catholic vote', *Historical Journal*, x (1967), p.184.
75   Petri Mirala, ' "A large mob, calling themselves Freemasons": Masonic parades in Ulster', in Jupp and Magennis (eds.), *Crowds in Ireland*, p.131.
76   L.M. Cullen, 'The internal politics of the United Irishmen' in David Dickson, Daire Keogh & Kevin Whelan (eds.), *The United Irishmen: republicanism, radicalism and rebellion* (Dublin, 1993), pp 192–3; L.M. Cullen, 'Alliances and misalliances in the politics of the Union', *Transactions of the Royal Historical Society*, x (6th series, Cambridge, 2000; hereafter, Cullen, 'Alliances and misalliances in the politics of the Union'), pp 234–7.
77   Lord Altamont, 27 June 1796 (NAI, State of the country papers, SOC 101521); Patrick Tohall, 'The Diamond fight of 1795 and the resultant expulsions' in *Seanchas Ardmhacha*, iii, no. 1 (1958), pp 17–50; Tomás Ó Fiaich,'Migration from Ulster to County Mayo in 1795–6', *ULS*, xii, no.2 (Winter 1990), pp 7–19.
78   James and Jane Burns of Brackly townland to James Burns, Washington, Pennsylvania, 2 May 1796, in Miller, *Peep O'Day Boys*, document 42, pp 128–9.
79   W.H. Crawford, 'The Linen Triangle in the 1790s' in *ULS*, xviii, no. 2 (Spring 1997), pp 43–51. Dr Crawford delineates the 'Linen Triangle' as the region within vertices at Lisburn, Dungannon and Newry and centred on Loughgall; Miller, *Peep O'Day Boys*, particularly documents 6, 10, 44, 45; D.W. Miller, 'Politicisation in revolutionary Ireland', *Ir. Econ. & Soc. Hist.* xxiii (1996), pp 12–13.
80   Cullen, 'United Irishmen', p.15.
81   Thomas Bartlett, *The fall and rise of the Irish nation: the Catholic Question, 1690–1830* (Dublin, 1992; hereafter, Bartlett, *The fall and rise of the Irish nation*), pp 216–23; *NS*, 23 Nov. 1795.
82   Camden to Gosford, 7 Nov. 1795 (PRONI, Gosford papers, D/1606/1/1/180B).
83   *BNL*, 28 Dec. 1795–1 Jan. 1796.

84 *House of commons report from the select committee on Orange lodges, associations or societies in Ireland*, xv, session (377) 1835; Bartlett, *The fall and rise of the Irish nation*, p. 219.
85 Gosford to Pelham, 25 Feb. 1796 (NAI, Rebellion papers, 620/23/37).
86 Under-secretary Edward Cooke to Gosford, 7, 8 July 1796 (PRONI, Gosford papers, D/1606/1/1/185A, 186).
87 Gosford to Cooke, 10 July 1796 (PRONI, Gosford papers, D/1606/1/1/185B); Gosford to Camden, 13 July 1796 (ibid., D/1606/1/1/188).
88 Bartlett, *The fall and rise of the Irish nation*, pp 218–9.
89 Allan Blackstock, '"The invincible mass": loyal crowds in mid Ulster, 1795–6', in Jupp and Magennis (eds.), *Crowds in Ireland*, pp 105–6.
90 Hereward Senior, *Orangeism in Ireland and Britain, 1795–1836* (London, 1966) pp 36–45, 94.
91 Crawford & Trainor (eds.), *Aspects*, document 76, pp 179–80.
92 Rev. James Jones to Cooke, 7 Sept. 1796 (NAI, Rebellion papers, 620/25/32); General Dalrymple to Cooke (ibid., 620/25/33) in which an enclosure from Warrenpoint reported 'that one Alexander Graham keeps an unlicensed public house at the Tullyhappies [probably Tullyhappy townland north-west of Newry] ... where the United and the Orangemen of Newry and Loughgall [?Loughgilly] assemble by night'.
93 Allan Blackstock, ' "A dangerous species of ally": Orangeism and the Irish yeomanry', *IHS*, xxx (May 1997; hereafter, Blackstock, 'A dangerous species of ally'), p. 394.
94 Gosford to Isaac Corry, 20 July 1796 (NAI, Rebellion papers, 620/24/48).
95 Lieutenant HI. Stuart to Colonel L Barber, 7 Sept. 1796 (enclosure in) Barber to Cooke, 24 Sept. 1796 (NAI, Rebellion papers, 620/25/104).
96 Blackstock, 'A dangerous species of ally', pp 397–8.
97 McAnally, *Irish militia*, p. 60.
98 Cullen, 'The United Irishmen', p. 7; Littlehales to Wickham, 3 June 1803 (PRONI, Wickham papers, T/2627/5/L/75); Crawford and Trainor (eds.), *Aspects*, p. 180.
99 Pelham to Gosford, 13 Dec. 1796 (PRONI, Gosford papers, D/1606/1/1/190B).
100 Corry to Cooke, 23 July 1796 (NAI, Rebellion papers, 620/24/48); T.G.F. Paterson to Dr Chart, 19 Nov. 1928 (PRONI, Paterson deposits, D/259/1).
101 Gosford to Camden, 21 Dec. 1796 (TCD, MIC 56, KAO, Camden papers, U840/0173/9).
102 Lord Carhampton, commander-in-chief, to Gosford, 7 Nov. 1796 (PRONI, Gosford papers, D/1606/1/1/189); *Irish Statutes*, 36 Geo. III (1796), C. 20.
103 Camden to Gosford, 26 Nov. 1796 (TCD, MIC 56, KAO, Camden papers, U840/0173/6); correspondence between Camden and Charlemont, 22 Nov.–1 Dec. 1796 (*HMC Charlemont*), ii, 289–90.
104 Leslie, *Armagh clergy*, p. 41 gives Bissett as prebendary of Loughgall 1791–1807, successor to Charles Warburton as rector of Loughgilly 1807–22, and later bishop of Raphoe in 1822. Clerics Bissett, Hugh Hamilton, dean of Armagh and Warburton were strong on law-and-order issues, supporters of Gosford and regular correspondents with Dublin Castle.
105 Gosford to Camden, 30 Nov. 1796 (TCD, MIC 56, KAO, Camden papers, U840/0173/7).
106 Camden to Gosford, 24 Dec. 1796 (ibid. U840/0173/10).

7
The election contests of 1797 and 1799; contention over Union in County Armagh 1798–1800

INTRODUCTION: THE POLITICS OF SECURITY AND PROTEST,
JANUARY TO JUNE 1797

By 1797, politics in Armagh, as elsewhere, had become increasingly polarised as a result of the extreme reactions to the national security situation. Recurring rumours of French landings led to further repressive measures against the United Irishmen and dragooning of the Northern District for arms by Lieutenant General Gerard Lake, including Armagh county by Brigadier General John Knox. In March, army searches for arms brought resentment, reprisals and rising fears of isolated loyalist residents such as Charles Warburton, rector of Loughgilly who appealed to Dublin Castle and to Lord William Bentinck's 24th Dragoons stationed at Armagh for military reinforcements against increasingly hostile neighbours.[1] Local resentment escalated when military over-reaction resulted in United Irishman Thomas Birch being killed in custody at Ballymacnab by the Royal Dublin City Militia in March 1797.[2]

Gosford's report to Dublin Castle in late March was pessimistic about the security situation in the county. A meeting called by General Knox was adjourned to allow better attendance. Those present had proposed that the area proclaimed should be extended to facilitate disarmament.[3] The increasing militarisation of the United Irishmen and reaction of the security forces had left politics so polarised that it was doubtful whether scheduled parliamentary elections could be held.

The ideological struggle for hearts and minds increased in spring 1797. In April, James Dawson and General Knox separately reported increasing support for the United Irishmen among civilians and armed forces alike.[4] Knox informed Dublin Castle of reported daily defections from the Dublin City Militia to the United Irish cause and later reported that yeomanry corps at Armagh, Keady and Dungannon – and Arthur Macan, sovereign of Armagh – were suspected of having United Irish sympathies.[5]

Episcopalian landlord Alexander Thomas Stewart of Acton shocked the prosecuting authorities when his evidence on 15 April at Armagh assizes helped to acquit two suspected United Irishmen on trial and appeared to approve the principles of the United Irish Society.[6]

The growing concerns of the ruling élite for national security were further increased by events at a protest meeting of Armagh freeholders on 19 April 1797. The Armagh meeting was but one in a series of meetings in spring and early summer 1797 against the government's draconian measures, part of a Whig campaign in the counties and several corporations to prepare petitions to the throne for the removal of government ministers and redress of repressive legislation. Some freeholders, as in Down, also called for parliamentary reform and Catholic Emancipation.[7]

But the most militant of these meetings followed Lord Francis William Caulfeild's requisition in Armagh to Sheriff Robert Sparrow, Lord Gosford's son-in-law,[8] for a meeting to discuss the state of the county and prepare an address to the throne. The twenty nine signatories on the requisition included persons of wide-ranging political views and agenda: Whig reformist agitators such as young Caulfeild and Joshua McGeough of Drumsill; wary, moderate Whig county MPs William Richardson and William Brownlow; Church of Ireland clergy Warburton and William Bissett, concerned at the security situation; and advanced radicals, including United Irish sympathisers such as Macan, sovereign of Armagh, and Stewart of Acton.

The concern of the government interest that extreme radicals might control the meeting may be gauged by the plethora of official correspondence before and after the meeting. Gosford, Sparrow and Sir Walter Synnot all communicated apprehensions and strategies to Chief Secretary Pelham who briefed another concerned government supporter James Dawson – since 1794, an official conduit of communication between Armagh and Dublin Castle – and directed him to attend the meeting and support Gosford's resistance to anticipated radical proposals for parliamentary reform and Catholic Emancipation.[9]

Independent accounts by Dawson and Alexander Hamilton of the sessions-house meeting in Armagh city are sufficiently similar to be taken as an accurate outline of proceedings. Three distinct political groups were evident at the capacity meeting chaired by Sheriff Sparrow. A pro-government group was led by Gosford, Dawson, Warburton and a partisan Sparrow. A moderate Whig reformist group was led by Caulfeild and Lord Charlemont protégés Richard Mountney Jephson MP and Joshua McGeough. An advanced radical group including Alexander Thomas Stewart, James Stewart, an attorney from Armagh city, Hen. [?Henrith or Hendrick] Cope, a captain in the Armagh militia, contained United Irish infiltrators and agitators who attempted to inflame passions against the government with calls for its dismissal and for radical reform. With revolutionaries exploiting divisions among politicians, it was a situation fraught with danger. Gosford's attempt to hold the line for government with a proposal of loyalty to king and country got little support. Even Caulfeild's call for parliamentary reform, Catholic Emancipation and dismissal of government ministers, was swept aside when young lawyer James Stewart seized the moment and stood on the table to read an inflammatory address which was enthusiastically carried and passed to county members Brownlow and Richardson for transmission to the lord lieutenant and the king.

Alarming conclusions and recriminations followed the Armagh meeting. General Knox predictably attributed events to the softening of security policy against attacks from 'very many of the Engagees [sic]' attending, the weakness of Sparrow as chairman and supineness of the Armagh magistracy in the face of mob rule 'headed by Mr Stewart and Mr Hen. Cope'. Jephson from the Caulfeild camp blamed 'poor generalship ... by the Gosford party', including Dawson and Sparrow. Gosford blamed Caulfeild for being the dupe of radicals and requesting the meeting in such dangerous times. Warburton saw the meeting as 'a collection of United Irishmen' and reported he was moving his family to Armagh city for protection.[10]

Dublin Castle was alarmed by proceedings at the Armagh freeholders' meeting. Pelham expressed concern that 'persons of property' were taking the United Irish oath and hoped that Lord Charlemont had learned his lesson.[11] Thereafter Charlemont's influence with Camden on security issues in Armagh decreased and that of Gosford and Knox was restored.

Lord Caulfeild may have called the freeholders' meeting in Armagh as launching-pad for his general election campaign. But the initiative had been seized by advanced radical interests whose election prospects seemed the more promising. Thereafter, however, the radical political challenge diminished for a number of reasons. Adherents of radical views were despairing of achieving change by constitutional methods. When W.B. Ponsonby's resolution for parliamentary reform on 15 May 1797 was defeated by 117 votes to 32 on a motion of adjournment, Grattan's followers withdrew with the words: 'we shall trouble you no more, and after this day shall not attend the house of commons'.[12] Their secession from constitutional politics left the field to the United Irishmen to seek change by physical force

In the weeks following the 19 April freeholders' meeting, the political situation changed in Armagh county when General Knox's movement of troops there, his disarming of parishes and imposition of an Oath of Allegiance to counter-act the United Irish Oath of Secrecy, wrested support from the United Irishmen and eased the immediate threat of insurrection in the county.[13] Warburton was encouraged to return to Loughgilly parish for the administration of the Oath of Allegiance and collection of arms. His neighbour, Rev James Archibald Hamilton was similarly engaged in Mullaghbrack parish.[14] In June when the archbishop of Armagh expressed his concerns to Gosford about security and recommended extended proclamation,[15] Gosford had already reported to Dublin Castle an upturn in the security situation in his own area exemplified by the conversion of former United Irishmen to Orangemen, illegal arms handed in, and *c.* 900 Mullaghbrack parishioners taking the Oath of Allegiance.[16]

With the army now in control of Armagh county it was possible to hold a general election. It was an achievement for Gosford's governorship as the postponement of an election had seemed inevitable earlier in the year. But the events of the 19 April 1797 freeholders' meeting had suggested that supine politicians would be swept aside by active radicals, and four of the six sitting MPs in Armagh county in 1797 were open to criticisms of passivity and/or old age. Sir Annesley Stewart was seventy two years old and had served Charlemont borough for thirty four years. Armagh borough member Sackville Hamilton was nearing retirement. He had replaced George Rawson, who died on 8 January 1796 after eighteen years of steadfast support to government. Thus in 1797, there was a vacancy in Armagh borough for a new pro-government MP.[17] The craven response of county members Richardson and Brownlow to the demands of the radicals would seem to have lost the respect of both radical and conservative wings of Armagh political thinking in 1797. The political stage was set for the emergence of young and vibrant constitutional politicians.

THE GENERAL ELECTION CONTEST
IN ARMAGH COUNTY, JULY–AUGUST 1797

The proceedings and outcome of the 19 April 1797 meeting of the Armagh freeholders had another significance for the general election in the county. It revealed that the Whig party was split on the issue of abstentionist politics. Unlike Leinster where Whigs, advanced radicals and United Irishmen had united behind an abstentionist policy against constitutional politics, in Armagh Whigs following Charlemont were prepared to oppose both advanced radical and Gosford's government party and to contest the election.[18]

A number of factors influenced that decision. One was the tradition of independence in Armagh which did not suffer dictation from outside gladly. A proximate factor in 1797 was the emergence of Caulfeild as a young Whig politician impatiently waiting his chance to break into parliamentary politics, and promoted by a father eager to extend the family political interest by representing Armagh county in the house of commons.

Lord Charlemont, for long a father figure of Whig politics, would not be following Grattan's lead into abstentionism in 1797 and expected other Whigs in Armagh county to deliver electoral support for his son.

Government supporter Lord Gosford was also anxious to introduce his son, the Hon. Archibald Acheson, to Armagh parliamentary politics. Acheson is not mentioned among those present at the freeholders' meeting of 19 April and seems to have maintained a low profile pre-election. There is no reason to doubt that he was still in his father's pro-government camp and was the government candidate in the election.

Thus the 1797 general election was regarded as an opportunity not to be missed to launch the parliamentary careers of the eldest sons of two peers anxious to extend family influence in high politics in Armagh county. The several holdings of both peers in the Catholic-orientated southern half of the county, enhancing the potential of their political interests by the late 1790s, seemed to identify their sons as the Armagh county politicians of the future. Acheson declared as candidate on 10 July 1797, Caulfeild two days later.[19]

Initially, not all Armagh MPs or potential candidates in the county, were prepared to step aside and allow two new county members to be returned unchallenged. Indeed five persons were prepared to offer their candidatures at different stages. Both sitting members, Richardson and Brownlow, considered standing again. But they had lost the support of, and were being pressurised by radical political activists in the county. When 'a card' in the press on 10 May questioned whether they had conveyed the 19 April address of the Armagh freeholders to the lord lieutenant and king as directed, Brownlow and Richardson assured the Armagh freeholders that they had delivered it to the lord lieutenant, though felt obliged to explain why they had not publicised the fact: 'but we thought it unnecessary, trusting you could not but be convinced that it was our duty, as well as our inclination to pay prompt obedience to any commands you honour us with'. But the tenor of the 'card' had suggested that the writers did not trust their two county MPs to transmit the radical address.[20]

Criticism of the two Armagh county MPs continued with pointed reference to the coming election. In the same edition of the Dublin newspaper in which Brownlow and Richardson had replied to the Armagh freeholders, a reference made to their inactivity, as compared to others, in the recent parliamentary debate and division on W.B. Ponsonby's motion for parliamentary reform, seemed to be promoting Caulfeild as candidate:

> The electors of the county of Armagh will perceive that Lord Charlemont's friends took a very active part in the debate on Mr Ponsonby's motion for reform on Monday night last [15 May 1797]. Mr Jephson spoke very ably on the subject – whereas their county members were silent, and either divided against the motion, or moved away before the division.[21]

Brownlow was the first to accept he was no longer wanted as candidate. When Caulfeild made an election pact with fellow Whig Richardson, Brownlow whose political image never had the appeal of his late father resigned from the Armagh county contest on 11 July, thus honouring his promise to Lord Charlemont in 1794. Richardson declared his candidature on 13 July 1797 for the county seat he had held since 1783.[22]

Acheson was at a distinct disadvantage in a three-cornered contest and needed an election partner or at least a 'running horse' to prevent his second votes going to the opposition. Lord Charlemont's election pact with Richardson caused consternation in the Gosford camp and Gosford's supporter, James Harden of Harrybrook advised Gosford strongly that 'Mr. Acheson must set up a person to take off his second voices or, at the beginning vote, all the split interests he has'.[23] Others had similar thoughts and were willing to serve as Acheson's 'running horse'. On 26 July, Michael Obins of Portadown, Acheson's uncle and major in the Armagh militia, declared his candidature for the Armagh election at relatively short notice. Obins's hasty decision without consultation upset Acheson's election mentors. On the day his candidature appeared in the press, they asked Obins to withdraw – which he did, with apologies, only five days after declaration.[24] The candidate being lined up as running horse for Acheson was 'Mr. Cope' – presumably Robert Camden Cope who had polled well in 1795 and had been asked then for reciprocal support for Acheson at the general election. Why Cope's candidature was not declared earlier is conjectural and does not seem to have been advertised in the press which was taken by surprise at his eleventh hour declaration.[25]

The poll opened on Monday 31 July 1797. By standards of previous elections, voting was heavy on the first day. Acheson got off to a flying start and at the close of opening day led the field: Acheson 122 votes, Caulfeild 61, Cope 35 and Richardson 23.[26] It seemed that Acheson had drawn votes from the other candidates – possibly from all three – to support his own first votes, many of which were probably plumpers. Richardson's low poll was something of a shock for a sitting member since 1783 and certainly adversely affected Caulfeild's vote. It sent a message that the subdued political style of the older Whigs was out of fashion in Armagh in the late 1790s.

By Thursday 3 August, the rate of voting had eased somewhat. By close, two clear leaders had emerged with Acheson on 203 votes and Caulfeild on 99. A disappointed Richardson withdrew from the contest with the following statement to the press:

> Finding, at the beginning of the election, that a system which I had laid down, and from which I was determined not to depart, was likely to prove unfavourable to my pursuit, I resolved at once to

retire. In times like the present, nothing short of a moral certainty of success could warrant any man in involving his county in a tedious contest; how ill then should I have requited the many favours I have received from mine had I continued to disturb the peace of it by a perseverance in a poll, the event of which was at least doubtful.[27]

Whether Richardson's unsuccessful 'system' referred to his election alignment or low-profile campaign in the interests of community peace, is unclear. But he reminded the electorate he would be available as candidate if required at a future election.

Cope also retired from the 1797 contest at this time. He disappeared as unobtrusively and mysteriously as his unheralded entry, his late intervention successfully completed and leaving the field to Acheson and Caulfeild. Lord Charlemont had cause to be relieved at the early closure to the contest as he was experiencing difficulty in borrowing cash to finance it.[28]

RETURNS FOR BOROUGHS IN 1797–8

Both sitting Armagh borough members were succeeded at the 1797 general election by two other government supporters viz. Chief Secretary Thomas Pelham and controversial barrister Patrick Duigenan. Pelham had started his political career as chief secretary to Lord Northington in late 1783–4 – in Charlemont's view 'just starting in the career of office, and who seemed to resort hither as to a proper school where the business of a statesman might be studied'. He now returned for a second term under Lord Camden from March 1795 and continued under Lord Cornwallis in 1798 until ill-health forced him to give way to Robert Stewart. He opposed Catholic Emancipation against which he had voted in May 1795, a view he had in common with lapsed Catholic, Duigenan.[29] The latter was more vociferously so, prompting Grattan to observe that Duigenan's anti-Catholic rhetoric was a double-edged sword which left Catholics slashed by its attack and Protestants with wounds of embarrassment by its use. Duigenan's support for government had earned him Arthur Acheson's Old Leighlin seat when Acheson entered the house of lords in 1791, and Primate William Newcome's Armagh borough seat in 1797. The return of Pelham and Duigenan secured the continued support of Armagh borough for government.[30]

In Charlemont borough, Jephson continued as MP in 1797 but, when he was appointed judge advocate of Gibraltar later in that year, Charlemont replaced him with the colourful Francis Dobbs, sworn on 23 January 1798. The ageing Sir Annesley Stewart did not stand again in the general election. Initially, Lord Francis William Caulfeild took Stewart's seat but when

Caulfeild opted for the Armagh county seat he won at the 1797 poll, the Charlemont borough seat was passed to William Conyngham Plunket KC who was sworn on 6 February 1798. With both members for Charlemont borough professional lawyers, Lord Charlemont had engaged an able team to articulate opposition to the Dublin administration in the house of commons.[31]

Isaac Corry had a double return for the boroughs of Newry and Randalstown in 1797, opting for Newry. His continued contributions on behalf of government would bring his promotions to government posts of ever-increasing importance in the period 1798–1800. But John Moore, the other member of the Armagh gentry who had supported government in the previous parliament, was not returned by Lord Drogheda at the 1797 general election. With the support of the marquis of Downshire, however, Moore would be returned as an anti-government member at a by-election for Newry borough following the death of Robert Ross. Another Armagh resident, James Verner of Churchhill, who would play a significant part in Armagh and national politics between 1798 and 1800 and who had first been returned to parliament for the Knox borough of Dungannon in the Abercorn interest at a by-election in 1794, was again returned in 1797 as government supporter.[32]

DISPOSITIONS OF ARMAGH MPs IN KEY NATIONAL ISSUES 1797–9; PROPOSALS FOR UNION, APPEAL TO PUBLIC OPINION, AND BY-ELECTION CONTESTS IN 1799

The absence of violence in Armagh over the period of the general election continued into late 1797 and 1798. United Irishmen were kept at bay in the county by a combination of factors: government propaganda and revitalised espionage network, enhanced military surveillance and support from the Orange Order and loyalist yeomanry.[33] Nicholas Maginn, 'the Saintfield informer', was reporting on United Irish meetings in Armagh, Samuel Turner providing similar information from Newry. Significantly Maginn's report on a provincial meeting held at Armagh on 14 October 1797 revealed that the only county delegate who reckoned his county unit would be unable to 'disarm the military' in the event of a rising was from Armagh. Orangeism spread rapidly as a counter-insurgency force in late 1797 swelling the ranks of the yeomanry corps of north Armagh and south Tyrone in early 1798, especially following Castlereagh's permission for emergency recruitment.[34]

In early 1798, with Grattan and his followers having withdrawn from parliament, opposition there to government measures was taken up by Sir Laurence Parsons and Armagh members Plunket, Dobbs and Caulfeild.

Plunket and Dobbs, in a vain attempt to protect the liberty of the press in early March, spoke out against further government measures to suppress seditious writing.[35] Parsons, concerned that government policies would provoke armed rebellion, moved on 5 March 'for a committee of the whole house' to examine the causes of public discontent and how to allay them and restore tranquility. His motion was seconded by Caulfeild in a maiden speech, supported by Dobbs and Plunket but heavily defeated by 156 votes to 19.[36]

At this time, Lord Gosford and sons were pre-occupied with militia duties. Earlier security measures had insured that when insurrection broke out in summer 1798, neither Armagh nor south Down rose despite the presence of United Irishmen. Colonel Gosford, Lieutenant Colonel Robert Camden Cope and Major Archibald Acheson, with security assured at home, could concentrate on leading the Armagh militia to early summer success in Leinster, and to September victories in Connacht and at Ballinamuck against General Humbert's expedition.[37]

National security achieved, Gosford was drawn back into national politics. The two great political issues at the turn of the eighteenth century were the legislative union of the London and Dublin parliaments, and Catholic Emancipation. Before 1800, most Armagh politicians opposed the latter.[38] Initially most also opposed parliamentary union. Threatened by rebellion in and invasion of Ireland, Pitt had adopted a policy of legislative union of the British and Irish parliaments in early summer 1798 and in autumn a draft Union bill was sent from London to Dublin. The November draft bill initiated a paper war of pamphlets, printed addresses and ballads, newspaper articles, petitions, resolutions, satirical cartoons, based on Under-secretary Edward Cooke's advice to British Postmaster-general Lord Auckland: 'If you are serious as to Union, it must be written up, spoken up, intrigued up, drunk up, sung up and bribed up'.[39]

As elsewhere, Armagh resented the proposed diminution in sovereignty, the loss of influence and patronage by the proposed reduction of members to an imperial parliament, and the uncertainty over the future of Irish textiles, particularly linen, in a Union; but would become sharply divided as its delivery appeared inevitable.[40] Gosford, as governor of the county and leader of the government caucus there, was expected by Dublin Castle to deliver support for Union. It was a daunting task in a county proud of its tradition of political dissidence. Among the few supporters of Union in Armagh at the beginning of 1799, were Primate William Newcome, the bigoted Duigenan – whose support of government was diluted by his criticism of new Lord Lieutenant Cornwallis's lenient line towards Catholics, Charles Warburton, rector of Loughgilly, and James Verner of Church Hill, one of the few Orange leaders to support Union, albeit on the direction of his patron.[41]

The anti-Union opposition was led by Lord Charlemont, his protégés and friends. These included Lord Caulfeild, Plunket and Dobbs in the house of commons, former county members Brownlow and Richardson, Sir Capel Molyneux, fourth baronet, who had inherited his father's patriotic zeal with his title when the third baronet died in 1797 aged eighty, and were supported by most Orangemen as individuals.[42] Armagh anti-Unionists anticipated the later canvass of public opinion when they called for a county meeting to be held on 22 January 1799 in Armagh courthouse; but other counsels (presumably government-oriented) managed to have the Armagh meeting postponed until after the debate in the Irish parliament scheduled to meet on that date. Professor Cullen has reminded us that government had a tactical advantage in the county meetings campaign in 1799–1800 in that, under the prevailing legislation, it could officially ban meetings which it deemed might break the peace. Hudson's comment to Charlemont – 'From what had been hinted to me of the means used to prevent a meeting of Armagh' – suggests the Gosford-led government interest in the county may have brought pressure to bear to have the meeting scheduled for Armagh on 22 January, cancelled.[43]

When the lord lieutenant's 'speech from the throne' on 22 January 1799 was attacked by veteran George Ponsonby – returned to parliament for the Union debate – who moved an amendment that 'the undoubted birthright of the people of Ireland to have a resident and independent legislature' be maintained, Plunket and Dobbs both supported him in the debate. A passionate Plunket threatened to resist Union 'to the last gasp of my existence, to the last drop of my blood'.[44] In the division on Ponsonby's amendment on 23 January, the government found itself with a majority of only one, i.e. 106 votes to 105. On the following day, Sir Laurence Parsons moved for the deletion of 'the Union paragraph' which was carried on Friday 25 January by 111 votes to 106, including tellers, the first defeat of government since the regency crisis of 1789.[45]

It was at this time that Gosford's campaign for Union in Armagh received an embarrassing setback with the defection of his son Archibald to the opposition in the 25 January division.[46] The general incredulity at Acheson's decision to vote anti-Union was echoed in Rev. Hudson's comment to Charlemont: 'I was surprised to see Mr. A[cheson]'s name amongst the patriots, and I suspect I was misinformed'.[47] But Hudson had not been misinformed. A few weeks after the 25 January division, Acheson was one of 'the gentlemen of the opposition in the house of commons' with Lord Caulfeild, Richard Dawson, et al. who celebrated their victory in a Dublin restaurant. A newspaper reported: 'It is allowed that the glorious anti-Unionists who dined at Daly's on Tuesday, did much justice to the cause of – good eating and drinking.' Molyneux could not resist gloating to Gosford: 'I congratulate you on the Major's Patriotic conduct [sic]'.[48]

In the parliamentary division on 25 January, four Armagh MPs had voted against Union proposals: both county members plus both Charlemont borough members. Isaac Corry and James Verner had voted for the measure but neither Armagh borough member, Pelham or Duigenan, is listed as having voted, suggesting that Castlereagh had miscalculated the vote for Union. Pelham had departed Ireland in May 1798 in recurring ill-health on less onerous secondment to the lord lieutenant's household staff. With every vote vital in further divisions on Union, Castlereagh later arranged that the absent Pelham should be replaced as Armagh borough representative by another Englishman, General Lake. Duigenan's absence is less clear. None of the division lists for 25 January includes Duigenan who was committed to Union and would have been expected to vote for it.[49]

So momentous was the issue of parliamentary union and so close the divisions of 22 and 25 January 1799 that it was argued in the parliamentary debates, particularly by anti-Unionists, that the final outcome should be endorsed by public mandate. Thus both sides embarked upon an appeal to the country in 1799 in attempts to win public opinion behind their respective cases. Charlemont reminded supporters that the anti-Union victory of 25 January was only one battle in a long campaign ahead and of the importance of winning public opinion to maintain momentum:

> I now begin to perceive that our victory, though glorious, is not absolutely decisive, and that our arch-enemy, enraged at a defeat to which he is wholly unaccustomed, may yet rally his discomfited mercenaries, and again attack us, and this he will most probably do unless he shall find us armed with our only genuine defence, the declared sense of the people.[50]

He attempted to whip up public support to hold the postponed rally against Union in Armagh: 'I have been labouring in Armagh, and still hope for success, though thwarted by many obstacles. The freeholders, indeed, are willing, but many of the gentlemen are supine, and the sheriff [Kendrick Cope] is absent'.[51]

Charlemont's efforts in Armagh were not in vain. Despite Rev. Hudson's opinion that government had prevented the Armagh county meeting scheduled for 22 January 1799 and that there would not be another, an anti-Union meeting was re-scheduled for February 1799. Major General George Nugent, commanding the northern district, stationed at Armagh and personal friend of the Acheson family, conveyed his disappointment to Lord Gosford but concluded that Cornwallis, having permitted meetings in other counties, would be unwilling to change that precedent in Armagh unless there was danger of violence which, he felt, the anti-Union side in Armagh would guard against. Nugent suggested that the Union propositions needed public airing before decisions were made in the Irish parliament but feared initial discussions would be heated.[52]

Leaders at the Armagh meeting of 19 February 1799 were Richardson, Brownlow, Moore and a bellicose Molyneux. Wary of the government's suppressive powers from recent legislation, the emphasis of the meeting was on low-key moderation and absence of press publicity. The loquacious Molyneux was made chairman to prevent his speeches monopolising the meeting, his 'violent' resolutions were not seconded and the more moderate anti-Union motions proposed by Richardson and seconded by Brownlow were accepted unanimously to be conveyed to Charlemont and Caulfeild for presentation in parliament. The anticipated opposition from pro-Union supporters did not materialise. Indeed, Colonel Robert Sparrow, Gosford's son-in-law, surprised the meeting by condemning the proposed Union, while other pro-government gentry absented themselves.[53]

An embarrassed Gosford felt obliged to write to Cornwallis apologising for his son's affiliation and professing his own loyalty on Union. Cornwallis replied that he had told Major Archibald that 'a man might be both a friend to the Union and to the interests of Ireland' and had warned him against being led astray by false friends.[54] Acheson, from Dublin, where the regiment awaited a review by General Trench, attempted to reassure his father that the lord lieutenant's admonition had not indicated that the son's anti-Union sins would be visited upon the father. But General Nugent, with an ear to the ground, was less convinced and advised Gosford to banish Archibald from the Irish parliament to join his younger brother Edward in the duke of York's army abroad until Union was carried if Gosford hoped to be made a representative peer in the proposed imperial parliament![55]

Acheson was not for turning and would oppose Union to the end.[56] The Union issue divided several families and political groups. Some families, like Archibald's friend Richard Dawson and his father Lord Cremorne of Monaghan, were split, with the head of family supporting Union from the house of lords while their son opposed it in the commons.[57] Gosford had much to lose by government disfavour and was all too aware of the importance of government influence in his promotion as representative peer in an imperial parliament. Both Cooke's list of proposed inducements to Irish peers in 1800 and Hardwicke's copy in 1804 of the list of 'Union engagements' reveal that Gosford had been offered the carrot of an earldom.[58]

Following the reverses of January 1799, the government would exert greater pressure on placemen, on opponents to come over and on those members who had abstained on 25 January to support Union in future divisions. The terms of union were made more palatable to those interests who stood to lose by the extinction of the Irish parliament. Catholic support was canvassed by both sides with promises of Emancipation. The courting of Catholics by Dublin Castle brought a resolution supporting

Union from a January meeting of Catholic prelates at Lord Fingall's residence in Dublin signed by Archbishop Richard O'Reilly of Armagh and nine other prelates, though their early resolutions were kept secret at Cornwallis's request lest they proved counter-productive.[59]

Two by-election contests in February 1799 in which two Armagh gentry were involved in the neighbouring pot-walloping borough of Newry illustrated trends. Following Cornwallis's sacking of Sir John Parnell from his post as chancellor of the exchequer – as an example to the rest – for not supporting Union and his appointment of Isaac Corry as Parnell's successor, Corry was required to seek re-election. Corry was opposed by Drogheda anti-Unionist pamphleteer Charles Ball. With Lord Downshire's backing, Ball seemed to have the beating of Corry until the intervention of Dr Thomas Troy, archbishop of Dublin and political spokesman for the Catholic hierarchy, and Dr Matthew Lennon, bishop of Dromore, to request the Newry Catholics to vote for Corry who was the local man and espoused Catholic Emancipation. Lennon reported results to Troy:

> Mr Ball, with his partisans, after canvassing the town for eight days, declined the poll and surrendered yesterday. The Catholics stuck together like a Macedonian phalanx, and, with ease, were able to turn the scale in favour of the chancellor of the exchequer ... He is very sensible of the efficacy of your interference and their steadiness.[60]

Corry's retention of the Newry seat – he was sworn on 11 February 1799 – was a significant morale-booster for the pro-Union side. But this was soon offset by the election of Lord Downshire's anti-Union candidate for the second Newry seat following the death of Colonel Robert Ross. Ball, Colonel Sparrow and Sir Capel Molyneux all let it be known they were available as candidates but were by-passed by Downshire in favour of John Moore junior of Drumbanagher who had the advantages of parliamentary experience and a family estate situated close to Newry town. Moore defeated the dauntless Ball who ran a second time within weeks, being beaten this time by 112 votes to 52 after a three-day poll from 6th to 8th March 1799.[61]

The government campaign for Union in the country was more active than that of the anti-Unionists in the country following the adjournment of parliament on 1 June 1799. Cornwallis's promotion tours of mid and southern Ireland in summer 1799 and of the north in autumn, sought support from the propertied classes in the country. On his whirlwind tour of the north in October, he visited the principal landlords to drum up support. On 8 October, his party of three stayed overnight at Gosford Castle and met the corporation and clergy in the Primate Newcome controlled city of Armagh en route to Belfast, apparently their only stop in

Armagh county which was generally anti-Union, though one deferred return on their visit was a later declaration in favour of Union from the corporation of Armagh City.[62]

From summer 1799 to winter, Gosford took his lead from Cornwallis and canvassed support for his declaration for Union from other men of property – resident and absentee – in the county, as preparation for a county address. Lords Sandwich, Cremorne, Dungannon, Colonel Sparrow, Count de Salis and Isaac Corry declared for Union, and some opponents, like John Moore of Drumbanagher, seemed to be wavering.[63]

A breach was made in the solid anti-Union front of Armagh county members at a by-election in October 1799. When Francis William Caulfeild was elevated to the Irish house of lords, following the death of his father James, the first earl of Charlemont, on 4 August 1799, at the subsequent by-election for his vacated county seat, Sir Capel Molyneux – ever-eager for a parliamentary seat – and Colonel Robert Camden Cope declared their candidature. In a fifteen day contest, from 12th to 30 October, presided over by High Sheriff Archibald Eyre Obins, Cope defeated Molyneux by 1810 votes to 1282.[64]

Despite the wide winning margin, a dogged Molyneux contested the result by parliamentary petition amid allegations and counter-allegations. Molyneux alleged that a number of voters had been bribed by Cope or his agents to vote more than once, using different names on different days, at different venues. Such impersonation had been facilitated, he suggested, by Sheriff Obins's arrangement of appropriating separate buildings in Armagh City as hustings for the poll of seven baronies. Obins had sworn six deputies to assist him. Molyneux also alleged that Cope – 'aided by a peer of the realm' – had illegally created freeholders merely to vote at the election and had rewarded them by funding 'houses of entertainment' for the duration of the election. A counter allegation from Cope cited Richard Dawson as claiming the petition would only be initiated – and financed by 'two noble lords' – if Cope voted for Union. Dawson denied Cope's allegation. Molyneux's petition was presented by James O'Donnell to parliament on 17 February 1800 and heard by select committee in the following weeks. The verdict on 26 March was that Cope had not been returned by corrupt means and his election upheld.[65]

THE STRUGGLE IN ARMAGH OVER UNION IN 1800

The Armagh county by-election in 1799 influenced the struggle for Union. Initially, both candidates had been anti-Union, typifying the disposition of the Armagh gentry generally. But the support of Gosford and the Unionists had guaranteed victory for Cope, and, as a quid pro quo, Cope was subsequently recruited to the Unionist side by James Verner and Gosford. Cornwallis congratulated Gosford on the satisfactory outcome.[66]

At the return of parliament in January 1800, a pro-Union coalition of Gosford, Verner, Cope, Duigenan plus General Lake – who was nominated by the primate to replace Pelham and sworn as Armagh borough representative on 15 January 1800 – was now ranged against the anti-Union front led by Charlemont, Dobbs, Plunket, Acheson, Moore, Brownlow, Richardson and Molyneux. Parsons's motion – to maintain an independent Irish parliament – attacking the speech from the throne on 15 January 1800, was supported in debate by Plunket. In the division on the following day, Acheson, Dobbs, Plunket and Moore supported Parsons's amendment which was defeated by 98 votes to 140. Cope, Lake, Verner and Corry voted against the amendment. Again, Duigenan was not in the press list of members who voted. Cope felt obliged to publicly give reasons to his Armagh electorate for voting anti-amendment:

> Whenever a legislative union is moved in parliament, I pledge myself to promote a full discussion of the terms on which that grand system is proposed to be established: ultimately to ratify or reject it as the interests of my country shall require.[67]

At the turn of the century, both sides were conducting tit for tat campaigns outside parliament. When, on 4 December 1799, two hundred and seventy seven 'merchants and freeholders' of the manors of Richhill and Mullalelish led by William Richardson, assembled and signed a declaration of 'most decided disapprobation' against Union, Sovereign George Perry and the burgesses of Armagh City forwarded the delayed freedom of the city to Cornwallis with a declaration for Union.[68] Cornwallis, through General Nugent, advised Gosford on a wide range – and order of presentation – of signatures required for a pro-Union declaration from the county to offset that of Richardson. Gosford's declaration in early January 1800, was headed by Primate Newcome and Lords Gosford, Sandwich, Lifford, Cremorne, Caledon and Count de Salis, and had *c.* 1,000 names of 'noblemen, gentlemen, clergy, merchants and freeholders' of Armagh county. Other major landed families on it included Sparrow, Copes, Blackers, Ogles, Hamiltons and Verners. Missing from Gosford's list were the names of Charlemont, Archibald Acheson, Richardson, Brownlow, Molyneux, Moore, Hall and Obré.[69]

Nugent wrote encouragingly from Dublin to Gosford that Armagh country gentlemen such as Sparrow had been converted to Union while others remaining neutral were only holding out for better terms for their support. Gosford's county declaration was soon followed by published support from 'the inhabitants' of Seagoe Parish led by Colonel Sparrow and the Blacker family, and from the 'Roman Catholic inhabitants of the Parish of Lower

Creggan' led by their parish priest Rev P. Quinn. When Gosford's declaration was attacked by anti-Union interests a list of landowners and inhabitants of Tandragee, headed by Sparrow, re-affirmed support for Union.[70]

A counter-offensive from a meeting in Charlemont's Dublin residence on 18 January 1800 led by Charlemont, Downshire and Foster against Castlereagh propaganda – that eighteen or nineteen counties had declared pro-Union and that anti-Unionists had been reduced to a mere 'faction' – launched a campaign of county meetings and petitions to whip up public opinion against Union before parliament resumed on 3 February.[71] Armagh county answered Charlemont's call with an anti-Union rally on 28 January 1800 and declaration by 7,000 names reasserting:

> ... their fixed and unalterable aversion to that pernicious measure, and their abhorrence of the means which had been resorted to in the prosecution of it ... A measure insulting to the sense and feelings of Irishmen, and whose adoption would hazard the peace, impede the prosperity, and annihilate the liberties of their country.[72]

Their petition was presented to the house of commons on 7 February 1800.[73]

The relative numerical strengths of pro and anti-Unionist members were put to the test soon after the resumption of parliament. Castlereagh's motion of 5–6 February 1800 formulating the lord lieutenant's Union proposals brought the largest-ever division in the Irish house of commons and victory for the government by 158 votes to 115. Duigenan and Lake supported the motion, Dobbs and Plunket opposed; but the Armagh county members were divided with Acheson opposing and Cope supporting the motion. Isaac Corry and James Verner supported while John Moore opposed.[74]

In an attempt to whip up public opinion against Union, many northern Orange lodges repudiated the official policy of neutrality and published declarations against the proposed Union. These included a newspaper notice in March 1800 following a meeting at McKean's Hotel, Armagh, of representatives of the Orange lodges of Armagh and Monaghan counties containing 2,100 members, carrying virulent anti-Union resolutions.[75]

But the initiative remained with government after the momentous result of 5–6 February and undercut preparations of anti-Unionists for the debates on the three readings of the Union bill in May and June. A meeting of Armagh magistrates and magistrates called in May 1800 by Charlemont, Molyneux, Brownlow, Richardson et al. was postponed.[76] Castlereagh's timely offer of £15,000 compensation for borough proprietors deprived of both parliamentary seats, eased the passage of Union. Despite expressions of disgust in debates by Dobbs and Plunket that representative rights could be sold like pieces of property, both sides accepted that borough political franchise was a marketable commodity – as private assets to be cashed in the event of their nationalisation through Union. Castlereagh saw his role: 'to buy out and secure to the crown forever the fee-simple of Irish corruption'. Borough patrons took the opportunity to cash in on the deal; and the second earl of Charlemont, leading opponent to Union, accepted like the rest his £15,000 for the representative rights of Charlemont borough.[77]

With Charlemont borough disfranchised by the Act of Union, the parliamentary career of Francis Dobbs was ended. Initially, W.C. Plunket also was left without a parliamentary seat but made a come-back – briefly as MP for Midhurst in 1807 and then as MP for TCD from 1812–27 – in the imperial parliament where he championed Catholic Emancipation.[78]

Archibald Acheson and Robert Camden Cope continued after Union – without election – as members for County Armagh in the imperial parliament. Acheson, having been returned at the general elections of 1802 and 1806, continued to serve in the British house of commons until he succeeded as second earl of Gosford in 1807, when he was replaced in the commons by William Brownlow. Cope did not contest the general election of 1802, relinquishing his Westminster seat to Lord Charlemont's younger brother, Henry Caulfeild.[79]

Other MPs in the Irish Parliament who resided in Armagh had mixed fortunes at the Union re-allocation of seats in the imperial parliament. James Verner lost out in Dungannon's single-member constituency to Major General Hon. John Knox. Isaac Corry's similar fate in Newry – losing by lot to John Moore – created the problem of how his budget was to be presented. Using an age-old precedent, the government turned to the primate, newly appointed Archbishop William Stuart, for an Armagh borough seat for Corry.[80] But Armagh's single seat was occupied by the rabid Protestant Duigenan who refused to stand down to accommodate Corry whom he considered a Catholic-phile. A constitutional furore ensued when Lord Chancellor Loughborough, himself opposed to Catholic relief, leaked the proposal to George III who interpreted the recommendation of Corry for Armagh borough seat as part of a conspiracy by Pitt and Castlereagh to introduce Catholic Emancipation. The king angrily requested Speaker Addington to remonstrate with Pitt for so dangerous a scheme and the archbishop of Canterbury promised to inform Castlereagh of his opposition to the election of Corry for Armagh. Pitt resigned over the king's interference and Addington was called to form a ministry.[81]

Duigenan retained his Armagh seat until his death in 1816. The government found a seat for Corry in Dundalk until he won back his Newry seat at the general election of 1802. In 1804 Pitt replaced Corry as chancellor of the Irish exchequer with John Foster. In May 1805 Corry voted for the unsuccessful Catholic petition – Grattan's maiden speech at

Westminster – which Duigenan had buffoonishly attacked. Corry lost his seat to General Francis Nedham in 1806 but was sponsored by Lady Downshire to a seat for Newport. The fall of Grenville's government in 1807 ended Corry's parliamentary career. Having contested the Newry seat again, unsuccessfully, he led an isolated life until his death in 1813.[82]

CONCLUSION: ARMAGH ELECTIONS IN THE FINAL IRISH PARLIAMENT, 1797–1800

The struggle for political control of Armagh county was intensified during the final Irish parliament. In the general election of 1797, the two sitting members were swept aside in a short contest by Francis William Caulfeild and Archibald Acheson, two new young candidates eager to continue active family political dynasties by restoration of a presence in the Irish house of commons. Their return was facilitated by the emergence, post-1793, of Catholic voting freeholders on Gosford and Charlemont estates situated in the southern half of the county. Acheson's election seemed a breakthrough for Gosford's pro-government caucus, giving an even division, for and against government, of the six members returned for Armagh constituencies. Isaac Corry and John Moore, two Armagh gentry returned for the neighbouring potwalloping borough of Newry, were also divided in allegiance; while James Verner of Churchhill, returned for the Knox borough of Dungannon in the Abercorn parliamentary interest, supported government.

The traditional 'independence' in the county was given a new dimension by the break of Lord Charlemont's anti-government parliamentary protégés with the official Whig policy of abstention from 1797 when Caulfeild, Jephson – later replaced by Dobbs – and Plunket, took leading roles in opposing government in debates and in divisions in the house of commons. Their decision would seem to have been vindicated when Grattan, Ponsonby et al. felt obliged to return to parliament for the Union debates.

Government proposals for a parliamentary union in 1799 sharpened political divisions in Armagh county. Initially the anti-Union caucus held the initiative. Its morale was high following the government reverses of 22 and 25 January 1799, and initial government pressure to prevent anti-government meetings in the county only enhanced determination to organise more. Archibald Acheson's inclusion in the parliamentary red list of 25 January was a major coup for the anti-Union side, for which an embarrassed Gosford felt obliged to apologise to Cornwallis. In that division four members returned for Armagh constituencies had voted against Union proposals, and none for. The absence of both Duigenan and Pelham from the division suggests a serious miscalculation by Castlereagh and evidence of his inexperience in parliamentary management.

With anti-Union opinion rife in Armagh, the emergence of the Catholics as an organised political force supporting Union was an important ally to government in the late 1790s. The resolutions of the Catholic bishops at the January 1799 meetings in Dublin showed a willingness to co-operate with government in response to the latter's proposals to make financial provision for Catholic clergy.[83] In County Armagh, and neighbouring Newry, initiatives and leadership were provided by Catholic church leaders rather than laity as in the intervention of Archbishop Troy and Bishop Lennon to organise Catholic votes for Isaac Corry in the Newry by-election of February 1799, and in the overt organisation of Catholic inhabitants of Lower Creggan by its parish priest in public support of Union just under one year later. Both instances heralded the arrival of Catholics as a force in high politics and Catholic Emancipation as a major political issue. In November 1800, Archbishop Richard O'Reilly was seeking information from the Presbyterian assembly at Richhill on the operation of the regium donum which 'will be of use in adjusting the business now pending between government and the Catholic prelates with respect to a provision for our clergy'.[84]

The appeal to the country which continued throughout 1799 into 1800 brought declarations for and against Union at different levels of politically conscious society: resolutions from county meetings of gentlemen and freeholders, addresses and petitions from local corporations – usually reflecting the dispositions of the patron, petitions from individual landlords signed by his tenantry, and declarations from grand juries, for many the most influential measure of public opinion, but least frequent. That government rated declarations from propertied gentlemen above popular demonstrations – to show the weight of landed and propertied gentlemen on its side and control of enfranchised freeholders – was evident in the advice of Cornwallis and Castlereagh to Gosford through General Nugent on 23 December 1799 on drawing up signatures for a declaration of support. Thus Gosford's declaration list was regarded as more influential than Charlemont's much more numerous list which followed.

The point was further illustrated in Cope's press notice which emphasised the influence of 'one body of my electors, highly respectable for their numbers, their property, and consequently their serious interest in the prosperity of this kingdom' when choosing the Unionist side in Armagh. Cornwallis's selective promotion tour of the north in autumn 1799 was restricted to areas and landlords known to support Union. Thus, apart from an over-night stay at Gosford Castle and a brief visit to Primate Newcome's Armagh, the lord lieutenant's entourage moved quickly through a largely anti-Union Armagh county to Belfast. A conclusion would seem to be that Dublin Castle, while realising public opinion could not be ignored, was confident that the landed and propertied classes disposed to government would decide the fate of Union, if they gave the lead.

Given the tradition of independence and patriotism in Armagh county, it was hardly surprising if a majority of freeholders remained opposed to Union. Thus Lord Gosford could take much credit for managing an even split of MPs returned for the county in the final parliamentary divisions on Union. And his success rate would have been better had his son not defected to the opposition. Why Archibald joined the anti-Union caucus is conjecturable. His opposition may have been due to a generational factor and/or the fashion of many of Archibald's younger anti-Union contemporaries such as Caulfeild and Richard Dawson. The 'x' annotation against Acheson's name on Castlereagh's red list of 25 January 1799 suggests the government was hopeful of his changing sides – hopes unfulfilled.[85]

But the political difference between Lord Gosford and son may have been more apparent than real, and both may have been anticipating a time when Archibald could bring Gosford leadership of the county another step forward by attempting to reconcile traditional dissidence with the ruling orthodoxy. The scars of resentment caused by the government's extraordinary use of 'engagements' to carry Union – particularly on those who had missed out on Union 'honours' and felt deprived by the loss of patronage, possibly forever – were sensitive reminders to Armagh political society after 1800. Lord Gosford had a promised earldom deferred in December 1800 and again in 1803, presumably to avoid re-opening still fresh wounds of anti-Union neighbours. Lord Hardwicke concluded that there had been collusion between Gosford and son on the deferment until an earldom might no longer be seen as a tainted reward for supporting Union. It is equally plausible to assume earlier collusion between them in taking opposing sides on Union to appease and be accepted within Armagh society afterwards.[86]

The sins of the son were not visited upon the father by officialdom. Lord Arthur Gosford finally accepted his earldom from the 'Ministry of all the talents' some five years after Union and was created first earl of Gosford on 10 February 1806. And the son was also shown to have been forgiven when he succeeded as second earl following his father's death in Bath on 15 January 1807, his phase of political dissidence well behind him.[87] By then, Archibald had already revealed he was no less pragmatic in accepting government promotion than the second earl of Charlemont had been in accepting compensation for lost borough patronage.

Despite his opposition to Union, Archibald did not allow its passage to interfere with his own political career nor with continuation of the Gosford political dynasty. From March 1800 he held the post of custos rotulorum for County Armagh. His father would seem to have aided him build a power base, resigning in April 1801 as colonel of the Armagh militia to allow Archibald to succeed him. From 1801 to 1807 Archibald served as

MP for County Armagh in the imperial parliament. He had powerful English connections from 1803 when his sister Mary married Lieutenant General Lord William Bentinck, governor-general of India and son of the third duke of Portland, and through his own marriage to heiress Mary Sparrow of Worlingham Hall, Beccles, in 1805. In that year the supremacy of the Gosford political dynasty in Armagh was copper-fastened when Archibald was appointed governor of the county which post he held until his death in 1849.[88]

The constitutional dispute over the attempt to place Corry in Armagh borough seat highlighted Armagh's involvement in imperial politics. Modern research has reminded us that the recommendation of Isaac Corry to the Armagh seat held by Patrick Duigenan by Pitt and the Irish administration was central to the constitutional contretemps between Pitt and the king in January 1801, though Geoghegan argues that Bolton was inaccurate in suggesting that that recommendation triggered off the king's fury.[89] The incident typified the continued importance of Armagh politics in Irish and British politics in the eighteenth century.

Notes

1. Lake to Pelham, 17 Mar. 1797 (PRONI, Pelham papers, T/755/4B/iv/ p.189); Rev. Charles Warburton to Dublin Castle, 15, 16, 17 Mar. 1797 (NAI, Rebellion papers 620/29/76, 81, 85).
2. Colonel H.G. Sankey to General Nugent, 16 Mar. 1797 (PRONI, Pelham papers, T/755/4B/iv/p.172); Reamonn Ó Muirí, 'The killing of Thomas Birch, United Irishman' in *Seanchas Ardmhacha*, x, no. 2, (1982), pp 267–319.
3. Gosford to Pelham, 30 Mar. 1797 (NAI, Rebellion papers, 620/29/152).
4. Dawson to Pelham, 11 Apr. 1797 (ibid. 620/29/219); Knox to Pelham, 11 Apr. 1797 (PRONI, Pelham papers, T/755/4B/iv/ pp 256–7).
5. Knox to Pelham, 19 Apr. 1797 (ibid. T/755/iv/2/p.289); same to same, 17 May 1797 (ibid. T/755/v/ pp 57–76).
6. Alexander Hamilton's diary entries for 15 Apr. 1797 (PRONI, Harmwood papers, C/5/1). Alexander Hamilton MP, of Knock, Co. Dublin and Newtownhamilton, Co. Armagh, was the eldest son of Hugh Hamilton, bishop of Clonfert 1795–9, previously dean of Armagh 1768–95.
7. Francis Plowden, *An historical review of the state of Ireland*, ii (London, 1803), Appendix xcix, pp 269– 75; *BNL*, 12 May, 2 June 1797.
8. Brigadier General Robert Bernard Sparrow of Brampton Park, County Huntingdon and Tandragee Castle, County Armagh, had married Lord Arthur Gosford's daughter Olivia, on 14 March 1797, see *Burke's peerage*, p.1139.
9. Pelham to Dawson, 17 Apr. 1797 (NAI, Rebellion papers, 620/29/274).
10. Knox to Pelham, 19 Apr. 1797 (PRONI, Pelham papers, T/755/iv/2/ pp 286–7); Jephson to Charlemont, 19 Apr. 1797 (*HMC Charlemont*), ii, 399; Gosford to Pelham, 21 Apr. 1797 (NAI, Rebellion papers, 620/29/292); Warburton to Pelham, 20 Apr. 1797 (ibid., 620/29/290).

11 Pelham to Gosford, 22 Apr. 1797 (PRONI, Gosford papers D/1606/1/1/192A).
12 *DEP*, 18 May 1797; *BNL*, 22 May 1797.
13 Knox to Gosford, 2 May 1797 (PRONI, Gosford papers, D/1606/1/1/192C).
14 Warburton to Pelham, 31 May 1797 (NAI, Rebellion papers, 620/30/258); Rev. J.A. Hamilton to Dublin Castle, 15 June 1797 (ibid. 620/31/100).
15 Primate William Newcome to Gosford, 22 June 1797 (PRONI, Gosford papers, D/1606/1/1/193B).
16 Gosford to Camden, 19 June 1797 (TCD, MIC 56, KAO, Camden papers, U840/0173/12).
17 J.C. Sainty, 'The secretariat of the chief governors of Ireland', *RIA Proc*, lxxvii (1977), sect. C, p. 24. Under-secretary Hamilton, the quintessential civil servant and bureaucrat had been a clerk in the revenue department since 1746 succeeding Thomas Waite as under-secretary in the civil department in 1780. Thereafter his expertise in government finance had provided indispensable support for chief secretaries and lord lieutenants for which he had been rewarded with the safe government parliamentary seats of St Johnstown, County Longford, 1780–3 and Clogher bishop-borough from 1783 until dismissed by Fitzwilliam in February 1795. His dismissal had brought protests from high-level politicians probably contributing to Fitzwilliam's recall a few weeks later. Hamilton had been reinstated on 15 May 1795. He had been sworn for Armagh archbishop-borough in January 1796 and retired a year later aged sixty-five.
18 Cullen, 'Alliances and misalliances in the politics of the Union', pp 236–7.
19 *BNL*, 31 July 1797.
20 *DEP*, 13, 18 May 1797.
21 *DEP*, 18 May 1797.
22 Harden to Gosford, 13 July 1797 (PRONI, Gosford papers, D/1606/1/1/194); *BNL*, 31 July 1797.
23 Same to same, 13 July 1797 (ibid. D/16/160/1/194).
24 *BNL*, 31 July 1797, 4 Aug. 1797. Michael Obins of Castle Obins, Portadown, had married Archibald Acheson's aunt Nichola in 1763, see Lodge, *Peerage of Ireland*, vi, 84.
25 *FJ*, 5 Aug. 1797.
26 Ibid.
27 *BNL*, 7 Aug. 1797.
28 Charlemont to Malone, 19 Aug. 1797 (*HMC Charlemont*), ii, 280–1.
29 Memoirs (*HMC Charlemont*), i, 104; *Commons jn. Ire.* (Grierson), xvii, 185–9; *NS*, 4–7 May 1795.
30 Johnston-Liik, *Irish parliament*, iv, 86; ibid. vi, 38–9; *Commons' jn. Ire.* (Bradley), xxviii, 91; *Commons' jn. Ire.* (Grierson), xvii, 185.
31 *Commons' jn. Ire.* (Grierson), xxvii, 185; Rev. Edward Hudson to Charlemont, 11 Mar. 1798 (*HMC Charlemont*), ii, 316; Charlemont to Haliday, 20 Mar. 1798 (ibid. ii, 317).
32 *Commons' jn. Ire.* (Grierson), xxviii, 5–8.
33 Cullen, 'United Irishmen', p. 20.
34 Reports of Nicholas Maginn, Oct. 1797 (PRONI, Cleland papers, D/714/2/8, 9); C.F. McGleenon, 'Patterns of settlement in the parishes of Ballymore and Mullaghbrack in the seventeenth and eighteenth centuries' in *Seanchas Ardmhacha* xv, no.2 (1993) pp 75–6; Blackstock, 'A dangerous species of ally', p.20.
35 *BNL*, 5, 8 Mar. 1798.
36 *FJ*, 6 Mar. 1798.

37 *A list of the officers of militia, 1799* (Dublin, 1800), p. 18 shows that Archibald Acheson had received a commission as major in his father's regiment, the Armagh Militia, on 10 Feb. 1798; Richard Musgrave, *Memoirs of the different rebellions in Ireland from the arrival of the English* (2nd ed., Dublin, 1801), pp 233–4; McAnally, *Irish militia*, pp 129, 132; Journal of Lt. Col. William Blacker, 1777–1855 (Armagh County Museum, Blacker MSS, 7 vols), i, 240; *Journal of the society of army historical research*, iii, no. 13 (Sheffield, July 1924), pp 106–7.

38 Francis Dobbs's resolution in the house of commons on 5 Mar. 1799 calling for Catholic emancipation was an exception, see *BNL*, 8 Mar. 1799.

39 Cooke to Auckland, 27 Oct. 1798 (PRONI, Sneyd papers, T/3229/2/37).

40 Gosford to the marquis of Cornwallis, 22 Feb.1799 (PRONI, Gosford papers, D/1606/1/1/205).

41 Armagh resident James Verner was MP for Dungannon borough 1794–1800, courtesy of George Knox who managed the Abercorn interest. Verner put his parliamentary seat before his Orange ideology and followed his patron's direction in divisions, e.g. voting for the Catholic Emancipation bill in 1795, see *NS*, 11–14 May 1795.

42 The official policy of the Grand Orange Lodge of Ireland in 1799 and 1800 was given as neutrality on Union, see *BNL*, 28 Jan. 1800.

43 Rev Nathaniel Alexander to Alexander Knox, assistant private secretary to Castlereagh, 17 Jan. 1799 in Charles Vane, marquess of Londonderry (ed.), *Memoirs and correspondence of Viscount Castlereagh, second marquess of Londonderry* (London, 1848; hereafter, Vane, *Castlereagh correspondence*), ii, 123; Hudson to Charlemont, 3 Feb. 1799, (*HMC Charlemont*), ii, 345–6; Cullen, 'Alliances and misalliances in the politics of the Union', p. 229.

44 James Moore (ed.), *A report of the debate in the house of commons in Ireland on Tuesday and Wednesday, 22nd and 23 January 1799 on the subject of an Union* (Dublin, 1799), p. 53; G.C. Bolton, *The passing of the Irish Act of Union: a study in parliamentary politics* (London, 1966; hereafter, Bolton, *Union*), p. 111.

45 Division list on Union, 25 Jan. 1799 (PRONI, Castlereagh papers, D/3030/ 552A); *BNL*, 29 Jan. 1799.

46 Division list 25 Jan. 1799 (PRONI, Castlereagh papers, D/3030/552A); *BNL*, 1 Feb. 1799.

47 Hudson to Charlemont, 3 Feb. 1799 (*HMC Charlemont*), ii, 345.

48 *FJ*, 14 Feb. 1799; Molyneux to Gosford, 14 Feb.1799 (PRONI, Gosford papers, D/1606/1/1/204).

49 Division list, 25 Jan. 1799 (PRONI, Castlereagh papers, D/3030/ 552A); Barrington, *Irish nation*, pp 289–99; *BNL*, 1 Feb. 1799; *Commons jn. Ire.* (Grierson), xix, 5.

50 Charlemont to Haliday, 2 Feb. 1799, (*HMC Charlemont*), ii, 345.

51 Ibid.

52 General Nugent to Gosford, 7 Feb. 1799 (PRONI, Gosford papers, D/1606/1/1/203C).

53 Robert Boyd to Charlemont, 20 Feb. 1799 (*HMC Charlemont*), ii, 346; Printed anti-Union petition from Armagh freeholders to parliament, 1799 (PRONI, Foster/Massereene papers, D/207/10/4).

54 Gosford to Cornwallis, 22 Feb. 1799 (PRONI, Gosford papers, D/1606/1/1/205); Cornwallis to Gosford, 5 Mar. 1799 (ibid., D/1606/1/1/206).

55 Major Archibald Acheson to Gosford, 8 Mar. 1799 (ibid. D/1606/1/1/207); General Nugent to Gosford, 21 Apr. 1800 (ibid., D/1606/1/1/228).

56   Barrington, *Irish nation*, p. 576.
57   Bolton, *Union*, p. 158.
58   Under-secretary Edward Cooke's draft list of the government's 'engagements to Irish peers', 1800 (PRONI, Castlereagh papers, D/3030/1356); Michael McDonagh (ed)., *The Viceroy's Postbag: correspondence of the earl of Hardwicke, first Lord Lieutenant of Ireland after the Union* (London, 1904; hereafter, *Hardwicke correspondence* in McDonagh, *Viceroy's Postbag*), p. 50.
59   Resolutions of Roman Catholic prelates, 17, 18, 19 Jan. 1799, cited in J.R. Ardill, *The closing of the Irish parliament* (Dublin, 1907; hereafter, Ardill, *The closing of the Irish parliament*), p. 29; Archbishop Troy to J.C. Hippisley (Emancipationist MP for Sudbury) 9 Feb.1799 (PRONI, Castlereagh papers, D/3030/598).
60   Bishop Lennon to Archbishop Troy, 7 Feb. 1799 (PRONI, Castlereagh papers, D/3030/595).
61   *BNL*, 1, 5, 8, 12 Mar. 1799; *Commons' jn. Ire.* (Grierson), xviii, 5–8; Ball's persistence in pursuit of a parliamentary seat was rewarded in 1800 when he was accepted as representative for Clogher borough – albeit only from 29 March to August when the borough was disfranchised under the Act of Union, see *Commons jn. Ire.* (Grierson), xix, 122–3.
62   General Nugent to Gosford, 30 Sept. 1799 (PRONI, Gosford papers, D/1606/1/1/220B); Colonel Littlehales to Gosford, 29 Sept. 1799 (ibid., D/1606/1/1/220A); Cornwallis to Portland, (private), 22 Oct. 1799 in Charles Ross (ed.), *Correspondence of Charles, first Marquis Cornwallis* (3 vols., London, 1859; hereafter Ross, *Cornwallis correspondence*), iii, 139; Ardill, *The closing of the Irish parliament*, p. 72.
63   Lord Sandwich to Gosford, 20 Aug. 1799 (PRONI, Gosford papers, D/1606/1/1/215); Lord Cremorne to Gosford, 17 Oct. 1799 (ibid., D/1606/1/1/220C); General Nugent to Gosford, 23, 24, 27 Dec. 1799 (ibid., D/1606/1/1/225 B, C, D); Count de Salis to Gosford, 4 Jan. 1800 (ibid., D/1606/1/1/226A).
64   *Commons' jn. Ire.* (Grierson), xix, 46–7; 'Figures for contested elections in Co. Armagh 1783–1826' (NLI, MS 2716) give the result as 1,795 votes to Cope against Molyneux's 1,277. Cope who had been appointed high sheriff of Armagh for 1799 was required to resign from post when standing for parliamentary election, and was succeeded as sheriff by Archibald Obins of Portadown.
65   *Commons' jn. Ire.* (Grierson), xix, 46–7. The six deputies sworn by Sheriff Obins are listed as: Samuel Cuming, John Wolsey, Curren Woodhouse, James Fulton, James Taggart and William Cross. The 'peer of the realm' mentioned in allegations probably referred to Lord Gosford; ibid. pp 62, 100, 113, 117; *BNL*, 21 Feb. 1800.
66   Warburton to Castlereagh, 13 Oct. 1799 (PRONI, Castlereagh papers, D/3030/1017); Littlehales to Castlereagh, 31 Oct. 1799 (ibid., D/3030/1043); Cornwallis to Gosford, 31 Oct. 1799 (PRONI, Gosford papers, D/1606/1/1/225A); James Verner to Castlereagh, 16 Dec. 1799, in Vane, *Castlereagh correspondence*, iii, 18.
67   *BNL*, 24 Jan. 1800.
68   *BNL*, 20, 27 Dec. 1799.
69   General Nugent to Gosford, 23 Dec.1799 (PRONI, Gosford papers, D/1606/1/1/225B); *FJ*, 11 Jan. 1800.
70   Nugent to Gosford, 5 Jan. 1800 (PRONI, Gosford papers, D/1606/1/1/226C); *BNL*, 17 Jan. 1800; *FJ*, 25 Jan. 1800.
71   Cooke to Auckland, 20 Jan. 1800 (PRONI, Sneyd papers, T/3229/2/2/52).

72 Cited in Ardill, *The closing of the Irish parliament*, p. 85; Anti-Union petition from County Armagh freeholders to Irish parliament (PRONI, Foster/Massereene papers, D/207/10/4).
73 *Commons' jn. Ire.* (Grierson), xix, 34.
74 Division list cited in Ardill, *The closing of the Irish parliament*, pp 91–103.
75 *BNL*, 21 March 1800.
76 Printed notice of postponement of meeting, 20 May 1800 (PRONI, Castlereagh papers, D/3030/1329); Gosford to Castlereagh, 21 May 1800 (ibid., D/3030/1328).
77 Castlereagh to Cooke, 21 June 1800 (Vane, *Castlereagh correspondence*, iii, 330–3); *Irish Statutes*, 40 Geo. III (1800) C. 34; 'A return from the commissioners of all claims for compensation on account of representative franchises which they have admitted and to what account' from general index to commons journals, cited in *Liber Munerum Publicorum Hiberniae*, Report by Rowley Lascelles (2 vols, 7 parts, London, 1824–30; hereafter *LMPH*), vii, 172; list of boroughs disfranchised in (Ross, *Cornwallis correspondence*, iii, 321–4). No compensation was allowed for boroughs retained as single-member constituencies 'as one seat in the imperial parliament was considered quite equal to two in the Irish' (ibid., iii, 324).
78 Johnston-Liik, *Irish parliament*, vi, 70–2.
79 B.M. Walker (ed.), *Parliamentary election results in Ireland, 1801–1922* (Dublin, 1978; hereafter, Walker, *Parliamentary election results*), p. 196; R.G. Thorne (ed.), *The house of commons 1790–1820* (5 vols, London, 1986; hereafter, Thorne, *House of commons*), ii, 627.
80 Primate Stuart, a son of George III's old mentor the earl of Bute and former bishop of St. David's who had been chosen for Armagh by the king without consultation with Pitt or the Irish administration, was unwilling to accede meekly to the latter's request.
81 Bolton, *Union*, pp 210–2.
82 Johnston-Liik, *Irish parliament*, iii, 513–4; Walker, *Parliamentary election results*, p. 234.
83 Resolutions of Catholic bishops, 17,18, 19 Jan. 1799 (Dublin Diocesan Archives, Troy papers 1797–9, AB2/116/7/126); handwritten copies of deliberations on the Veto question, 17, 18, 19 Jan. 1799 (ibid. MS 128); signed statement of Catholic prelates, 28 Jan. 1799 (ibid. MS 127).
84 Archbishop O'Reilly to his Vicar-General Dr. Henry Conwell, 4 Nov. 1800 (Cardinal Ó Fiaich Library & Archive, Archbishop O'Reilly correspondence).
85 Division list, 25 Jan. 1795 (PRONI, Castlereagh papers, D/3030/552A).
86 *Hardwicke correspondence* in McDonagh, *Viceroy's Postbag*, pp 11–50; Ross, *Cornwallis correspondence*, iii, 319; A.A. Aspinall, 'Acheson, Hon.Archibald' in Thorne, *House of commons*, iii, 17.
87 Ross, *Cornwallis correspondence*, iii, 319; *BNL*, 23 Jan. 1807.
88 *LMPH*, iii, 144; Littlehales to Gosford, 5 Apr. 1801 (PRONI, Gosford papers, D/1606/1/1/236); Walker, *Parliamentary election results*, pp 1–14; Arthur Wellesley, London, to Gosford, 25 Jan. 1809 (*Wellington supplementary despatches*, v, 542); *Burke's peerage*, p. 1139; Aspinall entry in Thorne, *House of commons*, iii, 17. The title 'governor' of the county changed to 'lord lieutenant' from 1831.
89 Bolton, *Union*, pp 210–2; P.M. Geoghegan, *The Irish Act of Union: a study in high politics 1798–1801* (Dublin, 1999), p. 165.

Conclusion

The political infrastructure in County Armagh which facilitated the return of six members to the Irish parliament had been laid in the Ulster Plantation of the early seventeenth century. A Protestant political community which became established in different waves of settlement during the seventeenth and early eighteenth centuries, returned two borough MPs committed to supporting the Dublin administration, two borough MPs committed to the Irish interest, and two county members, elected from a Protestant political élite, who were independent. In the period 1750–1800, the primate-borough of Armagh provided seats for key officers and supporters of government as required. MPs returned for Charlemont borough were the relations and political friends of the first earl of Charlemont who, following their patriot patron's lead, were normally opposed to government in parliamentary debate and divisions.

The two county members held the political balance of power in Armagh. County seats were coveted by the leading political families – Brownlows, Copes, Achesons, Richardsons and Caulfeilds – none of whom had sufficient freeholders to elect an MP without conjunction with other political interests. After a quiet second quarter of the eighteenth century with politics dormant and no election contests, a new generation of impatient Armagh politicians forced a practice general election campaign in 1752 and a tumultuous by-election contest the following year. The violence and expense of the 1753 contest persuaded the Armagh political élite to avoid election polls for thirty years, and county returns were decided by canvass and negotiation among the leading political interests in the county in the general elections of 1761, 1768 and 1776.

However, pressure from another generation of Armagh political families led to polls for the county seats in the general elections of 1783, 1790 and 1797 and in the by-elections of 1795 and 1799. By the late eighteenth century, Armagh county members had a national reputation of being independent of government control, and the county generally of being opposed to government, with four of the six Armagh parliamentary seats returning members opposed to the Dublin administration. In the 1797 general election poll, the emergence of Catholic freeholders from the

Charlemont and Gosford estates of south Armagh may have tipped the balance to return the first Acheson as county member in almost thirty years and a Caulfeild for the first time in almost forty.

The documents suggest *why* men stood for parliament. The motivation spurring Armagh families to stand for county seats was complex. The social prestige and power of leadership within the county were constant incentives to country gentlemen such as Rt Hon. Sir Archibald Acheson, Rt Hon. William Brownlow, Rt Hon. Sir Capel Molyneux and William Richardson, the first three privy councillors, and all, trustees of the Linen Board. For some, like the Achesons, county seats also provided opportunity for material reward for their family and friends and, in Namier's phrase, 'honour with ease' for themselves. By 1760, Acheson was friendly with Chief Secretary Richard Rigby and courting him for favours, even into the 1760s when Rigby had left the chief secretary's office. In the first Octennial parliament Acheson was wooed out of opposition to support Lord Lieutenant Townshend's administration with whom he engaged in personal correspondence, relentlessly seeking favours. In 1772 alone, he requested employment for his bankrupt son-in-law Alex Macaulay and an annual pension for Macaulay's wife, the appointment of his brother-in-law Walter Cope as bishop of Clonfert and, within months, Cope's translation from Clonfert to Ferns and Leighlin – which could provide two bishop-borough seats for Gosford's sons – and a peerage for himself. Townshend's removal delayed delivery of these, and Sir Archibald had to provide further government political service before most of the favours were granted to him by Townshend's successors. Harcourt obtained a peerage for him in 1776. Cope was not translated to the bishop-borough of Ferns and Leighlin until 1782 through which Gosford's son Arthur was introduced to parliament in 1783. Arthur repaid government patronage when he succeeded to the Gosford title in 1790 by promoting a government caucus in Armagh county to challenge the traditional independent opposition to government.

Brownlow's political value-system appeared to differentiate between government favours for himself – which he did not seek, and those for his family and friends which he did. Thus, while publicly disavowing the possibility of a title – to appease his patriot supporters – he negotiated promotions in the army for his young sons and a plethora of jobs for his friends in return for erstwhile support for the Harcourt administration. Sir Capel Molyneux, usually in patriot opposition, dallied long enough with the Harcourt administration to obtain his desired appointment to the privy council in 1776.

Members with the financial security of land and/or property, could afford a political independence denied to less wealthy members pursuing a parliamentary career. Thus, while the first earl of Charlemont could remain aloof from government enticements, his impoverished younger brother Francis was considered vulnerable to offers from Harcourt's administration in the mid-1770s. And, a decade later, Lord Gosford's son Arthur took soundings from a range of potential patrons to determine a route for his parliamentary career. By the late 1790s the generational dissidence of the sons of Lords Gosford and Charlemont mellowed after Union when the latter, having succeeded to second earl, readily accepted compensation for Charlemont borough seats, and the former prepared to succeed his father as governor of the county and leader of the government party there.

Perhaps the parliamentary careers of Thomas Dawson, George William Molyneux and Isaac Corry best illustrate the vulnerability of men of little or no property. Dawson, elected on the popular vote in 1776, succumbed to career opportunities afforded by the government's fencible regiments which threatened and were opposed by the Volunteer movement. The administration was aware of and played upon Dawson's financial insecurity, illustrating the difficulties facing young professionals pursuing a parliamentary career without government patronage. Molyneux, son of a patriot father, was enticed out of flamboyant opposition by a government post. Isaac Corry and he were examples of young barristers who sought to impress the administration and attract offers from government by able opposition.

But Armagh members were also moved by loftier motives than material gain and self-interested careerism. Most were actively involved in the public interest in the major political issues of the day. Their involvement was significant in national movements such as Volunteerism and the campaign for free trade in 1779, and provided leadership and initiative in east Armagh to re-kindle the dying fire of Volunteer politics, leading to the Dungannon Convention and the constitution of 1782. Given the broad divisions in the county between the political dispositions of the primate's protégés, those of Lord Charlemont, and the independent county members, it was inevitable that Armagh MPs would be divided on most major national issues, though most tended to be in opposition. They split on the issues of renunciation and fencible regiments, the latter division being crucial to Dawson losing his seat to Richardson in 1783. They were divided over parliamentary reform. Brownlow, Richardson, Grattan and Stewart, who supported moderate reform, were uneasy with the proposed inclusion of measures for Catholic relief and successfully campaigned for their omission from the reform programme submitted to parliament. Their opposition to Orde's commercial proposals of 1785 contributed to the withdrawal of Orde's bill, though politicians in Armagh were divided further between those who opposed the proposals for constitutional reasons and the linen interests who supported them on economic grounds. Armagh members were also prominent in the campaign to elect John Foster as speaker in 1785, and most defied Lord Lieutenant Buckingham to vote for a regency in 1789.

Armagh society experienced outbreaks of violence impinging upon the political process in every decade of the second half of the eighteenth century, occasionally threatening the operation of elections. Violence in 1753 was perpetrated by over-zealous supporters in the stormy by-election contest in that year. More widespread was the violence in 1763 and again in 1772 with insurrections by Oakboys in protest against what they perceived as unfair rises in – and frequent misuse of – county cess, tithes and rent in times of economic recession. Initially, violence was allowed to spread by weak policing by a supine or absent magistracy and was only suppressed by the intervention of the army on both occasions. Peace was restored without undue recrimination, partly due to a belief in some government quarters that the rises in taxes had been unfair, and that the protest had some moral justification. Research suggests that the membership of the Oakboys was cross-denominational but led by armed Protestants from levels of society just below the ruling landed élite. While Oakboy violence in 1763 and 1772 was rooted in cross-community socio-economic grievances, that arising in Armagh society from the mid-1780s was essentially sectarian in nature, and unique in its intensity and duration. This violence was an expression of increasing fears by the Protestant ruling élite of Catholic political and social advances. In the late 1780s, an absent governor Charlemont, with magistrates reluctant to act against neighbours, had found it difficult to keep the peace. When sectarian violence recurred in the mid-1790s, resident governor Lord Arthur Gosford also struggled to cope against a background of the increasingly militarised United Irish Society and increasing polarisation of Armagh politics through the rise of popular societies such as the Orange Order and Catholic Defenders. As national security became increasingly threatened by rebellion and French invasion, Gosford was converted to the formation of local yeomanry units and acceptance of the Orange Society as support for the militia and regular army. In such adverse conditions, the political process did well to survive in County Armagh and parliamentary elections were held.

In the 1790s, most Armagh MPs continued in the Armagh tradition of independence and constitutional oppositon despite the best efforts of new governor Lord Gosford to promote a government caucus in the county. The Charlemontite Whigs in the county defied the national Whig policy of abstentionism from May 1797 to continue opposition in parliament and to have Francis William Caulfeild and Archibald Acheson returned in the 1797 general election. A majority of Armagh MPs opposed proposals for Union until October 1799 when Gosford's support enabled Robert Camden Cope to win an Armagh by-election and subsequently join the Unionist side. Gosford was also successful in recruiting the principal gentry of the county in declarations of support for Union and obtaining similar support from the Catholic archbishop of Armagh and Catholic parishioners.

The narrative reveals *how* members were elected. The dynamics driving the process of election have been outlined earlier. The key relationship was that between the landlord and his freeholders. The 1753 election had shown that freeholders would be led, not driven, to the polls. In the final quarter of the eighteenth century, Armagh freeholders, however small their holdings, were buoyed by the prosperity afforded by the linen industry and would not be ignored or taken for granted in parliamentary elections. They continually reminded those landlords who were complacent and dilatory at election time that they expected to be canvassed and opposed any attempt by interests such as grand jurors or Volunteer groups to usurp or by-pass the decision-making role of freeholders in the return of county members. The key to a successful relationship between the landlord and his freeholders in Armagh elections in the period 1750–1800, was mutual respect.

The liberal Lord Charlemont defined his ideal relationship between landlord and freeholder at elections. Citing his own support for Molyneux in the 1776 general election and his attitude to five of his freeholders who voted for Dawson, Charlemont rationalised:

> Every freeholder has an absolute right to give his vote as to him shall seem best. It is a positive unalienable property vested in him by the constitution. … But if he should happen to have a landlord who has in every respect performed his duty towards him and towards the public … the recommendations of that landlord ought to have the greatest weight with him. [1]

Freeholders repeatedly reminded landlords of their political power. In 1768 Brownlow's freeholders forced this most independent of MPs to abort negotiations with Armagh grand jurors who were attempting to have county MPs returned by selection by them rather than by election by freeholders; and Brownlow felt obliged to submit himself to his freeholders' approval. In 1776 when conjunctions of leading interests to decide MPs were being deemed unconstitutional by many freeholders, Brownlow agreed to avoid such coalitions. Repeatedly, freeholder meetings imposed their 'instructions' on MPs in parliamentary votes. Despite the intervention of other pressure groups on occasion such as grand jurors, Volunteers and popular societies, it was the power of the freeholders which moulded political public opinion, forced the numerous election polls and earned the reputation for County Armagh of being one of the most 'independent' counties in Ireland in the period 1750 to 1800.

This book researches parliamentary politics and elections in a small but prosperous Irish northern inland county. The evidence reveals a vibrant political community passionately involved in electoral politics, making an important contribution to – and being influenced by – parliamentary politics at national level. It was a community comprised of political magnates, MPs divided between those supporting the Dublin administration, those opposing it and those independent, and a politically conscious freeholder electorate determined to have its say in the return of its county MPs and decisions on key national issues. This study of County Armagh provides new perspectives on and fresh insights into parliamentary elections and associated high politics in the second half of the eighteenth century.

Notes
1   Memoirs (*HMC Charlemont*) i, 150.

Appendix 1
List of elections to Armagh county 1715–1800

Estimated number of voters: *c.* 834 in 1738, 1180 in 1753, 2540 in 1789, 2630 in 1795, 3,092 in 1799.

DATE OF RETURN	CANDIDATES	POLLING FIGURES
24 Oct. 1715	William Brownlow William Richardson	No poll[1]
2 Oct. 1727	William Brownlow Robert Cope	No poll[2]
8 Nov. 1739	William Richardson vice William Brownlow, deceased	No poll[3]
9 Nov. 1753	Rt. Hon. William Brownlow vice Robert Cope, deceased Hon. Francis Caulfeild	637 543[4]
28 Mar. 1758	Hon. Francis Caulfeild vice William Richardson, deceased	No poll[5]
27 Apr. 1761	Rt. Hon. Sir Archibald Acheson, 6th Bt Rt. Hon. William Brownlow	No poll[6]
18 July 1768	Rt. Hon. Sir Archibald Acheson, 6th Bt Rt. Hon. William Brownlow	No poll[7]
3 June 1776	Rt. Hon. William Brownlow Thomas Dawson William Richardson withdrew 17 Jan. 1776[9] Arthur Cope withdrew 18 May 1776[10] Sir Capel Molyneux, 3rd Bt withdrew 3 June 1776[11]	No poll[8]
6 Sept. 1783	Rt. Hon. William Brownlow William Richardson Thomas Dawson	1,414 800 755[12]

DATE OF RETURN	CANDIDATES	POLLING FIGURES
14 May 1790	Rt. Hon. William Brownlow	820
	William Richardson	820
	John Moore junior	619[13]
c. 1 Feb. 1795	William Brownlow jun. vice Rt. Hon. W. Brownlow, dec.	1,356
	Robert Camden Cope	1,274[14]
3 Aug. 1797	Rt. Hon. Archibald Acheson	205
	Rt. Hon. Francis William Caulfeild	99[15]
	William Richardson withdrew	
	Robert Camden Cope withdrew	
	Poll aborted after 4 days	
30 Oct. 1799	Robert C. Cope vice Rt. Hon. F.W. Caulfeild, succeeded as 2nd earl of Charlemont to house of lords	1,810
	Sir Capel Molyneux, 4th Bt.	1,282
	Petition by Molyneux; Cope's election upheld by parliament on 26 March 1800.[16]	

Notes

1. PRONI, ENV. 5/HP/2/1, p. 2.
2. Ibid.
3. Ibid.
4. 'County Armagh Poll-Book' (PRONI, T/3324/2B/Acc.12465). Following a petition by Caulfeild, Brownlow was declared duly elected by parliament on 10 Dec. 1753 by 120 votes to 119. See Sackville to Wilmot, 11 Dec. 1753 (PRONI, Wilmot papers, T/3019/2222).
5. PRONI, ENV.5/HP/2/1, p. 2; *BNL*, 28 Feb., 10 Mar., 7 Apr. 1758.
6. PRONI, ENV.5/HP/2/1, p. 3; *BNL*, 5 May 1761.
7. PRONI, ENV.5/HP/2/1, p. 3; *BNL*, 22 July 1768.
8. PRONI, ENV.5/HP/2/1, p.3.
9. *BNL*, 26–30 Jan. 1776.
10. Ibid, 21–14 May 1776.
11. Ibid, 4–7, 14–18 June 1776.
12. 'Figures for contested elections in Co. Armagh, 1783–1826', (NLI, Co. Armagh Townlands' MS 2716, on fly-leaf).
13. Ibid., *BNL*, 14–18 May 1790.
14. Ibid., Thomas Prentice to Charlemont, 31 Jan. 1795 (RIA, Charlemont correspondence, MS 12, R.18, vii, No. 62).
15. *BNL*, 7 Aug. 1797.
16. *Commons' jn. Ire.*, Grierson (ed.), xix, pp 46–7, 117.

Appendix 2
List of elections to Armagh borough 1715–1800

Right of election: in the corporation
Number of voters: 13
There were no polls.

DATE RETURNED	CANDIDATES
Pre-12 Nov. 1715	Samuel Dopping Silvester Cross Charles Bourchier vice Dopping, chose to sit for University of Dublin[1]
Post-18 May 1716	John Eyre vice Bourchier, deceased 18 May 1716[2]
Pre-28 Nov. 1727	Edward Knatchbull Ambrose Philips[3]
Post-18 June 1749	General Philip Bragg vice Ambrose Philips, deceased 18 June 1749[4]
Pre-16 Oct. 1759	Hon. Francis Russell vice General Bragg, deceased 6 June 1759[5]
18 Apr. 1761	Hon. John Ponsonby Robert Cuninghame[6]
13 Nov. 1761	Hon. Barry Maxwell sworn vice Ponsonby, chose to sit for Co. Kilkenny[7]
25 July 1768	Hon. Sir George Macartney Hon. Philip Tisdall[8]
Pre-17 Oct, 1768	Charles O'Hara vice Tisdall, chose to sit for Univ. of Dublin[9]

DATE RETURNED	CANDIDATES
26 June 1776	Hon. Philip Tisdall Henry Meredyth[10]
Post-11 Sept. 1777	George Rawson vice Tisdall, deceased 11 Sept. 1777[11]
Post-26 July 1783	Henry Meredyth George Rawson[12]
Pre-1 Feb. 1790	Henry Duquery sworn 1 Feb. 1790 vice Meredyth, deceased 10 Dec. 1789[13]
Pre-7 May 1790	George Rawson Hon. Major Robert Hobart[14]
Pre-13 Oct. 1796	Hon. Sackville Hamilton sworn 15 Oct. 1796 vice Rawson, deceased 8 Jan. 1796[15]
Pre-9 Jan. 1798	Hon. Thomas Pelham *Patrick Duigenan*[16]
Pre-15 Jan. 1800	Lieutenant General George Lake sworn 15 Jan. 1800 vice Pelham, appointed to Lord Lieutenant's household staff[17]

Notes

1. *Commons' jn. Ire.*, Bradley (ed.), iv, 7.
2. Johnston-Liik, *Irish Parliament*, iii, 225.
3. *Commons' jn. Ire.*, Bradley (ed.), v, 859.
4. Johnston-Liik, *Irish Parliament*, vi, 62.
5. *Commons' jn. Ire.*, Bradley (ed.), xi, 287.
6. *BNL*, 24 May 1761.
7. *Commons' jn. Ire.*, Bradley (ed.), xii, 9.
8. *BNL*, 29 July 1768.
9. *Commons' jn. Ire.*, Bradley (ed.), xiv, 576.
10. *BNL*, 28 June–2 July 1776.
11. Johnston-Liik, *Irish Parliament*, vi, 405.
12. *Commons' jn. Ire.*, Bradley (ed.), xxi, 3–4.
13. Johnston-Liik, *Irish Parliament*, iv, 94.
14. *BNL*, 7–11 May 1790.
15. *Commons' jn. Ire.*, Grierson (ed.), xvii, 5.
16. Ibid., p. 185.
17. Ibid., xix, 5.

Appendix 3
List of elections to Charlemont borough 1715–1800

Right of election: in the corporation
Number of voters: 13
There were no polls.

DATE RETURNED	CANDIDATES
Pre-12 Nov. 1715	Hon. James Caulfeild Humphrey May[1]
Post-11 Sept. 1722	Hon. John Caulfeild vice May, deceased 11 Sept. 1722[2]
Pre-28 Nov. 1727	Hon. John Caulfeild John Moore[3]
Post-6 May 1752	Thomas Adderley vice Moore, deceased 1 May 1752; writ issued 5 May 1752[4]
Pre-5 May 1761	Hon. Francis Caulfeild Henry William Moore[5]
Pre-27 Oct. 1763	Sir Annesley Stewart sworn 27 Oct. 1763 vice Moore, deceased May 1762[6]
Pre-19 July 1768	Sir Annesley Stewart Hon. Francis Caulfeild[7]
Post-27 Nov. 1775	Henry Grattan vice Hon. Francis Caulfeild, lost at sea[8]
26 June 1776	Sir Annesley Stewart Henry Grattan[9]

DATE RETURNED	CANDIDATES
4 Aug. 1783	Sir Annesley Stewart Rt Hon. Henry Grattan[10]
Pre-1 May 1790	Sir Annesley Stewart Richard Sheridan[11]
Pre-31 Jan.1794	Richard Mountney Jephson sworn 31 Jan. 1794 vice Sheridan, deceased, 12 Dec. 1793[12]
Pre-9 Jan. 1798	Hon. Francis William Caulfeild Richard Mountney Jephson[13]
Pre-23 Jan. 1798	Francis Dobbs sworn 23 Jan. 1798 vice Jephson, appointed Judge-Advocate of Gibraltar[14]
Pre-6 Feb. 1798	William Conyngham Plunket sworn 6 Feb. 1798 vice Caulfeild, chose to sit for County Armagh[15]

Notes

1. *Commons' jn. Ire.*, Bradley (ed.), iv, 7.
2. Johnston-Liik, *Irish Parliament*, v, 230.
3. *Commons' jn. Ire.*, Bradley (ed.), v, 859.
4. *Commons' jn. Ire.*, Bradley (ed.), viii, 303.
5. *BNL*, 5 May 1761.
6. Johnston-Liik, *Irish Parliament*, vi, 333.
7. *BNL*, 19 July 1768.
8. Ibid., 1–5 Dec. 1775.
9. Ibid., 28 June–2 July 1776.
10. *BNL*, 8–12 Aug. 1783.
11. Ibid., 30 Apr. –4 May 1790.
12. Johnston-Liik, *Irish Parliament*, iv, 483.
13. *Commons' jn. Ire.*, Grierson (ed.), xvii, 185.
14. Ibid.
15. Ibid.

Appendix 4
Brief biographical details of MPs returned to Armagh constituencies 1715–1800

ACHESON, Rt Hon. Sir Archibald, b. 1 Sept. 1718; d. 5 Sept. 1790
MP for TCD 1741–60; Co. Armagh 1761–8–76; Enniskillen 1776 [r. Killyleagh 1768]
HONOURS: PC, sworn 7 May 1770.
PEERAGES: Succ. as 6th Bt 1749; cr. Baron Gosford 1776; Viscount Gosford 1785.
RESIDENCES/ESTATES: Gosford Castle, Markethill, Co. Armagh; Sackville St., Dublin; Arvagh, Co. Cavan, estates in Counties Armagh and Cavan
CAREER/MAJOR OFFICES: Estates owner; High Sheriff of Co. Armagh 1751; Deputy Governor 1756–71; High Sheriff of Co. Cavan 1761; Trustee of the Linen Board for Leinster 1760–89; Trustee of the Inland Navigation for Ulster, May 1768; Commissioner of the Tillage Act for Ulster, 1769–84. Director of the Royal Corporation for … Collieries of Ireland[1]

ACHESON, Rt Hon. Archibald, b. 1 Aug. 1776; d. 27 Mar. 1849
MP for Co. Armagh 1797–1800; [UK] 1800–7
HONOURS: PC, [UK] 3 Sept. 1834; GCB (Civil) 19 July 1838.
PEERAGES: Styled Lord Acheson 1806–7; succ. as 2nd earl of Gosford 1807; cr. Baron Worlingham [UK] 1835, Rep. Peer 1811–49.
RESIDENCES/ESTATES: Gosford Castle, Markethill, Co. Armagh; Sackville St., Dublin; Arvagh, Co. Cavan; Worlingham Hall, Beccles, Suffolk; estates in Counties Armagh, Cavan and Suffolk.
CAREER/MAJOR OFFICES: Estates owner, Governor of Co. Armagh 1790, 1798, 1805; Trustee of the Linen Board for Leinster 1799; Lord-in-Waiting 1834; Governor of Lower Canada 1835–8; Custos Rot. Co. Armagh 1800, 1818; Lord Lieutenant of Co. Armagh 1831–49.
MILITARY: Major in Armagh Militia 1798, Colonel 1801; Captain of the Yeomen of the Guard July–Nov. 1834, Apr.–June 1835.[2]

ADDERLEY, Thomas, b. *c.* 1713; d. 28 May 1791
MP for Charlemont B. 1752–60; Bandon B, 1761–8–76; Clonakilty B. 1776–83–90–1
RESIDENCES: Innishannon, Co.Cork; Granby Row and 34 Rutland Square, Dublin.
CAREER/MAJOR OFFICES: Estate owner Co. Cork, Freeman of the Corporation of Taylors 1753; Burgess of Kinsale 1755; Burgess of Bandon 1756; Commissioner and Overseer of the Barracks and Public Works 1759–69; High Sheriff of Co. Westmeath 1761; Treasurer to the Barrack Board 1773–82; Director of the Tyrone Collieries 1768–9, 1773.[3]

BOURCHIER, Charles, b. 1665; d. 18 May 1716
MP for Dungarvan B. 1692–3, 1695–9, Armagh B. 1715–6
RESIDENCE: [?] London.
CAREER: Professional soldier.
MILITARY: Officer in the Regiment of Horse commanded by Lord Windsor.[4]

BRAGG, Philip, b. 1684; d. 6 June 1759
MP for Armagh B. 1749–59
RESIDENCE: Dublin, [?] Henry Street.
CAREER: Professional soldier.
MILITARY: Appointed to the Irish staff in 1751; had rank of Lieutenant General at the time of his death.[5]

BROWNLOW, William, b. (bapt. 31 Dec.) 1683; d. 27 Aug. 1739
MP for Co. Armagh 1711–13–14, 1715–27–39
RESIDENCES/ESTATES: Lurgan, Co. Armagh; estates Co. Armagh.
CAREER/MAJOR OFFICES: Estate owner; High Sheriff of Co. Armagh 1711; Trustee of the Linen Manufacture for Ulster 1711.[6]

BROWNLOW, Rt Hon. William, b. 10 Apr. 1726; d. 28 Oct. 1794
MP for Co. Armagh 1753–60, 1761–8–76–83–90–4 [r. Strabane 1768]
HONOURS: PC 1765.
RESIDENCES/ESTATES: Lurgan, Co. Armagh; 12 Merrion Square, Dublin; estates in Counties Armagh, Louth and Monaghan.
CAREER/MAJOR OFFICES: Estate owner; High Sheriff of Co. Armagh 1750; Trustee of the Linen Board for Ulster 1752–93, Commissioner of the Tillage Act for Ulster 1759–84; Freedom of Dublin 1760; Freedom of the Guild of Merchants 1760.
MILITARY: Captain of the Lurgan Volunteers 1779, Lieutenant Colonel of the Northern Battalion of Volunteers, 1780.[7]

BROWNLOW, William, b. 1755; d. 10 July 1815
MP for Co. Armagh 1795–7; [UK] 13 Mar. 1807–10 July 1815
RESIDENCES/ESTATES: Lurgan; estates in Co. Armagh *c.* 22,270 acres.
CAREER/MAJOR OFFICES: A banker; High Sheriff of Co. Armagh 1787; Trustee of Linen Board 1808.
MILITARY: Captain of Lurgan Yeomanry 1797.[8]

CAULFEILD, Hon. Francis, b. *c.* 1730; d. 20 Oct. 1775 (lost at sea)
MP for Co. Armagh 1758–60; Charlemont B. 1761–8–75
RESIDENCES/ESTATES: Dublin.
CAREER/MAJOR OFFICES: Professional soldier; High Sheriff of Co. Galway 1764; Magistrate and Portreeve of Charlemont 1768.
MILITARY CAREER: Ensign 27th Foot 1746; appointed Major of Horse 1755; Cornet in Lord George Sackville's Regiment of Horse 1756; Major of Light Dragoons 1768.[9]

CAULFEILD, Rt Hon. Francis William, b. 3 Jan. 1775; d. 26 Dec. 1863
MP for Co. Armagh 1797–9; [r. Charlemont B. 1797]
HONOURS: PC, sworn 13 Feb. 1832; Knight of St Patrick 19 Oct. 1831.
PEERAGES: Succ. as 2nd earl of Charlemont 1799; cr. Baron Charlemont [UK] 1837 (with special remainder to his brother); Rep. Peer 1806–63.
RESIDENCES/ESTATES: Castle-Caulfeild, Co. Tyrone; Charlemont House, Rutland Square, Dublin; Clontarf, Co. Dublin; estates in Counties Armagh and Tyrone.
CAREER/MAJOR OFFICES: Estate owner in Co. Armagh; A member of the Royal Irish Academy 1799; Freedom of the City of Dublin 1800; Lord Lieutenant of Co. Tyrone 1839; Custos Rot. Co. Tyrone 1841–d.
MILITARY: Captain in Keady Yeomanry Corps of Cavalry 1796; 1st Captain in the Armagh Cavalry 1800, vice his dec. father.[10]

CAULFEILD, Hon. James, b. July 1682; d. 21 Apr. 1734
MP for Charlemont B. 1703–5 (resigned to travel abroad), 1713–14, 1715–26
PEERAGES: Succ. as 3rd Viscount Charlemont 1726.
RESIDENCES/ESTATES: Castle-Caulfeild, Co. Tyrone; large estate in Co. Armagh.
CAREER/MAJOR OFFICES: Estate owner; Trustee of Linen Board for Ulster, 1732–d.[11]

CAULFEILD, Hon. John, b. c. 1690; d. 19 Oct. 1764
MP for Charlemont B. 1723–7–60
RESIDENCES: Jervis Street, Dublin; London.
CAREER/MAJOR OFFICE: Civil servant, Chancery Clerk in Lord Privy Seal's office.[12]

COPE, Robert, b. 1679; d. 17 Mar. 1753
MP for Lisburn B. 1711–13; Co. Armagh 1713–14, 1727–53
RESIDENCES/ESTATES: Loughgall Manor and Mountnorris estates in Co. Armagh.
CAREER/MAJOR OFFICES: Estate owner; High Sheriff of Co. Armagh 1736; Trustee of the Linen Board for Ulster 1732–d.; Commissioner of the Tillage Act for Ulster 1735, 1739–1753.[13]

COPE, Robert Camden, b. c. 1771; d. 5 Dec. 1818
MP for Co. Armagh 1799–1800, [UK] 1801–2
RESIDENCES/ESTATES: Loughgall Manor and Mountnorris estates in Co. Armagh.
CAREER/MAJOR OFFICES: Estate owner; Sheriff of Co. Armagh 1799.
MILITARY: Lieutenant Colonel of the Armagh Militia 1795.[14]

CROSSE, Silvester, b.1671; d.1730
MP for Callan B. 1703–13–14; Armagh B. 1715–27; Clogher B. 1727–30
RESIDENCES/ESTATES: Crosse's Green, Co. Cork
CAREER/MAJOR OFFICES: Civil servant; Private Secretary to the Duke of Ormonde 1703–7.[15]

CUNINGHAME, Rt Hon. Robert, b. 18 Apr. 1726; d. 6 Aug. 1801
MP for Tulsk B. 1751–60; Armagh B. 1761–8; Monaghan B. 1768–76–83–90–6; [GB] E. Grinstead B. 1788–9
HONOURS: PC, sworn 7 June 1782.
PEERAGES: Cr. Baron Rossmore 1796; Rep. Peer Jan. –Aug. 1801.
RESIDENCES/ESTATES: Mount Kennedy, Co. Wicklow; Monaghan town; estates in Counties Wicklow and Monaghan.
CAREER/MAJOR OFFICES: Estate owner, Governor of the Hibernian Society 1769–1800; Trustee of the Linen Board for Leinster 1794–1800.
MILITARY CAREER: Professional soldier (fought at Culloden); Captain and aide-de-camp to Primate Stone when Lord Justice 1751 and to the Lords Justices 1753–4, 1755–61; rose to Colonel (Lieutenant General) 1788, 16th Foot 1789, of 5th Regiment of Dragoons 1790–1, 1793; Commander-in-Chief 1795–6.[16]

DAWSON, Thomas, b. (bapt. 19 Mar.) 1744/5; d. 15 Sept. 1812
MP for Co. Armagh 1776–83; Sligo B. 1783–90; Enniscorthy B. June–Aug. 1800
RESIDENCES: Clare-Castle, Tandragee, Co. Armagh (leased from the Fane family); Abbey Street, Dublin; little or no landed estate.
CAREER/MAJOR OFFICES: Lawyer, soldier; High Sheriff of Co. Armagh 1770.
MILITARY: Captain of Clare Company of Volunteers 1779–82 and Lieutenant Colonel of the Southern Battalion of Volunteers 1780–2; Colonel of the Royal Ulster Fencible Regiment 31 Aug. 1782–1 Oct. 1783.[17]

DOBBS, Francis, b. 27 Apr. 1750; d. 1811
MP for Charlemont B. 1798–1800
RESIDENCES: Acton, Co. Armagh; Summerhill, Dublin.
CAREER/MAJOR OFFICES: Lawyer, called to Irish Bar 1775, Commissioner of Bankruptcy 1777–83, listed in Judges and Barristers 1789–1800.
MILITARY CAREER: Captain of Tyrone's Ditches Volunteers 1779–82; Major in the Northern Battalion of Volunteers 1780–2; Major in the Royal Ulster Fencible Regiment Sept. 1782–1 Oct. 1783.[18]

DOPPING, Rt Hon. Samuel, b. 1671; d. 17 Sept. 1720
MP for Armagh B. 1695–9, 1703–13–14; TCD 1715–20 [r. Armagh B. 1715].
HONOURS: PC, sworn 17 July 1711, 6 Aug. 1714, omitted 30 Sept. 1714.
RESIDENCES/ESTATES: Dublin; purchased estates in Co. Meath.
CAREER/MAJOR OFFICES: Lawyer; Trustee of Linen Manufacture for Leinster 1711.[19]

DUIGENAN, Rt Hon. Patrick, b. 1735; d. 11 Apr. 1816
MP for Old Leighlin B. 1791–7; Armagh B. 1797–1800; [UK] 1801–11 Apr. 1816
HONOURS: PC, sworn 2 Aug. 1808
RESIDENCE: Lilliput Lodge, Sandymount, Dublin.
CAREER/MAJOR OFFICES: Professor of Laws 1766, Feudal and English Laws 1766, Civil Law 1769–74; called to the Irish Bar 1767; Bencher of the Honorable Society of King's Inns 1783, 1798–d; King's Counsel 1784; Comptroller of Sorting Office (Postal Service) July 1790; King's Advocate General of the High Court of Admiralty 1790–1800; Judge 1792–1800; Commissioner of Appeals 1795–7; Commissioner of Union Compensation 1801.[20]

DUQUERY, Henry, b. *c.* 1749–51; d. 9 June 1804
MP for Armagh B. Jan. –Apr. 1790; Rathcormack B. 1790–7
RESIDENCES: Leinster Street and Lower Mount Street, Dublin
CAREER/MAJOR OFFICES: Professional lawyer; Surveyor of Dun Laoghaire to 1770, of Custom House Quay 1770–81; King's Counsel 1780–1800; listed in Judges and Barristers 1789–1800; 3rd Sergeant 1789–91; 2nd Sergeant 1791–3; Commissioner of Appeals 1795–7; Bencher of the Honorable Society of King's Inns 1798–d.[21]

EYRE, John, b. *c.* 1682–6; d. Oct. 1745
MP for Co. Galway 1713–14; Armagh B. 1716–27; Co. Galway 1727–45
RESIDENCE/ESTATE: Eyrecourt, Co. Galway
CAREER/MAJOR OFFICES: Estate owner and soldier; Mayor of Galway 1707; Trustee of the Linen Board for Connacht 1711, 1732–44; High Sheriff of Co. Galway 1724; Governor 1735.
MILITARY: Ensign, Colonel of Royal Regiment of Foot 1723–39.[22]

GRATTAN. Rt Hon. Henry, b. June 1746; d. 4 June 1820
MP for Charlemont B. 1775–6–83–90; Dublin City 1790–7; Wicklow B. Jan.–Aug. 1800; [UK] Malton B. 1805–6; Dublin City 1806–4 June 1820
HONOURS: PC, sworn 19 Sept. 1782, dismissed 6 Oct.1798, restored 9 Aug. 1806.
RESIDENCE/ESTATE: Tinnehinch, Bray, Co. Wicklow; Moyanna, Stradbally, Queen's County; 56 St. Stephen's Green, Dublin.
CAREER/MAJOR OFFICES: Lawyer, called to the Irish Bar 1772; Governor of the Foundling Hospital and Workhouse 1782; listed in Judges and Barristers 1789–1800.
MILITARY: Colonel in Dublin Independent Volunteers.[23]

HAMILTON, Rt Hon. Sackville, b. 14 Mar. 1732; d. 29 Jan. 1818
MP for St. Johnstown B. (Longford) 1780–3; Clogher B. 1783–90–5 [r. Rathcormack B. 1783]; [Escheator of Munster 21 Mar. 1795]; Armagh B. 1796–7
HONOURS; PC, sworn 6 June 1796
RESIDENCE: Dublin Castle.
CAREER/MAJOR OFFICES: Civil servant: Clerk to Revenue Department 1746–61; Joint Principal Clerk in the Revenue Board 1762–7, Joint 2nd Secretary 1767–72, Joint Secretary of Customs 1772–3, Secretary for Port Business 1774–9; Under-Secretary (Civil Department) 7 Feb. 1780 vice Thomas Waite, removed by Lord Lieutenant Fitzwilliam 7 Feb. 1795, reinstated 15 May 1795, retired 5 June 1796; listed in Judges and Barristers 1789–d.; Commissioner of Treasury Accounts 1795–6; Commissioner to assess Compensation for the Union 1800.[24]

HOBART, Rt Hon. Robert, b. 6 May. 1760; d. 4 Feb. 1816
MP for Portarlington B. 1784–90; Armagh B. 1790–7; [GB] Bramber B. 1788–90; Lincoln B. 1790–6
HONOURS: PC, sworn 21 Apr. 1789, [GB] 1 May 1793.
PEERAGES: Styled Lord Hobart 1793–8; cr. Baron Hobart [GB] 30 Nov. 1798; succ. as 4th earl of Buckinghamshire [GB] 1804.
RESIDENCE/ESTATES: Norton, Lincolnshire; Park Castle, Dublin.
CAREER/MAJOR OFFICES: Professional soldier and civil servant: Chief Secretary to marquess of Buckingham 6 Apr. –23 Oct.1789, to Lord Westmorland 24 Oct. 1789–15 Dec. 1793; Clerk of the Pleas of Court of Exchequer 25 Dec. 1793, May 1798–1816; Treasury Commissioner 25 Dec.1793; Governor of Madras 1794–1798; [UK] Secretary of State for War and the Colonies 1801–1804; Joint Postmaster General 1806–1807; President Board of Control 1812–1816; Chancellor of the Duchy of Lancaster Jan.–July 1805, May–June 1812.
MILITARY CAREER: Ensign, 59th Foot 1776; served in America 1777; Lieutenant 7th Foot 1778; Captain 30th Foot 1778; Major 18th Light Dragoons 1783; aide-de-camp to Lord Lieutenant and Inspector of Recruits 1784–9; Major 1785–6; Colonel Lincolnshire Supplementary Militia 1803.[25]

JEPHSON, Sir Richard Mountney, b. 1 May 1765; d. 1825
MP for Charlemont B. 1794–7–8
HONOURS: Cr. Bt [UK] 1 June 1815.
RESIDENCE: Ely Place, Dublin.
CAREER/MAJOR OFFICES: Lawyer, called to the Irish Bar 1790; Commissioner of Bankrupts 1796; Judge of the Admiralty, Judge-Advocate of Gibraltar 1797; listed in Judges and Barristers 1799–1825.[26]

KNATCHBULL, Sir Edward, b. 12 Dec.1704; d. Nov. 1789
MP for Armagh B. 1727–60
HONOURS: Succ. as 7th Bt [E] 1763.
RESIDENCE: Mersham Hatch, Kent.
CAREER/MAJOR OFFICES: Lawyer and civil servant; an Englishman who made his career in Ireland, Secretary to Lord Chancellor Wyndham 1726–38; Exigenter of the Court of Common Pleas 1735–68; Master in Court of Chancery 1737–9; Trustee of the Linen Board for Munster 1739–d.[27]

LAKE, Gerard, b. 27 July 1744; d. 20 Feb. 1808
MP for Armagh B. 1799–1800; [GB] Aylesbury 1790–1802
PEERAGES: Cr. Baron Lake [UK} 1804, Viscount Lake 1807.
RESIDENCE/ESTATE: Aston Clinton, Buckinghamshire.
CAREER/MAJOR OFFICES: Professional soldier; Ist Equerry etc. to Prince of Wales 1780–6, 1787–96; Gentleman Attendant to same 1796–1808; Receiver General of Duchy of Cornwall, 1807–8.
MILITARY: Rose in 1st Foot Guards from Ensign 1758 to Lieutenant Colonel 1792; aide-de-camp to the King 1782; Colonel 53rd Foot 1794–6, 73rd Foot 1796–1800; Lieutenant General 1797; Colonel 80th Foot 1800–08; General 29 Apr. 1802.[28]

MACARTNEY, Rt Hon. Sir George, b. 3 May 1737; d. 31 Mar. 1806
MP for Armagh B. 1768–76; [GB] Cockermouth B. 1768–Mar. 1769; Ayr Burghs 1774 –Jan. 1776; Bere Alston B. 1780–Feb. 1781
HONOURS: Knight 1764; Knight of the White Eagle of Poland 1766; Knight of the Bath 1772; PC, sworn 23 Mar. 1769–d., [GB] 2 May 1792.
PEERAGES: Cr. Baron Macartney 1776, Viscount Macartney 1792, Earl Macartney 1794, [GB] Baron Macartney 1796.
RESIDENCE/ESTATES: Lissanoure, Co. Antrim, estates at Loughuile and Dervock; Henry Street, Dublin; Curzon Street, London.
CAREER/MAJOR OFFICES: Diplomat and colonial administrator; estate owner; Envoy to St. Petersburg 1764–7; Ambassador to Russia 1767; Chief Secretary to Lord Townshend 1769–72; Captain General of Southern Caribbean 1775; Governor of Grenada 1775–9; President of Madras 1781–5; Ambassador to China 1792–4; Envoy (unofficial) to Louis XVIII at Verona 1795–6; Governor of Cape of Good Hope 1796–8; Custos Rot. Co Antrim 1770–1806, Constable of Toome Castle 1774, Trustee of the Linen Board for Ulster 1769–d.
MILITARY: Colonel of a Regiment of Militia Dragoons.[29]

MAXWELL, Rt Hon. Barry, b. 1723; d. 7 Oct. 1800
MP for Co. Cavan 1756–60; Armagh B. 1761–8, Co. Cavan 1768–76–9
HONOURS: PC, sworn 6 June 1796.
PEERAGES: Succ. as 3rd Baron Farnham 1779, cr. Viscount Farnham 1781, earl of Farnham 1785.
RESIDENCES/ESTATES: Farnham, Co. Cavan, Palace Row, Dublin.
CAREER/MAJOR OFFICES: Estate owner; lawyer, called to the Irish Bar 1748; Prothonotary of Court of Common Pleas 1741–d.; Bencher of the Honorable Society of King's Inns 1766–d.; listed in Judges and Barristers 1789–d.; Burgess of Sligo B. 1756, resigned 1786; Trustee of the Linen Board for Munster 1778–d.; Commissioner of the Tillage Act for Munster 1779–84.[30]

MAY, Humphrey, b. 1674; d. 11 Sept. 1722
MP for St. Johnstown B. (Donegal) 1695–9; Charlemont B. 1715–22
CAREER/MAJOR OFFICES: Civil servant; 2nd Secretary (Capel) 1695–6, Chief Secretary to Lords Justices 1699–1701; Comptroller of Customs, Limerick 1698–1702; Clerk of Crown and Peace, Ulster 1700–02, 1714–15; Searcher, Waterford 1716–22.[31]

MEREDYTH, Henry, b. post 1708; d. 10 Dec. 1789
MP for Armagh B. 1776–83–9
RESIDENCES/ESTATES: Dollardstown, Co. Meath; Broadstone, Co. Dublin; Armagh.
CAREER/MAJOR OFFICES: Agent to the Archbishop of Armagh and civil servant; 1st Clerk to Chief Secretary 1753–1772; Deputy Auditor General 1757–75; Secretary to the Master General in the Ordnance, Civil Branch 1769–d.; 2nd Secretary (Buckinghamshire) Dec. 1776–June 77; Under-Secretary (Military Department) 1777–8; Corrector and Supervisor of Printing Press 1764–d.[32]

MOORE, Henry William, b. 26 Dec. 1725; d. (May) 1762
MP for Charlemont B. 1761–2
RESIDENCES/ESTATES: Drumbanagher, Co. Armagh.
CAREER/MAJOR OFFICES: Estate owner; High Sheriff of Co. Armagh 1756; High Sheriff of Co. Down 1757.
MILITARY: Captain in Captain James McCullough's Troop of Militia Dragoons 1756.[33]

MOORE, John, b. May 1675; d. 1 May 1752
MP for Charlemont B. 1727–52
RESIDENCES/ESTATES: Drumbanagher, Co. Armagh.
CAREER/MAJOR OFFICES: Estate owner; High Sheriff of Co. Armagh 1704; Burgess of Carlingford 1722, 1742; Portreeve of Charlemont 1740; Commissioner of the Tillage Act for Ulster 1735, 1739–d.[34]

O'HARA, Charles, b. 1715; d. 3 Feb. 1776
MP for Ballynakill B. 1761–8; Armagh B. 1769–76
RESIDENCES/ESTATES: Nymphsfield, Co. Sligo; Annaghmore House, Collooney, Co. Sligo; Clare Street, Dublin.
CAREER/MAJOR OFFICES: Estate owner; civil servant; High Sheriff of Co. Sligo 1740; Ranger of the Curragh of Kildare 1762–c. 1775; Commissioner of Accounts 1771–6; Commissioner of Stamps 1774; Commissioner of Imprests 1774; Commissioner for Paving the Streets of Dublin.
MILITARY: Captain RN[35]

PELHAM, Rt Hon. Thomas, b. 28 Apr. 1756; d. 4 July 1826
MP for [GB] Sussex 1780–1801; Carrick B. 1783–90; Clogher B. 1795–7; Armagh B. 1797–9 [r. Naas 1797]
HONOURS: PC, sworn 13 Sept. 1783, [GB] 11 Mar. 1795; FRS. 24 Apr. 1800
PEERAGES: Cr. Baron Pelham [UK] 1801, 2nd earl of Chichester [UK] 1805.
RESIDENCES/ESTATES: Stanmer, Lewes, Sussex; estates in Counties Londonderry and Donegal
CAREER/MAJOR OFFICES: Estate owner; civil servant; Chief Secretary 1783–4, 1795–8; Commissioner of the Treasury 1795, 1796, 1797; Secretary of State 1796–1801; Home Secretary [UK] 1801–03; Commissioner on the Board of Control for India 1801–02; Chancellor Duchy of Lancaster 1803–04; Joint Postmaster General [UK] 1807–23; Postmaster General 1823–6.
MILITARY: Surveyor General of the Ordnance [GB] 1782–3; Captain Sussex Militia 1778; Lieutenant Colonel Sussex Militia 1794–1803; Lieutenant Colonel in Pevensey Regiment 1810[36]

PHILIPS, Ambrose, b. 1675; d. 18 June 1749
MP for Armagh B. 1727–49
RESIDENCE: Dublin.
CAREER/MAJOR OFFICES: Civil servant; Secretary to Lord Chancellor, Dec. 1726; Judge of Prerogative Court 1733; Registrar of Prerogative Court 1734–47; JP for Westminster.[37]

PLUNKET, Rt Hon. William Conyngham, b. 1 July 1764; d. 5 Jan. 1854
MP for Charlemont 1798–1800; [UK] Midhurst Jan. –Apr. 1807; TCD 1812–27
HONOURS: PC, sworn 6 Dec. 1805, [GB] 10 May 1827.
PEERAGES: Cr. Baron Plunket [UK] 1 May 1827.
RESIDENCE: Old Connaught, Bray, Co. Wicklow.
CAREER/MAJOR OFFICES: Lawyer, called to the Irish Bar 1787; listed in Judges and Barristers 1789–1800; King's Counsel 1796; Solicitor General 1803–5; Bencher 1804; Attorney General 1805–7, 1822–7; Chief Justice of the Common Pleas 1827–30; Lord Chancellor 1830–4; 1835–41.[38]

PONSONBY, Rt Hon. John, b. 29 Mar. 1713; d. 16 Aug. 1787
MP for Newtownards B. 1739–60; Co. Kilkenny 1761–8–76–83 [r. Armagh B. 1761, Newtownards and Gowran 1768; Carlow B. 1776]; Newtownards B. 1783–7
HONOURS: PC, sworn 1748, 1760, 1761 (removed 7 May 1770).
RESIDENCES/ESTATES: Bishop's Court, Co. Kildare; Inchiquin, Castlemartyr/ Youghal, Co. Cork.
CAREER/MAJOR OFFICES: Estates owner; Secretary to Lord Lieutenant Devonshire 1741; Secretary to the Revenue Commissioners 1741–4; First Commissioner of the Revenue 1744–70; Speaker of the House of Commons 1756–71; Lord Justice 1758, 1760, 1761, 1762, 1764, 1765, 1766; Collector of Cork 1739, Trustee of the Linen Manufacture for Leinster 1744–d.; Commissioner of the Tillage Act for Munster 1749–d.; Freedom of Cork 1752, Waterford 1752, Carlingford 1756, Fethard (Tipperary) 1774.
MILITARY: Colonel of Iverk Corps of Volunteers; Gentleman of the Horse Volunteers 1745–6; Colonel 1745–6.[39]

RAWSON, George, b. ante-1746; d. 8 Jan. 1796
MP for Armagh B. 1777–83–90–6
RESIDENCES/ESTATES: Belmont, Bray, Co. Wicklow; Dawson Street, Dublin.
CAREER/MAJOR OFFICE: Professional soldier; Stamps Commissioner 1789–d.
MILITARY CAREER: Lieutenant Colonel of 3rd Regiment of Foot 1766–9; Lieutenant Colonel 1776; Barracks Commissioner 1788.[40]

RICHARDSON, William, b.1656; d.1 June 1727
MP for Co. Armagh 1692–3; Hillsborough B. 1703–13; Co. Armagh 1715–27
RESIDENCE/ESTATE: Richhill, Co. Armagh.
CAREER/MAJOR OFFICE: Estate owner; professional soldier; High Sheriff of Co. Armagh 1690.
MILITARY CAREER: Major 1717, 1719.[41]

RICHARDSON, William, b.1710; d. 22 Feb. 1758
MP for Co. Armagh 1739–58
RESIDENCE/ESTATES: Richhill, Co. Armagh.
CAREER/MAJOR OFFICES: Estate owner; lawyer, called to the Irish Bar 1733; Bencher c. 1734; High Sheriff of Co. Armagh 1737; Commissioner of the Tillage Act for Ulster 1747–d.; Trustee of the Linen Board for Munster 1750–d.[42]

RICHARDSON, William, b.1749; d. 23 Mar. 1822
MP for Co. Armagh 1783–90–7; [UK] 1807–20
RESIDENCE/ESTATES: Richhill, Co. Armagh.
CAREER/MAJOR OFFICES: Estate owner; lawyer; High Sheriff of Co. Armagh 1777–8; Foreman of Grand Jury of Co. Tyrone 1786; of Co. Armagh 1792; Trustee of the Linen Board for Leinster 1796–1801; listed in Attorneys of the King's Bench, Common Pleas, Court of Exchequer 1798–1800; Advocate and Proctor in the Court of Delegates, Prerogative, Admiralty and Consistory 1799.
MILITARY: Captain of Richhill Volunteers 1779, Major in the Northern Battalion of Volunteers; Lieutenant Colonel in Armagh Militia 1793–4; Captain of Richhill Yeomanry Corps of Cavalry 1796, 1797.[43]

RUSSELL, Hon. Francis, b. 27 Sept. 1739; d. 22 Mar. 1767
MP for Armagh B. 1759–60; [GB] Bedfordshire 1761–7
PEERAGES: Styled Marquess of Tavistock 1739–67.
RESIDENCES/ESTATES: Woburn Abbey, Bedfordshire; Houghton Park House, Ampthill.
CAREER/MAJOR OFFICES: Heir to estates, surviving son and heir of Lord Lieutenant John Russell, 4th duke of Bedford; little interested in politics, his great interest was in strengthening the army against invasion; nominated for eight committees in Irish parliament; died following a hunting accident in 1767.[44]

SHERIDAN, Richard, b. 1750; d. 12 Dec. 1793
MP for Charlemont B. 1790–3
RESIDENCE: Dominick Street, Dublin.
CAREER/MAJOR OFFICES: Lawyer; called to the bar 1774; Governor of the Hibernian Marine Society 1776; received freedom of the City of Dublin 1780; King's Counsel 1783; listed in Judges and Barristers 1789–93.[45]

STEWART, Sir Annesley, b. 1725; d. Mar. 1801
MP for Charlemont B. 1763–8–76–83–90–7 [r. Ballynakill B. 1783]
HONOURS: Succ. as 6th Bt 14 Aug. 1769 on d. of his cousin, 1st earl of Blessington.
RESIDENCES/ESTATES: Fort Stewart, Co. Donegal; Eccles Street, Dublin; Ramelton
CAREER/MAJOR OFFICES: Banker; Director of Tyrone Collieries 1768–d.; member of Hibernian Fire Insurance Company 1772–84; Freeman of Fethard (Tipperary) 1774.
MILITARY: Lieutenant Colonel in the Volunteers.[46]

TISDALL, Rt Hon. Philip, b. Mar. 1703; d. 11 Sept. 1777
MP for TCD 1739–60, 1761–8–76 [r. Armagh B. 1768]; Armagh B. 1776–7
HONOURS: PC, sworn 28 Feb. 1764.
RESIDENCES/ESTATES: Leinster Street, Dublin; Stillorgan Park, Co. Dublin; Bawn, Co. Louth.
CAREER/MAJOR OFFICES: Lawyer; called to Irish Bar 1733; 3rd Sergeant of King's Counsel 1741–5; Justice of Assize, Connaught 1744–52; Judge of Prerogative Court 1745–d.; Solicitor General 1751–60; Attorney General 1760, 1761–d.; Secretary of State 1763–d.; Keeper of Privy Seal 1763; Register in Chancery; Bencher in Honorable Society of King's Inns 1768–74; Freeman of Ardee 1721, Burgess 1721; Burgess of Carlingford 1734; Freedom of Dublin 1760, of the Guild of Merchants 1760, of Cork 1761.[47]

Notes

1. Johnston-Liik, *Irish parliament*, iii, 49–51.
2. Ibid., iii, 51–2.
3. Ibid., iii, 99, 56–9.
4. Ibid., iii, 225.
5. Ibid., iii, 259–60.
6. Ibid., pp 292–3.
7. Ibid., pp 293–6; Paterson, 'Armagh Volunteers' in *UJA*. (1941–4), 3rd series, vi (1943), p. 80; iv, (1941), p. 103.
8. Johnston-Liik, *Irish parliament*, iii, 296–7.
9. Ibid., iii, 386–8.
10. Ibid., iii, 388–9.
11. Ibid., iii, 389.
12. Ibid., iii, 390.
13. Ibid., pp 505–6.
14. Ibid., iii, 506.
15. Ibid., iii, 554.
16. Ibid., iii, 565.
17. Ibid., iv, 31–2.
18. Ibid., iv, 67–8.
19. Ibid., iv, 76–7.
20. Ibid., iv, 84–7.
21. Ibid., iv, 93–4.
22. Ibid., iv, 125–6.
23. Ibid., iv, 302–10.
24. Ibid., iv, 351–3.
25. Ibid., iv, 430—2.
26. Ibid., iv, 483.
27. Ibid., v, 37.
28. Ibid., v, 50–2.
29. Ibid., v, 154–6.
30. Ibid., v, 220–2.
31. Ibid., v, 230.
32. Ibid., v, 245–6.
33. Ibid., v, 298.
34. Ibid., v, 299.
35. Ibid., v, 395–6.
36. Ibid., vi, 37–9.
37. Ibid., vi, 62–3.
38. Ibid., vi, 70–2.
39. Ibid., vi, 89–96.
40. Ibid., vi, 149–50.
41. Ibid., vi, 158.
42. Ibid., vi, 159–61.
43. Ibid., vi, 161–2.
44. Ibid., vi, 203.
45. Ibid., vi, 270–1.
46. Ibid., vi, 333–4.
47. Ibid., vi, 405–8.

Bibliography

PRIMARY SOURCES

A. MANUSCRIPTS
1. *Armagh County Museum*
The Blacker Manuscripts, journal of Lieutenant Colonel William Blacker, 1777–1855, 7 volumes, Records of the Armagh Militia.
T.G.F. Paterson transcript, 'An impartial account of the late disturbances in the county of Armagh; containing all the principal meetings, battles, executions, whippings &c of the Break-O'Day-Men and Defenders, since the year 1784 down to the year 1791; with a full and true account of the nature of the rising of both parties; by an inhabitant of the town of Armagh, signed J. Byrne, Dublin, 1792'.

2. *Armagh Public Library*
County Armagh Poll Book, 1753, Johnston Collection.

3. *Cardinal Ó Fiaich Library and Armagh Diocesan Archive, Armagh*
Correspondence of Richard O'Reilly, Archbishop of Armagh, Drogheda, to Rev. Henry Conwell, Vicar-General, Dungannon, 1793–1820.

4. *Dublin City Library and Archive, Pearse Street, Dublin (formerly Gilbert Archive)*
Harcourt correspondence, MSS, 93, 94.

5. *Dublin Diocesan Archive*
Archbishop Troy papers, correspondence 1797–9 (AB2/116/7/1–).

6. *National Archives Ireland, Dublin*
Rebellion papers (620/–).
State of the Country papers, County Armagh (SOC – series 1 and 2).
Townshend papers (M. 648–735).

7. *National Library of Ireland, Manuscripts Department, Dublin*
Bolton papers (MSS 15,891–, 15,917–9, 16,350).
Heron papers (MSS 13034–7).
County Armagh townlands (MSS 2716).

8. *Nottingham Archives Office*
Brownlow papers.

9. *Public Record Office of Northern Ireland*
Abercorn papers (T/2541/–).
Armagh Diocesan papers (D10/4).
Ashbourne papers (T/2955/–).
Bedford papers (T/2915/–).
Brownlow papers (D/714/–).
Castlereagh papers (D/3030/–).
Castleward papers (D/2092/–).
Drennan papers (T/765/–).
Drennan-Bruce papers (D/553/–).
Emly papers (from Henry Huntington Library), T/3052/–.
Gosford papers (D/1606/–).
Grand jurors, Armagh corporation lists (T/636/–).
Grand jury presentments books (C & P ARM/–).
Groves's transcript of the 1766 religious census (T/808/–).
Harmwood papers (C/5/1).
High sheriffs of County Armagh (T/2704/–).
Hobart papers (T/2627/–).
Home Office, Ireland civil correspondence (MIC/224/–).
History of the Irish parliament papers (ENV/5/HP/1–3).
Macartney papers (D/572/– MIC/227/–).
Massereene-Foster papers (D/562/–).
O'Hara papers (T/2812/–).
Paterson deposits (D/259/–).
Paterson transcript of John Byrne's 1792 pamphlet, 'An impartial account of the late disturbances of the county of Armagh' (T/3575/1).
Pelham papers (T/2876/–).
Shannon papers (D/2707/–).
Sneyd papers (T/3229/–).
Stewart papers (D/3167– MIC/509/–).
Townshend Letter-Book (T/3590 MIC437).
Transcript of County Armagh Poll Book, Johnston Collection, Armagh Public Library, (T/3324/2B/Acc.12465).
Wickham papers (T/2627/–).
Wilmot papers (T/3019/–).

10. *Royal Irish Academy, Dublin*
Original Charlemont correspondence, 2nd series, 10 vols (MSS 12 R.18–).

11. *Trinity College, Dublin*
Camden papers U.840/0173/1–12, MIC 56 (from Centre for Kentish Studies).

B. PUBLISHED CORRESPONDENCE, MEMOIRS, ETC.

Castlereagh: Vane, Charles (ed.), *Memoirs and correspondence of Viscount Castlereagh, second marquess of Londonderry* (5 vols, London, 1848).

Charlemont: Hardy, Francis (ed.), *Memoirs of the political and private life of James Caulfeild, earl of Charlemont* (2nd edition, 2 vols, London, 1812).

Cornwallis: Ross, Charles (ed.), *Correspondence of Charles, first marquis Cornwallis*, vol iii (3 vols, London, 1859).

Drennan: Chart, D.A. (ed.), *The Drennan Letters ... 1776–1819* (Belfast, 1931).

Grattan: Memoirs of the life and times of the Rt. Hon. Henry Grattan by his son Henry Grattan, MP (5 vols, London, 1849).

Hardwicke: McDonagh, Michael (ed.), *The Viceroy's Postbag* (Dublin, 1904).

Orrery: Countess of Orrery, (ed.), *The Orrery Papers* (2 vols, Dublin, 1903).

Plunkett: Hanley, John (ed.), *The letters of Saint Oliver Plunkett 1625–81, archbishop of Armagh and primate of all Ireland* (Dublin, 1979).

Wellington: Duke of Wellington (ed.), *The supplementary dispatches, letters and memoranda of Arthur Wellesley, first duke of Wellington*, v (15 vols, London, 1858–72).

Wilmot: Walton, James (ed.), *"The King's business": letters on the administration of Ireland 1740–61, from the papers of Sir Robert Wilmot* (New York, 1996).

C. PUBLICATONS OF THE HISTORICAL MANUSCRIPTS COMMISSION

HMC Charlemont MSS, 12th Report, appendix 10, i (London, 1891).

HMC Charlemont MSS, 13th Report, appendix 8, ii (London, 1894).

HMC Emly MSS, 8th Report, appendix I, (London, 1881).

HMC Eyre-Matcham MSS, Reports on various collections (London, 1909).

HMC Fortescue MSS, 13th Report on the manuscripts of JB Fortescue, appendix 3, i (London, 1892).

HMC Rutland MSS, 14th Report, appendix, part I, iii (London, 1894).

HMC Stopford-Sackville MSS, Report on the manuscripts of Mrs Stopford-Sackville of Drayton House, Northamptonshire (2 vols, London, 1904–10).

D. PUBLICATONS OF THE PUBLIC RECORD OFFICE OF NORTHERN IRELAND

Bartlett, Thomas, *Macartney in Ireland 1768–72*, Belfast, 1978.

Collins, Peter, *County Monaghan sources in the Public Record Office of Northern Ireland*, Belfast, 1998.

Cooke, A.B. and Malcomson, A.P.W. (eds.), *The Ashbourne papers: a calendar of the papers of Edward Gibson, first Lord Ashbourne*, Belfast, 1974.

Crawford, W.H. and Trainor, Brian (eds.), *Aspects of Irish social history 1750–1800*, Belfast, 1969.

Educational facsimiles of manuscripts on selected topics, Belfast, 1969 –.

Gillespie, R.G. (ed.), *Settlement and survival on an Ulster estate: the Brownlow leasebook 1667–1711*, Belfast, 1988.

Hewitt, Esther (ed.), *Lord Shannon's letters to his son*, Belfast, 1982.

Malcomson, A.P.W. (ed.), *Eighteenth Century Irish official papers in Great Britain: private collections, volume II*, Belfast 1990.

Malcomson, A.P.W., *Isaac Corry 1755–1813: 'An adventurer in the field of politics'*, Belfast, 1974.

Miller, D.W., *Peep O'Day Boys and Defenders: selected documents on the County Armagh Disturbances 1784–96*, Belfast, 1990.

Thompson, F.M.L. and Tierney, D. (eds.), *General Report on the Gosford estates in County Armagh 1821 by William Greig*, Belfast, 1976.

E. PARLIAMENTARY REPORTS, JOURNALS, STATUTES etc.

House of commons report from the select committee on Orange lodges, associations, or societies in Ireland, xv, session (377), 1835.

Journals of the house of commons of the kingdom of Ireland (Bradley edition, 28 vols, Dublin, 1782–95; Grierson edition, 19 vols, Dublin, 1796–1800).

Journal of the [Irish] house of lords, 1634–1800 (8 vols, Dublin, 1779–1800).

The Statutes at Large Passed in the Parliaments Held in Ireland, 1310–1800 (20 vols, Dublin, 1789–1800).

F. ROLLS

Erck, J.C., *A repertory of the enrolments of the patent rolls of chancery in Ireland*, Dublin, 1846.

Murray, L.P. (ed.), 'Hearth money roll, County Armagh, A.D. 1664' in *Archivium Hibernicum*, Maynooth, 1941, viii, 122–36.

G. STATE PAPERS AND GOVERNMENT REPORTS

Calendar of home office papers of the reign of George III, 1760–75 (4 vols), London, 1878–99.

Calendar of the state papers of Ireland 1611–47, London, 1880.

Lists of the officers of militia, issued by Dublin Castle, Dublin, 1796–1800.

Lascelles, Rowley (ed) *Liber munerum publicorum Hiberniae*, (2 vols), London, 1824–30.

H. CONTEMPORARY NEWSPAPERS AND PERIODICALS

Armagh Local Studies Library
Belfast News-Letter.
Freeman's Journal.
Northern Star.

Dublin City Library & Archive
Dublin Evening Post.
Hibernian Journal.
The Irish Builder.
Universal Advertiser.

Linen Hall Library, Belfast
Belfast Mercury or Freeman's Chronicle.

I. PAMPHLETS (in chronological order)
A letter from a free citizen of Dublin to a freeholder in the county of Armagh (QUB Library, Foster Collection, Dublin, 1753), vol xiii.
A second letter from a free citizen of Dublin to a freeholder in the county of Armagh by the author of the first (RIA, Haliday, Tracts, Dublin, 1753), Box 212, No. 27.
Seasonable advice to the freeholders of Armagh; by a brother freeholder (QUB, Foster pamphlets), vol. xiii.
A fifth letter from a free citizen of Dublin to a freeholder of the county of Armagh, containing an examination of a pamphlet entitled Seasonable Advice &c.
... recommended to the perusal of those who would form a fair and clear judgement of the candour and veracity of the author of that paper (RIA, Haliday, Dublin, 1753) vol. 250, No. 4.
Observations on the free citizen's fifth letter; by the author of The Seasonable Advice (RIA, Haliday, Tracts, Dublin, 1753), vol x, Box 210, No. 1.
A letter from a gentleman in the county of Armagh to his friend in Dublin; occasioned by the late robbery of the northern mail (RIA, Haliday, Dublin, 13 October 1753), No. 2.
Case of the Hon. Francis Caulfeild, Esq (RIA, Haliday collection, Dublin, 1753), 3B53–56/219
A letter from a freeholder of the county of Armagh to a friend in Dublin, bearing date October 31st, 1753 (RIA, Haliday, Tracts, Dublin, 1753) box 212, No. 15.
An extract of a letter from Armagh, dated October the 31st, 1753 (RIA, Haliday collection, Dublin, 1753), 3B53–56/220.
An impartial account of the whole proceedings at Armagh during the election, with the causes of the late disturbances at that place (RIA, Haliday collection, Dublin, 10 November 1753, 3B53–56/221; PRONI, Chilham papers, T/2519/4/225, 226).
Layman's sermon at Patriot Club of County Armagh (RIA, Tracts, 1749–64, Dublin, 1755), vol x, Box 220, No. 9.
Francis Dobbs, *A letter to the Right Honourable Lord North on his propositions in favour of Ireland* (Dublin, January, 1780).
Francis Dobbs, *A history of Irish affairs from 12 October 1779 to 15 September 1782* (Dublin, 1782).
John Byrne, *An impartial account of the late disturbances in the county of Armagh ... by an inhabitant of the town of Armagh* (Armagh County Museum and PRONI, T/3575/1, Dublin, 1792).
James Moore (ed.) *A report of the debates in the house of commons in Ireland on Tuesday and Wednesday, 22 and 23 January 1799 on the subject of an Union* (Dublin, 1799).

J. CONTEMPORARY WORKS
Beaufort, D.A., *Memoir of a map of Ireland*, Dublin, 1792.
Bradshaw, Thomas, *General Directory of Newry, Armagh 1820*, Newry, 1819.
Coote, Sir Charles, *Statistical Survey of the County of Armagh*, Dublin, 1804.
'Falkland' [Rev. J.R. Scott], *A review of the principal characters of the Irish house of commons*, Dublin, 1789.
Musgrave, Sir Richard, *Memoirs of the different rebellions in Ireland from the arrival of the English*, (2nd edition), Dublin, 1801.
Plowden, Francis, *An historical view of the state of Ireland*, London, 1803.
The post chaise companion or traveller's directory through Ireland (1sted.), Dublin, 1786.
Stuart, James, *Historical memoirs of the city of Armagh*, Newry, 1819.

Swift, Jonathan, 'A vindication of His Excellency John, Lord Carteret ...' in Walter Scott ed. *The works of Jonathan Swift DD ... with notes and a life of the author*, (2nd ed.), Edinburgh, 1824.

Taylor, George and Skinner, Andrew, *Maps of the roads of Ireland*, Dublin, 1778, (reprint, Shannon), 1969.

Tyner, George, *The traveller's guide through Ireland; being an accurate and complete companion to Captain Alexander Taylor's Map of Ireland*, Dublin, 1794.

Wakefield, Edward, *An account of Ireland, statistical and political*, (2 vols), London, 1812.

SECONDARY SOURCES

A. BOOKS

Ardill, J.R., *The closing of the Irish parliament*, Dublin, 1907.

Bardon, Jonathan, *A history of Ulster*, Belfast, 1992.

Barrington, Jonah, *Rise and fall of the Irish parliament*, Dublin, 1843.

Bartlett, Thomas, *The fall and rise of the Irish nation: the Catholic Question 1690–1830*, Dublin, 1993.

Bartlett, Thomas and Hayton, D.W. (eds.), *Penal Era and Golden Age: essays in Irish history 1690–1800*, Belfast, 1979.

Beckett, J.C., *The making of modern Ireland 1603–1923*, London, 1966.

Blackstock, Allan, *An Ascendancy Army: The Irish yeomanry, 1796–1834*, Dublin, 1998.

Bolton, G.C., *The passing of the Irish Act of Union: a study in parliamentary politics*, London, 1966.

Burns, R.E., *Irish parliamentary politics in the eighteenth century*, 2 vols, Washington, 1989–90.

Clarkson, L.A. and Crawford, E.M., *Ways to wealth: the Cust family of eighteenth century Armagh*, Belfast, 1985.

Connell, K.H., *The population of Ireland*, Oxford, 1950.

Connolly, S.J, *Religion, law and power: The making of Protestant Ireland 1660– 1760*, Oxford, 1992.

Craig, M.J., *The Volunteer Earl, being the life and times of James Caulfeild, first earl of Charlemont*, London, 1948.

Cullen, L.M., *Anglo-Irish trade 1660–1800*, Manchester, 1968.

Cullen, L.M., *An economic history of Ireland since 1660*, London, 1972.

Davis, Thomas, *The Patriot Parliament of 1689, with its statutes, votes and proceedings*, (3rd ed.), Dublin, 1893.

Drogheda, Countess of, *The family of Moore*, Dublin, 1906.

Evans, E.E. (ed.), *Harvest home, the last sheaf: a selection from the writings of T.G.F. Paterson*, Dundalk, 1975.

Foster, R.F., *Modern Ireland 1600–1972*, London, 1988.

Geoghegan, P.M., *The Irish Act of Union: a study in high politics 1798–1801*, Dublin, 1999.

Hill, Rev. George, *An historical account of the plantation in Ulster at the commencement of the seventeenth century, 1608–20*, Belfast, 1877.

Hughes, A.J. and Nolan, William (ed.), *Armagh history and society: interdisciplinary essays on the history of an Irish county*, Dublin, 2001.

Hunt, William (ed.), *The Irish parliament 1775, from an official and contemporary manuscript*, Dublin, 1907.
James, F.G., *Lords of the Ascendancy: The Irish house of lords and its members 1600–1800*, Dublin, 1995.
Johnston, E.M., *Great Britain and Ireland 1760–1800*, Edinburgh, 1963.
Johnston, E.M., *Ireland in the eighteenth century*, Dublin, 1974.
Jupp, Peter, *British and Irish elections 1784–1831*, Newton Abbot, 1973.
Jupp, Peter and Magennis, Eoin (ed) *Crowds in Ireland c. 1720–1920*, Basingstoke, 2000.
Kelly, James, *Henry Flood: Patriots and politics in eighteenth-century Ireland*, Dublin, 1998.
Kelly, James, *Prelude to Union: Anglo-Irish politics in the 1780s*, Cork, 1992.
Kerr, Rev. W.G., *The parish of Mullaghbrack*, Armagh, 1953.
Killen, Rev. W.D., *History of congregations of the Presbyterian Church in Ireland*, Belfast, 1886.
Lecky, W.E.H., *Ireland in the eighteenth century*, (4 vols), London, 1892.
Macaulay, Rev. Ambrose, *Archbishop Crolly: Archbishop of Armagh 1835–49*, Dublin, 1994.
Magennis, Eoin, *The Irish political system 1740–1765: The golden age of the Undertakers*, Dublin, 2000.
Malcomson, A.P.W., *John Foster: the politics of the Anglo-Irish Ascendancy*, Oxford, 1978.
Malcomson, A.P.W., *Archbishop Charles Agar: churchmanship and politics in Ireland 1760–1810*, Dublin, 2002.
Malcomson, A.P.W., *Primate Robinson 1709–94*, Belfast, 2003.
McAnally, Henry, *The Irish militia 1793–1816: a social and military study*, Dublin, 1949.
McClelland, Aiken, *The formation of the Orange Order* (N.D, N.P.).
McCracken, J.L., *The Irish parliament in the eighteenth century*, Dundalk, 1971.
McNally, Patrick, *Parties, Patriots and Undertakers: parliamentary politics in early Hanoverian Ireland*, Dublin, 1997.
Moody, T.W. and Vaughan, W.E. (eds.) *A new history of Ireland. IV: Eighteenth-century Ireland 1691–1800*, Oxford, 1986.
Moore, H.H., *Three hundred years of congregational life: the First Presbyterian Church in Markethill*, County Armagh, Armagh, 1909.
Namier, L.B., *England in the age of the American Revolution*, (2nd ed.), London, 1961.
Namier, L.B., *The structure of politics at the accession of George III*, (2nd ed.), London, 1965.
O'Connell, M.R., *Irish politics and social conflict in the age of the American Revolution*, Philadelphia, 1965.
O'Gorman, Frank, *Voters, patrons, and parties: The unreformed electoral system of Hanoverian England 1734–1832*, Oxford, 1989.
Ó Gráda, Cormac, *Ireland: a new economic history of Ireland, 1780–1939*, Oxford, 1994.
Pares, Richard, *King George III and the politicians*, Oxford, 1967.
Paterson, T.G.F., *Derrymore, County Armagh*, Belfast, 1963.
Perceval-Maxwel, M., *The Scottish migration to Ulster in the reign of James l*, London, 1973.
Phillips, J.A., *Electoral behaviour in unreformed England: plumpers, splitters and straights*, New Jersey, 1982.
Robinson, Philip, *The plantation of Ulster*, Dublin, 1984).
Roebuck, Peter (ed.) *Public service and private fortune: the life of Lord Macartney 1737–1806*, Belfast, 1983.

Rogers, Patrick, *The Irish Volunteers and Catholic Emancipation 1778–93*, London, 1934.
Seaver, George, *History of the Seaver family formerly of Heath Hall in the county of Armagh and their connections*, Dundalk, 1950.
Senior, Hereward, *Orangeism in Ireland and Britain 1795–1836*, London, 1966.
Simms, J.G., *Jacobite Ireland*, London, 1969.
Simms, J.G., *The Williamite confiscation in Ireland 1690–1703*, London, 1956.
Simms, J.G., *William Molyneux of Dublin 1656–98*, Dublin, 1982.
Steven Watson, J., *The reign of George III, 1760–1815*, Oxford, 1960.
Swords, Liam (ed.), *Protestant, Catholic and Dissenter: the clergy and 1798*, Dublin, 1997.
Williams, Basil, *The Whig supremacy 1714–1760*, (2nd ed.), Oxford, 1962.
Wylie, J.C.W., *Irish land law*, (2nd ed.), Abingdon, 1986.
Young, Arthur, *Tour in Ireland 1776–9*, (Hutton, A.W. ed., 2 vols), London, 1892.

B: ARTICLES
Bartlett, Thomas, 'The Townshend viceroyalty, 1767–72' in Bartlett & Hayton (ed.), *Penal Era and Golden Age*, (above), pp 88–112.
Baskerville, S.W., Adman, Peter and Beedham, K.F., 'The dynamics of landlord influence in English county elections, 1701–34: the evidence from Cheshire' in *Parliamentary History*, xii, (1993), pp 126–142.
Bigger, F.J., 'Castledillon and the Molyneux family' in *BNL*, 12 Oct. 1923.
Blackstock, Allan, ' "A dangerous species of ally": Orangeism and the Irish yeomanry' in *IHS*, xxx (May, 1997), pp 393–405.
Blackstock, Allan, ' "The invincible mass": loyal crowds in mid-Ulster, 1795–6' in Jupp & Magennis (ed.), *Crowds in Ireland c.1720–1920*, pp 83–114.
Bodkin, Rev. M., 'Notes on the Irish parliament of 1773' in *RIA Proc.*, xlviii, sect. C, (1942–3), pp 145–223.
Clarkson, Leslie, 'Armagh 1770: portrait of an urban community' in David Harkness and Mary O'Dowd (eds.), *The town in Ireland*, Belfast, 1981, pp 81–102.
Coyle, E.A., 'Talbot's fencibles and the Drogheda mutiny' in Journal of the County *Louth Archaeological and Historical Society*, xxiv (1997) pp 39–50.
Crawford, W.H., 'Change in Ulster in the late eighteenth century' in Bartlett & Hayton (ed.) *Penal Era and Golden Age*, pp 186–203.
Crawford, W.H., 'Economy and society in south Ulster in the eighteenth century' in *Clogher Record*, viii, no. 3 (1975), pp 241–58.
Crawford, W.H., 'Evolution of towns in County Armagh' in Hughes and Nolan (ed.), *Armagh history and society*, pp 851–80.
Crawford, W.H., ' "The Linen Triangle" in the 1790s', *ULS*, xviii, no. 2 (Spring, 1997), pp 43–53.
Cullen, L.M., 'Alliances and misalliances in the politics of the Union' in *Transactions of the Royal Historical Society* (6th series, x, Cambridge, 2000), pp 221–41.
Cullen, L.M., 'The internal politics of the United Irishmen' in David Dickson, Daire Keogh & Kevin Whelan, *The United Irishmen: republicanism, radicalism and Rebellion*, Dublin, 1993, pp 176–96.
Cullen, L.M., 'The United Irishmen: problems and issues of the 1790s' in *ULS*, xviii, no. 2 (Spring, 1997), pp 7–27
Donnelly, J.S., 'Hearts of Oak, Hearts of Steel' in *Studia Hibernica*, xxi (1981), pp 7–73.
Geoghegan, Patrick, 'The Catholics and the Union' in *Transactions of the Royal Historical Society* (6th series, x, Cambridge, 2000), pp 243–58.

Hayton, D.W., 'The beginnings of the "Undertaker" system' in Bartlett & Hayton (ed.), *Penal Era and Golden Age*, pp 32–54.

Hayton, D.W., 'Introduction: the long apprenticeship' in *Parliamentary History*, xx (2001), pp 1–25.

Hayton, D.W., 'Introduction: Ireland after the Glorious Revolution, 1692–1715' in *PRONI, Educational Facsimiles 221–240*, pp 2–25.

Hayton, D.W., 'Notes and documents. A debate in the Irish house of commons in 1703: a whiff of Tory grapeshot' in *Parliamentary History*, x (1991), pp 151–63.

Hughes, J.L.J., 'The chief secretaries in Ireland, 1566–1921' in *IHS*, viii, (March, 1952), pp 59–72.

Hunter, R.J., 'County Armagh: a map of plantation *c.* 1610' in Hughes and Nolan (ed.), *Armagh history and society*, pp 265–294.

Hunter, R.J., 'Towns in the Ulster Plantation' in *Studia Hibernica*, (1971), xi, pp 40–79.

Johnston, E.M., 'Members of the Irish parliament, 1784–7' in *RIA Proc.*, lxxi, sect. C (1971), pp 167–246.

Johnston, E.M., 'The state of the Irish house of commons in 1791' in *RIA Proc.*, lix, sect. C (March, 1957), pp 1–56.

Jones, S.R., 'Presbyterianism in County Armagh' in Hughes and Nolan (ed.), *Armagh history and society*, pp 693–712.

Jupp, P.J., 'County Down elections 1783–1831' in *IHS*, xviii, (Sept., 1972), pp 177–206.

Jupp, P.J., 'Irish parliamentary elections and the influence of the Catholic vote, 1801–20' in *The Historical Journal*, x, (1967), pp 183–96.

Kelly, James, 'The parliamentary reform movement of the 1780s and the Catholic Question' in *Archivium Hibernicum*, xliii (1988), pp 95–117.

Kelly, James (ed.), 'Select documents XLIII: A secret return of the Volunteers of Ireland in 1784' in *IHS*, xxvi, (May, 1989), pp 268–92.

Lammey, David, 'The free trade crisis: a reappraisal' in Gerard O'Brien (ed.) *Parliament, politics and people: essays in eighteenth-century Irish history*, Dublin, 1989, pp 69–92.

Lammey, David, 'The growth of the "Patriot Opposition" in Ireland during the 1770s' in *Parliamentary History*, vii, (1988), pp 257–81.

Large, David, 'Select documents: xix. The Irish house of commons in 1769' in *IHS*, xi, (March, 1958), pp 18–45.

Magennis, Eoin, ' "A Presbyterian insurrection"? Reconsidering the Hearts of Oak disturbances of July 1763' in *IHS*, xxxi (Nov. 1998), pp 165–88.

Magennis, Eoin, 'All politics, no religion: a loyalist view of the "Armagh Troubles", 1796' in *Seanchas Ardmhacha*, xix, no. 2 (2003), pp 102–17.

Magennis, Eoin, 'In search of the "moral economy": food scarcity in 1756–7 and the crowd', in Jupp and Magennis (ed.), *Crowds in Ireland*, pp 189–211.

Malcomson, A.P.W., 'Absenteeism in eighteenth century Ireland', in *Irish. Econ. Soc. Hist.*, i (1974), pp 15–35.

Malcomson, A.P.W., 'The gentle leviathan: Arthur Hill, second marquess of Downshire 1753–1801' in Peter Roebuck (ed.), *Plantation to Partition*, Belfast, 1981, pp 102–18.

Malcomson, A.P.W., ' "The parliamentary traffic of this country" ' in Bartlett & Hayton (ed.) *Penal Era and Golden Age*, pp 137–61.

McNally, Patrick, 'The Hanoverian accession and the Tory party in Ireland' in *Parliamentary History*, xiv (1995), pp 263–83.

Miller, D.W., 'The Armagh troubles, 1784–95' in Samuel Clark and J.S. Donnelly, Jr (eds), *Irish peasants, violence & political unrest 1780–1914*, Dublin, 1983, pp 155–91.

Miller, D.W., 'Politicisation in revolutionary Ireland: the case of the Armagh troubles' in *Irish. Econ. Soc. Hist.*, xxiii (1996), pp 1–17.

Mirala, Petri, ' "A large mob calling themselves Freemasons": Masonic parades in Ulster' in Jupp and Magennis (ed.) *Crowds in Ireland*, pp 117–138.

Muhr, Kay, 'Territories, people and placenames in County Armagh' in Hughes and Nolan (ed.), *Armagh history and society*, pp 295–332.

O'Donovan, Declan, 'The money bill dispute of 1753' in Bartlett & Hayton (ed.) *Penal Era and Golden Age*, pp 55–87.

Ó Fiaich, Rev. Tomás, 'Migration from Ulster to County Mayo in 1795–6' in *ULS*, xii, no. 2 (Winter, 1990), pp 7–19.

Ó Muirí, Rev. Reamonn, 'The killing of Thomas Birch, United Irishman' in *Seanchas Ardmhacha*, x, no. 2 (1982), pp 267–319.

O'Sullivan, Harold, 'Land confiscations and plantations in County Armagh during the English Commonwealth and Restoration periods, 1650 to 1680' in Hughes and Nolan (ed.), *Armagh history and society*, pp 333–80.

Parkinson, Edward, 'The Wests of Ballydugan' in *UJA*, 2nd series, xii (1906), pp 135–41, 159–65.

Paterson, T.G.F., 'The County Armagh Volunteers of 1778–93' in *UJA*, (3rd series, Belfast, 1941–4).

Paterson, T.G.F., 'The Chamberlains of Nizelrath, the Brownlows' in *The County Louth Archaeological Journal*, xi (1947), pp 173–85.

Paterson, T.G.F., 'County Armagh in 1622: a plantation survey' in *Seanchas Ardmhacha*, iv, no. 1 (1960–1), pp 103–40.

Paterson, T.G.F., 'Presbyterianism in Armagh' in *Seanchas Ardmhacha*, xix, no. 2, (2003), pp 140–63.

Power, T.P., 'Parliamentary representation in County Kilkenny in the eighteenth century' in William Nolan and Kevin Whelan (eds.) *Kilkenny: history and society* (Dublin, 1990), pp 305–32.

Sainty, J.C., 'The secretariat of the chief governors of Ireland', *RIA Proc.*, lxxvii, sect. C (1977), pp 1–33.

Sayles, G.O., 'Contemporary sketches of the members of the Irish parliament in 1782' in *RIA Proc.*, li, sect. C (1954), pp 227–86.

Schlegel, Donald, 'The MacDonnells of Tyrone and Armagh' in *Seanchas Ardmhacha*, x, no. 1 (1980–1), pp 193–219.

Simms, J.G., 'Dean Swift and County Armagh' in *Seanchas Ardmhacha*, vi, no. 1 (1971), pp 131–40.

Smyth, P.D.H., 'The Volunteers and parliament, 1779–84' in Bartlett & Hayton, *Penal Era and Golden Age*, pp 113–36.

Thomas, P.D.G., 'Two voting lists for the Irish house of commons in 1773' in *Parliamentary History*, vii (1988), pp 313–27.

Tohall, Patrick, 'The Diamond fight of 1795 and the resultant expulsions' in *Seanchas Ardmhacha*, iii, no. 1 (1958), pp 17–50.

Walker, B.M., 'Landowners and parliamentary elections in County Down 1801–1921' in Lindsay Proudfoot (ed.) *Down: history and society* (Dublin, 1997), pp 297–325.

Wall, Maureen, 'The rise of a Catholic middle class in eighteenth century Ireland' in *IHS*, xi (Sept. 1958), pp 91–115.

Whyte, J.H., 'Landlord influence at elections in Ireland 1760–1885', in *EHR*, lxxx (Oct.1965), pp 740–60.

C: REFERENCE WORKS

Ball-Wright, Rev. W. (ed.), *Records of Irish families of Ball compiled from public and private sources*, Dublin, 1887.

Burke, A.P. (ed.), *History of the landed gentry of Ireland by Sir Bernard Burke*, London, 1904.

C[okayne], G.E. (ed.), *The complete peerage* (6 vols, Gloucester reprint), 1982.

Connolly, S.J. (ed.), *The Oxford companion to Irish history*, Oxford, 1998.

Cotton, Henry (ed.), *Fasti Ecclesiae Hibernicae: the succession of the prelates and members of the cathedral bodies in Ireland* (5 vols), Dublin, 1849.

Crone, J.S., *A concise dictionary of Irish biography*, Dublin, 1928.

Johnston-Liik, E.M., *History of the Irish Parliament 1692–1800: commons, constituencies and statutes* (6 vols), Belfast, 2002.

Leslie, J.B., *Armagh clergy and parishes*, Dundalk, 1911.

Lodge, John (ed.), *The peerage of Ireland*, (7 vols), London, 1789.

Presbyterian Historical Society of Ireland, *A history of congregations in the Presbyterian Church in Ireland*, Belfast, 1982.

Stephenson, Leslie and Lee, Sidney (eds.), *Dictionary of National Biography*, (22 vols), London, 1967–8.

Thorne, R.G. (ed.), *The History of Parliament: The House of Commons 1790–1820*, (5 Vols), London, 1986.

Townshend, Peter (ed.), *Burke's Peerage, Baronetage and Knightage* (105th edition), London, 1970.

Walker, B.M., *Parliamentary Election Results in Ireland 1801–1922*, Dublin, 1978.

D: UNPUBLISHED THESES

Beaumont, D.M., 'The gentry of the King's and Queen's Counties: Protestant landed society 1690–1760' (2 vols, Ph.D. thesis, TCD, 1999).

Gourley, R.S., 'The social and economic history of the Gosford estates 1610–1876' (Ph.D. thesis, QUB, 1973).

Magennis, Eoin, 'Politics and government in Ireland during the Seven Years War, 1756–63' (Ph.D. thesis, QUB, 1996).

Nelson, I.F., 'The Irish Militia, 1793–1802' (Ph.D. thesis, QUB, 2001).

Smyth, P.D.H., 'The volunteer movement in Ulster: background and development 1745–85' (Ph.D. thesis, QUB, 1974).

Index

Abbey of SS. Patrick and Mary, Newry 16
Abbey of SS. Peter and Paul, Armagh 9
Abbey Street, Dublin 289
Abercorn family 256, 266
Abercorn, eighth earl of, *see* Hamilton, James, eighth earl of Abercorn
Acheson family 2, 13, 14, 17, 21, 22, 30, 32, 40, 67, 73, 76, 156, 189, 230, 239, 259, 274, 275
Acheson, Anne 41
Acheson, Archibald, first Baronet 13
Acheson, Archibald, first Viscount Gosford 23–4, 25, 32, 38, 39, 40–1, 41–2, 43, 44, 51, 52, 54, 56, 57, 58, 60, 69, 71, 72, 73, 74, 75, 77, 84, 85, 87–9, 90–1, 92–3, 95–6, 97, 99, 100–1, 103, 104, 105–6, 107–9, 110, 111, 112–15, 118, 119–20, 122–4, 125, 126–7, 128, 129–30, 132, 133, 144, 145, 149, 150–1, 152, 154, 155, 156, 158, 167, 169, 173, 187, 189, 190, 205, 206, 207, 208–9, 213, 215, 223, 225, 226, 228, 232, 275, 280, 286
Acheson, Archibald, second earl of Gosford 4, 235, 236, 237, 241, 253, 254–5, 257, 258, 260, 263, 264, 265, 266, 268, 277, 281, 286
Acheson, Arthur (of Mourne) 53
Acheson, Arthur, fifth Baronet 13, 23, 32, 38, 44
Acheson, Arthur, first earl of Gosford 4, 123, 155, 156, 189–90, 194, 197, 201, 202–3, 205, 206, 207, 208, 209–10, 213, 214, 223, 224, 228, 230, 231, 232–3, 233–5, 236, 237, 238–40, 241–2, 243, 244, 249, 250–1, 252, 253, 254, 255, 257, 258, 259, 260, 262–3, 263–4, 266, 267, 268–9, 275, 276, 277–8
Acheson, George, third Baronet 13
Acheson, Henry 13
Acheson, Lady Anne (*née* Savage) 23
Acheson, Lady Anne (*née* Taylor) 13
Acheson, Lady Mary (Bentinck) 269
Acheson, Lady Mary (*née* Sparrow) 24
Acheson, Lady Millicent (*née* Pole) 123
Acheson, Lord Edward 260
Acheson, Mary (*née* Richardson) 24
Acheson, Nicholas, fourth Baronet 13, 23
Acheson, Patrick, second Baronet 13
Acton, Co. Armagh 15, 16, 24, 25, 30, 58, 72, 73, 146, 158, 160, 200, 225, 233, 250, 289
Adderley, Thomas 21, 38, 39, 40, 42, 43, 45, 49, 69, 71, 72, 73, 85, 89–90, 91, 93, 94, 98, 284, 286

Adderton, Captain Henry 16
Addington, Speaker 265
Agar, Archbishop Charles 154
Airthir 7
Aldercorn, Colonel 75
Alexander family 235
Alexander, James, first earl of Caledon 263
Allott, Rev. Dr Richard 209, 215
Altnamackin, Co. Armagh 61
America 109, 122, 128, 129, 130, 133, 143, 149, 150, 153, 155, 171, 192, 227, 237, 291
American War of Independence 128, 129, 130, 133, 144, 149–50, 153, 155, 168, 171, 183
Ampthill, Bedfordshire 295
Anabaptists 17
Andrews, Provost Francis 91, 95, 116, 151
Anglesey, earls of, *see* Annesley family
Annaghmore House, Co. Sligo 293
Annasamry, Co. Armagh 61
Anne, Queen 10, 18, 19, 20, 21, 22, 23
Annesley family 16, 23, 30
Annesley, Sir Francis 12, 14, 16
Antrim, Co. 17, 52, 53, 54, 85, 120, 121, 146, 185, 198
Archdall, Mervyn 185
Ardee, Co. Louth 295
Ardgonnell, Co. Armagh 22, 56
Ardress, Co. Armagh 59
Armagh borough 2, 9–10, 13, 18–20, 21–22, 31, 76, 86, 94, 107, 115–16, 117, 133, 151, 173, 188, 208, 212, 229, 252, 255, 259, 263, 265, 269, 274, 282–3, 287, 288, 289, 290, 291, 292, 293, 294, 295
Armagh Royal School 8, 158
Armagh, barony of 8, 25, 27, 29, 30, 31, 55, 59
Armaghbreague, Co. Armagh 27, 28
Arvagh, Co. Cavan 13, 71, 88, 96, 108, 112, 114, 286
Ashenhurst, J.T. 195
Aston Clinton, Buckinghamshire 291
Athy, Co. Kildare 61
Auckland, first Baron, *see* Eden, William, first Baron Auckland
Audley, Lady Elizabeth, Dowager of Castlehaven 16
Audley, Lord, *see* Tuckett, George, Lord Audley of Orior and earl of Castlehaven
Aughmuty, Dean James 43
Australia 210
Aylesbury, Buckinghamshire 291
Ayr Burghs 292
Ayrshire 13

Bagnal, Arthur 16
Bagshawe, Colonel 91
Balbriggan, Co. Dublin 199
Baleek, Co. Armagh 56
Ball family 25, 30, 58, 67
Ball, Abraham 53
Ball, Charles 261
Ball, John 54
Ball, Lieutenant Thomas 17
Ball, Thomas (of Cullyhanna) 223
Ball, Thomas (of Wexford) 54, 61
Ballinamuck, Co. Longford 257
Ballintoy, Co. Antrim 16, 24–5, 41
Ballyclare, Co. Armagh 14, 25, 58, 109, 187
Ballydonaghy, Co. Armagh 59
Ballydugan, Co. Down 16
Ballyhannon, Co. Armagh 59
Ballyheridan, Co. Armagh 14, 22, 57
Ballymacnab, Co. Armagh 249
Ballymascanlon, Co. Louth 54
Ballymore, Co. Armagh 12, 14, 24, 26, 30, 44, 54, 56, 60, 114, 158
Ballymoyer, Co. Armagh 13, 30
Ballynaghy, Co. Armagh 59
Ballynakill, Co. Laois 117, 133, 152, 184–5, 189, 213, 293, 295
Ballynemoney, Co. Armagh 10
Ballynewry, Co. Armagh 61
Ballyoran, Co. Armagh 12, 26, 30
Ballyshannon, Co. Donegal 116
Bandon, Co. Cork 21, 286
Bandon-bridge, Co. Cork 69, 89, 94
Bangor, Co. Down 69
Bann, River 30, 115, 120, 121
Barrington family 117, 185
Barrington, Jonah 146
Barrington, Rev. Benjamin 59, 61, 69, 91, 96, 101, 104
Bartlett, Thomas 102, 237, 238, 239
Bath, Avon 41, 86, 99, 108, 115, 199, 215, 268
Bath, fifth earl of, *see* Bourchier, Henry, fifth earl of Bath
Bawn, Co. Louth 295
Beaulieu, Co. Louth 25, 53, 58
Beccles, Suffolk 269, 286
Bedford, fourth duke of, *see* Russell, John, fourth duke of Bedford
Bedfordshire 295
Belfast 50, 61, 62, 63, 85, 114, 121, 145, 155, 167, 170, 183, 185, 197, 198, 199, 204, 226, 227, 233, 261, 267
Bell, Captain Benjamin 171
Bell, George 61
Bell, James 71
Bellew, Jane 62
Bellew, Sam 62
Bellomont, first earl of 108
Bellurgan, Co. Louth 25, 58

Belmont, Co. Wicklow 294
Belturbet, Co. Cavan 69
Bentinck family 190
Bentinck, Lady Mary (*née* Acheson) 269
Bentinck, Lieutenant General Lord William 249, 269
Bentinck, Lord Edward 189–90, 201
Bere Alston, Devon 292
Beresford, John 206
Beresford, Marcus, first earl of Tyrone 84, 108
Bernard, Elizabeth (Caulfeild) 21
Bernard, Francis 94
Bernard, Sir John 24, 89, 90
Bernard, Stephen 69
Bessborough, earl of 73, 117
Bessbrook, Co. Armagh 213
Birch, James 185
Birch, John 53
Birch, Thomas 249
Bishop's Court, Co. Kildare 294
Bissett, Rev. William 241, 250
Black, Captain James 171, 172
Blacker family 26, 263
Blacker, Counsellor Samuel 41, 44, 52, 56, 85, 89, 95–6, 101, 103, 114
Blacker, William 59, 61, 104
Blackhall, Captain John 121, 158, 166, 172, 187, 195, 196, 197, 198–9, 200, 202, 204, 215
Blackstock, Allan 239
Blackwater, River 7, 25, 57, 58
Blackwatertown, Co. Armagh 25, 145, 223
Blackwood family 111
Blackwood, John 121
Blackwood, William 114
Blaquiere, John, first baron de Blaquiere 119, 124, 125, 126–7, 128, 129, 143, 152
Blessington, first earl of 295
Bolton Street, Dublin 62
Bolton, Archbishop Theophilus 19
Bolton, G.C. 269
Bond family 26, 59, 67
Bond, John 63
Bondsville, Co. Armagh 26
Botany Bay, Australia 210
Boulter, Primate Hugh 19, 20, 49
Bourchier, Charles 20, 282, 287
Bourchier, Henry, fifth earl of Bath 14–15
Bourchier, Sir John 14
Bourke, John 91
Bourke, Joseph 123
Bowes, John 87
Boyd, Adjutant Andrew 155
Boyle family 74
Boyle, Bellingham 70
Boyle, Co. Roscommon 15
Boyle, Henry, first earl of Shannon 39, 40, 42, 43, 44, 50, 58, 64, 67–8, 69, 72, 73, 74, 77, 94, 95, 98

Boyle, John, fifth earl of Cork and Orrery 24, 25, 41, 54, 58, 60, 90
Boyle, Richard, second earl of Shannon 107, 118, 119, 125, 132, 154, 162
Boyne, battle of the 10
Bragg, General Philip 20, 39, 76, 282, 287
Bramber, West Sussex 291
Bramhall, Primate 18
Brampton Park, Huntingdon 24
Bray, Co. Wicklow 290, 294
Brenoge, Co. Armagh, *see* Acton, Co. Armagh
Bristol 105, 115
Bristol, Lord, *see* Hervey, Frederick, earl-bishop of Derry
Broadstone, Co. Dublin 292
Brodrick, Alan 18
Broughshane, Co. Antrim 183
Brown, John 13
Browne, Thomas, fourth Viscount Kenmare 191
Brownlow family 2, 10, 21, 22, 30, 31, 32, 40, 43, 48, 49, 55, 67, 76, 109, 150, 237, 274
Brownlow, Arthur (Chamberlain) 10–11, 22, 47, 48
Brownlow, Eleanor (*née* O'Dogherty) 10
Brownlow, John 10
Brownlow, Lady Betty 109
Brownlow, Letitia (Cope) 22
Brownlow, Lettice (Chamberlain) 10
Brownlow, Lieutenant Charles 127, 153, 163, 275
Brownlow, Sir William (d. 1661) 10
Brownlow, William (1683–1739) 22, 23, 47, 48, 109, 280, 287
Brownlow, William (1726–94) 22, 32, 38, 39–40, 42, 43–69, 71, 73, 74–5, 77, 84, 85, 87–8, 89, 90, 92–3, 96, 97, 98–9, 100, 104, 105–6, 107, 108, 109–11, 112–13, 114, 115, 118, 119–20, 121, 122, 126–7, 130, 131, 132, 133, 144, 145, 147–8, 150, 152, 153, 154, 156, 157, 158–9, 160–1, 162, 163–4, 165, 166, 167, 171, 172–3, 174, 180, 181, 182, 184, 185, 186–7, 187–8, 191, 192, 193, 194, 195, 196, 197, 199, 200, 201, 202, 203–4, 205, 206–7, 208, 211, 212, 213–14, 215, 222, 224, 225, 226–9, 231, 234, 236, 242, 243–4, 254, 275, 276, 278, 280, 281, 287
Brownlow, William (1755–1815) 200, 232, 234, 235, 236, 241, 243, 244, 250, 251, 252, 253, 254, 258, 260, 263, 264, 265, 275, 281, 287
Brownlow's-Derry, Co. Armagh 10, 12, 30, 54, 55, 195
Bruce, William 71
Buckinghamshire 291
Buckinghamshire, fourth earl of, *see* Hobart, Robert, fourth earl of Buckinghamshire
Buckinghamshire, second earl of, *see* Hobart, John, second earl of Buckinghamshire
Burgh, General 170
Burgh, Prime Sergeant Hussey 152, 153, 159, 163
Burleigh, George 62
Bushe, Gervaise 161, 163
Bute, third earl of, *see* Stuart, John, third earl of Bute
Butler family 88, 94
Butler, Brinsley, second earl of Lanesborough 88, 92, 96, 97, 106, 108, 112, 114, 119
Butler, Elizabeth 15
Butler, Humphrey, first earl of Lanesborough 69, 112
Butler, James, first duke of Ormonde 15
Butler, James, second duke of Ormonde 18, 288
Butler, Thomas 15
Butler, Tom 69
Byrne, Chris 62
Byrne, J. 208, 209, 215

Caledon, Co. Tyrone 25, 41, 58
Caledon, first earl of 263
Callan valley, Co. Armagh 28
Callan, Co. Armagh 288
Calvinists 18
Camac, Mr 231
Cambridge, University of 12
Camden, first Marquis, *see* Pratt, John, first Marquis Camden
Camlough, Co. Armagh 30
Camoley [Camly], Co. Armagh 46, 59
Campbell, Lord Frederick 107, 108, 116
Campbell, Rev. William 158, 191, 198, 200, 210, 215
Canada 286
Canavan, Daniel 62
Canterbury, archbishop of 265
Cape of Good Hope 292
Carlingford, Co. Louth 22, 69, 127, 293, 294, 295
Carlisle, fifth earl of, *see* Howard, Frederick, fifth earl of Carlisle
Carlow, Co. Carlow 294
Carmichael, William 105
Carrickblacker, Co. Armagh 26, 59, 61, 293
Carrickfergus, Co. Antrim 21, 85
Carson, Samuel 155
Carter, Thomas 74
Carteret, John, second Earl Granville 23, 47
Casey, Charles 72
Cashel, diocese of 19
Castlebellingham, Co. Louth 54
Castle Bernard, Co. Cork 21
Castle-Caulfeild (estate), Co. Tyrone 288
Castle-Caulfeild (village), Co. Tyrone 21

Castle-Dillon, Co. Armagh 12, 16, 30, 57, 89, 116, 119, 145, 157, 212
Castlehaven, earl of, *see* Tuckett, George, Lord Audley of Orior and earl of Castlehaven
Castlemartyr, Co. Cork 294
Castlereagh, Viscount, *see* Stewart, Robert, Viscount Castlereagh
Castle Stewart, Co. Tyrone 94
Castleward, Co. Down 41
Caulfeild family 9, 15, 20–1, 30, 32, 38, 40, 43, 44, 47, 57, 59, 67, 73, 76, 89, 94, 117, 274, 275
Caulfeild, Anne (Davys) 21
Caulfeild, Anne (Moore) 94
Caulfeild, Colonel John 21
Caulfeild, Elizabeth (*née* Bernard) 21
Caulfeild, Francis 38–9, 40, 41–2, 42–69, 71, 72, 75, 77, 84, 85, 87, 88, 89, 90, 92, 93–4, 97, 98, 107, 108, 109, 110, 111–12, 117, 118, 120, 126, 127–8, 132, 133, 226, 276, 280, 284, 287
Caulfeild, Francis William, second earl of Charlemont 4, 234, 236, 241, 242, 250–1, 252, 253, 254, 255–6, 257, 258, 260, 262, 263, 264–5, 266, 267, 268, 276, 277, 281, 285, 288
Caulfeild, Henry 265, 288
Caulfeild, James, first earl of Charlemont 2, 4, 17, 21, 31, 38, 45, 47, 48, 49, 54, 56, 72, 73–4, 75, 84, 86, 87, 89–90, 91, 93, 94, 95, 97, 99, 100, 101–2, 103, 107, 109, 110, 111–12, 117, 118, 128, 132, 144, 145, 147, 148, 151, 152, 154, 155, 156, 157, 158, 162, 164–5, 166–8, 168–9, 170, 171, 173, 174, 180, 183, 184, 185, 186, 187, 189, 191, 192, 193–4, 195, 196, 197, 198, 199–200, 202, 203, 204, 205, 206, 207, 210, 211–12, 213, 215, 222, 223, 226, 228, 230, 231, 232–3, 234, 235, 236, 240, 241, 242–3, 244, 250–1, 252–3, 254, 255–6, 257–8, 259, 260, 262, 266, 274, 276, 277, 278, 288
Caulfeild, James, third Viscount Charlemont 21, 25, 284, 288
Caulfeild, John 21, 49, 53, 71, 72, 73, 85, 90, 94, 284, 288
Caulfeild, Mary (Moore), *see* Moore, Mary (*née* Caulfeild)
Caulfeild, Rev. Charles 53, 94
Caulfeild, Tobias, first Baron Charlemont 9, 12
Caulfeild, William, second Baron Charlemont 9–10
Caulfeild, William, second Viscount Charlemont 10, 21
Cavan, Co. 14, 71, 87, 88, 91, 93, 94, 95, 99, 108, 110, 112, 114, 115, 198, 286, 292
Cavendish, William, fourth duke of Devonshire 73, 74, 89

Cavendish, William, third duke of Devonshire 73, 294
Cavendish-Bentinck, William Henry, third duke of Portland 166, 168, 169, 170, 174, 180, 189–90, 208, 211, 213, 224, 269
Chamberlain, Arthur, *see* Brownlow (Chamberlain), Arthur
Chamberlain, Lettice (*née* Brownlow) 10
Chamberlain, Patrick 10
Chambré, Hunt 61
Charlemont borough, Co. Armagh 2, 3, 9–10, 15, 17, 18, 20–1, 25, 31, 47, 49, 53, 71, 86, 89, 90, 93–4, 95, 107, 117, 128, 151–2, 173, 185, 188, 189, 193, 212, 230, 231, 252, 255–6, 259, 265, 274, 276, 284–5, 286, 287, 288, 289, 290, 291, 292, 293, 295
Charlemont Fort, Co. Armagh 9, 84, 155, 156
Charlemont House, Co. Tyrone 288
Charlemont, Co. Armagh 57, 68, 101, 287, 293, 294
Charlemont, first Baron, *see* Caulfeild, Tobias, first Baron Charlemont
Charlemont, first earl of, *see* Caulfeild, James, first earl of Charlemont
Charlemont, Lady Mary (*née* Hickman) 112
Charlemont, second Baron, *see* Caulfeild, William, second Baron Charlemont
Charlemont, second earl of, *see* Caulfeild, Francis William, second earl of Charlemont
Charlemont, second Viscount, *see* Caulfeild, William, second Viscount Charlemont
Charlemont, third Viscount, *see* Caulfeild, James, third Viscount Charlemont
Charles II 11, 14
Charlesfort, Co. Wexford 146
Cherry, Rev. George 85
Cheshire 76
Chester, Cheshire 99, 105
Chichester, Arthur 7
China 292
Church of England 17, 19
Church of Ireland 22, 26, 27, 39, 47, 49, 71, 91, 99, 100, 103, 104, 130, 146, 158, 197, 198, 199, 250
Churchhill, Co. Armagh 26, 92, 101, 256, 257, 266
Clancarny, Co. Armagh 13, 17, 30
Clandeboye, Co. Down 13
Clanrye, River 7, 25
Clare Street, Dublin 145, 293
Clare, Co. Armagh 15, 18, 30, 45, 59, 90, 101, 105, 157, 160, 187, 235, 289
Clare-Castle, Co. Armagh 145, 146, 149, 158, 174, 181, 187, 188, 223, 289
Clarke family 59, 67
Clarke, Henry 61
Clements, Nathaniel 107

Clermont, Viscount, *see* Fortescue, William Henry, first Viscount Clermont
Clogher, Co. Tyrone 24, 89, 116, 117, 152, 182, 189, 212, 288, 290, 293
Clogher, diocese of 24, 89, 92, 96, 99, 189
Clogheran Church, Co. Dublin 50
Clonakilty, Co. Cork 94, 286
Clonfeacle, Co. Armagh 239
Clonfert and Kilmacduagh, diocese of 122, 123, 189, 275
Clonmakate, Co. Armagh 101
Clonmel, Co. Tipperary 102
Clontarf, Co. Dublin 288
Clontylew, (variants Clontyclew and Clantilew), Co. Armagh 11, 26, 30, 59, 61
Clony, Co. Cavan 13
Close, High Sheriff Maxwell 160, 162
Coalisland, Co. Tyrone 46
Cockermouth, Cumbria 115, 292
Coghill, Marmaduke 20
Cole, John, first Baron Mountflorence 150
Colebrook, Sir George 151
Coleraine, Co. Londonderry 86
College Green, Dublin 1, 157
Colooney, Co. Sligo 293
Comber, Co. Down 170
Conlon, James 62
Conolly, Thomas 95, 116, 152, 154, 162, 164, 207
Conway, Edward, second Viscount Conway 15, 22
Cooke, Edward 230, 239, 240, 257, 260
Cooke, Francis 14
Coolmalish, Co. Armagh 56
Coolmilis, Co. Armagh 13, 30
Coote, Charles, first earl of Bellomont 108
Coote, Sir Charles 6, 29
Cope family 2, 16, 21, 24, 30, 31, 32, 40, 43, 67, 76, 121, 187, 197, 200, 228, 263, 274
Cope, Anne (*née* Acheson) 41
Cope, Arthur 42, 104, 106, 108, 110, 112, 114, 144, 145, 147, 148, 158, 173, 200, 202, 228, 234, 280
Cope, Bishop Walter 24, 25, 41, 54, 58, 60, 75, 88, 96, 97, 106, 107-8, 122-3, 189, 190, 213, 224, 275
Cope, Dean Anthony 'Nanty' 42, 43, 44, 45, 54, 55, 56, 58, 60, 61, 65, 66, 71, 72, 88, 89, 92, 101, 104, 110, 112
Cope, Hen. 250, 251
Cope, Henry 11, 12
Cope, John 165
Cope, Kendrick 259
Cope, Letitia (*née* Brownlow) 22
Cope, Richard 11, 12
Cope, Robert 22-3, 24, 38, 39, 42, 55, 280, 288
Cope, Robert Camden 234, 235, 236, 237, 243-4, 254, 255, 257, 262-3, 264, 265, 267, 277, 281, 288

Cope, Sir Anthony 11
Corcrain, Co. Armagh 59
Cork, Co. 21, 40, 43, 94, 286, 294
Cork, Co. Cork 183, 294, 295
Cornwallis, Charles, first Marquis Cornwallis 255, 257, 258, 259, 261, 262, 263, 264, 266, 267, 283
Corodownan, Co. Cavan 13
Corry, Edward 53, 152
Corry, Isaac (I) 53, 61
Corry, Isaac (II) 152, 153, 154, 157, 159, 161, 163, 184, 193, 194, 197, 201, 202, 204, 206, 207, 208, 213, 214, 231, 240, 256, 259, 261, 262, 263, 264, 265-6, 267, 269, 276
Coulter, Thomas 54
County Armagh Patriot Club 70
Covenanters 100
Coyns, Tim 62
Craig, Sir James 13
Cranagill, Co. Armagh 59
Crawford, W.H. 215, 237, 239
Creggan, Co. Armagh 18, 26, 27, 263-4, 267
Cremorne peers, *see* Dawson family
Cremorne, first Baron, *see* Dawson, Thomas, first Baron Cremorne
Cromie, Sir Michael 150
Cromwell, Oliver 6, 17, 29
Crosse, Silvester 20, 282, 288
Crosse's Green, Co. Cork 288
Cuffe, James 168
Cullaville, Co. Armagh 46
Cullen, L.M. 237, 258
Culloden, battle of 45, 73, 289
Cullyhanna, Co. Armagh 223
Cumberland 115
Cumberland, duke of, *see* William, Prince, duke of Cumberland
Cuming, Samuel 172
Cuninghame, Colonel Robert 39, 91, 92, 94, 97, 107, 115, 126, 282, 289
Cuppage, Adam 195
Curragh, the, Co. Kildare 293
Curran, J.P. 208, 231
Curriator Pass, Co. Armagh 15
Curzon Street, London 292
Cusher, River 14
Custom House Quay, Dublin 290

Dalrymple, General William 238
Dartrey, earls of, *see* Dawson family
Davys, Anne (*née* Caulfeild) 21
Davys, John 21
Dawson family 25, 67, 146, 158, 174
Dawson Street, Dublin 294
Dawson, Captain James 146, 158, 161, 164, 165, 167, 172, 174, 186, 192, 195, 235, 236, 249, 250

Dawson, Chapell 19
Dawson, Richard 'Dick' 224, 228, 258, 260, 262, 268
Dawson, Thomas (magistrate) 19
Dawson, Thomas (MP) 145–6, 147, 148, 149–50, 152, 153, 154, 157, 158, 159, 160–1, 163–4, 165, 166, 169, 170, 171, 172, 173, 174, 180, 181, 182, 183, 184, 185–7, 187–8, 197, 203, 207, 208, 211, 212, 276, 278, 280, 289
Dawson, Thomas Townly 59, 61, 166
Dawson, Thomas, first Baron Cremorne 145, 260, 262, 263
Dawson, Walter 145–6
Dawson's Grove, Co. Monaghan 25, 87, 145
de Salis, Jerome, second Count 25, 109
de Salis, Madame Mary (*née* Fane) 25, 109, 146, 149, 187
de Salis, Peter, third Count 235, 262, 263
de Zuylestein, William Henry, fourth earl of Rochford 120, 125, 143
Defenders 208, 211, 215, 237, 238, 239, 240, 244, 277
Derry, Co. Londonderry 121, 164, 194, 199
Derry, diocese of 191
Derrycreevy, Co. Armagh 11
Derrycrew, Co. Armagh 197
Derryhale, Co. Armagh 61
Derrymore, Co. Armagh 152, 157, 184, 213, 231
Derrynoose, Co. Armagh 26
Dervock, Co. Antrim 292
Devonshire, third duke of, *see* Cavendish, William, third duke of Devonshire
Dewcorran, Co. Armagh 10
Dickie, William 63
Dillon, Henry 12
Dillon, John 12
Dobbin, Leonard 61
Dobbs, Francis 146, 150, 158, 160, 164, 165, 166, 167, 169, 170, 171, 172, 174, 188, 222, 227, 255, 256, 257, 258, 263, 264, 265, 266, 285, 289
Dobbs, Jane (*née* Stewart) 146
Dodington, George 21
Dollardstown, Co. Meath 292
Dominic Street, Dublin 295
Donaghhenry, Co. Tyrone 53
Donaldson, Randal 26
Donegal, Co. 157, 184, 198, 204, 293
Donegall family 120
Doogary, Co. Armagh 59
Dopping, Samuel 20, 282, 289
Dorset, first duke of, *see* Sackville, Lionel, first duke of Dorset
Douglas, James, fourteenth earl of Morton 116
Douglas, Sir James 12–13

Down, Co. 4–5, 7, 17, 27, 30, 41, 52, 53, 58, 73, 85, 96, 109, 114, 117, 121, 122, 148, 152, 163, 184, 185, 198, 208, 232, 239, 241, 250, 257, 293
Downshire, Lady Mary 266
Drennan, Dr William 233
Drogheda, Co. Louth 53, 62, 96, 170, 189, 261
Drogheda, first marquis of, *see* Moore, Charles, first marquis of Drogheda
Drogheda, first Viscount, *see* Moore, Garret, first Viscount Drogheda
Dromara, Co. Down 185
Dromisken, Co. Armagh 15
Dromore, diocese of 75, 96, 106, 107, 122, 123, 261
Drumbanagher, Co. Armagh 2, 15, 21, 25, 30, 58, 93, 117, 133, 157, 183, 189, 209, 211, 213, 223, 225, 226, 227, 261, 262, 293
Drumcar, Co. Louth 184
Drumcree, Co. Armagh 12, 26
Drumglass, Co. Tyrone 46
Drumilly, Co. Armagh 11, 12, 25, 30, 41, 58, 197
Drumsill, Co. Armagh 61, 250
Dublin Castle (administration) 3, 4, 7, 19, 20, 23, 31, 38, 43, 46, 64, 66, 68, 70, 73, 75, 76, 77, 86, 88, 95, 96, 97, 101, 102, 105, 116, 118, 121, 122, 123, 124, 125, 126, 130, 133, 143, 150, 151, 153, 154, 164, 169, 170, 171, 181, 189, 193, 198, 201, 203, 204, 206, 207, 208, 209, 213, 214, 215, 222, 229, 232, 237, 238, 239, 241, 243, 249, 250, 251, 252, 256, 257, 260, 267, 274, 279, 290
Dublin University, *see* Trinity College, Dublin
Dublin (city of) 1, 12, 18, 21, 22, 23, 42, 43, 45, 46, 49, 50, 51, 52, 53, 57, 59, 61, 62, 64, 67, 71, 74, 75, 85, 88, 90, 93, 94, 95, 96, 99, 100, 102, 103, 107, 108, 110, 121, 122, 124, 128, 145, 153, 155, 157, 162, 165, 182, 189, 190, 192, 194, 195, 200, 202, 207, 209, 222, 225, 226, 230, 231, 232, 233, 234, 236, 242, 249, 253, 257, 258, 260, 261, 263, 264, 267, 286, 287, 288, 289, 290, 291, 292, 293, 294, 295
Dublin, Co. 233
Dublin, diocese of 19, 105, 191, 261
Duigenan, Patrick 255, 257, 259, 263, 264, 265, 266, 269, 283, 289
Dun Laoghaire, Co. Dublin 290
Dundalk, Co. Louth 16, 27, 53, 54, 62, 100, 265
Dundonald, Co. Down 163
Dungannon, Co. Tyrone 127, 165, 166, 167, 170, 174, 184, 186, 192, 193, 239, 240, 249, 256, 265, 266, 276
Dungannon, second Viscount 262

Dungarvan, Co. Waterford 287
Dunleer, Co. Louth 62
Duquery, Henry 208, 229, 283, 290
Durham 43

East Grinstead, West Sussex 289
East Lothian 13
Eastwood, Francis 53
Eccles Street, Dublin 295
Edall, James 63
Eden, William, first Baron Auckland 163, 166, 257
Edenaveys, Co. Armagh 13
Edinburgh 12
Elizabeth I 9
Ellis, Robert junior 41
Ely Place, Dublin 291
English Civil War 11, 12, 13, 14, 15, 17
Enniscorthy, Co. Wexford 289
Enniskillen, Co. Fermanagh 150, 173, 193, 230, 286
Essex, earl of 9
Established Church, *see* Church of England; Church of Ireland
Evans, Francis 165, 167, 172
Ewer, Bishop John 105
Eyre, John 20, 282, 290
Eyrecourt, Co. Galway 290

Fane family 24, 30, 45, 109, 145, 149, 150, 289
Fane, Charles, first Viscount Fane 15, 25, 109, 146
Fane, Charles, second Viscount Fane 25, 42, 54, 58, 60, 90, 109
Fane, Dorothy (Sandwich), *see* Sandwich, Lady Dorothy (*née* Fane)
Fane, Henry 15
Fane, John, tenth earl of Westmorland 208, 222, 229, 231, 233, 235, 237, 238, 291
Fane, Lady Rachel 15
Fane, Lady Susanna 146, 149, 187
Fane, Mary (de Salis), *see* de Salis, Madame Mary
Farlow, James 53
Farnham, Co. Cavan 292
Farnham, first earl of (first creation), *see* Maxwell, Robert, first earl of Farnham
Farnham, first earl of (second creation), *see* Maxwell, Barry, first earl of Farnham
Ferguson, Rev. George 103
Fermanagh, Co. 52, 53, 185
Ferns and Leighlin, diocese of 91, 92, 122, 123, 189, 190, 213, 275
Fethard, Co. Tipperary 294, 295
Fews Barracks, Co. Armagh 26
Fews, barony of, Co. Armagh 7, 8, 9, 12–14, 17, 25, 26, 27, 30, 56, 58, 59, 67, 98, 99, 101

Fiennes, Richard, Lord Saye and Sele 11, 12
Fingall, eighth earl of, *see* Plunkett, Arthur, eighth earl of Fingall
FitzGerald, James, first duke of Leinster 40, 64, 68, 73, 88–9, 91, 125, 126, 127
Fitzgerald, Lord Henry 230
FitzGerald, William, second duke of Leinster 152, 154, 157, 162, 204
Fitzherbert, Alleyne, first Baron St Helens 210, 229
Fitzpatrick, Richard 166, 189
FitzRoy, Augustus, third duke of Grafton 124
FitzRoy, Charles, second duke of Grafton 23
Fitzwilliam, William, fourth Earl Fitzwilliam 238, 244, 290
Flanders 12
Flood, Attorney General Henry 67, 125, 132, 165, 167, 168, 174, 193, 194, 195, 197, 201, 202, 213–14
Forbes, George, sixth earl of Granard 212
Forbes, George, third earl of Granard 69, 72
Forbes, John 201, 206–7
Forde, First Lieutenant James 85
Forkhill, Co. Armagh 16, 30, 101, 146, 211, 223
Forster, Rev. Nicholas 230
Fort Stewart, Co. Donegal 94, 295
Fortescue, Faithfull 15
Fortescue, James 125
Fortescue, William Henry, first Viscount Clermont 53, 61, 113–14, 115
Foster, Speaker John 161, 195, 205–6, 214, 231, 232, 264, 265, 276–7
Fox, Charles James 180–1, 196, 201, 205, 207, 213
Fox, Henry 95
France 32, 48, 73, 75, 84, 85, 124, 147, 153, 155, 229, 233, 240, 244, 249, 277
Free and Independent Club of the County of Armagh 71, 74
French family 24
French, Robert 69, 98

Galway, Co. 42, 49, 68, 69, 70, 171, 287, 290
Galway, Co. Galway 20, 102
Gamble, William 116
Gardiner, Luke 154, 168, 200–1
Gardiner, Mr 63
Gardiner's Row, Dublin 145
Garnett, Bishop John 24, 89, 91, 92, 96, 112, 116, 117, 152, 189, 212
Gellespie, James 62
Geoghegan, P.M. 269
George I 11, 19, 20, 21, 22, 23
George II 22, 39, 45, 84, 85, 87, 91
George III 105, 107, 119, 123, 124, 129–30, 149, 153, 160, 161, 167, 168, 185, 204, 206, 207, 214, 251, 253, 265, 269

George IV 207, 214, 291
Germany 129
Gibraltar 255, 285, 291
Gilford, Co. Armagh 67, 121, 196
Gisbourne, General 121
Glenville, Co. Antrim 122
Godley, Rev. William 61
Gordon, Mr 231
Gordon, Robert 153
Gore, Sir Ralph 23
Gormanston, twelfth Viscount 191
Gosford Castle, Co. Armagh 261, 267, 286
Gosford, first earl of, *see* Acheson, Arthur, first earl of Gosford
Gosford, first Viscount, *see* Acheson, Archibald, first Viscount Gosford
Gosford, Haddingtonshire 13
Gosford, second earl of, *see* Acheson, Archibald, second earl of Gosford
Gowran, Co. Kilkenny 294
Grafton, second duke of 23
Grafton, third duke of 124
Graham family 14, 24, 57
Graham, Arthur 166
Graham, Arthur (of Ballyheridan) 22, 57
Graham, Colonel Arthur 54, 57, 60, 61, 89
Graham, Rev. Isaac 57
Graham, Richard 59
Granard, Co. Longford 189
Granard, sixth earl of 212
Granard, third earl of, *see* Forbes, George, third earl of Granard
Granby Row, Dublin 286
Granby, marquis of 105
Grandison, Viscount, of Limerick, *see* St John, Oliver, Viscount Grandison of Limerick
Grange, Co. Armagh 23, 55
Granville, second Earl, *see* Carteret, John, second Earl Granville
Grattan, Henry 128, 132, 152, 153, 154, 155, 157, 158, 159, 161, 163, 164, 165, 166, 167–8, 171, 174, 184, 188, 189, 191, 193, 194, 197, 200, 201, 202, 203, 204, 205, 206, 207, 208, 212, 214, 222, 230, 231, 232, 243, 251, 253, 255, 256, 265, 266, 276, 284, 285, 290
Grattan, James 128
Grenada 292
Grenville, George 104, 105
Grenville, William Wyndham 169, 180, 181, 182, 189
Grenville, William, first Baron Grenville 266
Griffiths, Richard 225
Grueber, Rev. Dr Arthur 158

Haddingtonshire 13
Haliday, Dr Alexander 203, 204, 222, 226

Halifax, second earl of, *see* Montagu-Dunk, George, second earl of Halifax
Hall family 24, 30, 126, 235, 263
Hall, Christina (*née* Poyntz) 16
Hall, Francis 16
Hall, Roger 16, 25, 53, 54, 56, 58, 72, 88–9, 109
Hall, Savage 223
Hall, William 62
Hallsmill, Co. Down 53
Hamilton, Alexander 24, 26, 59, 250
Hamilton, Chief Baron 198–9
Hamilton, Claude 13
Hamilton, Dean Hugh 158, 198–9, 208, 215
Hamilton, George 69
Hamilton, Hans 14
Hamilton, James, eighth earl of Abercorn 43, 110–11, 114
Hamilton, John 13, 14
Hamilton, Margaret (Orrery) 25
Hamilton, Rev. James Archibald 252
Hamilton, Sackville 167, 181, 252, 283, 290
Hamilton, Sir Hans 11, 14, 17, 22
Hamilton, Sir James 13
Hamilton, William 17
Hamilton, William Gerard 'Single-speech' 91, 96–7, 196
Hamiltonsbawn, Co. Armagh 11, 14, 22, 56, 57
Hampton Hall, Co. Dublin 199
Hampton, Primate 18
Hanover Club 20
Hanwell, London 11
Harcourt family 3
Harcourt, Simon, first earl Harcourt 84, 124–9, 132, 133, 143, 144, 145, 150–1, 152, 275–6
Harden, Henry 59, 61
Harden, High Sheriff Henry 166, 167, 171
Harden, James 223, 254
Hardwicke, third earl of, *see* Yorke, Philip, third earl of Hardwicke
Harrybrook, Co. Armagh 59, 61, 166, 254
Hartington, marquis of, *see* Cavendish, William, fourth duke of Devonshire
Hartley, Travers 207
Hatton, George 225
Hawkshaw, Mr 227
Hazleton, William 121
Headfort, marquis of 13, 24
Hearts of Oak, *see* Oakboys
Hearts of Steel, *see* Steelboys
Heasty, Catherine 62
Hely-Hutchinson, John 84, 85, 107, 120, 132, 151, 152, 154
Henderson, Mrs 62
Henderson, Thomas 19
Henley, Robert, second earl of Northington 181, 189, 190, 191, 193, 196, 201–2, 203, 205, 213, 230, 255

Henry Street, Dublin 287, 292
Herbert, Thomas, eighth earl of Pembroke 21
Heron, John 11
Heron, Sir Richard 150, 151, 152, 156, 163
Hertford, first marquis of, *see* Seymour-Conway, Francis, first marquis of Hertford
Hervey, Frederick, earl-bishop of Derry 191, 193, 194, 196, 197, 198, 199, 213
Hewitt, James, first Viscount Lifford 154, 162
Hewitt, James, second Viscount Lifford 263
Hickman, Mary (Charlemont) 112
Hill family 23
Hill, Arthur 72
Hill, Arthur, second marquis of Downshire 256, 261, 264
Hill, Dr Hugh 59
Hill, Thomas 73
Hill, Wills, first marquis of Downshire 108–9, 184, 232
Hillsborough, Co. Down 23, 294
Hillsborough, first earl of, *see* Hill, Wills, first marquis of Downshire
Hill-Trevor, Arthur, second Viscount Dungannon 262
Hinchingbrooke, Cambridgeshire 105, 109
Hoadly, Primate John 19
Hobart, John, second earl of Buckinghamshire 151, 152–4, 155, 156, 162, 163, 229
Hobart, Robert, fourth earl of Buckinghamshire 222, 229, 231, 283, 291
Hockley, Co. Armagh 12, 57
Hotham, Bishop John 189
Houghton Park House, Bedfordshire 295
House, Archdeacon George 53
Hovenden, Walter 10
Howard, Frederick, fifth earl of Carlisle 163, 164, 166
Hudson, Rev. Edward 211, 223, 258, 259
Humbert, General 257
Hunter, David 59
Huntingdon, Cambridgeshire 24, 106

Inchiquin, Co. Cork 294
India 269, 293
Ingram, Captain John 166
Innishannon, Co. Cork 89, 286
Iron Acton, Gloucestershire 15
Irwin, Sir John 163
Irwin, William 59, 61
Italy 48

Jackson family 25, 146
Jackson, Bishop Charles 91
Jackson, Richard 16, 54, 58, 61, 86, 101, 118
Jackson, Robert 155, 195
James I 6, 7, 9, 12, 13

James II 10, 11, 13, 19, 47, 226
Jenny, Rev. Henry 23, 44
Jephson, Richard Mountney 230, 232, 250, 251, 253, 255, 266, 285, 291
Jersey, earls of 14
Jervis Street, Dublin 288
Jocelyn, Viscount 67, 73
Johnson, Arthur 114
Johnson, Baptist 49
Johnston family 67
Johnston, Henry 51
Johnston, James 89, 228, 223
Johnston, John 61
Johnston, Joseph 61
Johnston, Lieutenant Colonel George Hamilton 51, 52
Johnston, Mr. 206
Johnston, Nicholas 158
Johnston, R. 224
Johnston, Sir Richard 121, 152, 196
Johnston-Liik, Edith Mary 2
Johnstown, Co. Armagh 171, 181
Jones, Captain William Todd 183, 185, 191, 192, 196, 199, 213, 225
Jones, High Sheriff Thomas Morres 54, 58, 61, 158, 167
Jones, Robert 62
Jonesborough, Co. Armagh 26, 58, 61
Jones-Nevill, Arthur 64, 65, 67, 70
Jupp, Peter 146

Keady, Co. Armagh 18, 28, 170, 171, 172, 241, 249, 288
Keane, Bishop Edmund 105
Kells, Co. Meath 13
Kelly, Daniel 87, 93
Kenmare, fourth Viscount 191
Kent 15, 17, 291
Kernan, Co. Armagh 12, 14, 24, 30, 44, 54, 56, 60, 114
Kerry, Co. 241
Kilcluney, Co. Armagh 55
Kilcurly, Co. Louth 53
Kildare, Co. 52, 53, 204, 293
Kildare, Co. Kildare 16, 40
Kildare, diocese of 52, 53, 204, 293
Kildare, earl of, *see* FitzGerald, James, first duke of Leinster
Kilkenny, Co. 53, 94, 282, 294
Killala, diocese of 91
Killevy, Co. Armagh 15, 16, 26, 61
Killileagh, Co. Down 26, 111, 114, 286
Killylea, Co. Armagh 101
Killymoon, Co. Tyrone 96
Kilmacantry Bridge, Co. Armagh 101
Kilmore, Co. Armagh 12, 26
Kilmore, Co. Cavan 91, 99

Kilrudden, Co. Armagh 13
Kiltubbrid, Co. Armagh 59
King family 24
King, Archbishop William 19
King, Dorothy (Moore) 15
King, Sir John 15
Kingsborough, Lord 207
Kinsale, Co. Cork 286
Knappagh, Co. Armagh 61, 223
Knatchbull, Sir Edward, seventh baronet 20, 282, 291
Knox, George 232
Knox, Major General John 249, 251, 256, 265, 266
Knox, Thomas 127, 239, 240

Lagan, River 120, 121
Lake, Gerard, Viscount Lake 249, 259, 263, 264, 283, 291
Lambeg, Co. Antrim 183
Lanesborough, first earl of, see Butler, Humphrey, first earl of Lanesborough
Lanesborough, second earl of, see Butler, Brinsley, second earl of Lanesborough
Lauder, William 13
Lawson, Robert 171
Lecale, Co. Down 27
Lee, Mr 188
Lees, John 118, 123, 124
Legacorry, Co. Armagh 11, 30, 56, 145, see also Richhill, Co. Armagh
Leinster Street, Dublin 290, 295
Leinster, first duke of, see FitzGerald, James, first duke of Leinster
Leinster, second duke of, see FitzGerald, William, second duke of Leinster
Leith, Edinburgh 13
Leixlip, Co. Kildare 74
Lennon, Dr Matthew 261, 267
Leslie, Rev. Henry 23, 114
Levinge, Rev. Robert 53, 59
Levinge, Sir Richard 18, 20, 21, 22
Lewes, Sussex 293
Lifford, first Viscount, see Hewitt, James, first Viscount Lifford
Lilliput Lodge, Dublin 289
Limerick, Co. 126
Limerick, Co. Limerick 292
Lincoln, Lincolnshire 291
Lincolnshire 11, 291
Lindsay, Primate Thomas 19, 20
Linlithgow, West Lothian 12
Lisburn, Co. Antrim 22, 170, 183, 184, 185, 192, 213, 225, 228, 231, 288
Lisdrumgullion, Co. Armagh 25, 30
Lissanoure, Co. Antrim 115, 123, 124, 292
Livingstone, Robert 158

Llandaff, diocese of 105
Lloyd, Andrew 21
London (Westminster administration) 11, 18, 31, 65, 86, 88, 98, 116, 121, 124, 125, 127, 143, 153, 154, 156, 161, 180, 182, 201, 204, 207, 208, 257, 265, 266, 293
London (city of) 21, 49, 53, 67, 68, 69, 86, 88, 90, 104, 108, 116, 121, 124, 128, 130, 153, 207, 208, 287, 288, 292
Londonderry, Co. 52, 53, 99, 121, 198, 239, 293
Longthorpe, Northants 24
Loughborough, first Baron 265
Loughbrickland, Co. Down 15
Loughgall Manor, Co. Armagh 12, 16, 22, 23, 24, 30, 45, 54, 55, 57, 60, 67, 108, 110, 121, 144, 145, 187, 228, 234, 236, 243, 288
Loughgall, Co. Armagh 26, 58, 158, 166, 172, 184, 186, 195, 197–8, 199, 200, 204, 215, 238
Loughgilly, Co. Armagh 26, 55, 58, 122, 208, 249, 251, 257
Loughguile, Co. Antrim 292
Louis XVIII 292
Louth, Co. 7, 30, 52, 53, 61, 114, 125, 146, 232, 287
Lowry, Galbraith 69
Lowther, Sir James 115
Lucas, Dr Charles 90, 94, 97–8
Lucas, Francis 59
Lurgan, Co. Armagh 18, 22, 27, 28, 30, 45, 47, 48, 55, 58, 62, 67, 71, 72, 73, 85, 92, 93, 109, 114, 120–1, 130, 157, 159, 185, 195, 203, 241, 287
Lylo, Co. Armagh 85

Macan, Arthur 249, 250
Macarell, Johnny 69
Macartney, George, Earl Macartney 115–16, 117, 118, 120, 122, 123, 124, 132, 133, 151, 282, 292
Macaulay family 123, 124
Macaulay, Alexander 122, 128, 230, 275
Macaulay, Mrs 123, 124, 275
MacBrian, Tirlough 17
MacDonnells 13
Madras, India 291, 292
Magenis, Richard 61
Magheryentrim, Co. Armagh 13
Maginn, Nicholas 256
Mahon, Co. Armagh 26
Malcomson, A.P.W. 146, 231
Malone, Anthony 73, 74
Malone, Edmond 230
Malton, North Yorkshire 290
Manners, Charles, fourth duke of Rutland 190, 196–7, 201, 202, 203, 206, 208, 209, 211, 213, 214, 215, 229

Manners, John, marquis of Granby 105
Mansfield, first earl of 162
Markethill, Co. Armagh 13, 17, 23, 44, 62, 67, 99, 100, 101, 103, 122, 156, 164, 170, 172, 189, 198, 201, 209, 232, 237, 238, 241, 286
Marlay, Bishop George 96
Marsh, Epaphroditus 20
Marsh, Primate Narcissus 18, 19, 20
Marshall, John 195
Marshall, Robert 72
Marston House, Somerset 41
Martin, Robert 72
Mary, Queen 10, 11, 13, 23
Matchett, Rev. James 12, 14
Maxwell family 88
Maxwell, Barry, first earl of Farnham (second creation) 88, 94, 95, 107, 108, 112, 115, 282, 292
Maxwell, Henry 91, 106
Maxwell, High Sheriff John 202, 203, 204
Maxwell, Robert, first earl of Farnham (first creation) 39, 74, 87, 88, 91, 95, 108, 115
Maxwell, Samuel 155, 195, 200
May, Humphrey 21, 284, 292
Mayo, Co. 235, 237, 243
McCall, Hamilton 172
McCamon, John 166
McCann, Arthur 59
McCann, Mr 62
McCann, Thomas (hostelry owner) 62
McCann, Thomas (magistrate) 209
McClintock, John 184
McComb, Alexander 61
McCombe, Rev. Alexander 26
McCord, John 72
McCullough, Captain 227
McCullough, Captain James 26, 46, 59, 94, 293
McGeough family 235
McGeough, Joshua 61, 166, 250
McGeough, Samuel 61
McKinstry, John 187
McKinstry, Lee 155
McKinstry, Robert 62, 93
McNeale, Malcolm 53–4
McTrew, Charles 62
Meath, Co. 289
Meath, diocese of 105, 106
Mellifont, Co. Louth 15
Meredyth, Henry 69, 91, 151, 153, 154, 158, 159, 161, 163, 173, 188, 194, 197, 203, 207, 208, 212, 213, 229, 283, 292
Meredyth, Lieutenant John 91
Merrion Square, Dublin 287
Mersham Hatch, Kent 291
Methodists 27
Middletown, Co. Armagh 22, 56, 67
Midhurst, West Sussex 265, 294

Miller, D.W. 215, 237
Minden, battle of 84
Moira, Co. Down 191
Moira, earl of 154
Moira-Castle, Co. Down 183
Molyneux family 12, 16, 24, 30, 40, 76
Molyneux, George William 189, 193, 194, 196, 197, 203, 207, 208, 212–13, 214, 227, 276
Molyneux, Samuel (I) 12
Molyneux, Samuel (II) 116
Molyneux, Sir Capel, fourth baronet 189, 195, 200, 258, 260, 261, 262, 263, 264, 281
Molyneux, Sir Capel, third baronet 12, 24, 41, 42, 54, 57, 60, 72, 89, 112, 116, 119, 126, 133, 144, 145, 147, 148–9, 152, 153, 154, 157, 158, 159, 161, 173, 189, 192, 195, 200, 203, 207, 212, 227, 228, 258, 275, 276, 278, 280
Molyneux, William 12, 24, 116
Monaghan borough 49, 50, 115, 289
Monaghan, Co. 7, 27, 30, 50, 53, 54, 59, 99, 146, 182, 198, 260, 264, 287, 289
Monaghan, Co. Monaghan 289
Monella, Co. Armagh 11, *see also* Hamiltonsbawn, Co. Armagh
Moneyglass, Co. Antrim 61
Monivea, Co. Galway 24, 69
Monroe, General 15
Montagu-Dunk, George, second earl of Halifax 91, 96, 98, 106
Montague, John, fifth earl of Sandwich 235, 262, 263
Montague, John, fourth earl of Sandwich 25, 105, 109, 111, 145, 149, 187
Montgomery, George 112, 115
Montgomery, William 117
Moore family 2, 15, 24, 25, 30, 40, 76, 117, 189, 227, 235
Moore, Acheson 69
Moore, Anne (*née* Caulfeild) 94
Moore, Arthur 15
Moore, Charles, first marquis of Drogheda 84, 111, 117, 118–19, 133, 152, 183, 184, 185, 207, 213, 225, 231, 256
Moore, Dorothy (*née* King) 15
Moore, Garret, first Viscount Drogheda 15
Moore, Henry William 90, 93–4, 97, 117, 118, 284, 293
Moore, John (1675–1752) 15, 21, 25, 54, 56, 58, 60, 284, 293
Moore, John (1726–1809) 117, 118–9, 120, 126, 133, 152, 153, 154, 157, 159, 161, 163, 185, 189, 213, 223
Moore, John junior 183, 184–5, 189, 194, 197, 203, 207, 208, 209, 211, 213, 223, 225–6, 227–8, 231, 236, 243, 256, 260, 261, 262, 263, 264, 265, 266, 281

Moore, Mary (*née* Caulfeild) 21, 25, 117
Moore, Sarah (Stewart), *see* Stewart, Sarah (*née* Moore)
Moore, Sir Edward (I) 15
Moore, Sir Edward (II) 15
Moore, William 117
Mornington, Co. Louth 96
Morton, fourteenth earl of 116
Mount Hall, Co. Down 58, 223
Mount Hamilton, Co. Armagh 22
Mount Kennedy, Co. Wicklow 289
Mount Street, Dublin 290
Mountflorence, first Baron 150
Mounthill, Co. Louth 44, 58, 223
Mountirwin, Co. Armagh 59, 61
Mountnorris, Co. Armagh 12, 14, 16, 18, 23, 30, 44, 45, 54, 55, 56, 60, 61, 65, 66, 110, 112, 166, 200, 288
Mountnorris, Lords, *see* Annesley family
Mourne, Co. Down 53
Moyanna, Co. Laois 290
Mullabane, Co. Armagh 12, 57
Mulladry, Co. Armagh 11
Mullaghbrack, Co. Armagh 26, 61, 208, 252
Mullaghglass, Co. Armagh 16, 25, 30, 58, 88, 223
Mullalelish, Co. Armagh 11, 54, 263
Mullingar, Co. Westmeath 23, 69
Murray, William, first earl of Mansfield 162
Murrell, Rev. Samuel 121
Mussenden, Isabella 75

Namier, Sir Lewis 275
Naples, Italy 48
Narrowwater, Co. Down 16, 53, 58, 88, 126
Navan, Co. Meath 69
Neagh, Lough 7, 11, 27, 30
Nedham family 17, 24, 25, 30, 58, 184, 235
Nedham, General Francis, first earl of Kilmorey 266
Nedham, Sir Francis 41, 54, 60, 72, 109
Nedham, William 152, 224, 228
Needham family, *see* Nedham family
Newburgh, Mr 112
Newcastle, first duke of, *see* Pelham-Holles, Thomas, first duke of Newcastle
Newcome, Primate William 255, 257, 261, 263, 267
Newenham, Sir Edward 154, 196
Newry Canal 27, 46
Newry, Co. Down 7, 13, 15, 16, 20, 25, 27, 30, 53, 55, 58, 59, 61, 62, 72, 73, 101, 152, 157, 159, 184, 199, 213, 224, 227, 231, 256, 261, 265, 266, 267
Newry, Lordship of 16–17
Newry, River 109
Newton, Bishop 105

Newtown, Lord, *see* Butler, Brinsley, second earl of Lanesborough
Newtownards, Co. Down 294
Newtownhamilton, Co. Armagh 26–7, 28, 59, 209, 210
Nicholas, Charles 59
Nine Years War 7, 9, 14, 15, 29
Nizelrath, Co. Louth 10
Noble, Adam 26
Noel family 30
Noel, Baptist 16
Norfolk 12
North, Frederick, Lord North 74, 125, 126, 128, 159, 160, 166, 180–1, 196
Northington, second earl of, *see* Henley, Robert, second earl of Northington
Northumberland, second duke of 96, 103, 105, 115, 116, 132
Norwich, Norfolk 11
Nottinghamshire 10
Nugent, Major General George 259, 260, 263, 267
Nugent-Temple-Grenville, George, first marquis of Buckingham 150, 169, 170, 174, 180–1, 184, 189, 190, 207, 208, 209, 213, 214, 224, 229, 277, 291
Nymphsfield, Co. Sligo 293

Oakboys 3, 98, 99–104, 120–2, 125, 130, 277
Oaktate, Co. Louth 53
Obins family 26, 30
Obins, Captain Hamlet 167
Obins, High Sheriff Archibald Eyre 262
Obins, Michael (of Ballyoran) 12
Obins, Michael (of Portadown) 115, 254
Obins, Mr 169
Obré family 26, 30, 263
Obré, Edward 11, 54, 59, 61
Obré, Eleanor 11
Obré, High Sheriff Francis 113, 114
O'Dogherty, Eleanor (Brownlow) 10
O'Dogherty, Sir Cahir 10
O'Donnell, James 262
O'Donnell, Rev. Hugh 197
Offaly, Co. 10
Ogle family 263
Ogle, George 205
Ogle, Mr 62
Ogle, Thomas 19
O'Hanlon, Hugh Boy 17
O'Hanlons 7, 8, 9, 14
O'Hara, Charles 117, 120, 126, 127, 132–3, 151, 282, 293
Old Connaught, Co. Wicklow 294
Old Leighlin, Co. Carlow 91, 123, 190, 203, 208, 213, 224, 230, 255, 289
Oliver, Silver 125–6

O'Moore, Rory 16
O'Neill, Art MacBaron 8, 16
O'Neill, John 185
O'Neill, Sir Henry MacShane 8, 17
O'Neill, Sir Phelim 13, 17
O'Neill, Sir Turlough MacHenry 8
O'Neill, Tirlough Og 17
Oneilland, barony of, Co. Armagh 8, 10, 11, 12, 14, 23, 24, 25–6, 27, 30, 55, 59, 98, 102, 103, 104, 120–1
O'Neills 7, 8, 9, 14, 15, 17
Orange Order 237, 238–40, 241, 244, 252, 256, 257, 258, 264, 277
Orde, Thomas 190, 196, 197, 198, 199, 201, 202, 203, 205, 206, 209, 214, 276
O'Reilly, Archbishop Richard 261, 267
Orior, barony of, Co. Armagh 7, 8, 9, 13, 14–17, 23, 24, 25, 26, 27, 30, 56, 58, 88, 98, 99, 100, 101, 158, 160, 164, 165, 169, 242
Ormonde, first duke of, *see* Butler, James, first duke of Ormonde
Ormonde, second duke of, *see* Butler, James, second duke of Ormonde
Orrery, fifth earl of, *see* Boyle, John, fifth earl of Cork and Orrery
Orrery, Lady Margaret (*née* Hamilton) 25
Oxford, University of 145, 241
Oxfordshire 9, 11

Palace Row, Dublin 292
Palace Street, Dublin 194
Paris 205
Park Castle, Dublin 291
Parker, Mr 114
Parkgate, England 128
Parnell, Sir John 261
Parsons, Sir Laurence 256, 257, 258, 263
Peep O'Day Boys 208–10, 215, 223, 237, 239
Pelham, Henry 64, 73
Pelham, Thomas, second earl of Chichester 194, 208, 224, 241, 250, 251, 255, 259, 263, 266, 283, 293
Pelham-Holles, Thomas, first duke of Newcastle 19, 32, 73, 91, 92, 105, 117
Pembroke, eighth earl of, *see* Herbert, Thomas, eighth earl of Pembroke
Perry, George 263
Pershore, Worcestershire 11
Pery, Speaker Edmund Sexton 74–5, 84, 98, 120, 126, 151, 152, 153, 154, 173, 190, 205
Pevensey, East Sussex 293
Philips, Ambrose 20, 282, 293
Phipps, Sir Constantine 18, 21, 22–3, 47
Phoenix Park, Dublin 170
Pitt, William, the Elder 74, 75, 92

Pitt, William, the Younger 190, 196, 201–2, 204, 211, 214, 257, 265, 269
Plunket, William Conyngham, Baron Plunket 256, 257, 258, 263, 264, 265, 266, 285, 294
Plunkett, Arthur, eighth earl of Fingall 191, 261
Plunkett, Oliver 18
Pole, Millicent (Acheson) 123
Pollock, Counsellor 227
Ponsonby family 73, 74, 75
Ponsonby, George 207, 208, 258
Ponsonby, Speaker John 74, 75, 86, 87, 94, 95, 107, 108, 118, 119, 120, 124, 132, 151, 282, 294
Ponsonby, William Brabazon 205–6, 231, 232, 251, 253, 266
Portadown, Co. Armagh 12, 26, 30, 45, 56, 59, 61, 67, 72, 74, 115, 167, 238, 254, *see also* Ballyoran, Co. Armagh
Portarlington, Co. Laois 229, 291
Portland, third duke of, *see* Cavendish-Bentinck, William Henry, third duke of Portland
Potter, John 31–2
Powell, William 12
Power, Richard 210
Poyntz family 15, 30
Poyntz, Christina (Hall) 16
Poyntz, Christina (*née* Puleston) 15
Poyntz, Elizabeth 15
Poyntz, Lucas 15
Poyntz, Sarah (Stewart) 15–16
Poyntz, Sir Charles 15
Poyntzpass, Co. Armagh 15
Pratt, John, first Marquis Camden 238, 239, 240, 241, 242, 244, 251, 253, 255
Pratt, Mr 112
Prentice, Thomas 155, 195
Presbyterians 17–18, 19, 22, 26–7, 71, 99, 100, 103, 121, 128, 155, 158, 185, 191, 198, 209–10, 215, 267
Preston, Jenico, twelfth Viscount Gormanston 191
Preston, John 69
Pringle family 235
Pringle, Robert 59
Puleston, Christina, *see* Poyntz, Christina

Quakers 10, 17, 22, 27
Queen's College, Oxford 145
Quilca, Co. Cavan 230
Quinn, Rev. P. 264

Ramelton, Co. Donegal 2, 295
Randalstown [Reynaldstown], Co. Louth 53, 61, 256
Rathcormack, Co. Cork 229, 290

Rawes, Co. Monaghan 59
Rawson, George 151, 153, 154, 158, 159, 161, 163, 188, 194, 197, 203, 207, 208, 212, 213, 229, 231, 252, 283, 294
Reresby, Leicestershire 11
Reynoldstown, Co. Louth 114
Richardson family 2, 11, 21, 30, 31, 32, 40, 67, 76, 145, 150, 185, 235, 274
Richardson, Ann (née Sacheverel) 11
Richardson, John 24
Richardson, Major Edward 11
Richardson, Mary (Acheson) 24
Richardson, Rev. William 239
Richardson, William (1656–1727) 11, 22, 23, 32, 280, 294
Richardson, William (1710–58) 23, 38, 39–40, 41, 45, 49, 50, 54, 56, 57, 60, 70, 71, 73, 75, 280, 294
Richardson, William (1749–1822) 145, 147, 158, 160, 164, 166, 173, 182, 183, 185, 186–7, 187–8, 193, 194, 195, 197, 201, 202, 203, 204, 205, 206, 207, 208, 211, 212, 214, 222, 224, 225–6, 227–9, 231, 232, 234, 236, 241, 242, 243, 244, 250, 251, 252, 253, 254–5, 258, 260, 263, 264, 275, 276, 280, 281, 295
Richhill, Co. Armagh 11, 22, 45, 56, 57, 67, 85, 100–1, 103, 155, 166, 182, 185, 237, 238, 263, 267, 294, 295
Richmount, Co. Armagh 11, 22, 30, 54, 55
Rigby, Richard 74, 84–5, 86, 87, 88, 90–1, 93, 95, 96, 97, 99, 105, 108, 109, 115, 124, 128, 149, 275
Riversdale, Lord 229
Robinson, Hugh 59
Robinson, John 129, 143
Robinson, Judge Christopher 122
Robinson, Primate Richard 27, 91, 105, 115, 116, 125, 131, 132, 151, 153–4, 158, 188, 198, 199, 208, 212, 215, 229
Robinson, Septimus 105
Rochford, fourth earl of, see de Zuylestein, William Henry
Rockingham, marquis of 125, 166
Rolleston, Rev. Richard 12, 16
Rome, Italy 47, 48
Roscommon, Co. 24, 71
Ross, Colonel Robert 127, 129, 184, 230, 256, 261
Rossmore, Baron, see Cuninghame, Colonel Robert
Rostrevor, Co. Down 184
Rowe, High Sheriff Thomas 101, 102, 103
Rowley, Hercules 185
Russell, Francis, marquis of Tavistock 76, 282, 295
Russell, John, fourth duke of Bedford 74, 75, 76, 84, 86, 87, 88, 89, 91, 92, 105, 295

Russia 124, 292
Rutland Square, Dublin 286, 288
Rutland, fourth duke of, see Manners, Charles, fourth duke of Rutland

Sacheverel family 10
Sacheverel, Ann (Richardson) 11
Sacheverel, Francis 11
Sackville Street, Dublin 232, 286
Sackville, George, first Viscount 39, 42, 64–5, 67, 69, 70, 73, 84, 91, 94, 287
Sackville, Lionel, first duke of Dorset 19, 39, 50, 68, 70, 71, 73, 91, 105
Saintfield, Co. Down 256
Salisbury, Wiltshire 27
Sandford, General 102
Sandwich, fifth earl of, see Montague, John, fifth earl of Sandwich
Sandwich, fourth earl of, see Montague, John, fourth earl of Sandwich
Sandwich, Lady Dorothy (née Fane) 25, 109, 146, 149
Sandymount, Dublin 289
Savage, Philip 23
Saye and Sele, Lord, see Fiennes, Richard, Lord Saye and Sele
Scotch Street, Armagh 19
Scott, Attorney-General 152, 162, 165
Seagoe, Co. Armagh 14, 104, 263
Seaver family 25, 235
Seaver, Thomas 61
Seceders 100
Senior, Hereward 239
Seven Years' War 98
Seymour-Conway, Colonel Henry 73
Seymour-Conway, Francis, first marquis of Hertford 73, 86, 106, 183, 184, 185, 225
Shanagoolan, Co. Armagh 11
Shannon, first earl of, see Boyle, Henry, first earl of Shannon
Shannon, second earl of, see Boyle, Richard, second earl of Shannon
Sharman, Lieutenant Colonel William 183, 185, 192
Shaw's Lough, Co. Armagh 110, 112
Sheitrim, Co. Monaghan 59
Sheridan, Richard 230, 231, 232, 243, 285, 295
Shrewsbury, first duke of, see Talbot, Charles, first duke of Shrewsbury
Singleton, Henry 43, 44, 72, 75
Sligo, Co. 117, 293
Sligo, Co. Sligo 188, 289, 292
Smith, Captain Anthony 16
Smith, Dr Arthur 106
Somerset 41
Southwell, Thomas, first Viscount Southwell 155

Spain 153, 155
Sparrow family 263
Sparrow, Colonel Robert 250, 251, 260, 261, 262, 263–4
Sparrow, Mary (Acheson) 24
St George, G. 117
St James Street, London 116
St James's Palace, London 167
St John family 14, 24, 30, 45, 48, 76, 114
St John, Barbara 14
St John, Oliver, Viscount Grandison of Limerick 12, 14
St John, Sir Francis 24, 41, 42, 43–4, 46–7, 54, 56, 60, 72, 90
St Johnstown, Co. Donegal 69, 292
St Johnstown, Co. Longford 290
St Petersburg, Russia 292
St Stephen's Green, Dublin 290
Staffordshire 12
Stanhawe family 10
Stanhawe, Eleanor 11
Stanhawe, William 11
Stanmer, Sussex 293
Stannard, Eaton 67, 71–2
Staples, John 116, 117
Steelboys 120–2
Stevenson, John 53
Stewart family 2, 16, 24, 30, 40, 56, 76
Stewart, Mr (of Killymoon) 96
Stewart, Alexander (of Acton) 24–5, 41–2, 54, 58, 63, 73, 146
Stewart, Alexander (of Co. Down) 184
Stewart, Alexander Thomas 200, 225, 228, 233, 250
Stewart, Colonel Robert (of Co. Down) 184, 185
Stewart, James 165, 193, 204, 207, 230, 231, 250, 251
Stewart, Jane (Dobbs) 146
Stewart, Major Charles 16
Stewart, Rev. Archibald 16
Stewart, Robert, Viscount Castlereagh 255, 256, 259, 264–5, 266, 267, 268
Stewart, Sarah (née Moore) 94, 118
Stewart, Sarah (née Poyntz) 15–16
Stewart, Sir Annesley, sixth baronet 94, 97, 107, 117, 118, 126, 128–9, 132, 151–2, 153, 154, 157, 158, 159, 161, 163, 173, 184–5, 188–9, 193, 194, 197, 201, 202, 203, 204, 206, 207, 208, 212, 214, 222, 227, 230, 231, 243, 252, 255, 276, 284, 285, 295
Stillorgan Park, Co. Dublin 295
Stone, Andrew 19, 105
Stone, Primate George 19, 20, 39, 42, 43, 46, 60, 64, 65, 69, 70, 71, 72, 73, 74, 76, 77, 84, 86, 88, 91, 94–5, 96, 98, 102, 104, 105, 106, 115, 116, 117, 131, 151, 289
Strabane, Co. Tyrone 110, 111, 114, 120, 287
Stradbally, Co. Laois 290

Stringer, Thomas 71, 72, 90, 93
Strong family 26
Strong, Rev. James 59, 61
Stuart, Charles Edward 31–2
Stuart, James 198
Stuart, John, third earl of Bute 105, 115, 116
Stuart, Primate William 19, 265
Suffolk 286
Summerhill, Dublin 289
Summerisland, Co. Armagh 67
Sussex 293
Sweetman, Mr 187
Swift, Dean Jonathan 19, 23, 32, 44
Swords, Co. Dublin 12, 50
Synnot, High Sheriff Sir Walter 181, 183, 185, 186, 187, 188, 192–3, 195, 209, 210, 250

Talbot, Charles, first duke of Shrewsbury 18
Talbot, Richard 170
Talbot, Richard, first earl of Tyrconnell 10
Tallbridge, Co. Armagh 59
Tandragee Castle, Co. Armagh 158
Tandragee, Co. Armagh 14, 28, 30, 41, 45, 56, 72, 85, 89, 90, 101, 114, 145, 158, 159, 160, 166, 202, 264, 289
Tartaraghan, Co. Armagh 101
Tavistock, marquis of, see Russell, Francis, marquis of Tavistock
Tawnavaltiny, Co. Armagh 14, 15, 25, 30, 58, 109, 187, 235
Taylor, Anne (Acheson) 13
Taylor, Sir Thomas 13
Taylor, William 171
Teemore, Co. Armagh 12, 16, 30, 57, 171, 181
Tegart, James 73
Temple, third Earl, see Nugent-Temple-Grenville, George, first marquis of Buckingham
Thurot, François 85
Thynne, Thomas, first marquis of Bath 119
Timmons, John 62
Tinnehinch, Co. Wicklow 290
Tipping family 25, 44, 58
Tipping, Edward 26
Tipping, Francis 223
Tipping, Thomas 44, 53, 54, 61
Tisdall, Philip 67, 107, 116, 117, 126, 132, 151, 152, 173, 282, 283, 295
Todd, Rev. James 182, 185
Toler, John 210
Toome Castle, Co. Antrim 292
Toome, Co. Antrim 115
Townshend family 3
Townshend, George, fourth viscount 84, 106, 107–8, 115, 116, 117, 118–20, 121–3, 124, 125, 127, 129, 130, 131, 132, 133, 143, 144, 151–2, 189, 275, 292

Townshend, Thomas, first Viscount Sydney 169, 182, 196–7
Trainor, Brian 239
Tremble, William 240
Trench, Frederick 49
Trench, General 260
Trevor, Bishop Richard 43
Trevor, Edward 16
Trewman, John 53
Trinity College, Dublin 8, 20, 24, 30, 32, 73, 116, 119, 132, 133, 145, 146, 151, 152, 154, 265, 282, 286, 289, 295
Troy, Archbishop John Thomas 191, 261, 267
Tuckett, George, Lord Audley of Orior and earl of Castlehaven 16
Tullybrick, Co. Armagh 59
Tullydowey, Co. Tyrone 21
Tullyhappy, Co. Armagh 16
Tullyvallen, Co. Armagh 59
Tulsk, Co. Roscommon 289
Turner, Samuel 256
Turnley, John 54
Tutbury, Staffordshire 12
Tynan, Co. Armagh 26, 59, 61
Tyranny, barony of, Co. Armagh 7, 8, 9, 10, 14, 17, 26, 30, 31, 55, 58, 59, 98, 99
Tyrconnell, earl of, see Talbot, Richard, first earl of Tyrconnell
Tyrone, Co. 7, 10, 13, 25, 27, 30, 52, 53, 54, 57, 58, 69, 99, 110, 160, 165, 198, 204, 239, 286, 288, 289, 295
Tyrone, first earl of, see Beresford, Marcus, first earl of Tyrone

Ulster Plantation 6, 13, 29, 31, 274
United Irish Society 229, 233, 236, 238, 239, 240, 241, 244, 249–50, 251, 252, 256, 257, 277
Upton family 120
Ussher, Primate James 18

Valentia, Viscounts, see Annesley family
Verner family 26, 263
Verner, High Sheriff Thomas 52, 59, 92, 101, 103, 200
Verner, James 256, 257, 259, 263, 264, 265, 266
Verona, Italy 292
Villiers, Barbara 14
Villiers, Edward 14
Volunteers 3, 143, 144, 155–72, 173–4, 180, 181–4, 185–6, 191–2, 193–4, 195–6, 197–9, 200–1, 202, 203, 204, 209, 210, 211–12, 213, 214, 215, 223, 225, 227, 230, 232, 233, 238, 239, 240–1, 243, 244, 276, 278

Waite, Thomas 20, 68, 69, 70, 86, 87, 100, 118, 123, 124, 290
Waldron family 11
Waldron, John 11
Wales, Prince of, see George IV
Walpole, Horace, fourth earl of Orford 105
Walpole, Robert, first earl of Orford 19, 31, 32
Walsh, Captain 75
Warburton, Charles 249, 250, 251–2, 257
Warburton, George 49
Ward, Edward 185
Ward, Judge Michael 41, 44
Waringstown, Co. Down 53
Warren, William 53
Waterford, Co. Waterford 292, 294
Wedderburn, Alexander, first Baron Loughborough 265
Wesley, John 27
West family 16
West, Roger 16
Westmeath, Co. 286
Westmorland, Francis, first earl of 15
Westmorland, tenth earl of, see Fane, John, tenth earl of Westmorland
Weston, Edward 20
Wexford, Co. 53, 146
Wexford, Co. Wexford 61
Weymouth, third Viscount 119
Whaley, Richard Chapel 61, 63
Wharton, Thomas 18
Whitechurch, Dame Mary 15
Whitechurch, Marmaduke 16
Wicklow, Co. 151
Wicklow, Co. Wicklow 290
Wigley family 16
William III 6, 10, 11, 13, 23, 29, 47
William, Prince, duke of Cumberland 45, 73
Williams, Sir Thomas 16
Wilmot, Sir Robert 31–2, 64–5, 67, 68, 70, 86
Wilson, Patt 62
Wiltshire 14
Windsor, Lord 287
Wisdom, Ob. 62
Woburn Abbey, Bedfordshire 295
Woodward, Rev. Dr Charles 158
Worcester, Worcestershire 11
Workman family 26, 67
Workman, Arthur 53
Workman, High Sheriff Meredyth 50, 51, 52, 61–2, 63, 65–6, 67, 70, 71
Workman, Richard 59, 61
Workman, William 61
Worlingham Hall, Suffolk 269, 286
Worlingham, Baron, see Acheson, Archibald, second earl of Gosford
Wride, Thomas 27
Wyndham, Thomas 20, 291

Yelverton, Barry, first Viscount Avonmore 154, 161, 163, 164, 194
York, Frederick, duke of 260
Yorke, Philip, third earl of Hardwicke 260, 268
Yorke, William 72

Youghal, Co. Cork 294
Young Pretender, *see* Stuart, Charles Edward
Young, Arthur 27
Young, Bishop Edward 122